Contact: Countdown to Transformation

The CSETI Experience – 1992-2009

By Steven M. Greer, M.D.

Copyright: Steven M. Greer, M.D.

September 2009

All rights reserved.
No part of this book may be reproduced in any form
or by any electronic or mechanical means
including information and retrieval systems
without prior permission from the publisher in writing.

Greer, Steven M

Contact: Countdown to Transformation – The CSETI Experience from
1992-2009

ISBN: 9780967323831
Library of Congress Control Number: 2009907457

Cover design and Graphics:
Bryan Dechter/Dancing Eyes Design
873 Silverleaf Rd.
Zionville NC 28698
www.dancingeyes.com
Printed in United States of America

Address all inquiries to:
Crossing Point, Inc.
PO Box 265
Crozet, VA 22932

Produced by:
123PrintFinder, Inc.
27702 Crown Valley Pkwy. #148, Suite D-4
Ladera Ranch, CA 92694

This book is dedicated to the loving memory of Shari Adamiak. Her tireless work and devotion to Universe Peace still inspires us all and we are eternally grateful for everything she did for CSETI and humanity.

Other books by Dr. Greer

"Extraterrestrial Contact: The Evidence and Implications" – 1999

"Disclosure: Military and Government Witnesses Reveal the Greatest Secrets in Modern History" – 2001

" *Hidden Truth- Forbidden Knowledge* " - 2006

Companion materials available at www.DisclosureProject.org

DVDs:
The Disclosure Project – 2001 National Press Club Event
The Disclosure Project – 2 hour Witness DVD with Briefing Document and Executive Summary
The Disclosure Project – 4 hour Witness Testimony

CDs:
Hidden Truth – Forbidden Knowledge – 2 Guided Meditations
Cosmic Consciousness: A Course in Advanced Mantra Meditation – 2 CD set

For more information about Dr. Greer's work:
www.DisclosureProject.org
www.CSETI.org
www.TheOrionProject.org

CSETI – Center for the Study of Extraterrestrial Intelligence
PO Box 265 • Crozet, VA 22932

Table of Contents

Acknowledgements 8
Foreword 9
Participants 12
Introduction 17
Chapter 1 ---1992 29
Chapter 2 ---1993 38
Chapter 3 ---1994 50
Chapter 4 ---1996 56
Chapter 5 ---1997 73
Chapter 6 ---1998 119
Chapter 7 ---1999 159
Chapter 8 ---2000 188
Chapter 9 ---2001 211
Chapter 10 –2002 232
Chapter 11 –2003 242
Chapter 12 –2004 250
Chapter 13 –2005 275
Chapter 14 –2006 298
Chapter 15 –2007 324
Chapter 16 –2008 356
Chapter 17 –2009 375
Chapter 18 – The Orion Transmissions 378
Appendix – Briefings with Questions and Answers 403
Index 443

Acknowledgements

This book would not have been possible without the help of many people.
My apologies to anyone I may have inadvertently forgotten.

I thank:

- All those who participated in the dictation,
- Norm Fletcher who recorded the original dictation,
- Kay Gibson who transcribed the original dictation,
- Janet Brook who transcribed subsequent dictations,
- Jack Auman and Steve Graf who edited, fact checked, proofread and indexed,
- Ellen Costantino who edited and formulated the dictated material into something that conveyed the beauty and excitement of the events,
- Bryan Dechter who designed the truly inspirational cover art,
- Todd Goldenbaum, videography of CSETI events and editing for the DVD,
- Linda Willitts, my personal assistant,
- Debbie Foch, the CSETI coordinator who so ably organizes the Ambassador to the Universe Trainings,
- Dr. Jan Bravo, devoted friend and supporter,
- All those who have participated throughout the years in the trainings that have facilitated these experiences,
- My wife, Emily, my lifelong companion – who is always there,
- And the ETs who continue to communicate with us and to reach out to humans in the spirit of Universal Peace.

Foreword

This book is the result of two and a half years of collaborative effort with many people who have been on the CSETI Contact Team over the past 19 years. It is an oral history project and most of this book was created by the CSETI Team sharing their collective experiences in Palm Springs CA in February of 2007. The individuals who spoke at that event have been on many CSETI Expeditions to make contact with interstellar civilizations. The transcript has been edited for length and readability. Events after February 2007 described in the book were the result of later collaborations and reports.

As a largely unfunded, all-volunteer citizen's diplomatic project, the CSETI CE-5 Initiative is a world encircling effort to train ordinary people to make open contact with Visitors from other star systems. We have been amazed at the degree to which these ET visitors have cooperated with such an effort- a clear signal that they would like further contact with humanity – once we are prepared.

Many of the experiences described in this book sound mystical and beyond the scope of current science. But could it be anything else? After all, any civilization capable of interstellar travel at multiples of the speed of light would manifest in such extraordinary ways as to appear to us on Earth today as mystical and even unbelievable. But think for a moment: if we on earth today were to go back to the time of Thomas Jefferson in the late 1700s with cell phones, fiber optics, plasma TVs and rockets, would not most or all of these technologies seem like magic? I suspect if you merely possessed an ordinary cell phone in that era you would risk being burned at the stake as a witch!

This brings to light the central question of how might such advanced ET civilizations appear to us? This book, in part, is an attempt to answer that question. It is not what many would expect. If these events had met our preconceived expectations, the events would be manmade and out of Hollywood, and not ET.

Any civilization capable of reaching our solar system from another will manifest technologies so advanced as to look like magic to us. Such civilizations can shift beyond the speed of light and solid matter as easily as we call home on a cell phone. Their communications technologies travel through 'infraspace' – from trans-dimensional realms where thought, consciousness, light, and electromagnetism intersect and come together.

Thus, our experiences have been awe-inspiring and beautiful – and at times unbelievable, even to those who have borne witness to these historic, early diplomatic contact events between humanity and Extraterrestrial peoples.
These Visitors have made contact with us in a thousand different ways – using technologies, materialized spacecraft, thought, consciousness, sound, light and more.
Now, we have been approached by senior officials in other countries to learn – and experience – the techniques associated with Contact. Soon open and official Contact will be made…

The Rosetta stone of ET Contact is non-local consciousness: awareness that is transpersonal, transcendental and that opens the individual awareness to the omnipresent Mind. It is this field of unbounded Mind that is the ultimate Internet for interstellar communications. These advanced ET civilizations have technologies that interface with coherent thought emanating from this expanded state of mind – and this is the central technology of the CSETI CE-5 Contact protocols. We will soon discover, I believe, that the most important science of the next 1000 years will be the science of consciousness.

Of course, this is controversial – but so is every new idea, and we are looking to the potential future of humanity, not its past. For we have entered a universal moment – an era wherein humanity will attain first world peace and then Universal Peace. And then we will travel among the stars together.

In the meantime, these ET civilizations are here, watching,

waiting – hoping – for the maturation of the human race. Some of us have decided to reach out to them and welcome them to the good humanity has to offer – to pioneer open contact now. Will you join us?

Participants
The CSETI Experience
Palm Springs, California
February 2007

Dr. Ted Loder

Dr. Loder, a Ph.D. scientist, oceanographer, and professor emeritus at the University of New Hampshire, lives in Barrington, New Hampshire. He attended his first training at Crestone, Colorado in 1997 and has been to about 35 week's worth of trainings. He is CSETI's science adviser and helped to put together the briefing summary for the 2001 Disclosure Project. He's also been a key player helping to ferret out and investigate energy and propulsion technologies that AERO has been pursuing.

Linda Willitts

Linda, a biologist by training, has had a life-long interest in ETs. She saw Dr. Greer at an expo in Sacramento in September of 1996. Unlike most researchers who simply talked about what happened at Roswell or explored abductions, she was struck by Steven's introduction of spirituality and geo-politics to the ET topic, as well as practical applications and technologies that could save our world. She attended the first Joshua Tree conference in November 1996, and has been to all but one CSETI training since then — over 40 week's worth of experiences. When Shari Adamiak passed away in 1998, Linda stepped into the breach as an assistant to Dr. Greer.

Debbie Foch

Debbie is from Largo, Maryland. Her college degree was in Space Science, and she worked for NASA contractors at NASA's Goddard Space Flight Center. She found out about CSETI at the International Forum on New Science in 1992, where she met both Dr. Greer and Ricky Butterfass. Her interest in cosmology found a match with CSETI. Debbie has been the coordinator for all CSETI expeditions and trainings since 1998, handling the logistics after Shari Adamiak died. She has been to over 40 weeks of CSETI trainings. She's also webmaster for cseti.org and disclosureproject.org. Debbie also prints out and monitors the satellite pass-overs for each fieldwork location and date.

Dr. Jan Bravo

Dr. Bravo is from Santa Clara, California and started with CSETI in 1998. She has over twenty years of practice as an emergency room physician. She felt drawn to attend Dr. Greer's presentation in Hawaii of '98. Since that time she has been a key and stalwart supporter of both CSETI and the Disclosure Project, attending most CSETI trainings. Only through her financial commitment was the National Press Club Disclosure possible.

Trudy Guyker

Trudy is a housewife and grandmother residing in Chandler, Arizona. After attending a lecture and workshop at a Whole Life Expo in Santa Fe, New Mexico in 1993, she realized that CSETI with its spiritual emphasis was how she could best utilize her own spiritual knowledge with her interest in the UFO phenomenon. She has attended over ten months worth of CSETI events.

Charlie Balogh

Charlie Balogh, from Phoenix, Arizona, has been a member of CSETI since 2000, after he heard Dr. Greer's talk at The Prophet's Conference in Phoenix. Charlie is a professional musician who specializes in the pipe organ. He purified the crop circles tones used in CSETI protocols that were originally recorded by the British Broadcasting Corporation while videotaping a trip through a fresh crop circle in July of 1992. More recently, Charlie composed music for and produced the meditation and mantra recording of "Cosmic Consciousness," the course in advanced mantra meditation by Dr. Greer offered on compact disk through CSETI.org.

Dr. Raven Nabulsi

Dr. Nabulsi lives in Orange County, California. She first saw Dr. Greer at a MUFON meeting in Costa Mesa in 1998. She attended the CSETI Training in Sedona, Arizona in November 1998. She has become one of the CSETI team members and attends most of the trainings. She is a healer and holds a doctorate in her field as a licensed acupuncture therapist. She also owns a candy company specializing in chocolates.

Ricky Butterfass

Ricky met Dr. Greer in 1991, when both were speakers at the International Association for New Science Forum in Fort Collins, Colorado. Ricky listened to Dr. Greer's presentation and particularly liked the idea that in CSETI, everyone could be – and was expected to be – a part of the team. Butterfass has been a part of CSETI expeditions around the globe.

Kay Gibson

Currently living in Mexico, Kay was born and raised in California. She first met Dr. Greer in Sacramento in September of 1996 at the Whole Life Expo. She signed up and went to the training in November 1996 at Desert Hot Springs. Since then she has traveled with CSETI frequently, including expeditions/trainings in England, Hawaii, Sedona, Crestone, Mt. Shasta, and Joshua Tree.

Jan Brook

Jan, from Broken Arrow, Oklahoma, first heard about CSETI through the Internet when Debbie Foch was part of a UFO forum on CompuServe. Although they never met personally, Shari Adamiak was also instrumental in getting Jan involved, and she has stayed active with CSETI since 1998.

Dr. Warren Wittekind

Warren, from Seattle, Washington, has been with CSETI since December of 2002. He is a nuclear engineer, who earned his PhD at the University of Wyoming, and has attended numerous trainings, beginning with the Consciousness Training at Joshua Tree in 2003.

Greg Heller

Greg is from San Mateo, California, and has been with CSETI since 2003. He heard about CSETI through Art Bell first and then the National Press Club web broadcast – he saw it live and was fascinated by it.

Dwynne "Arnie" Arneson

Arnie was a Disclosure Project witness and wanted to come to Joshua Tree to learn more about Close Encounters of the 5th Kind.

He spent 26 years in the USAF. He had an above top-secret SCI-TK (Special Compartmented Tango Kilo) clearance. He worked as a computer systems analyst for Boeing and was the Director of Logistics at Wright-Patterson AFB. At one point he was the cryptography officer for the entire Ramstein AFB in Germany and while there received a classified message that a UFO had crashed in Spitsbergen, Norway. At Malmstrom AFB in Montana, he saw another message describing a metallic circular UFO seen hovering near the silos whose missiles went off-line so they could not be launched.

Other Participants

David Alfassi, Dr. Bill Clendenin, Norm Fletcher, Pam Fletcher, Daniel Krevitsky, Chuck Schnibben, Randy Tielking, & Terry Underwood.

Todd Goldenbaum

Todd is the webmaster for The Orion Project. His additional tasks with the project are data collection, fund raising, and organization. Involved with CSETI and The Orion Project since 2007, he has attended many trainings and is the chief videographer for the fieldwork during these trainings. He has donated countless hours and equipment to both The Orion Project and CSETI. Todd holds BA and BS degrees from the University of Kansas in journalism and East Asian Languages and Cultures.

Ellen Costantino

Ellen is the Personnel Support Coordinator for The Orion Project. She spent many hours editing and proofreading this manuscript. Having attended several Ambassador to the Universe trainings she has also given public presentations about Dr. Greer's work. Ellen majored in Microbiology and minored in Psychology at Oregon State University. She is a licensed Medical Technologist/Microbiologist, a licensed Kelley-Radix and Radix Institute Teacher, and an Upledger Certified Craniosacral therapist.

Notes, Previous Reports and Publications

Shari Adamiak, Al Dunaway, Dr. John R.M. Day

Introduction

Introductory Remarks By Steven M. Greer MD

This effort represents the fourth book in a series that deals with contact between humans and extraterrestrial peoples. This book is unique because the individuals who have been on these expeditions throughout the world share what they recall – not just the experience of what they saw and heard, but what they felt and what that meant to them. It presents objective and subjective experiences, and amounts to a no-holds-barred look at the meaning of contact. This book also provides a permanent record of historic and paradigm-changing encounters that the world does not yet know about. The details have only been implied in my other books.

To the readers of this book, I suggest that you also read _Disclosure: Military and Government Witnesses reveal the Greatest Secrets in Modern History._ It details the facts from government documents, military and corporate witnesses who have had first-hand knowledge on the subject of UFO encounters. The philosophical basis for the CE-5 contact protocols and some of CSETI's early experiences are in the first book, _Extraterrestrial Contact: The Evidence and Implications_. My own personal journey, which started when I was a child of eight or nine, is in the third book, _Hidden Truth – Forbidden Knowledge_. These books are available at www.DisclosureProject.org.

Extraterrestrial Contact

This book shares with the world what it has been like for a group of people on the vanguard of interplanetary contact in the late 20th and early 21st century. As such, it creates a new paradigm for increasing contact between human civilizations and non-human or extraterrestrial civilizations in the near future. It goes beyond anything that has been available to the public before. Since 1990 thousands of sightings and hundreds of separate encounters involving thousands of people have occurred during these CSETI expeditions. On dozens and dozens of these expeditions there have been interactions, sightings and repeated anomalous, extraordinary manifestations of advanced extraterrestrial intelligence.

Phenomena vs. Expressions of Intelligence

I would like to make a comment here about avoiding the use of the term "phenomena" in relation to these events. First, a phenomenon connotes a mystery, while the subject of contact is now known and partially understood. Second, and most importantly, the word "phenomenon" refers to natural events such as ball lightning or weather phenomena – something that happens randomly as a course of nature. An interaction experience cannot be called a phenomenon after we have deliberately invited the extraterrestrial intelligence to come to a particular place on the Earth! When they respond to our intentions and arrive, that is an "encounter." Specifically, it is a **close encounter of the fifth kind**, or CE-5, meaning that humans initiated or cooperated with the contact. So it is not just some random, natural phenomenon. It is an actual, extraterrestrial manifestation of advanced intelligence. For this reason, we are calling these events "expressions of intelligence" as opposed to "phenomena." They encompass a wide range of categories, which we will summarize briefly.

These expressions of intelligence range from completely manifested extraterrestrial vehicles at close range to anomalous omni-directional sounds emanating around us. We have been in field groups where we have broadcast the CSETI tones into the atmosphere and have had anomalous tones come back. The first time this happened, in England in the early 1990s, I had the idea to get a radio transmitter so we could transmit those tones out into space. Meanwhile, the group was in a state of non-local consciousness vectoring the extraterrestrial vehicle to the site. Within minutes of transmitting the tones on a wind-swept hill, a tone came back for several minutes. It was an omni-directional, non-local tone. We could not find its source. It was their way of saying, "Yes, we are receiving your transmission, and we are here monitoring what you are doing." That was not a natural phenomenon, but rather an interaction that originated from advanced extraterrestrial civilizations who were signaling back to us their reception of our signal. Incidentally, it turns out Marconi had sent the first telegraph message from the very same hill!

Deliberate Contact

Transmitting tones was deliberate contact, planned and executed by humans to invite extraterrestrial civilizations to interact with us in whatever way seemed safe and appropriate for that time and place. We always transmit these tones we recorded to these visitors as part of our CSETI protocol. Contact comes in myriad forms of intelligence and technology, from lights to tones and objects.

Materialization and Neutrino Light

Sometimes objects will not be fully materialized, even though they are visible and giving off sparkling light. This "sparkle," what one scientist has called "neutrino light", represents an advanced, inter-dimensional technology that is bumping up against the fabric of linear space/time. Other objects can be completely seen as materialized spacecraft, fully visible but not completely "solid." You could walk right through them because they are spin/shifted slightly out of what is called the "linear space/time concretion" or the fixedness of linear space/time and the material structure of the cosmos. These have all taken place within the context of the CE-5 Initiative.

The Center for the Study of Extraterrestrial Intelligence

In 1990 I founded the Center for the Study of Extraterrestrial Intelligence. After studying what was happening in the non-classified world with this subject, I discovered that there were many groups that went on "sky watches" and there were many retrospective efforts to document events *after* they happened. For example, UFO groups of various types around the world would take a report from someone who had a sighting last night or last week. However, there was nothing happening on Earth that was a real-time, conscious attempt to contact these visitors with the specific purpose of peaceful, diplomatic and open communication. Not at the UN, and certainly not within classified projects, because those are all oriented towards shooting these objects down. No peaceful attempts were occurring within any overt government programs such as the State Department of the United States or the foreign ministries of European or any other nations on Earth.

Eisenhower 1954 Meeting with ETs

So 60 years after obtaining definitive proof that we are being visited by advanced extraterrestrial life forms, no group on Earth had – up to that time – taken upon itself the task of openly reaching out and communicating with these ETs. Attempts made during the 1950s were quickly shut down by transnational industrial and financial interests. We have a document sent to me by a European Ministry of Defense that quotes a first-hand witness who states that President Eisenhower did meet with extraterrestrial beings in 1954 near Edwards Air Force Base (Muroc). The military-industrial complex did not want him to announce that he had this meeting with an extraterrestrial biological entity. So in spite of President Eisenhower's attempts, that initiative to make *open* contact failed.

Science Fiction or Docudrama?

If you look at the original movie *The Day the Earth Stood Still*, you will understand why the Eisenhower effort died. Even though the movie is a B-rated movie, there is a wonderful message in it. Some covert interests within the State Department of the United States even supported its production. The meta-message in that movie is that there are completely benign, but more importantly, quite enlightened, advanced, and evolved extraterrestrial people trying to make contact with the Earth. This contact became necessary because we had developed weapons of mass destruction: atomic and hydrogen weapons. The extraterrestrial peoples wanted contact. They wanted us to find a way to live together in peace with each other and in peace with them. Destruction was the direction we were traveling in the early days of the space race, and they knew it. In "The Day the Earth Stood Still," humans responded to an ET emissary with a violent, military reaction. Responding to what they did not understand from a sense of fear, xenophobia, and paranoia, this militaristic response was an enormous tragedy that continues to this day.

Arrested Evolution

Unfortunately, we never recovered from the power grab within the vast and highly secretive corridors of industrial and economic interests. These interests hijacked the ET subject as well as our economic and technological development and thereby arrested the evolution of the human race. For 60 years, this power grab has thwarted not only peaceful contact with visitors from other planetary systems, but also the human potential to live peacefully on this planet with a civilization using advanced technologies. These new energy and propulsion technologies do not damage the Earth's biosphere and would create enormous abundance. The energy and propulsion systems used by the so-called "UFOs" do not cannibalize the atmosphere in order to generate enormous amounts of power, and this fact has been known for over half a century.

Futuristic or Catch Up?

While many people view the CE-5 Initiative as futuristic, in reality we are trying to catch up with where human evolution was intended to be 50-70 years ago. The same holds for all the other projects associated with the CSETI effort: the Disclosure Project, AERO Inc., and The Orion Project (see www.TheOrionProject.org). In 1954 human evolution was hijacked, and left in a global cul-de-sac, and we have been going around in circles ever since. The consequences of this have been enormous: geo-political instability, oil wars, biosphere degradation, global warming, polar ice caps melting, environmental collapse and social disruption. This includes the unfair and unsustainable condition where 80% of the world's population is living in terrible poverty. All because of the zero sum game necessitated by the fundamental operating system of the planet — the internal combustion engine and fossil fuels — which should have been retired decades ago.

Col. Corso 1956 Meeting with ET

I am reminded of something that I saw in the personal papers of Col. Phillip Corso when I was at his home shortly after his death. His son showed me a stack two or three feet high of papers and information that the Colonel eventually wanted to get out to the public. Much of what he knew was not included in his first book, *The Day After Roswell*. One of the papers was an account of his being present at the landing of an extraterrestrial vehicle in 1956, two years after Eisenhower had his meeting at Edwards. The Colonel went out to where the vehicle had landed on the Holloman

Range in New Mexico near White Sands. He saw a spaceship that was fully materialized, but would shift energetically, appearing as a shadowy mirage, similar to when heat rises up from the desert. Then the craft would "tune back in" to material space/time, and it would fully materialize again!

Eventually an extraterrestrial person emerged and communicated with an electronic device that interfaced directly with thought – their technologies are capable of this – and Colonel Corso asked, "What do you want with me? Why are you here?" The extraterrestrial asked the Colonel to have the military switch off some of the high-powered radar systems that had been configured to interfere with the electronics of their craft moving through the atmosphere. (This is the reason behind the so-called "Roswell crash" in New Mexico in 1947. We have a document from an FBI field agent to J. Edgar Hoover describing how those ET craft were downed. ETs do not come here from interstellar space and then just accidentally run into each other and crash! All of the extraterrestrial propulsion and guidance systems are very sensitive, high tech electronics, particularly when they are fully materialized in the linear space/time dimension, and these early electronic warfare systems were embedded in radar arrays.)
Colonel Corso turned to this extraterrestrial person and asked, "Well, what's in it for *me* if I do this?" And the extraterrestrial said, "A new world, if you can take it!"

So here we are, over 50 years after Col. Corso's encounter - and I suggest that we learn to take it, because the world needs this knowledge and needs to know that we can live peacefully with our interplanetary neighbors. We can not develop further as a civilization with the continued suppression of this information- and the 'black shelving' of these new energy technologies that would give us a new world, completely sustainable, without poverty, and with abundance for all.

What is the CE-5 Initiative?

The CE-5 Initiative uses a set of protocols that invite extraterrestrials to interact with us openly, within the framework of universal peace. It began in 1991, and has become a journey for thousands of people. Now is the time for those people's voices to be heard and for them to share their experiences. It is important for everyone to understand that this is not only an experience of one person. There are thousands of people who have been on these expeditions, experienced contact and learned how real ET contact happens. People have gone out in small groups of two, three, or four and been able to create the conditions for encounters in Australia, Canada, England, Mexico, Japan, Africa and elsewhere.

The protocols for ET Contact are described in the books *Extraterrestrial Contact: The Evidence and Implications* and *Hidden Truth – Forbidden Knowledge*. A number of years ago I had a series of experiences involving a higher state of consciousness – similar to what's popularly called "remote viewing" – where I could see into space, bi-locate and connect with extraterrestrial vehicles. I would then vector them into a location. These experiences began after I had a near-death experience at age 17. I had been raised a very devout atheist but found out that, in fact, there was a Universal Consciousness and Being. The conscious mind within each of us is the same Universal Mind that is the Great Being. There is no separation except the separation that our intellect and ego creates. We build those barriers and only we can take them down.

Minds in the Universe

As Erwin Schrödinger stated, the total number of minds in the universe is one[1]. This single mind of consciousness, once experienced, can be used to see remote places. In the case of advanced extraterrestrial civilizations whose communications technologies are interfacing with consciousness and thought, one can connect to them, guide them and show them a specific location.

There was no such thing as a CE-5 until 1990/91 when I began to describe that concept[2]. There were Close Encounters of the First Kind, a sighting within a certain number of feet; Close Encounters of the Second Kind, where there was some sort of physical trace or evidence; Close Encounters of the Third Kind, like the movie,

---

[1] http://en.wikiquote.org/wiki/Erwin_Schrödinger
[2] The Wikipedia article on "Close Encounter" cites the CSETI type CE-5 and credits Steven Greer's CSETI group as originator (http://en.wikipedia.org/wiki/Close_encounter).

where there was some kind of interaction with an extraterrestrial biological life form; and Close Encounters of the Fourth Kind, where people had been taken on board a craft or had experiences that were more interactive. The Close Encounter of the Fifth Kind was a new level and also a completely new paradigm. Notice that all of the previous types of close encounters are passive. But in the CE-5, we are turning the situation around and empowering the human to *invite* open contact." Instead of being a *chance* encounter, it is a deliberate encounter and meeting with a peaceful, mutually beneficial and diplomatic purpose.

History of CE-5 Experiences

I began to look for other people who had had experiences like this. I found that in the literature there were hundreds of accounts of people who had had chance encounters of the First, Second, Third or Fourth Kind which then turned into a Close Encounter of the Fifth Kind. For example, they would see one of these extraterrestrial vehicles and signal to it. The object would stop, turn back and signal back to them.

Thought, Light and Sound Interactions

Then I found cases where people would see one of these objects and think, "I wish it would move to the right so I could see it better" and the object would move to the right. Then they would think, "I wish it would move to the left", and it would move to the left; "I wish it would move up" and it would move up. They found that the event was interactive and mediated through directed *thought* – with the consciousness of the individual connected to the object.

I also found that there were interactions that involved sound and light. Near the La Brea tar pits in Los Angeles there was a grand opening for a movie. The promoters put up a giant searchlight that attracted ET vehicles and there followed a big wave of sightings. The ETs were interested and interacting with the lights. So I discovered that there were *three* main modalities through which a human could engage in contact and interaction with these extraterrestrials: (1) consciousness and thought; (2) light or lasers, and (3) sound. These three components, consciousness, light and sound, became the basis of the CE-5 or Close Encounters of the Fifth Kind Initiative.

We have extraordinary beeping tones that were recorded in a crop circle in England by the BBC, which were given to us by Colin Andrews, as well as tones that were sent to us by the ETs and recorded by CSETI at Mt. Shasta, CA. We have lasers and lights that we send upward. And we train our groups to be able to go into a deep state of quiet consciousness which transcends the boundaries of linear space/time so we can enter into non-local or expanded states of consciousness. In this state of consciousness our groups can sense or see extraterrestrial spacecraft and objects, connect to them, and then vector them directly to our site via thought.

As soon as we began using these protocols, the extraterrestrials appeared. When I had these experiences as a young man of 18 or 19, I thought they were quirks peculiar to me. Then I found that other people had this type of experience. I wondered whether these experiences could be formalized into an expeditionary effort for diplomatic and peaceful purposes so that a whole group of people could do this. Thus began the CE-5 Initiative in 1990 and 1991.

The Purpose of CSETI

Since that time we have been all over the world using these protocols and making diplomatic contact, and we have not been disappointed. It is important to note that these efforts have been done with a higher purpose. They are far different from accidentally seeing a craft. These contact events represent a conscious effort to put humans in direct communication with extraterrestrial intelligence for peaceful, diplomatic and highly spiritual – not religious – purposes.

Recognizing that the total number of conscious minds in the cosmos is One, CSETI adopted the motto: One Universe – One People. This connotes several ideas. First, there exists one mankind that is interplanetary. Second, this is a universal phenomenon and a universal reality. Third, there are conscious, intelligent people on other planets capable of knowing the unbounded Being within us.

On "the plane of the Absolute," which the Sufi mystics refer to, the center point of consciousness is the unbounded field of mind. There is only one Great Being shining through the eyes of all people.

Success of CSETI

Understanding that motto is the foundation of our contact, and it is also the genesis of our success. Extraterrestrials are not interested in humans who are still living in the illusion of separation. It does not matter how many stars you have as a general or how many Ph.D.s you have, or how rich you are. They are interested in whether or not you have realized this single fact: that the conscious mind is a singularity, and that we are all one being, we are all one people. If you understand and experience this fact with clarity and purity of heart as you endeavor to become a diplomat from humanity to their people, these visitors will respond. They have never *not* responded. We have never gone on an expedition where some expression of this higher intelligence and these extraterrestrial civilizations has failed to occur.

Mind Control: The Term "UFO"

Many people have asked me how many times I have seen a UFO. I tell them I have never seen a UFO, because there is no such thing as a UFO. The term was concocted by those who knew exactly what the vehicles were and is a clever attempt at "mind-conditioning." There are two categories of vehicles. The first is ETVs, "extraterrestrial vehicles," the term used at the National Security Agency (NSA). The second is ARVs, "alien reproduction vehicles," which are man-made advanced anti-gravity craft that look like a "UFO." They do not actually "fly" in any normal aerodynamic sense of the word. They are using propulsion systems developed as far back as the 1920s by T. Townsend Brown et al. They employ what is known as the Biefeld-Brown Effect that involves high voltage, electromagnetic, and magnetic flux phenomena that allow an object to become weightless, levitate, and move in a virtually mass-free manner even though in the atmosphere of Earth. Advanced physicists in classified projects have understood this for at least 50 years and maybe longer.

So I tell people we have never seen a "UFO". We have, however, had thousands of sightings and interactions with extraterrestrial vehicles and their occupants. I have also had encounters with a few ARVs. We have seen both, and it is important to be able to distinguish between the two. If you ever see a craft and wonder what it is, ETV's are sleek seamless smooth craft with the ability to phase shift instantly. They are often luminous and appear as one smooth solid surface. ARV's do not phase shift, reflect light normally, and have visible nuts and bolt construction with visible seams etc.

Chapter 1

1992

First CSETI Expedition
Eupan, Belgium
February 1992

In Belgium we met with officials who loaned us air force property such as night scope binoculars during the big wave of sightings of huge triangular and other objects outside Eupan and the outskirts of Brussels. These sightings began in November of 1989, and we went there in February 1992 to make contact. As soon as we landed and went into the field, we had an encounter. What this said to me was that the extraterrestrial civilizations visiting Earth have been waiting with extraordinary patience for humans to do something rational and peaceful about their presence. Instead of tracking them on radar, sending F-16 fighters to shoot at them, or standing with mouths agape, we were there answering a deep need for humans to engage in some kind of rational response. When we began to walk through that door, it was flung wide open!

CE-5 Event with Lights
Dr. Steven Greer[3]
The team and I gathered in a pre-arranged field with a police officer and two members of Belgium's principal UFO research organization on 2-9-92 at 8:30 P.M. The policeman had had many experiences with various sites and large triangular craft. The weather was cold, with wind, mud and intermittent driving rain. We used high-powered searchlights, specific auditory tones played over our cars' stereo systems via cassette tape, and Coherent Thought Sequencing (CTS).

At approximately 8:50 P.M., we noticed several bright white lights hovering above a ridge on the other side of Eupan. This ridge was

---

[3] Adapted from Steven M. Greer, *Extraterrestrial Contact* (Crozet, VA: Crossing Point, 1999), pp. 189-199.

crossed by a road that led into Eupan and had been the location of a number of sightings in the past. As the weather cleared, with our infrared scope I was able to see first one and then eight lights hovering above the ridge. These lights were several miles away and no distinct craft were seen. However, their movement defied prosaic explanation. At times, these lights would move in a circular fashion, reverse their direction and appear to merge with one another. After five to ten minutes of these observations, one of the lights signaled back to us in the same sequence which we had used to signal to them. These observations lasted for about thirty minutes, at which time the weather became unfavorable for further observations.

Vibratory Rumble from Above

On a high ridge near the town of Henri-Chapelle, between 12:30-1:00 A.M. on 2-11-92, we observed a long convoy carrying a canister under tight security along the road. While observing this event, we noticed through a break in the clouds a bright, large yellow-white light appear which moved slowly and was larger than the full moon. We could see the moon through thin clouds in the opposite direction from this light. This light was in the clouds in the area of the transport convoy, and was soon obscured by rapidly moving clouds.

A few minutes later, after the convoy had moved out of sight, we heard and felt a deep vibratory rumble directly over our car which lasted 10-30 seconds. This vibration was coming from the clouds directly overhead (the ceiling of clouds was very low from our position on the ridge). It was unlike anything any of us had ever heard; it certainly was not the distant rumble of thunder or jets, nor was it a sonic boom. Each of us felt that this sound was emanating from an immense and powerful object directly overhead in the clouds — like a million transformers humming almost to a roar or boom. This sound did not appear to be coming from a moving object.

A second episode of vibratory rumbling occurred shortly after the first one. We all felt that was associated with the mysterious light previously observed. It emitted this sound once overhead to let us know it was there because it could not safely descend below the cloud cover. It appeared to be a sound that was intentionally turned on, then off, then on again.

CSETI Training Group
Pensacola, Florida
March 1992

Dr. Steven Greer
In March 1992 we went to an area outside Pensacola, Florida. There had been sightings at nearby Gulf Breeze. I gave a day-long workshop for 50 people, including two former air force pilots, in which I discussed and demonstrated the meditation technique and remote viewing protocols. That night we headed to the beach at the state park on Santa Rosa Island. We arrived, began the protocols and within minutes four silent, hovering extraterrestrial vehicles appeared.

We were signaling to them in intelligent sequences, and they were signaling back. Flashing the 500,000-candle-power light three times resulted in the lead craft flashing back three times. Then after two flashes, it returned a signal of two flashes, then five and so on. About this time, half a dozen people jumped in their cars and roared out of there exclaiming "Oh, my God, this is actually happening!"

My reaction was, "Of course. Why did you think you came out here?" The event, a true CE-5, lasted for 20 minutes. After all the craft "winked out," we drew a large equilateral triangle in the northwest sky with our light. Three of the craft visibly returned and formed, in clear response, an equilateral triangle. People from six different locations observed the event. It was reported on the front page of the Pensacola newspaper the next day. We also have photographs and video (see DVD).

What you would never read in those reports about that event was the fact that there were advanced extraterrestrial beings at the site. While objects were being seen in the sky a mile or two away, de-materialized but very palpable forms were moving around us.

Those who were sensitive enough to pick this up realized they were on the beach with us.

My reply was "Yes, of course, we have invited them here." These beings were present enough that you could sense them. If your eyes were trained to see the neutrino light level, you could see them shimmering as they moved about amongst us. A few more people from our group became frightened and left, causing me to realize I needed to train people more thoroughly.

Meeting with Military Intelligence
Atlanta, Georgia, USA
April 1992

Dr. Steven Greer
CSETI events that began in the 1992 era have continued to this day. Suppressive countermeasures have also been occurring at the expeditions ever since. Because of how these early events had been reported to the public, the head of Army intelligence, CIA Director R. James Woolsey, and others took our efforts very seriously. So seriously that after the events of 1992 in Pensacola, I was invited to a conference and then to a hotel room in the wee hours of the morning with the former head of Army intelligence and a number of other military intelligence folks. What occurred was an inquiry. This experience is recounted in my memoir, Hidden Truth – Forbidden Knowledge[4]. I was essentially asked, "What in the hell are you doing?" There was a great deal of interest but also a great deal of concern because, as one of them put it, "Who has authorized you to do this?"

I told them the visitors authorized us because we are citizens of the universe. The extraterrestrials are eager to have some people make peaceful contact with them, and that is what we are doing, and we will do it no matter how much they threaten us. I informed him that there was nothing he could do to stop it. No threats, no amount of money, and no amount of interference would frustrate our contact attempts. We are to become a peaceful, global civilization and an

---

[4] Steven M. Greer, *Hidden Truth-Forbidden Knowledge* (Crozet, VA: Crossing Point, 2006), pp. 82-83.

interplanetary civilization, and that is going to happen.

CSETI Expedition
Gulf Breeze, Florida
Summer 1992

Scan of Intent

Dr. Steven Greer
I will never forget our second trip in the summer of 1992 to the Gulf Breeze area. We were out at night waiting and nothing was happening. One person present had a prejudice against certain types of what he thought were extraterrestrial people. He finally left for some reason and within ten minutes of his leaving an object appeared. We had been watching this object, thinking it was an antenna, but it was actually an ET craft with a red light – hovering. A line of these antennas with red lights made up part of the landscape. Suddenly, what we had thought to be a red light on an antenna started moving and came over us. We signaled to it and it flashed. It was a glowing, red-orange orb, and it waited to show itself until the ufologist with the prejudices left.

We have had the same scenario happen numerous times. Clearly, a probe had been sent to assess our group coherence. Extraterrestrial reconnaissance involves a scan that is not only electromagnetic and bio-electromagnetic, but also seems to monitor consciousness, thought and a person's heart and intentions. It is a scanning of the intent of those people present, and it is very reliable.

CSETI Rapid Mobilization Investigative Team
Alton Barnes, England
July 1992

Dr. Steven Greer
The pièce de résistance of that era was a few months later. Shari Adamiak and I along with a few other people went to England to meet with Colin Andrews and other crop circle researchers. We went to the little town of Alton Barnes, an area in Wiltshire near Marlborough. This was ground zero for the most astonishing of the crop circles – truly fabulous circles that happened before all the hoaxing occurred.

A CE-5 Crop Circle[5]

Woodborough Hill is on an estate of 1500 acres in the Royal Trust Lands. We were given the use of the estate, and initially we went up there to do research. One night we went up with about twelve people. (I think several of these people retold this story on Art Bell's Coast to Coast AM in 2006.) When we got there, I thought, "These crop circles are obviously some type of an interaction, and obviously of intelligent control and design. What if we go up on top of that hill and decide on a shape?" With no one else knowing what we were going to do, we debated many shapes, finally settling on what is now known as the CSETI triangle – three circles with lines connecting them in an equilateral triangle. We went into a state of expanded consciousness with all of us projecting that shape to the extraterrestrial people who are responsible for crop circle phenomena.

In the wee hours of the next morning, within line sight of Woodborough Hill, a farmer came out in his field and found exactly the crop circle we had envisioned. The site was called Oliver's Castle. It was as if the pattern had been lifted from our minds and placed in that field. All of us had been together until 1 or 2 AM in the morning, and the farmer had come out at 4:00 AM because the weather was clear and he was trying to take in his wheat. When Shari Adamiak and I saw that crop circle, tears welled up within us as we knew that was exactly the image we sent them. This event was a CE-5 involving the crop circles and I realized then there were no limits to what we could do with the CE-5 initiative.

Craft Appears in Storm

Subsequently, we decided to do some work away from Woodborough Hill because we were being overrun by media, particularly Japanese and German. There were hilarious scenes of us racing through the countryside with media pursuing, trying to figure where we were going.

We located ourselves near Woodborough Hill, in a field where there had been a very beautiful crop circle about the time we

---

[5] http://www.ufoevidence.org/documents/doc237.html

arrived. Clouds formed and a rainstorm developed. From within the clouds there were swirling lights just above us. Rain did not occur anywhere else except over the fields in which we were located, and this weather chased off everyone who was there trying to interfere with our effort. A short time later, we moved from the fields to a one-lane, concrete farm road. It was barely wide enough for a car. The road went through the farm and was above a field that sloped gradually down to a creek.

Because of the cold, drizzly weather, I said, "Let's just stay here in our vehicles." By then, there were just four of us in two cars, one behind the other in a little pullout off the farm road. I had been told in an earlier meditation, "Later, a little later, we will be here later – stay." Everyone else left but I knew we should stay. The night was getting late, about 12:30. It was cold, and we had been out all day. Suddenly there was a banging on my car window. Chris Mansell was one of the people with us. I rolled the window down, and he said, "There is a spacecraft in the field lit up like a bloody Christmas tree."

I said, "Yeah, yeah, and I'm Santa Claus."

He insisted, "No, I'm serious." He moved aside and there it was – a completely materialized, disc-shaped craft with brilliant lights rotating counter-clockwise along its base. Some bleeding back and forth among the lights made the overall pattern very complex. I have never seen light or movement like that before or since. It was astonishing. The craft was about 10 feet above the field but at our eye level. I could see the metallic structure between the rotating lights at the base, which were blue-green, red, amber, and white. These lights were rotating counter-clockwise. The object rose to a high dome or cone on which sat three or four amber colored lights. I got out of the car and told the woman I was with, a Ph.D. psychologist, to get the light and signal to it while inviting them to come closer.

She said, "Are you kidding?" and was clearly terrified. I realized that she was someone who had steeped herself in the UFO subculture, at least 90% of which is disinformation designed to scare people. Most of what you read in the media defames and ridicules the subject to make it seem ridiculous. The specific purpose is to scare people so that eventually they will accept the price of interplanetary war, which of course, the controllers of the War Machine want. If you understand that, you have it figured out.

The psychologist had absorbed a great deal of this terrifying media imagery and information but had taken an intellectual by-pass around it. While she thought she was ready for contact, it was all in her head. She was the kind of person who says 'I would like to meet them at my house for bagels and lox', but when the reality presented itself, she fell apart. Subsequently the extraterrestrials, who are very aware of such reactions, left. Even though the ship was a few hundred feet away you could feel their consciousness at our site; their consciousness and presence was right beside us.

The electromagnetic effect of this fully materialized ship, rotating slowly, caused my compass to rotate slowly counter-clockwise. This continued for a full hour, until the compass had slowly rotated 360 degrees. At the end of this period, the same ET craft appeared above us in an opening in the clouds – at a safe distance for the frightened psychologist. It signaled with us, and then vanished into space… During the time the ET craft was in the field, all of us felt the hair on our bodies stand up because of the high electrostatic charges.

Word of the near landing spread through the media and the area. A Japanese television crew was producing a documentary on crop circles for a network in Japan. The producer in charge was a tiny Japanese lady named Michi Nakamora. At the Ivy Inn in Marlborough she was interviewing me about what had happened in the near landing event. I noticed that they had fabulous camera equipment, something that we did not have. Back then the state of the art for our group was Betacams. After the interview ended, I turned to her with her film crew still there, and I asked, "Would you like to come out with us? If more of these type events happen, it would be great if we had someone along with a really high quality camera for filming these things at night." Her eyes got as big as saucers and she said, in clipped English "Nooo, I be freaked out." I told her that I would keep her safe, but still she would not go.

Lesson Learned

At that point I realized most people were not ready for such an experience yet. They were not aware of their own limitations or subconscious fears. With that realization, we moved into an era beginning in 1993 of CSETI training expeditions in which we started preparing people much more extensively. Before that time, the trainings were just a few hours of briefings and discussion, and now there is much more involved in preparation for fieldwork.

Tones from Crop Circles
Charlie Balogh

The BBC was documenting a fresh crop circle in England in July 1992. While their film crew was videotaping their walk through the circle, they heard incredibly high-pitched tones that were carried on some sort of "other" frequency that fried all their video equipment. The only things the crew could salvage were the auditory tones.

Crop circle researcher Colin Andrews provided the tones to CSETI. We broadcast them during our contact protocols for a number of years. After listening to them for a while, I realized they had a musical quality to them. Colin slowed the recorded tones down so that we could hear each individual tone. The actual sound forms what we call a sine wave, which is the purest form of sound.

On the original tape there was excessive hiss and tape noise, and I thought the most important and salient parts of that recording were the actual tones. Out of curiosity, on my synthesizer at home, I decided to see if I could recreate those tones, and the result worked out beautifully. I was able to determine the pitches, the actual frequencies, and the rhythm they used. I recreated them electronically and re-recorded them. CSETI now uses these tones instead of the original ones.

Chapter 2

1993

First Experience in Crestone

Dr. Steven Greer
In the winter of 1993 I was invited to a meeting of UFO researchers in Crestone, Colorado. "UFO" activity had occurred for years near the Great Sand Dunes and in Crestone. I had never been there, so Shari Adamiak and I went. We were traveling near the outskirts of Crestone on the west to east road when suddenly a brilliant white light, like a strobe light, appeared. It tracked alongside our car, flashing like landing lights on a runway. It was a very powerful event, and we felt it was an ET way of saying "welcome."

Later Shari and I went out into the Baca, an immense expanse of desert surrounded by mountains. We were in the vehicle because it was winter and very cold, yet we had a series of amazing encounters with a craft. We first saw the craft in the sky, and it then came down into the Baca. It was not fully materialized, but more like a hologram. I knew that we needed to come back to Crestone to do a CSETI expedition.

Travis Walton Movie
During this time frame a horrible movie called *Fire in the Sky* came out. It was a distortion of the experience in Arizona of Travis Walton, whom I personally knew. The producer was at the meeting in Crestone. He was not amused when I pointed out that the frightening scene on board the spacecraft was not at all what had actually happened. I also told him that the movie was disinformation designed to sow fear in the public. I think that is why the movie was not popular, because it was full of disinformation and sought to frighten people. I was not shy about expressing my views on this subject because I get very concerned when major media people purposely distort a true story for its sensationalistic

and xenophobic value. People form images and beliefs about what they see in movies, and this movie was full of inaccurate and concocted material.

CSETI Expedition
Popo, Mexico
January-February 1993

Lucid Precognitive Dream
Dr. Steven Greer
In late January 1993 we went to Mexico where there had been a large number of sightings around the volcano named Popo[6]. Since this experience has been reported in my other books, I will not recount all of it here. One key fact is that seven days prior to arriving in Mexico I had a lucid, precognitive dream in which I was shown a specific place. I had never been to Mexico before, but from the dream I knew exactly what the place looked like. We found that exact place, and everything unfolded exactly as it appeared in the dream with an amazing series of contacts.

Bright Flash
On January 31, 1993, while engaging in CSETI protocols to vector ET spacecraft into the site, the entire team was briefly engulfed in a bright flash of light, which originated in the northwest sky. No conventional source for this beam was found. We had the sense the ETs were checking us out with some type of scanning procedure. This type of light scanning has since happened on numerous CSETI expeditions around the world.

Large Triangular Craft
On February 1, 1993, the team vectored onto the site a large triangular craft, measuring 300-800 feet on each edge and coming towards us from the volcano. I could see in my mind's eye the person in charge of the craft and other beings on board. All were extremely luminous and white, tall beings. We signaled to them with very bright lights. The craft responded to our signals, circled the area and descended with its leading edge fully illuminated.

---

[6] http://vulcan.wr.usgs.gov/Volcanoes/Mexico/Popocatepetl/framework.html

It was about 300 feet in elevation and under 5000 feet from our research site. It had a brilliant light at each corner of the triangle, and a red pulsating light in the center. It was accompanied by a small red-orange probe or scout craft. It circled the area, and as the craft left the area it repeatedly returned signals from the team, and then dipped out of sight below a ridge. The contact lasted about ten minutes. During this very close encounter, all electronic devices failed, as did all cameras, which have motors. We later wished we had with us an old-fashioned mechanical crank film camera!

ETs and Volcanoes

At another point on that same trip it became very quiet. The ETs indicated they were busy, and this proved to be true. Mt. Pinatubo[7] had erupted in the Philippines, and the ET craft were working at Popo because it is the 3rd or 4th largest volcano on the Earth. The volcano overshadows one of the most populated cities on the planet, Mexico City. Popo is short for Popocatepetl and is 18,000 feet high. We were told directly by the ET craft that Popo is a very unstable volcano.

First CSETI Training
March 1993
Wickenberg, Arizona, USA

Ricky Butterfass

The first CSETI training was like a boot camp. We had breakfast at 7:30 in the morning. We ate a strictly vegetarian diet for the entire week, and we were doing many meditations. We were going through the protocols intensively. For me, a CSETI training was similar to being back in Navy flight school where they downloaded everything they thought you could possibly handle.

I remember one incident in which we were out in the field. Dr. Greer had told us to report to him any observations or thoughts that we had. I told him, "There is a craft here right now, but you cannot see it because it is phase-shifted." I had the idea it was like a Polaroid lens because unless you have it synchronized correctly,

---

[7] http://vulcan.wr.usgs.gov/Volcanoes/Philippines/Pinatubo/description_pinatubo.html

you cannot capture an image of the object. I told Dr. Greer the craft was going to come over the hill, descend, and then stop over a particular hill. Dr. Greer listened to my account, and we all went to dinner.

Later, as I was setting up my camera down on the main site, Dr. Greer appeared and said to me, "What you saw was correct. A craft did come down over the hill. After moving around it went back and is still sitting over there." I said, "Yes," and from then on, a bond was formed between us.

Dr. Steven Greer
We were at the hotel at dusk. A red object, fully materialized, came down in front of a hill. First the object traveled in a straight line. The craft then descended before moving back over the hill. Everyone looking at this ship initially thought it had to be the rear lights of a car, but we realized that it was operating where there was no road. This was a case in which one of these objects was traveling in disguise. Several of us saw it.

Several women had gone out into the desert separate from the group. At this time I thought we could handle as many people as wanted to come. But with 80 people, the situation was rather hard to control. It turned out that these women had an encounter with fully materialized three-foot high extraterrestrial beings. It was our first attempt to start training people, and we had a sighting and an encounter right away. What an amazing experience!

Dr. Richard Haines, Ph.D., an Ames Research Center scientist for NASA, was attending this training. As a result of his experiences at this training and my urging, he wrote a book, <u>CE-5: Close Encounters of the Fifth Kind</u>. He collected cases from all over the world involving interactive contact events that happened serendipitously. I feel that Dr. Haines' effort produced a very good historical collection of CE-5s.

Ricky Butterfass
We had many events at that training. The first night Dr. Greer, Dr. Joe Burkes, and another person were setting up a demonstration

using lights. They wanted the strongest signaling light available. I suggested they go to an aircraft supply store and buy an aircraft landing light which could be hooked up to a car battery. Suddenly we saw a huge orange disc plasma light, about the size of a 737, and Dr. Greer turned on the landing light. The ET craft stopped over a hill a quarter mile away. I was standing next to Dr. Greer holding a green chemical light source. I waved this light, and from the orange disc came a focused beam of light that hit Dr. Greer and me three times. It seemed to be locked onto the two of us. I was ecstatic, thinking, "Yeah! That's what I'm here for."

During the week I saw a number of red probes fly in. They looked like old train lanterns or a tail light and were about the size of a bowling ball. When they flew in they were often hard to observe because they were dark. If I happened to look right in the center, I could see a red lens effect, like a tail light lens. Sometimes I could see something like an infrared light. I could not see these probes until I looked right at them. They would do a quick scan, and fly out. They would come in about 15 feet over us and scan the whole group to find out what was going on. Every night the extraterrestrials sent in an orange disc, which I felt was a scout ship.

One night we formed the CSETI triangle with three teams about 100 yards apart. Dr. Greer's team was the Blue Team and was down in front. I was part of the Green Team on the hill about 100 feet above ground level. There were about 30 people in my group. We had walkie-talkies and were talking to each other. The orange disc came flying in, and we could see it. Our coordinator radioed Dr. Greer, and I saw this disk. While it was still it dimmed down. This disk then went over a ridge and came out from behind a hill.

Unique and Shared Realities
Dr. Steven Greer
What often happens on these events is that a shared reality occurs, where everyone sees something. Then there are other expressions of extraterrestrial presence that are very idiosyncratic, wherein the

---

[8] Greer, *Extraterrestrial Contact* (1999), pp. 64-103.

ability to see something has to do with one's level of consciousness and perceptual abilities. For example, most of the time interstellar vehicles are not operating at a linear, fixed, materialized frequency. You cannot go faster than the speed of light as solid matter. What happens when the craft is resonating beyond the crossing point of light? The detailed answer to this question is addressed in entire chapters in my first book[8]. The vehicle exists in a form that closely approximates what the mystics have called "etheric" or "astral" energy. Once we achieve a deeper state of consciousness, and there are ET craft that everyone sees, people begin to perceive other expressions of the extraterrestrial presence, but not everyone sees such interactions. The event is not invalidated just because some did not see it. Even when completely materialized craft appear, many people will not see it because their minds are in a state of denial or shock. The phenomenon is interesting and has both psychological and perceptual aspects.

"Seeing" Beyond the Ordinary

The issue involves training one's perception to go beyond seeing only material objects. Many expressions of extraterrestrial intelligence occur beyond the crossing point of light and outside our narrow visible spectrum of perception. Interstellar capable means you must go beyond the speed of light. If you are beyond the speed of light, you are certainly not locked in linear space/time.

Manifestations of Advanced Technology

Consider for a moment the advanced electronics that permit interstellar communication and interstellar travel: What does it take to enable a huge spacecraft weighing millions of tons to shift/spin out of linear space/time, dematerialize and reappear in another star system? If that spacecraft has not yet fully materialized, but is in your environment, what would be the manifestations of that technology? Those manifestations are the types of things we experience and are trying to share. Any person can see a fully materialized spacecraft that comes into view and is tracked on radar. But this is not how they usually manifest.

For several decades now, all the air space around Earth has

been covered by a deep space network and a near Earth network reconnaissance system that can track and target extraterrestrial vehicles. Very powerful electromagnetic weapons systems have hit and destroyed numerous ET craft. Therefore, most of the time, these extraterrestrial vehicles are shifted beyond the crossing point of light. In the field with us, a craft will often materialize and then vanish. Yet during, before, and after materialization, many varied expressions of extraterrestrial communication and technology can occur around us. Some fall in the realm of subtle vision or celestial perception, what some physicists call neutrino light emissions. These manifestations of advanced technologies can have an effect on your body, thought, or visual perception. If you are not aware of these possibilities, you may see or feel nothing at all, even though these expressions are going on around you. How can that be?

The Crossing Point of Light

Most of what exists in the entirety of the cosmos resonates beyond the frequency of the speed of light. This is a really key point. Most of what exists in the relative cosmos is resonating beyond the frequency of the speed of light and is thus beyond the field of normal visual perception and material, solid matter. If a civilization has reached interstellar capability, most of their technologies, and most of their ability to communicate, transport, materialize and dematerialize, use spectra of energy that are beyond the crossing point of light.

Perception is related to a person's level of consciousness, as well as their training. Both can be developed over time. For example, whether or not you see anything under a microscope is highly dependent on your ability to learn and develop that skill.

Shari and I received many reports from locals who saw the lights and craft during the Wickenburg training. After we left the area, sightings of these craft continued and were reported in the local media. We seemed to have opened up a gateway that enlivened the whole area for an ongoing level of extraterrestrial activity that many people began to see.

The White Noise of Space/Time

I have had experiences that helped me realize the credibility of the idea that thought and consciousness created by humans in a given space becomes permanently encoded in that space. If you walk into a place that is very sacred, where much meditation or prayer has taken place, you can *feel* it. Or if you go to a place where deep grief has occurred, you can sense it. The experience becomes encoded in what some call "the white noise of space/time" or, as others would say, "the Akashic Record." Within the fabric of space/time and beyond linear space/time a level of reality exists where everything that is thought or experienced is recorded as frequencies.

In a greater sense, the CSETI Initiative is opening up this potential around the world. We have had the same pattern of experiences repeat many times in our expeditions. We have numerous sightings and expressions that occur and are seen by various people. After we leave an area, extraterrestrial activity often continues to be experienced by residents in that area, as well as with those who have been on the expedition. That has happened over and over again.

Our actions potentiate an area, and those actions affect the people in the local area. Remember Schrödinger's dictum that the total number of minds in the universe is one. Rupert Sheldrake's concept of morphogenic fields also relates to this dynamic (www.sheldrake.org). Like the 100th Monkey phenomenon, once an individual or group initiates some unique new behavior, that activity potentiates the pattern for others who are not in direct communication or contact with the person (or group). Others will begin to have the same experience via a non-local propagation effect. This effect happens because of the non-local integrative nature of consciousness. Consciousness always consists of a non-local field of awareness. One action or experience affects other people, the animals, the Earth, space, time – everything is perfectly integrated through the nonlocal aspect of conscious intelligence.

Training to Transcend Fear

1993 was also important in the sense that I came to understand how to set up expeditions and train people to do CE-5 type activities. We began to set up working groups of people who could go back to their local areas and continue the research and contact. I saw that this approach was necessary after what happened in 1992 at Alton Barnes when the psychologist with me became absolutely terrified and her fear stopped the event from progressing. The extraterrestrial craft actually stopped coming closer *because* of her fear. ETs are exquisitely sensitive to human emotion and fear, contrary to what has been portrayed in the general media. If extraterrestrial peoples perceive fear and unpleasantness, they just go away. It is the ARVs (Alien Reproduction Vehicles) and the secret government abduction squads that keep coming at you, no matter how terrified you are! Of course, those are not extraterrestrial at all.

CSETI EXPEDITION
England
Summer, 1993

Team Under Observation

In the summer of 1993, we went back to England. The Ministry of Defense in England had a UFO officer at that time named Nick Pope, and he knew about our 1992 experiences at Alton Barnes. The week before we arrived, Colin Andrews and his team got reports about activity on the hills surrounding the estate that we were using. Investigating more closely they found that military personnel dressed in camouflage were setting up antennas and reconnaissance electronics all over the area. Some of the farmers who owned the land asked them what they were doing installing such things. The response was, "It's a matter of national security and it's none of your business. Buzz off, bloke." From the moment we landed, and the entire time we were there, we were under constant observation, and even experienced interference.

Speech at Cambridge University
Cambridge, England
1993

While we were in England to do the CE-5 research, I was invited to give one of the keynote addresses for an international congress gathering at Cambridge for Mensa, a group for people with high IQs. The presentation was quite linear and evidence driven. I presented government documents, testimony and some photographic and video evidence. After the lecture, I took questions from the audience.

In the front row sat an esteemed scientist who had worked his entire life at Cambridge and on committees with the British government. He stood up in front of hundreds of people in the hall and said, "I'll have you know that if there was anything to this, I would have known about it!" He went off on a tirade with his face red and neck veins bulging. His blood pressure had to have been 250. He concluded by exclaiming, "I find it utterly depressing that a man of your intelligence should be wasting his life on such drivel!"

I said, "With all due respect, unless you had a need to know, you wouldn't have known about this. I don't care how many degrees you have. Secondly, if there is a ten percent chance that what we have discovered is real, and that we're being visited by civilizations that are ten to the sixth to ten to the seventh years more developed than we are, and these sorts of technologies are being studied, this is the most important event to happen in the known history of the human race. Next question?"

Later we had a luncheon in a very beautiful great hall at Cambridge. As I was leaving to rejoin our group in Wiltshire, I heard footsteps running up behind me. It was a couple of young scientists who worked with the agitated professor at Cambridge. They apologized for his behavior and explained that my comments had frightened him. I told them I was accustomed to that sort of thing, and that I hoped I had not given him the impression that these visitors were in any way hostile. They conveyed to me he was frightened because he really believed that what I said was *true, which meant* his entire career had been involved in studying things at the kindergarten level of science and had been a waste – all because he had not been allowed to know about this matter. My message collapsed his whole sense of who he was, so he attacked the messenger. We have since found that this happens with great regularity!

CSETI Expedition
Crestone, Colorado
1993

Dr. Steven Greer

1993 was the year we were outside Crestone looking toward the southwest when an enormous object appeared in a crystal clear, dark sky. The object looked like a jeweled crown. It had brilliant lights, blue, red, golden, and emerald green. I now refer to it as "the jewel in the sky at Crestone." Everyone in the group saw it, and we all were awestruck. The light of the object was of such purity and intensity that it conveyed its beauty in an evocative emotion.

Coherent Light from ET Vehicles

I have learned the reason the light was so unusual is that it consists of coherent light similar to that of a laser. The materials of extraterrestrial vehicles have emerged from an etheric template into the materialized, three-dimensional world. The elements are therefore extremely pure. This has been found from the analysis of samples acquired from ET vehicles targeted and shot down. Samples analyzed from the debris in South America represent one example of this extraordinary purity. There is no way today's conventional technology can mine and manifest that degree of purity from those elements. They are created through an ultra-sonic technique where a template is created in the astral and etheric level of energy[9]. The product emerges in three-dimensional form, hence it is seamless, and the elements are so very pure. The vehicles are not being cobbled together from existing materials. So the light source is of an intensity people will describe as " not of this world." The light is etheric and literally not from this world.

Shape-shifts in ET Vehicles

The "Jewel in the sky at Crestone" was low in the atmosphere, and it morphed from a crown shape to a triangular shape. Soon military jets came in, and suddenly the object shifted and began to move. At that point it looked *exactly* like an airplane with aviation

---

[9] Greer, *Hidden Truth* (2006), p. 314.

lights on it. We saw how these ET vehicles can appear as one shape, then shift to another and then shift again to suddenly look like something prosaic, such as a satellite. In this case the object ultimately appeared to be an aircraft. Everyone there was mystified by this transformation of a jewel like ET craft into something that looked like a jet in the night sky.

Emotional Components

Trudy Guyker
In many cases strong emotion occurs because the craft are very beautiful. There was, of course, ample excitement, but absolutely no fear.

Linda Willitts
I have felt deliberate expression of emotion from the ETs. They definitely send love to us sometimes, although not every time. I can feel the love when it occurs. Realizing they have come from interstellar space to have a connection with me on Earth is so incredible I feel emotion whenever they interact with me.

Dr. Steven Greer
People are most prone to be in fear and denial of the connection with ETs when an encounter is actually happening. They see the object and sense they are being seen because we can actually feel the consciousness of those beings connecting to you on the site where you are. People may think they are ready for connections with ET, but often their fear arises so fast they cannot tolerate the experience. That is what happened at Gulf Breeze in Pensacola where some of the people sensed what was really happening, became frightened, jumped in the cars and drove off. It also happened in England when we had a craft land in the field and the psychologist who thought she was ready for contact was so completely stunned and terrified.

Chapter 3

1994

CSETI Working Group in Arizona & New Mexico
1994

Trudy Guyker
I joined a working group in Santa Fe, New Mexico. The first time we got together we had a weekend workshop in the foothills. There were about nine of us. Jupiter was visible in the sky, and two satellites passed overhead, one from the north and one from the south, something you do not see very often. When they crossed, we flashed a million foot candle light on the northbound satellite. We were looking for a signal back, but none came. We flashed to the southbound and it flashed back at us with a light brighter than Jupiter. I was amazed, awed, and deeply affected. Just think, the people in that craft were communicating with us.

During 1994 our group went to Yuma, Arizona, and joined another group. One night I had a wonderful dream. I was in the middle of a group of what I thought were little children because the tops of their heads were at about the level of my waist. I could see myself in the dream. I was moving along and suddenly realized I was not walking. The whole group was moving me as I was gliding along. Then I realized they were not little children; they were ETs. It helped me realize that they communicate through dreams, and that was important to learn. I accepted the dream as real because it was very lucid. I just accepted it as what had happened. The ETs liked me.

During that year, I was very fortunate to be living outside Los Alamos, New Mexico. The night sky there is incredibly dark and beautiful. I was able to go out into my back yard and watch the sky almost every single night for one full year. So many wonderful things happened during that time— all kinds of things flying.

One night I was looking through the binoculars at a satellite going west to east. It came over me and I was watching it through my binoculars. This apparently ordinary satellite suddenly flashed and became a triangular-shaped craft. I could not see through it; it was like looking at a reflection. It was an elongated triangle distorted in the middle. I looked away because I thought my eyes were playing tricks. When I looked again there it was. At this time it disappeared for about ten seconds. Then it flashed again and turned into a cigar-shaped craft. It was a golden brown color, and I could see the rounded contours of the ends. Once again, I watched it for about ten seconds. Ten seconds is a long time when you are seeing this kind of thing. Then, flash, and the "alleged" satellite appeared again.

Another time I was out looking at the sky on a beautiful black night, when a beautiful light blue globe appeared. At arms length, it would have been the size of a dime. It just appeared and then very slowly sank. Those are a few of the things that happened before I met Dr. Greer.

The Challenge of Believing

I went home and was having second thoughts about what I had seen. My husband suggested it was probably a helicopter or a balloon. His comment made me determined to accept the event as real, and as soon as I did that, my confidence grew. After that I was able to look at everything else more firmly and not discount what I saw. That is an important realization. I believe the ETs make some appearances to help you build your confidence.

Dr. Steven Greer
You have to believe something is possible to perceive it. If you do not think you can become a medical doctor and resuscitate people you cannot. You have to know that you can. There is a saying: "As ye have faith, so shall your powers and blessings be." This is faith, not in the sense of religious belief, but is an affirmative confidence that something can be, and to that extent it will be. Knowing this helps people get out of their own way. Witness the Sufi Master

who asked his student to levitate and walk on water. The disciple protested he would sink and drown. The teacher replied, "Leave thyself behind and then walk upon the water." When taking on what seems to be an impossible task, you have to be able to get out of your own way to let it happen.

I was recently told by the former Minister of Defense in Canada that he met with a senior senator in the Canadian Parliament who told him that he could not help us because he was just the chairman of a Senate Committee. He said the task was too big— like having only a six-pound line and trying to reel in a 2,000-pound whale. Of course he could not do it, because he did not see it as possible.
The world advances through people knowing they can arise and do impossible things. That is the power of certainty, of genuine faith, and of a positive affirmation of what can be, even if it has not yet happened.

VIP Expedition with Rockefeller's People
Crestone, Colorado
1994

In 1994 we went to Crestone again with Laurance Rockefeller's people and a few others. CSETI conducted a VIP expedition at their request. A number of objects appeared in the sky and signaled to us at a distance, but the most astonishing event happened at the Great Sand Dunes. We were traveling north of the Dunes on a county road. The time of day was between 4:30- 5:00 PM, so it was broad daylight. I wanted to find a certain area north of the Great Sand Dunes because we had remote viewed that there was going to be an unusual encounter that would happen in that area during daylight.

ET Capabilities

We reached the spot with 20 people in four or five cars. We got out and were looking around the area. Suddenly from the west and flying directly east towards the Sangre de Cristo Mountains[10] was a small, private, single-engine airplane. It looked like a Cessna and

---

[10] Sangre de Cristo Mountains: http://en.wikipedia.org/wiki/Sangre_de_Cristo_Mountains

was only 100 feet above the ground. Everyone saw it, including George Lamb, Bootsie Galbraith, Sandy Wright, and others from New York. People were commenting that they did not hear any sound as the plane approached. It moved along above some power lines beside us and then flew over us. Some people saw it as yellow and white while others saw it as magenta. Everyone saw it, but perceptions of it differed, even though it was extremely close! It flew towards the Sangre de Cristo Mountains and went into a box canyon. We had people observing it through binoculars. George Lamb cried out, "If it doesn't pull up, it's going to crash!"

I said, "Just watch, George. Let's stay quiet and centered in a state of calm consciousness." With every single person watching, the plane merged into a mountain and disappeared. I explained it was not an airplane, but an ET craft that was *shifted* to look like an airplane. Expressions of extraterrestrial technological capabilities boggle the mind. The people in our group rubbed their eyes in disbelief. I repeated that they had just see an extraterrestrial vehicle that, to any casual person watching, looked like someone flying his personal airplane at a low altitude on a nice, sunny day in the Colorado Rockies. That is what you saw, but in reality it was an extraterrestrial vehicle. It made no noise. While it was near enough that you could see into the cockpit, there was nobody in there. The vehicle disappeared into a box canyon and never came out. Nothing obstructed our view of that range of mountains. The box canyon was fairly close to us, and the vehicle literally merged with and disappeared into the mountain as we watched[11].

Dr. John Altshuler's Experience[12]

Dr. John Altshuler shared with me an incident when he was flying his private plane. He was a well-regarded hematologist/pathologist in Denver and a dear friend. He was flying near the Great Sand Dunes on the east side of Blanca Peak, at 14,345 feet the third highest peak in Colorado. It was a sunny, crystal clear day. Suddenly an enormous, disc-shaped, metallic-looking extraterrestrial vehicle appeared reflecting the sun's rays. The craft, which he estimated as 100 yards across, came very close to his airplane and activated

---

[11] Shari Adamiak reported this same incident in *Extraterrestrial Contact*, pg. 249.
[12] Greer, *Extraterrestrial Contact* (1999), pg. 249.

his gyro and instruments, causing them to spin wildly.

Electromagnetic anomalies occurred in his cockpit. Then he had an encounter with the ETs where he was on board their craft in time/space suspension. Subsequently he found himself consciously in his plane again. The enormous craft flew towards the upper third of Blanca Peak and went 'straight into the mountain'. He was expecting to see an enormous collision, just as we were expecting with the little 'plane' in the box canyon. He said that it just seamlessly merged into the mountain. The craft was materialized enough to reflect the sun off its surface, yet it just merged into the mountain and disappeared.

The FAA (Federal Aviation Agency) monitoring his flight lost track of him for a short time, so he almost got into trouble over this very strange event. We later learned from our own experiences on Blanca Peak that it contains a major extraterrestrial base and spaceport. He never would talk about the event publicly.

States of ET Vehicles

Extraterrestrial vehicles can be materialized, dematerialized or in between those two states. The spin and resonance frequency can exist out of phase with linear space/time. The vehicle looks very physical and materialized, yet it can go straight through solid matter, because solid matter is mostly empty space. If you collapsed the solid matter of your body and removed all of the space, it would fit on the head of a pin. You are mostly empty space. Nothing prevents one bit of empty space from going through another bit of empty space if it can shift a little bit out of resonance frequency. That is how objects that appear to be solid, materialized objects can go straight through other solid, materialized objects. They can shift their resonance frequency and spin.

RMIT Report
Monterrey, Mexico
December 1994

CSETI learned of a major wave of activity in the large metropolis of Monterrey, Mexico. We contacted the investigator who had filmed many of the sightings, Sr. Santiago Yturria Garza. Santiago and his friend, television host Diana Perla Chapa, have been involved in the investigation of suspected spacecraft and ET presence since the 1970s.

The team in Monterrey consisted of Shari Adamiak, another person, me, and a woman who was a good friend of Boutros Boutros-Ghali and his wife. Boutros was the Secretary-General of the United Nations at that time. We went to the edge of a city in the mountains. This location was known to have had a great deal of ET activity. We also had a Mexican driver whose wife was with him to help us. We had a Suburban for our field gear and crew, and the driver stayed with the truck.

We engaged the CSETI CE-5 protocol, and suddenly on the mountain appeared a disc or egg-shaped craft sitting on the peak. This event was not an astral perception, but a materialized ship that was sitting on the jagged peak above us. No person could walk there. After a few moments an electric, cobalt blue light from the craft flowed down the mountain. This "liquid light" was similar to an effect that would also occur at Blanca Peak four years later in 1998. The light moved like tendrils and wrapped around all of our feet. This light was seen by everyone. While all of this was happening we were signaling to the ET craft, communicating with the occupants mentally, and the blue light swirling around our feet as the Mexican driver was watching from below. He was so overwhelmed by what he saw that he went screaming out of the truck and wanted to leave. The driver was absolutely terrified, but his wife calmed him and talked him into staying. He climbed inside the truck, locked the doors and rolled up the windows.

We remained there at the edge of Monterrey in a state of communion and connection with the ETs. The craft remained for two hours and 45 minutes signaling and communicating with us. The woman who had accompanied us — a very well-connected socialite, told Boutros-Ghali and his wife about this event after getting back to New York. The Secretary-General knew that CSETI was at the vanguard of making interplanetary contact and diplomatic communication with cosmic extraterrestrial beings, so at that time we were keeping him appraised of our expeditions and experiences.

Chapter 4

1996

Colby Incident
Rock Point, Maryland
April 1996

In the spring of 1996 a colonel surfaced who wanted to broker a meeting between us and the former CIA Director, Bill Colby. They were good friends – Colby had been on the inside of the secret government. Colby was advancing in years and wanted to help our effort before he passed away. He had offered to give us a functioning, extraterrestrial energy device, which was available to him in his intelligence 'cell', and $50 million in secured funding to get this information and technology out to the world. The very week a member of CSETI's board of directors was to meet with him, he was found dead in the waters of the Potomac River. The colonel who set up the meeting later told me personally that Colby had been assassinated[13]. This was very disturbing. The colonel came to Shari Adamiak's wake and told me that we can never look back- just keep moving forward, despite our unbearable grief. Perhaps you can see why after Shari died, and I had a very aggressive cancer, and Colby was murdered, I was close to shutting down all of these projects. But I vowed to persevere and not let these murderous people win. I realized that it is only when good people give up that these negative influences can prevail in the vacuum of leadership that we leave. So, NEVER give up.

Mexico
May 1996

Remote View of Plane Crash

---

[13] From Wikipedia, the free encyclopedia: http://en.wikipedia.org/wiki/William_Colby
"On April 27, 1996, Colby died in an apparent boating accident near his home in Rock Point, Maryland, although his body was actually found, underwater, on May 6, 1996. The subsequent inquest found that he died from (con't)

Linda Willitts
I recall you mentioning a Mexico trip where you and Bob Hairgrove remote viewed a plane crash.

Dr. Steven Greer
Yes. We were at a site, if I remember correctly, where a Native American avatar had appeared. We were in a deep meditation, and I sensed in real time that something terrible had happened. It was very specific, a man-made event resulting in loss of life. As I picked up this information, it overrode all of my other remote viewing because it was such a disturbance in the field of consciousness. I shared this with the others. Bob Hairgrove shared his experience that he saw a pilot in a jet that was broken and was going down. We shared this because our protocol is that no matter how seemingly meaningless a vision or a remote view may be, you need to share it with the whole group. This is particularly true when it is something that comes in spontaneously and overrides your total consciousness. We shared, but we did not know what to make of it. We tucked it away and went about what we were doing.

Several days later when I called home, my wife asked if I had heard about the terrible ValuJet crash in the Everglades[14]. We found out that the Valujet crash occurred at the precise moment, adjusted for time zones, that we were both having this remote view experience. I got the loss of life and some kind of man-made accident while Bob saw the jet going down. Putting the two together we got exactly what happened in real time to the minute.

The lesson here is the importance of people sharing their part of the message or image with everyone else even though it may not seem to make any sense. In reality something had happened that was catastrophic, and it was important that he shared his part because it came together with my part and made the whole. We remarked at the time that maybe some terrible plane crash had happened, but we did not know. It is a very important lesson in terms of being able to trust each other to share the information you get in a deep

---

drowning and hypothermia after collapsing from a heart attack or stroke and falling out of his canoe, and there was no further investigation."
Theories about death (con't)

remote view.

Winner of Art Bell RV Contest

I had trained Bob to remote view using the technique of going into unbounded mind. It involves the Vedic approach to unbounded Samadhi and then seeing from the inner sight of non-local awareness. Bob was also the person who won the Art Bell contest when Bell asked his audience to remote view an item he had put up on his refrigerator. Bob went into unbounded mind, went into Art Bell's house, looked at his refrigerator, called up the hot line and accurately described the item. He is the person who saw accurately out of all the millions of listeners. Art Bell was stunned and asked Bob how he did it. Bob said, "I've been on a few of these trainings for a few weeks with Dr. Greer at CSETI."

Day Training
Palm Beach County, California
1996

Dr. Steven Greer

In 1996 I took a small day training group out for fieldwork in Palm Beach County. As we walked out at dusk onto the beach at the state park, a beautiful, translucent, aquamarine blue globe about the size of a large grapefruit appeared along the back of the woman walking in front of me. This woman had worked with Gandhi. There were three women at this event who had been some of Gandhi's closest confidants. If you look at his autobiography, there were some blond women from Europe who became part of his household and cooked for him. Those three were in our group, and each had a lucid, pre-cognitive dream where they were given my name, this event and that they should be there. As we walked out onto the beach, this beautiful extraterrestrial orb appeared right along the center of this woman's back. Everyone saw the orb. It went out onto the beach with us and vanished. It did not fly off; it just disappeared.

The whole night there we were in a state of cosmic consciousness.

"Although the inquest into Colby's death found he had died of natural causes, there were some suspicious circumstances: he rarely went canoeing at night; he had not spoken to his wife of any plans to go canoeing; his house was unlocked, with the radio and computer on and the remains of a meal on the table; there was no sign of the

We knew that Gandhi was with us, though on the other side in the spirit world. He was very aware of CSETI's work and the state of universal peace and consciousness into which we were entering. You could tell these women were highly enlightened and pure hearted. They appeared in a most enigmatic way. We sat together on the beach, and they were in a high enough state of consciousness that we sat there the entire night without fatigue. Four hours went by in what felt like fifteen minutes. We were all in a state of God-consciousness/ cosmic consciousness with higher spiritual beings and extraterrestrial beings present. It was truly a beautiful evening!

CSETI Training
Crestone, Colorado
June 1996

Debbie Foch
In 1996 at Crestone we found a field site in the Baca within view of the Sand Dunes. One evening we saw an object with about ten lights lined up at the bottom of Mount Blanca near the Sand Dunes. The atmosphere was very hazy so you could only see them through binoculars. These lights were moving up and down like it was a solid craft coming toward us. Dr. Greer told us all to calm down and be prepared for some sort of interaction. I think Trudy remote viewed on board the craft.

Trudy Guyker
I went into the craft which was circular and darkly lit. As I walked along inside I saw lights on the floor, as a guide. At another point I saw several of the pilots who were looking toward us. As the craft was coming closer Dr. Greer told everyone to return to their seats and check what was in their hearts to see if they were ready for this. We all did that, and I guess there were some people who were fearful because the craft stopped.

Debbie Foch
We also saw many amber orbs that year that were moving along

---

life-jacket his friends said he usually wore; and his body was found approximately 20 yards from the canoe (itself found 100 yards from the house) after the area had been thoroughly searched several times."
[14] Wikipedia: http://en.wikipedia.org/wiki/ValuJet_Flight_592

the tree line toward the north of our location.

CSETI Expedition
Scotland, UK
October 1996

Dr. Steven Greer
There was a very wealthy person who was afraid to do anything too bold as far as extraterrestrial disclosure, but did let us use his private jet. We flew to Scotland with Sandy Wright, Shari Adamiak, my second daughter, Elisabeth, this gentleman and his pilot. We then went to the area called Bonny Bridge, north of Edinburgh, where many sightings had recently occurred. We went out for fieldwork and had an encounter during which one of the massive triangular ships common to Bonny Bridge dipped down out of the fog at night, became illuminated, circled the area, and then went back up into the clouds.

One of our main purposes in going to Scotland was to collect a series of original films and documents from encounters that had happened in the area and bring them back to the US. Another purpose was to do a CE-5 to welcome the ETs in Scotland[15].

By the time we landed back in the US counterintelligence agents, furious that we were collecting this kind of documentation, took pictures of "Dr. Greer landing in a private jet." They flooded the Internet with innuendo that I was a CIA agent who had gone to Scotland to abscond with UFO photographs and documents! They claimed I had stolen the UFO archives of Scotland and brought them back to America. It was just madness! When I got home and got online, there were 500 emails in my inbox calling me everything imaginable. This is typical of the type of psychological warfare and disruptive actions that continue to this day.

Shortly after the Scotland trip, I told Shari that it was time for me to share more of the underlying truth at the root of the

---

[15] Ironically, when we landed in a private jet, they rolled out the red carpet, and we did not get off the jet right away because we had a private customs exam. A customs and immigration person came on board to check our passports. He was cold and officious until he got my passport. When he saw that my name was Greer, he said,

extraterrestrial subject. I had realized that the process had to be a carefully planned progression, because you cannot strip away all the veils and provide all the information at once. For most people, it would just be too much to take.

Vision Quest
Crestone, Colorado
October 1996

Dr. Steven Greer
After telling Shari that the time had come to provide the world with more information, she and I privately went to Crestone to go on a vision quest. I remember that we enjoyed picnicking in the car on the gravlox she had saved from the Scotland trip. It was late October.

Unveiling the Next Level

I realized that to unveil more information about the extraterrestrial subject, I needed someone to listen. I knew you cannot teach unless you have receptive students. As the saying goes: 'The wise are those who speak not unless they have a hearer.' Shari was that person until the time of her death.
We went out to the Baca at 8,000 feet in very cold weather. The temperature must have been close to 0 degrees Fahrenheit and the moon was visible. Suddenly, an enormous, amorphous, sombrero-shaped craft appeared. It nearly materialized, like the scintillating blue-green teal one that came straight down at Joshua Tree. The craft had been hovering in the Baca in what looked like a fog, but it was actually awake, conscious, living technology. It approached us slowly but deliberately. We got out of the car and were standing there together when suddenly the ship lit up. The entire environment around us changed and was scintillating. In an instant, we found ourselves inside the dematerialized craft.

I said, "Now is the time for us to go to the next state." We sat and I took her into the state of God-consciousness in which you become aware of the cosmic mind. As you cross the veil of light you are

---

"Oh, the house of Greer." Apparently 'Greer' is a very prominent scion name— a Scottish name in the same clan as MacGregor. "Welcome to Scotland." When I said that I was American, he said, "But you're part of the clan." We could have had anything on that plane, but; he did not check a thing, and off we went.

able to see the celestial with your naked eyes. This effect is how children and some adults have been able to look at a flower, see its essence and know how it can be used for healing. All of the indigenous peoples have this ability to some extent – if it hasn't been beaten out of them by a misguided, materialistic educational system.

The New Cosmology

Shari had a small cassette recorder, and I told her to begin recording. I subsequently began a download of the entire cosmology resonating beyond the crossing point of light. That information became the paper "Extraterrestrials and the New Cosmology[16]." The dictation consisted of the real-time encounter with the ETs in that ship. The veils of denser light fell away so that I could perceive and describe the enfolded nature of linear space/time and the material cosmos. The astral, the etheric, the celestial, and the divine were all present and shining. This experience continued for hours as I observed and spoke.

Debbie Foch

Two papers came out of that transcription: "Extraterrestrials and The New Cosmology" and "The Crossing Point[17]." The vocal group, Enigma, must have picked up on that because they used that phrase, 'the crossing point of light,' in their third CD[18].

Dr. Steven Greer

When we returned to the Baca Townhouses the hour was quite late. Shari loved to make blue corn chip nachos after we had been out in the cold. As we sat eating the nachos by candlelight, I said, "They're back." We went out on the patio and looked toward Crestone Peak to our east. There, sitting on the peak in the moonlight in the wee hours of the morning, was an *enormous* sombrero-shaped ship totally visible. It had to be hundreds of feet in diameter. I connected to it in awareness and, with the moonlight, could see a fine celestial mesh of energy, or what I call the crystalline matrix of the astral energy field. These energies manifest within and as the basis of linear space, time and the material world. We could

---

[16] Greer, *Extraterrestrial Contact* (1999), pp. 64-80.
[17] Greer, *Extraterrestrial Contact* (1999), pp. 81-100.
[18] "Enigma 3: Le Roi Est Mort, Vive Le Roi!" The phrase 'crossing point of light' occurs at the beginning of track 11.

see it, and as we stood there awestruck, I told her that it was time for me to share this information with the group. She said, "Yes, this is the next level."

Slated for Extermination

She was not alive much longer. In just over a year she was in a coma. The question often arises as to why the ETs could not have saved Shari. I cannot answer that except to say that later when we went to England in July of 1997, we found out that we were slated for extermination by Majestic elements who were furious at what we were doing. We knew it and we had been told that. I had been told that we had pushed disclosure of the ET presence too far and that it had thrown the entire MJ-12 group into complete disarray.

So we were in the crosshairs of some very angry and powerful people. The dark forces were literally trying to kill us – all of us. A number of senior people involved with the disclosure of the ET presence were forced into near death, and many did die. The dark cabal forces were furious that we had aroused so much interest at the Pentagon, at the Joint Staff, Congress, and the White House. Secretary-General Boutros-Ghali had committed the facilities of the UN General Assembly for the Disclosure event before he was threatened and had to pull out. His advocacy for disclosure is why he was denied the traditional second term.

Cancer Episodes

During this same era, Congressman Steve Schiff of New Mexico, who was trying to get the Roswell information out, developed what seemed like a minor skin cancer and then quickly died. I got metastatic malignant melanoma and Shari got breast cancer at exactly the same time. She was dead within a year. Initially, I thought I would die first because I had the more aggressive and fatal type of cancer. Malignant melanoma that is metastatic is the most aggressive and deadly of all skin cancers[19]. I had multiples of these cancers. My wife and children were worried because if you have metastatic malignant melanoma and do not know where

---

[19] http://www.hemispherx.net/content/ftp/metastatic.htm

the primary is, the assumption is it could be fatal. It only takes one cell to go into your internal organs, and by the time it is detected, there is usually just enough time to be measured for the coffin. But ironically, I survived it and after three of them, I have had no more. Disturbingly, we could never find the primary site, because the primary was in a Petri dish in an underground facility in Utah. The primary can be radionically transmitted onto the person targeted[20]. I did everything possible to beat this cancer and had great people working for me. Shari and I had thousands of people praying for us, too, for which we are eternally grateful.

At Crestone we had broken through the veil and passed through the crossing point of light. I felt that it was time to share the cosmology – because I knew we could be out of time, and only a fool, given the diagnoses that we had, would have thought otherwise. So I thought it was important to get the information on the cosmology and crossing point of light as widely known as possible. We also knew that we were never alone and that somehow this was going to work out.

Q&A on Dynamics of Articulating the Cosmology
Greg Heller
On the Vision Quest with Shari in Crestone, was that when the whole cosmology solidified for you so that you could present it?

Dr. Steven Greer
The vision quest was a vehicle for me to articulate to other people what I had experienced since I was a boy, and which I knew and routinely experienced. So it was not anything new to me. What was new was Shari, who had the *capacity* to not only understand it but also experience it. That gave me the impetus and allowed me to articulate it in a way that others might understand. You know, we are trying to use language to describe experiences and perceptions that are vastly beyond linear speech. If Shari had been of lesser capacity, I would have never shared this information. It would be like talking calculus to someone who is in first grade. In this case,

---
[20] Thomas E. Bearden, *Oblivion: America at the Brink* (Santa Barbara: Cheniere Press, 2005), pp. 210-223.

Shari was completely ready and receptive. She understood and "got" it. She was in the correct state of consciousness in the Baca and back at the Baca Townhouse later when I articulated how the crystalline matrix interfaced with the astral and with the material cosmos.

I thought that since Shari understood the cosmology, other people could too. We had recorded it on tape, and we eventually turned it into the two papers. Up until that time I was reluctant to talk about it because I was unsure that it would have made any sense to anyone. There is no point talking about something that is incomprehensible. There is more I would still like to share... I still have not shared everything about the experiences and knowledge from my near-death experience in 1973 or the subsequent contact I had on the mountain in North Carolina in 1973 when I was taken on the ET craft. I understood a lot of this very well, but not in a way that is easy to explain, and the time must be right.

When I became a meditation teacher and a Siddha[21], I began to practice the siddhis[22] and once levitated and floated across the lawn at Livingston Manor in New York at a retreat. I began to have similar experiences on a routine basis, and I was only 18-21 years old. I had accessed considerable Vedic information, knew the reality of the extraterrestrial presence and understood how their technologies and knowledge of the science of consciousness interfaced with the material sciences.

Shari was someone of *very* high intelligence—but also very spiritual. She had been having more and more of these experiences with extraterrestrials because we had been doing expeditions and RMITs together for a number of years. Finally, the time had come when I felt I could really articulate it to her, and through her to others.

Steven Greer's Role

My role, having had these experiences, is to communicate them. I have been fortunate to have the gift to talk about these experiences in a way that larger and larger numbers of people will understand.

---

[21] Wikipedia: http://en.wikipedia.org/wiki/Siddha
[22] Wikipedia: Siddhi—a Sanskrit word that literally means "accomplishment", "attainment", or "success" [http://en.wikipedia.org/wiki/Siddhi]

That can take them to the next level of understanding, which is really my purpose.

CSETI Expedition
Joshua Tree, California
November 1996

Dr. Steven Greer
We had come to Joshua Tree in 1996 to do an expedition, and we stayed at a hotel in Desert Hot Springs.

Linda Willitts
Jamie Cromwell, the actor who had just done the movie, "Babe[23]," was there.

Dr. Steven Greer
Jamie also played the man who made first contact in the Star Trek movie, "First Contact[24]." He told us he was inspired by what we were doing to play that role. Many people in music and Hollywood follow our work. There was a musical group called "Blink-182." Founder Tom DeLonge[25] and his band came out with us in the Joshua Tree desert. We introduced them to the CSETI idea. They had been following our work for years, and had a song called "Aliens Exist[26]."

Linda Willitts
The first night we went to a place close to Desert Hot Springs near the hills. That was when a small, orange craft that looked like a cigarette flying in the dark scooted low near the mountain ridge making a spitting/hissing noise as it traveled.

Dr. Steven Greer
Jamie Cromwell just missed that, but the craft actually came right over us and it was so low that you could hear it moving through the air. It was an orange-colored ship; you could hear a 'shhhhh' noise, and it was spinning. It came from behind us at a very low altitude, maybe 300 feet.

[23] http://us.imdb.com/title/tt0112431/
[24] http://www.imdb.com/name/nm0000342/
[25] Wikipedia: http://en.wikipedia.org/wiki/Tom_DeLonge

Ricky Butterfass

Before the orange disc came in, we did a CTS. I did a remote view and saw a large craft. I was in communication with the commander of it. The craft was disc shaped and looked like a huge radio telescope antenna. It was not solid, but had a grid pattern, and underneath was a cluster of eight other discs. I had an exchange with the pilot in which I asked if he could land the craft in the mouth of the valley. He said no. I asked why not, and he said because the craft was about a half-mile wide and it would not fit. He also said that even if he could land it he would not because it was so big it would freak out the whole town.

I asked if he could send down an orange scout ship like the kind that we had in Phoenix in 1993. I asked him to send it down and light it up so we could see it without a doubt. Just then someone saw an orange disc come straight down, and I said, "Oh, yes. I just had a CTS and communicated with the commander and I asked him to send down a scout ship orange disc."

Linda Willitts

Yes, I remember that.

Ricky Butterfass

The thing came screaming right over the top of us at a few hundred feet, all lit up. It was at least 100 feet across, and it sounded like hair singeing. Sparks came out the sides with a trail about two miles long all lit up behind it.

The Rosetta Stone of ET Communication

Dr. Steven Greer

It is important to understand that there is always a consciousness and remote view connection to the vehicle and the occupants prior to these events. It is the key – the Rosetta stone – of interplanetary, extraterrestrial, interspecies communication.

People who want to dismiss the importance of the consciousness

---

[26] http://www.lyrics007.com/Blink-182%20Lyrics/Aliens%20Exist%20Lyrics.html

and the protocol of coherent thought sequencing are dismissing the Rosetta stone. They are really throwing out the main lesson. The beeping tones are important for giving the ETs a very precise vector in case we are not precise in our consciousness. The same is true of the lasers that we use now. While tones and lasers are important to give a precise vector, the key to really making contact is the ability to go into unbounded, non-local consciousness. This state enables one to see remote places, connect to the spacecraft and, as Ricky was describing, coherently thought-sequence our location. We invite them to that location in a spirit of interplanetary peace and diplomacy. We do it each afternoon, we do it at night before we go to bed, and we do it when we are out in the field with a group of people.

It is the part of CSETI protocol that has generated the most controversy and ridicule, but it is also the reason we have had these very successful events. To understand the trans-personal nature of consciousness is to realize that consciousness is nonlocal and this nonlocality is absolutely vital because inter-stellar civilizations have developed communications technologies that interface directly with thought and awareness.

Hershey's Kiss Craft to Underground Base
Linda Willitts
This was one of the most spectacular ET events we have ever seen. Dr. Greer had remote viewed that we were going to see something spectacular, quick, and it was going to happen very late in the evening. At about 1:30 in the morning we were leaving the park. There was a car in front of Dr. Greer and he, his daughter, and Shari were in the car ahead of me. Suddenly straight down out of the sky came a fluorescent teal- green, bluish object the size of my fist at arm's length. It was streaming out blue white plasma. It came down in two seconds from about half a mile away, and it looked like it was going to crash into the ground. As it made contact with the ground, the ground was illuminated for a great distance, but there was no crash or sound of any kind.

Dr. Steven Greer
Let me set the stage a little better for this event. A man with our

group had an RV that was always tying up traffic and created difficult situations. Whenever this fellow was around, nothing would happen. We later found out that he had infiltrated CSETI so that he could learn about the ET technology. His sole interest in the project was to become fabulously wealthy by being "the next Rockefeller of energy!" So whenever he was present there were never any encounters. It felt so quiet I knew something was not right. I had clearly remote viewed that there was going to be a major event, that it would be late and that it would be enigmatic and quick. I had shared this with 30 or 40 people. Finally I felt it was time to leave that place. As fate would have it, this man took a long time loading his gear and the rest of the vehicles in our group left. As we were going up a hill, a car was driving in front of me.

Suddenly all of the dashboard lights on the car dimmed. I immediately said to Shari and my daughter who was in the back seat, "They're here, heads up!" Straight out of the zenith came a 200'–300' diameter flat disc shaped like a Hershey's Kiss[27]. The tape that you pull on a Hershey's Kiss would be like the trail of scintillating light streaming behind the craft. It did not come in at an angle, but fell like a weight straight down out of the Zenith. As the disc approached the Earth, it illuminated the whole desert like daylight as far as you could see. We expected a huge boom because this craft was at the crossing point of light, not quite at the point of materialization. Instead it went right into the Earth, and I was told at that instant there was an ET underground base there.

After this spectacular event, the desert was dark again. I was trying to fix the location where the craft entered the earth while driving on a very rough dirt road. The vehicle in front of me was putting up a cloud of dust, so I passed it. The whole time I was driving, I was multi-tasking trying to keep in my mind's eye the exact impact location. When we got to that area I knew that that was the place. I could see the exact spot the enormous ET craft had gone straight into the desert.

---

[27] http://www.hersheys.com/kisses/about/

Globes over Parking Lot

Ricky Butterfass

One year we were in that parking area when three globes came in and formed a triangle. We were standing out on the road, talking to each other and signaling to them, but they were just glued there in the sky for about 20 minutes. I think they came in from three directions before merging into a triangle. The one in the center moved off, and I had my binoculars on it. When it flew over the top of us I could hear a low humming sound and I could see that it was an equilateral triangle with a red light in the center of it. Out from the red light that bisected each angle of the triangle, there were three blue lights. One of the others moved over the top of us, and it had orange lights under it. I have never seen any type of aircraft configuration with a cluster of a dozen orange lights under it. It went off in the opposite direction of the first one.

Smell of Ants

Kay Gibson

I would like to add that aside from the exciting experience of seeing lights and craft, there are other, more subtle, aspects of which one should be aware. This was my first CSETI training so it was interesting because I had no expectations. I did not know what was going to happen, and one of the things that happened was a smell that I associate from childhood with crushed ants.

Dr. Ted Loder

That would be formic acid.

Kay Gibson

I had no idea what that smell was except as ants, so there was a very strong scent of formic acid for a second and then it was gone. It was like someone put smelling salts under my nose.

I also sensed that there were beings that looked like grasshoppers at least three feet long out in the desert. I had no reason to think there would be such a thing. I have never thought of extraterrestrials looking like that. I did not report it because it felt too personal and too strange. Since then, however, I have had event after event where I have been with beings of this type.

A third experience was being touched. Somebody touched me physically on the arm. I turned to see who it was, and there was nobody there. When I reported that experience, Dr. Greer said when that happens to lock onto that touch and track back to who touched you and find out what they want.

I want to emphasize that there is a much richer combination of experiences happening than just the visual events. I was also interested to find that I felt no fear at any time. I even had the thought, you know that there are big grasshopper beings nearby in the desert and yet you feel no fear about that.

Dr. Steven Greer
Almost every time we do an expedition, one or more people will be physically touched. There seems to be nothing there, but there is an extraterrestrial biological life form on site, usually phased out of the visual spectrum. We may not always see them, but the beings are present, and they are very real.

When I was on the mountain in North Carolina in 1973, I could see and sense the being, and I could see the indentation from the touch on the sleeve of my ski jacket. All my hair stood on end, and then I floated onboard a craft. The rest you have heard[28].

People often think of such touch occurrences as transient phenomena that mean nothing. They are actually expressions of extraterrestrial intelligence interfacing with this world in a way that is safe or appropriate for that moment, and they are often a lesson.

Insect-like Humanoids

The insect-like beings are all humanoid. They have two arms and two legs but have heads and faces that are very much like an insect. One type is almost like a praying mantis. We have had a number of encounters with them, including ones that came into Shari's apartment in Denver around the time when she was beginning to get sick. They were incredibly gentle and compassionate, and

---

[28] Greer, *Hidden Truth* (2006), p. 24.

enormously intelligent. They do have the scent of formic acid. Some people might think how gross – but not so. Every type of biological life form on Earth could potentially evolve and become an intelligent humanoid type being. While humans went from mammalian to primate human, elsewhere higher life forms such as dolphins, cetaceans, reptiles, insects or birds have evolved into humanoid forms. For example, we have had major encounters with ET creatures that are bird-like with a bird-like head and face, but they are upright and have two arms and two legs and a kind of feathery covering.

Encounter with Cetacean Type ET

I had an amazing encounter once with a small whale-like cetacean —two arms, two legs, light fur, standing upright, and extremely intelligent. It was absolutely real and extraterrestrial. I saw it very clearly, not just in my mind's eye. I saw it and thought it looked like a whale that had evolved into a humanoid form.

Morphogenic Fields

The leitmotif involves morphogenic field propagation. Once a certain type of form succeeds in an environment, it propagates non-locally. There is enormous diversity in terms of the origin of the exact biological form of a humanoid. In reality, the same morphogenic field leads to the evolution of other higher intelligence life forms capable of reaching a critical mass of self-awareness. The hallmark of a higher intelligent life form is the ability to be aware of the Great Mind or the Godhead or Supreme Being.

Chapter 5

1997

RMIT
Mexico City, Mexico
March 1997

Something from the Car
Trudy Guyker
I was very fortunate to be in Mexico on the last RMIT with Dr. Greer, Shari Adamiak, and Bob Hairgrove. We went out to work at a gravel pit near Mexico City the first night before we had even unloaded our luggage. A million people lived in this valley, and we could hear music and people talking off in the distance. Bob was driving near a little ditch about two feet high, and suddenly from my right came a figure; a pearly, whitish, ghostly figure. It was hunched over as if it was riding a bike. It 'whooshed' to the left about 50 feet and then suddenly stopped. It stood up, and it looked like an angular Gumby figure. Bob saw it too, but it happened so quickly we had to describe it to Dr. Greer.

Light Inside Mount Popo
After a few days at the gravel pit site, we went to Mount Popo. Our site there was located at an old colonial ruin. It was dark and isolated, but near a village. As we were looking at Popo it was steaming. There were forest fires around and an awful feeling of violence. Looking at the volcano at night we could not see anything, even with binoculars. When we looked through the night vision scope, we saw a huge light inside the crater, like a huge spotlight. This light illuminated the other side of the volcano. Using your eyes or binoculars, you would see nothing. We came back the next night to find it gone, but on the third night it was back again.

Dr. Steven Greer
We had also seen many ET craft coming up out of the crater and flying around.

Kay Gibson

I currently live in Mexico, and these kinds of things are filmed and reported regularly in the news. When people who have had sightings are interviewed, the person interviewing does so in a serious manner, and it is treated as news. It is nice to see that happening as opposed to what happens in the US where it is all treated like a great joke.

Mexican Children Relate They Met ETs

Linda Willitts

When Dr. Greer, Shari, Trudy and Bob were in Mexico, they talked to some of the Mexican children. The people there were well aware of the ET craft and just accepted them. The children said that the ETs onboard the craft told them they did not need to worry. The ETs said that if Mt. Popo ever exploded, or any other type of disaster occurred, they would come in their craft and save them.

Dr. Steven Greer

These children had gone hiking into the forest beyond the last road past Atlimeyaya[29]. In 1993 we had gone hiking there and found a pyramid from an ancient civilization. The children, who ranged from six to ten years old, told us about having been in that area one day when they met a group of ETs. Both groups were about equal in stature. The ETs were very loving and talked to the children in their minds. They were told that there would be events that would happen on the Earth, but they should not be worried. The ETs would be there to protect them and take them on board their spacecraft. I do not believe these children could make this up. We were reminded of the Northridge earthquake when Dorothy Ives and her best friend simultaneously had a craft outside their windows getting the same message.

Trudy Guyker

One night the four of us camped out. The other three went to sleep but there was no way I was going to sleep. It was pitch black, and quiet, and a skunk passed right by me. As I was sitting there

---

[29] http://www.maplandia.com/mexico/puebla/atlixco/san-baltasar-atlimeyaya/

watching, suddenly I saw three light forms coming toward us. They were tall and looked pale white, with slashes like lightning. Then they moved off toward my right and were gone. I was awestruck. The three of them woke up, and Dr. Greer asked whether anyone had seen or experienced anything. Bob said that he had had the most bizarre dream: "I was sitting here and suddenly this man came toward me and laid down in front of me on his side. He put his face on his hand; he wore a plaid shirt and jeans and had a piece of grass in his mouth. He was a very nice fellow and I was aware that two more people were behind him. We had this wonderful conversation and exchanged information." Then I told what I had seen. I think I had seen those beings in their light form and Bob had seen them through the dream state.

Bob and I were happy because it was confirming our experiences and built up our confidence. Later Bob told me that Shari, the year before in Denver, had gone out with her working group. As she walked into the woods, she met a man dressed in a plaid shirt and jeans with a piece of grass in his mouth. Michael McClasky responded to this story by telling about an incident that happened to him a couple of years before, where he lived in Washington. He had been out, stopped and had a beer. He came home, walked around the side of his house and at the corner in the back of the house, came upon three people. Two of them were off to the side and the third seemed to be encased in a 'glow.' This third person was lying on a tree branch that was thick and low to the ground. He was lying on his side on the branch with his face in his hand, wearing a plaid shirt and jeans, and had a piece of straw in his mouth. They had a communication about something that Michael could not remember, and he was afraid that lapse was due to the beer. So when I told him about what happened in Mexico, he seemed totally liberated.

Q&A on Who Can Access an Event

Unidentified male voice - When you are experiencing these events, do people in the adjacent area not experience them because they are not consciously connected?

Dr. Steven Greer
Do you mean people who are not part of the CSETI contact group? It depends on whether we have an etheric, astral, celestial or fully materialized event. In Florida, for example, it was on the front page of the paper with many local people seeing it. During the Phoenix Lights, thousands of people saw that event. We have had events in Crestone where people from miles away saw the craft around us. It varies, but events are often seen and reported in the media following these CE-5s – not only here but in England and Mexico. It depends on whether the ETs are fully materialized, partially manifest as a light or plasma, or more subtle astral energy.

If something is just at the crossing point of light and barely in the visible spectrum, it is not going to be seen, even by people sitting right there. In Charlottesville 2006, when an ET probe came into our circle, no one actually saw it originate in the sky, fly into the group, and then stand there shimmering, but it was caught by an infrared shot on the camera. So it depends on the type of event that happens.

When there are CE-5s, we have had reports arrive a month or two later through the website. Someone will say, "Yes, I saw that happen." That has also happened many times when people had no idea we were in the area doing CSETI fieldwork. At Mt. Shasta in 1999, the year we saw the enormous triangle, it was reported all the way from Washington state to southern California. Thousands of people called in and saw it. It was a major CE-5 with an interplanetary craft that was at least hundreds to thousands of miles across on each side, moving as a single object.

Incident with the Federales
Trudy Guyker
Mexico was important to me because it was an indication that we had been brought to a new level. We were at our field site at the foot of Mount Popo and had been flashing the lights as Dr. Greer used his laser. Two things were happening. One was local. The volcano was active and smoking. It had been throwing out ash so officials had taped off areas around the volcano and were controlling these areas. At that time the United States was accusing Mexico of not

doing enough to stop the drugs coming into the U.S.

This evening we saw a police car coming across the valley and it passed by on the road a couple of hundred feet from our site. Soon they came back down the road pushing the police car, a little Beetle, onto the site. No engine, no lights, nothing. Just the four of us were there in the middle of nowhere in the middle of the night.

Dr. Steven Greer
Two people were walking in front of the police car with their guns drawn.

Trudy Guyker
They left the car beyond the site and there were at least eight policemen. As they came into the site, they cocked their rifles. It was very stark, and the whole situation felt full of potential violence; the volcano was steaming, the forest fires were burning, and the police were coming toward us with cocked rifles. I seriously wondered what I was doing there! It was frightening. The younger police came and checked out all of us. A couple of older police were checking the car. I think they were looking for drugs, and thought that we were waiting for a drug drop because we were flashing the lights. Then one of the young guys stood in front of me and asked me some questions and pointed at my binoculars. Dr. Greer knew a little Spanish and was trying to communicate with them telling them that we were there looking for the ETs.

It was scary, but I had an abnormal reaction to all this because instead of being afraid, I was very calm. It was like I was sitting in front of a TV watching a sitcom. Later, the young guys went over to their car, put down their guns, opened up the car trunk, took out a guitar and started singing and playing the guitar. The two older policemen were still out in the bushes looking for drugs. Dr. Greer told us to pack up our things quietly and efficiently leave, so we did. It felt surreal, but we thanked them for their music and left.

At the hotel we calmed down and went to bed. I was in bed falling off to sleep when suddenly I was back at the site. I was above and behind the group and I could see the four of us. I saw all the policemen, saw the older guys looking for drugs, saw the young man come over and ask me for my binoculars. They were standing there, but what I saw behind and slightly above each of these policemen was an angel, horizontally and slightly above and behind with their hands out. In front of us, slightly elevated, as if on a balcony, were two ETs. One was very human looking, plus a smaller ET with a little round head. To their right was a celestial being. That is what I was seeing.

I should go back a little. The first night at the site we had seen three amber colored lights in the shape of a triangle on a ridge of hills to the south, across the road. They were there all night. We weren't sure what they were because they looked like amber-colored streetlights. Around 12:00 they went out so we thought the people went to sleep. The next day we went into the village and were talking to a wonderful man who owned the restaurant. He knew Dr. Greer, and Dr. Greer asked if people lived over where we saw the lights. The man said, "Oh no. There is no electricity over there".

I figure that the lights were the craft sitting there. It was watching, guarding and protecting us. Then the night the police came, the ETs also came and we were inside a craft while this was happening. I saw the three pilots, and they and the celestials were watching us. We were inside the craft, and they were protecting us. I was not going to say anything about it because the others were not seeing it.

I thought, "My God, this is proof that this happened because the police put down their guns, went over to the truck, took out the guitar and started singing. It was as if those angels were just keeping things safe. It was at that point that I realized, this man – Dr. Greer – is protected beyond belief. This whole CSETI thing, the Disclosure Project is really important. Not only are people taking part in it, but also cosmic beings are taking part in it. It is a cosmic thing happening here, and that is why I say that I realized at that point that everything was taken up to a new level.

Dr. Steven Greer

My experience of the police encounter was a little different because I was the responsible person on the site. Also, as an emergency room physician who had been in mission-critical situations, I understood the body language and unspoken cues. As the police came around the site, the information flashed that they were going to kill and rob us. There is a lot of that going on – with roving bands of police – in Mexico. On a previous trip to Mexico, we had been stopped at gunpoint, had our passports and cash taken, and were going to be thrown in jail on trumped up charges. We managed to get out of that. So I knew that this current situation was really serious, and that we were extremely vulnerable.

I went into a state of divine consciousness and connected to the Godhead avatar being that I met when I had my near-death experience. I asked for protection for all of us and asked for blessing and peace on these intruders. That was what I actively did in that situation, and I have done the same in similar emergency situations. The behavior of the police changed, as Trudy correctly described. I also knew that an ET craft was there and was observing, but it was shifted energetically just beyond the visible on the other side of the crossing point of light. The police went into what psychologists call a 'fugue state,' – an altered state. Their whole demeanor and emotion changed from hyper-aggressive attack mode to little boys who went to the car, sat in a circle and began to sing and play the guitar! At that point, I turned to the group. This is precisely what I said, because I will never forget it: "Now, in one seamless motion, gather up everything and go to the car and leave in complete silence and peace."

I maintained this state of consciousness with the God-conscious being the whole time we were doing this. Then I went into consciousness like a secret service agent or a bodyguard would when they are moving someone important out of a dangerous situation. I took control of that vehicle and drove like you would if you were driving the US President out of an ambush. We flew down the road at the maximum possible speed without losing control, got into the gated compound where we were staying, and then I knew we were safe. After that, I am sure the police came out of their fugue state, and I would bet they did not even recall us leaving the site. They were in a suspended state of peace awareness the whole time.

That night I had a beautiful lucid dream of being with a group of varying types of extraterrestrial beings on a spacecraft. They were all aware of everything we were doing. I was communicating to them the upcoming briefings that we were planning with the leadership of the US government. The dream was crystal clear, lucid and real.

Best Evidence
Phoenix, Arizona
March 1997

Dr. Steven Greer
A number of events happened in rapid succession in March of 1997. We had prepared President Clinton and his staff, who had decided that they were not going to take on the task because they were terrified of the Majestic Group. So we were trying to get members of Congress to hold hearings on the ET subject. We were putting together a private briefing for members of Congress. To do this, we were collecting the best available evidence, including the best photos and videotapes of extraterrestrial vehicles that had ever been taken. We had thousands and thousands of them.

Friendly Nemesis

A picture editor for the BBC, Neil Cunningham, volunteered to help put the information together and came to Phoenix, Arizona from London. A member of the secret government offered us the use of a digital lab. He had been, in turns, both friendly and a nemesis. He had worked closely with Murder, Inc. This group had tried to kill as many people like me as possible. The group included "Dr. Death" along with a well-known billionaire. Some members of this group act friendly. It is in line with the old adage: keep your friends close but your enemies closer. So this person offered us the use of a digital lab in Phoenix, and we went there. We had no other means to put our summary of photographs together from the huge database. I had the executive function to choose which photos went into the best evidence video, but I did not have the ability to run the editing machines.

So, there we were. Shari had breast cancer, I had metastatic malignant melanoma, Colby had been murdered, and Clinton had refused to help. As I flew into Sky Harbor Airport in Phoenix, I felt I should go into cosmic consciousness and connect with the ETs, and ask for their help.

The Phoenix Lights

I went into the coherent thought sequencing protocols, and saw an enormous ET craft, connected to them and vectored them into Phoenix. I told them that if they could make an appearance so that someone could film them, I would greatly appreciate it. We needed evidence to put into the collection of videos and photographs that we were going to give to members of Congress in three weeks. That was around 5:30 PM on March 13, 1997.

That evening, about 3 hours later, events occurred which have collectively been called The Phoenix Lights. It was a mass-witnessed CE-5 that resulted in aircraft from Luke AFB being scrambled. It eventually became worldwide news[30]. What few people know is that it was a major CE-5 that was done at our request so that we could get that footage to give to Congress in April of 1997.

Trudy Guyker
I live in Chandler, Arizona, which is near Phoenix. I had the opportunity to meet Dr. Lynne Kitei, who wrote a book called *The Phoenix Lights*[31]. She had brought some photographs to Sedona, where I met her. Her life has been changed by the lights she had observed from her balcony in the hills of Phoenix. On the cover of her book is a photo of a triangular craft with three amber lights. I think that is the same craft we saw in Mexico and that it came to Phoenix when Dr. Greer was there. I think it is all connected. In August 2005, my husband Fred and I and several of the people in

---

[30] http://www.thephoenixlights.net/
[31] Lynne D. Kitei, *The Phoenix Lights: We Are Not Alone* (Charlottesville: Hampton Roads, 2004).

the area saw another craft exactly like that about ten miles from my house, and it was reported. I think it was also the same craft.

Dr. Steven Greer
Right. The epicenter of the Phoenix Lights event was right over the lab in Tempe where we were doing the work putting together the best available evidence of videos and photographs. At the time, someone came running in saying that there was a huge ET ship on the local news. So it was on the news in Phoenix that night, although it took a couple more months for it to get on the news nationwide. Eventually, the event did make it through the media filters (The main stream media is unimaginably corrupt…). We ended up being able to incorporate almost in real time the CE-5 of the Phoenix Lights into the film summary of the best evidence that we gave to members of Congress at our briefing in 1997 of April.

Briefings
Washington, D.C.
April 1997

Briefing for Congress

Dr. Steven Greer
The Congressional Briefing that we set up for the United States Congress in April 1997 has been described in my previous books. *Extraterrestrial Contact* contains the paper trail, with copies of the letters sent to President Clinton[32], Vice-President Gore[33], the invitation to Members of Congress[34], and a memo to the participants[35] as well as a confirmation of attendance memo[36].

Hidden Truth-Forbidden Knowledge describes other details, including the mind control, psychological warfare, and electromagnetic weapons system attempts made against us in a concerted effort to get us to abandon our plans[37]. I should also add, parenthetically, that not only members of Congress were at the congressional briefing. Senior White House staff members were also present, as well as senior Department of Defense people.

---

[32] Greer, *Extraterrestrial Contact* (1999), pp. 416-417.
[33] Greer, *Extraterrestrial Contact* (1999), pp. 420-421.
[34] Greer, *Extraterrestrial Contact* (1999), pp. 431-432.

Dr. Death said he wanted to come, and I told him that he was not invited. He said, "Well, I'll be there anyway," and he was – but not in person. As we conducted this event for Congress, I was on the stage presenting and was attacked by some kind of electromagnetic weapon. I felt like I was literally being cooked from the inside out, like a microwave, and almost lost consciousness.

Our military adviser was there, and he felt and sensed it also. He knows about this type of weapon because he was 'read into' them[38]. There were other people in the room from the DOD. I am certain they had some means of facilitating that attack, but the meeting went forward anyway. This briefing was part of the plan in preparation for ongoing disclosure.

Pentagon Briefings

Following that meeting, a group of us went to the Pentagon. There, in the E Ring, we met with the head of Intelligence, Joint Staff (J2), who at the time was an admiral. Prior to this meeting we had transferred to him some of the information, testimony and documents that we had. I had given him a secret NRO (National Reconnaissance Office) document that had not been declassified and that had been taken from Nellis Air Force Base. This document has the project code names and numbers from the early 1990s for black projects dealing with reverse engineering of ET craft and technology. (This document is in the Briefing Document on the 2 hour DVD of Disclosure Project witness testimony.)

The head of Intelligence used the code numbers and names in this secret document from Nellis to locate within the Pentagon one of the top secret, compartmented, intelligence operations. He asked to be read into the project. The admiral was told, "You don't have a need to know."

He became furious and said, "God damn it! I'm the head of Intelligence for the Joint Staff. If I don't have a need to know, who does?" At this point, they informed him they could not speak with him further, and cut the line. They never responded to his inquiries

---

[35] Greer, *Extraterrestrial Contact* (1999), pp. 433-435.
[36] Greer, *Extraterrestrial Contact* (1999), p. 436.
[37] Greer, *Hidden Truth* (2006), pp. 148-154.

after that, so by the time I got to this briefing he was hopping mad, agitated and actually frightened. The original stand-up briefing at the Pentagon was scheduled for about 45 minutes with the Admiral. We met for about two hours and could have gone on longer. He was steadily canceling downstream appointments, turning to his assistant to cancel other meetings. At the end of our meeting, we had a heart to heart discussion. He was extremely supportive.

He looked at me and said, "If there's a group that has this information and technologies, and they're lying to the President and to me and to the CIA Director, and if you have found people who have some knowledge in their capacity and have documents or information, then as far as I'm concerned, that group is illegal. It is rogue and you have my permission to go to the media and anyone else who will listen and put all of this information out to the public."

Later someone who has been close to me for a number of years was in a meditative state and remote viewed our group going into the Pentagon. This person saw ETs dematerialized but near us, and a row of angels escorting us in — and thus knew that we would be protected.

The Missing Piece of the ET Puzzle

Obviously my movements are being tracked. You are not going to walk into the offices of the head of Intelligence for the Joint Chiefs of Staff and drop a bomb like unveiling the code names of these projects without having everything you do tracked by such a group. But we felt protection as we walked in. The doors opened and things happened because of the state of consciousness at the foundation of the project. This has been the mystery of what has been achieved. We cannot talk about it much because people think this aspect of the ET topic gets too far "out there," but it is the *inner reality* of what is happening. It is the core and the missing piece of the puzzle. It is actually on these levels of higher consciousness and in these dimensions that real progress and evolution happen.

---

[38] "Read into" is military jargon for being briefed on something that is a classified or compartmented operation.

Second Pentagon Briefing

At a subsequent Pentagon meeting when I briefed General Patrick Hughes, head of the Defense Intelligence Agency (DIA), the same ET/angelic/celestial presence accompanied us. At the DIA they had to draw straws to see who from his staff could be in on the meeting because the General would only allow one person. Many people on his staff wanted to be at the meeting.

When people ask me who green-lighted the Disclosure Project, I tell them that one of the first to do so was the Head of Intelligence for the Joint Staff. In late 1997 I began to write letters to the effect that unless otherwise directed, we were going to move forward with bringing forward top-secret military and intelligence people's testimony and documents, some of which were not declassified through official channels.

CSETI Training
Crestone, Colorado
June 1997

Dr. Steven Greer
We went to Crestone in June 1997 and had an extraordinary encounter on Blanca Peak. No one except me knew that Shari was so sick at that time.

Debbie Foch
I want to share how we chose our specific site. We were in a training lecture at the White Eagle Lodge. We had done our meditation and remote viewing and were discussing which specific site we should use for our fieldwork. People "remote viewed" numbers and names. One of the names people viewed was a Mexican name, and combined with several images people saw, the information pointed to Zapata Falls on Mt. Blanca. We went there and encountered an extensive thunderstorm.

Linda Willitts
We often get large thunderstorms at the Zapata Falls site, but this storm was exceptional. There were frequent and powerful lightning

strikes as well as widespread magenta lightning flashes. We could see black, dimmed down, triangular-shaped craft flying without lights. In the Zapata Falls area we often get military suppression from NORAD at Cheyenne Mountain, near Colorado Springs, and the ETs cannot safely show themselves. But electrical storms often disable NORAD's detection equipment and the ETs can appear. So we were able to see these ET craft.

After the storm the air was clear. We left the vehicle and could see neutrino light appearing like fireflies all around us. The light was not quite materialized and looked like shooting sparks of colors—yellow, blue, red, and white sparks—in the trees.

Shari Adamiak[39]
We were fortunate to be treated to an hour and a half of the most spectacular displays of nature. Lightning struck almost continuously far and near. During the light show, Dr. Greer and I were looking directly out in front of us, across the northern half of the valley. Suddenly, a large metallic disc appeared momentarily in an opening in the clouds directly in line with our Jeep's windshield. Yellowish-white, it was absolutely crystal clear for the fractions of seconds that it was visible.

Dr. Ted Loder
The whole mountain was shimmering. Scintillating is probably the proper term. I remember walking out alone that evening before we went out to the site and thinking, "What am I doing here in the middle of the night in a rain storm looking at blinking lights on a mountain top?" That thought came from my analytic mind and shortly thereafter I realized that there was nowhere else I would rather be. From that point on things evolved for me.

After the Storm

Shari Adamiak[40]
After the lightning ran its course, it began to rain. Another hour and a half inside the stuffy vehicles produced some interesting

---
[39] Greer, *Extraterrestrial Contact* (1999), p. 250.
[40] Greer, *Extraterrestrial Contact* (1999), pp. 250-251.

events. One gentleman saw a large disc materialize momentarily. Another man sensed someone standing close to him, although he knew no one else was nearby in the rain. Other team members reported sensing and feeling energy forms close by.

Debbie Foch
Afterwards, those of us who weathered the storm got out of our vehicles. There were about 20 of us, and some of us went up the path that led to a waterfall. Perfectly visible amber orbs came over the mountain, and more subtle energies flashed and glowed. That was the first year Dr. Greer and Shari pointed out the subtle energy examples to the group. Dr. Greer said that it was time to do so; this was an opportunity after the storm. He was teaching about the subtle energies that were magnified after the storm excited the magnetic field of the craft around us. He also started sharing the cosmology with the whole group. Then he and Shari saw a glowing area on the path, and they went to investigate.

The Special Contact Site
Dr. Steven Greer
I knew all week that there was a special place, a clearing on Blanca Peak, which is the sacred mountain of the east for the Native American people. Many Native American traditions and stories are told about the Star People in that area. Many generations of native people have seen these Star People. We also knew from the vision quest that Shari and I had done in the area, that it was time to bring people to the next level of awareness about an integrated cosmology. We knew that raising people to the next level would help thin the veil, making it easier for people to see more and go further into contact.

While we were in the cars during the storm, we were in a meditative state. We were sitting there looking out at these triangular and disc-shaped craft with no lights. The craft moved in and out of the mountain which was silhouetted by the electricity around it. These craft traveled at the speed of light, and if you blinked you would miss them. Some large disc- and chevron-shaped craft were going in and out of the huge mountain cluster called Blanca Peak. After the storm abated, we left our cars and saw the entire mountainside and the space around us full of scintillating light. I knew that the light was extraterrestrial and that we were inside a large ship, which accounted for all the distortion. The air became very still and was very unusual. It was as if we were in a cocoon of silence, which has happened many times on these expeditions.

I knew that we would need to prepare. I walked up the trail with my eyes closed, turned to the right and remote viewed with my inner vision an opening on the hillside. I was told that this was the contact site. Shari and I came back down and joined the group. I asked everyone to follow me silently up to the site in a very high state of spiritual calmness and depth. As we walked up the path, I saw that there were sentries - scintillating forms that were extraterrestrial guards lining the path. Behind them, shifted to a higher frequency beyond the crossing point of light, were angelic guardian beings. When we arrived at the contact site, I went to a precise location. People were walking a little behind me as I led them to this specified area, and Shari was nearby. I asked people to stay so that they were in a semi-circle. I walked forward into a blinding white light that suddenly manifest immediately above me. As I stopped in the light, everything shifted.

Cosmic People Gathered

I realized that we were in an enormous extraterrestrial vehicle that was not fully materialized, but was present enough that the neutrino light was visible. Everyone saw shimmering, scintillating light. One did not have to be in a God-conscious state of celestial perception to see this light. I began to connect with a dozen extraterrestrial elders standing in a semi-circle mirroring the semi-circle of humans behind me. We were sharing within deep cosmic mind – it was an incredibly reverent contact that lasted about 40 minutes. These Beings appeared in a wide range of height and form. Having communicated with each of the elders, I learned that each extraterrestrial represented a group of planetary systems.

Beyond the group of ET elders was another group of beings who came from what I like to call the "Concourse on High" – the celestial, angelic realm of beings. Finally, straight up towards the mountain, was an enormous, luminous being. It was an avatar – a manifestation of the Godhead. In a state of awe, I was communicating with the avatar, the angelic beings and the ETs. The communication during this intense, emotional time was non-linear, non-local and non-verbal. I received the transmission in the form of packets of knowledge and information moving, flowing and connecting in the form of feeling and energy. The communication during the entire event was similar to what I encountered during my near-death experience that I wrote about in my third book[41].

Specific actions were communicated to me during this experience. I was specifically asked to use my contacts with the military and ask them stop the attacks that were happening to the extraterrestrial facility inside Blanca Peak. It was a very clear request, and I replied, "I will do everything I can to achieve this." (In some ways I thought the request was strange, but below I will share why the ET elders were so concerned.) As the event continued, I felt I would have disappeared or levitated if my frequency had risen any higher. I felt inexplicably light in a state of God-consciousness, beyond cosmic awareness.

It was a time of coming together of cosmic people and the cosmology. I clearly saw that not only were the extraterrestrial beings and the whole area enveloped in a quasi-materialized craft, but that its dimensions were visible. Celestial beings and an avatar were present, and I sensed that the whole event was being watched by the entire Cosmos – the great Cosmic Mind. This moving event remains difficult to describe in words.

As the event concluded, the beings began to recede and move back beyond the veil, but they were still present subtly. As I turned to leave I said to the semicircle of people, "Either you have seen or you have not seen, and you have understood or you have not understood." That was my only comment to the group. As we left I saw again the sentries, along with very powerful Native American elders who were present in their astral forms. These Native American beings have an ancient connection to the Star People and are guardians of the mountain.

---

[41] Greer, *Hidden Truth* (2006), pp. 20, 45, 195, 274.

Other Experiences of the Same Event
Shari Adamiak[42]
After the rainfall everyone began observing flashes of colored light occurring randomly around the mountaintop. Brilliant colors would flash momentarily and were seen by all of us. Soon an event began to unfold on the rocky path towards Zapata Falls. More than just light flashes began to manifest. Forms of light, balls of light, columns of light, scintillating shimmers and more were reported. We picked our way in the dark up the path to a clearing in which close encounters ensued. Some teammates said they felt a shortness of breath during this event and the time leading up to it, which ended once the encounters concluded. I saw a brilliant blue neon-like light appear in a very precise geometrical arrangement. Many of us observed light forms standing in front of us. It appeared that a meeting was to occur between Dr. Greer and other life forms. Before the rest of the team was called to join, we heard invisible moccasin-clad feet softly walking around us.

Debbie Foch
I was standing next to Shari, and we were in line with the path where Dr. Greer walked. The section of the path where he walked was lit, and he stood under the light. I saw him standing there, and he was in the light the whole time, moving and interacting with something that I could not see. I knew there were energies and beings at the location, and I also realized that the amazing happenings were very important.

Linda Willitts
We have returned to this site numerous times, every year since this event. The group is intuitive and knows to follow protocol when we go to a contact site at any location. Mount Blanca is really rocky, and we sense our way up there. We do not use flashlights, we do not speak, and we do not go ahead of Dr. Greer, who leads the way.

I felt a sense of the powerful sacredness in the place. Then, as we stood in the semi-circle I saw hoards of ETs, including what

---

[42] Greer, *Hidden Truth* (2006), p. 251.

I call "Caspers" – beings about three feet tall, shapeless and gray – something like the cartoon character, "Casper the Ghost." They were not totally materialized, but I could see them clearly. These beings scampered after Dr. Greer with great excitement, as if they were really happy to have him there. The feeling of great excitement touched me as well. In the distance among the trees I could see larger beings who resembled taller Caspers.

As I watched Dr. Greer, the edges of his body became indistinct. I sensed that he might disappear. Though it was not frightening, I wondered how long we should wait if he should disappear. Fortunately, he returned without disappearing. While I was standing in the semi-circle, someone put a hand on my shoulder as though about to whisper something to me. Yet when I looked around no one was near me.

By the end of the contact experience, the moon had risen above the trees, and it was shining a diffuse light. I saw a small, chevron-shaped, black craft shoot up across the moon. The night was a moving and amazing experience.

Debbie Foch
Was this the year that the clouds broke above us and a star appeared directly overhead at the end?

Dr. Ted Loder
Yes, the star was right over Dr. Greer. Halfway through the event, the clouds opened in a circle. This was my first year at Crestone. I saw the trail glowing as we walked along it – amazingly glowing. Those of you who have been to the contact site since our training there, know it still glows. There is white rock along the trail, but that night it was particularly amazing. The light in the sky and the scintillations that were occurring helped make the light more remarkable than usual. I saw Dr. Greer fade "in and out" similar to a radio station that is between stations. It was an incredibly emotional evening for me. I knew we were undergoing a major and important experience.

Trudy Guyker

While we were doing our first CTS I sensed a rolling gray cloud coming from right to left. It was a huge cloud that rolled through all the cars, depositing incredible energy. The "rolling cloud" occurred after the first CTS. Dr. Loder, his son Chris, the Craddocks and I performed the second CTS. I was in the back seat of the car, and during the CTS we all sensed powerful energy enter. On my chest I felt a sudden pressure. It felt like a huge brick sitting there, and I could hardly breathe. After we got out of the car, I still could not breathe very well, and it took all my energy to move. Then Dr. Greer and Shari called us to come up the trail. There were certain white rocks that lit up like lanterns that guided us. Because it was pitch black, I struggled up to the site and maneuvered over to the right side of the semi-circle to see what was happening.

As I looked at the clearing I saw what appeared to be a glowing shrub in the middle. I thought, "There is something here. What is this shrub doing here all of a sudden?" Then the shrub changed, became more solid and took on a pearl cast. I became aware that about twelve or fifteen feet to the left of this "shrub" were two smaller "shrubs" and a taller "shrub" behind them. That was my impression and then they became more solid. Dr. Greer went to the center form that was about one and a half feet taller than he was. I was amazed because he stood there and then put his arms around this shape. I thought, "Oh, my God, I really am seeing this." Dr. Greer next crossed his arms across his body and then stepped back putting his hands out at his sides. At one point he started to dematerialize.

Suddenly I received a communication saying, "Do not look at this event; do not stare at it. Do not try to understand what is being said. You are to be a witness to this." I sent out my greetings and my love. Dr. Greer came back, and I heard him say, "You have seen what you have seen and those who have not seen have seen nothing," and, "pray for peace." We started back down the trail, and, suddenly, the weight was off my chest. I was breathing normally again. When we arrived back down at the site, it was totally dark. I realized that during the whole event, the site had been illuminated like moonlight.

Dr. Steven Greer

These beings radiated infinite love and compassion. They also expressed a tremendous appreciation for what we were doing. Of course, we were grateful as well.

Material Evidence

Understanding the physics behind the magnetic flux field, the quantum vacuum, materialization and spin theory led to some evidence beyond witness testimony. I had a compass in the breast pocket of my down jacket. It was right over my heart chakra. The event involved the higher states of consciousness and chakras being opened and cosmic energy flowing through them. Shari and I went to the San Juan Hills for a day after the training was over. By then her cancer had metastasized to the lymph nodes, and we knew it was very serious. I took out my compass to get the directions of our location, and discovered that magnetic north had been shifted 120 degrees on this compass!

The magnetic field of my compass had shifted, and it stayed that way for about a month. We photographed it. This was the same compass that, in 1992 at Alton Barnes, had rotated counter-clockwise while an ET craft was moving in the same direction in the field. On Blanca Peak, I knew- because of the 120 degree shift- that not only was the ET craft very near, but it was also right at the edge of fully materializing. Many people saw the scintillating energy. An enormous ship had emerged and was overlaying our space/time at that place on the mountain. The ET craft was resonance frequency shifted just beyond a materialized form. But it was there strongly enough that during the encounter when I walked into the area of brilliant light, I was in a field of energy that altered the magnetic field of the compass!

I consider the electromagnetic phenomenon involving the 120-degree shift of the compass as proof of the real nature of this meeting. This phenomenon involves a reality beyond what most people can currently imagine within the field of science. We need to understand the new energy, the antigravity technologies, and how certain enlightened beings and people in the past have learned to levitate. It is all part of the same knowledge, physics and cosmology. The interstellar civilizations comprehend this. They certainly understand the relationship between higher states of consciousness, electromagnetism, mass effect, and material objects. To them my compass being altered for at least a month would be understood as basic science.

I should note that after about a month, the compass returned to being a normal, functioning compass.

Shari Adamiak[43]
Something very real, albeit not solidly physical, occurred on Mt. Blanca that night, and many people witnessed it. And a solidly physical trace remained. Dr. Greer had his compass with him, in the breast pocket of his jacket. This is the same compass he has carried in all of his fieldwork for the past six years. Two days after the events on Mt. Blanca we were stunned to see that the compass was altered. It no longer registered north as true. It was approximately 140 – 160 degrees turned and registered north as somewhere near due south. In July of 1997 at our training in England, the compass was still altered. We have photographs to prove and preserve this data.

Shari's Sacrifice
The meeting at Crestone was a singularly important event. As it turned out, it was the last time Shari would be at Crestone on Blanca Peak. I knew at the meeting that one of us was supposed to go. I knew that, and so it turned out to be. Within six months, Shari had passed on to the worlds of light – a Bodhi Satva[44].

Debbie Foch
Are you saying that the plan was to have Shari join the ETs to help us?

Dr. Steven Greer
It was just known that that was going to be – that that was the plan.

---

[43] Greer, *Extraterrestrial Contact* (1999), p. 251.
[44] http://en.wikipedia.org/wiki/Bodhisattva

One of us, apparently, would leave, and that's what happened.

Covert Program Surveillance

Dr. Ted Loder

I was relatively new to CSETI, and a linear scientific type. An event that really impressed me happened on Friday night of the training. It was clear enough that we could see Blanca Peak. Sometime between 9:30 and 10:30, an orb with orange amber light moved across Blanca Peak. We discussed whether or not it was an airplane. About fifteen minutes later, fighter planes were flying in from three different air bases, coming to the top of Mount Blanca. Looking through the night scopes, I counted eleven or twelve fighters flying around the top of Mount Blanca where the orb had been. It does not make sense that fighters from three air bases would fly around the top of Mount Blanca on a Friday night if nothing has happened. I thought "There may be something going on here after all."

Dr. Steven Greer

Every expedition since 1992 has been accompanied by military reconnaissance and military people on the ground nearby trying to suppress the events. This fact is something about which I am warning the world government that wants us to have a CE-5 for them. We have had this type of experience hundreds of times, and not just at a distance like Ted mentioned, but right overhead and circling us.

Shari Adamiak[45]

Our final night together as a team in Crestone was spent at a lovely hot springs facility. We met at our lodgings to caravan to the hot springs. When we pulled out of our lodgings and for the next twenty miles, the radar detector in our vehicle kept sounding. It would register on both X and K bands. There was no regularity to the signal or the time between signals. Only our team's vehicles were behind us, and we were in the vast emptiness of the San Luis Valley as we traveled.

---

[45] Greer, *Extraterrestrial Contact* (1999), pp. 251-252.

Dr. Steven Greer
While we were in the hot tubs, there were so many high altitude craft we lost count of how many were there in the crystal clear sky. We were in a meditative state together in the hot tub, and there had to have been dozens of craft that night. It was like a swarm of exoatmospheric ET craft.

Shari Adamiak[46]
As we pulled into the hot springs the rain began to stop, and we all enjoyed a beautiful night under the moon and stars together. A number of events occurred while we were all in the hot springs. Unusual satellite-like objects originated from the handle of the Big Dipper, began to travel south or west across the sky. They would vanish in a streak as they shot vertically out of sight. Tony Craddock clearly saw a black flash whizzing by at an altitude of several hundred feet coming from the direction of Mt. Blanca. I observed a dark or black object that streaked across just feet over our heads directly over the hot springs pool.

Dr. Ted Loder
After the hot springs session, Tony and Pat Craddock, Trudy and I decided to go back to Mount Blanca. We went back to the hotel, got our field gear and left for Blanca about midnight. We went back to the parking lot at the Blanca site, set up our four chairs in the normal protocol so that each one of us could look in a different direction and spent about three hours there. As I was sitting opposite Trudy, she was glowing and had a beautiful deep red aura around her. I checked my eyes by looking away and then back, and the aura was only on Trudy.
Later in the evening, we watched a long, black, rectangular cloud that was sitting right above Blanca. The night was exquisitely clear with no other clouds in the sky and no moon.

Trudy Guyker
All day long Pat Craddock had not seen anything, and she was disappointed. She was facing Blanca and saw a little black cloud. The night sky was perfectly clear but there was an oval shaped cloud, perfectly black, just to the left of the peak. The cloud did

---
[46] Greer, *Extraterrestrial Contact* (1999), p. 252.

not move, so we were watching it. Tony, Ted, and I turned and were watching something else in the valley, when Pat said, "The black cloud just went, zoom, into the peak." It was as if Pat was given something because she had not seen anything all day.

Dr. Ted Loder
After initially spotting it, about 30 seconds later, the cloud was gone. My perception was the black cloud enveloped a craft. The craft left and the cloud just disappeared.

Alleged Phenomena

Dr. Steven Greer
There have been a series of well-documented photographs of ET craft manufacturing clouds around them and then hiding in these clouds. A Navy Captain took a series of such photographs in Washington or Oregon years ago. We have had similar occurrences many times on our expeditions. There are times when something looks like a cloud. If it suddenly becomes an unusual shape or moves in a strange way, it may not be a cloud. This is why in CSETI we often say, an alleged cloud, an alleged star, an alleged aircraft, etc. An example: the alleged airplane that flew into the box canyon and disappeared silently (with no engine sound) after it had been 100 or 200 feet above us.

We have learned that we must question what we are seeing, and ask ourselves if the ET ships are masquerading as a cloud, or appearing as an aircraft or satellite. The object we saw last night provided a good example. We have checked the satellite charts, and no iridium satellites were in the area. When I connected to the object and asked it to do something a satellite cannot do, it turned course, got much brighter, and flew off toward Joshua Tree. Anyone casually looking at the night sky would have thought the object to be a satellite or an aircraft.

The Crestone training of 1997 really set the tone for all the trainings to follow. I knew that it was time to start going into these deeper aspects of the cosmology. The "alleged black cloud" event also indicated that it was time to move beyond the veil of light and beyond the obvious to what was really happening on a deeper level of cosmic awareness and cosmic being. We needed to move to a more profound level for another reason. Either Shari or I was not going to make it, so there was going to be a time of enormous transition in the whole project.

You have to understand that there were people who were not happy with what we had been doing. Between late 1993 and 1997 we had put our activities on the radar screen of the CIA Director, the President of the United States, the United Nations Secretary-General, and many members of Congress, including Senate Intelligence Committee members. We were putting sensitive information out to the public and having meetings with senior flag officers at the Pentagon, generals and admirals who were being deceived about the matter, and who were really angry about it. The powers-that-be who had been conducting the secrecy were not amused. We were in the midst of an enormous, cosmic struggle, and it continues to this day.

CSETI Expedition
England
July 1997

Shari Adamiak's Condition

Every year from 1992 through 2000 we went to England, and we often did a CSETI expedition in the crop circles. We worked with Colin Andrews, Ron Russell and others. By June and July of 1997 Shari's condition had deteriorated, and her cancer metastasized to multiple locations in her body. And so we arrived in England with heavy hearts. It was a sad and difficult time because she was my best friend and had worked with me since 1991 on the CSETI project.

Shari had done so much work and was such an enormous supporter- spiritually, emotionally and in so many other ways. She was a strong woman and very protective of the CSETI mission and purpose. If anyone tried to interfere with our operation, she would go after them like a lioness, yet she was also amazingly spiritual and sweet. Thus, it was very sad to know that she was getting so sick and deteriorating so rapidly.

We went to England with about a dozen people and rented a large manor house that was built in the 1700s.

Linda Willitts
Most of the CSETI group was picked up at Heathrow airport the morning of July 22, 1997 in a van by Ron Russell (a crop circle researcher, space artist, and CSETI friend) and Busty Taylor (a pilot & crop circle photographer). They took us to the large manor house where we stayed. Shari was already there and had picked flowers for our bedrooms. Dr. Greer came later in the day.

The house was a lovely 18th-Century house with some 18th-century problems. Although the plumbing had been modernized, it proved less than ideal. Ron told us that the night his first group left, he was outside ruminating on whether the house would be adequate for the CSETI team. He said that he sent a thought to the universe, asking if he had done the right thing in securing this house for our use. Ron said that immediately three lights appeared in the perfect shape of the CSETI triangle. Moreover, there were beams of light connecting all three orbs, making it a perfect depiction of the CSETI crop circle and logo He felt that he indeed had received confirmation that all would be well[47].

The ET Visit
Dr. Steven Greer
On the night of July 24th Shari and I were too tired for fieldwork. I was battling my own cancer situation. Shari was very sick, becoming more and more tired. I told everyone that they should go out without Shari and me that night, and that they should be out in the field no later than 10:30 PM. Shari and I needed to rest. The two of us stayed upstairs in the residential quarters of the estate. We did some meditation and talked about what the future might hold. It was very emotional because we knew that one of us, perhaps both of us, would be taken. We were dealing with and discussing many profound issues. Someone had given us a laser that was supposed to help with healing energy. We were using the laser on the areas where I had had repeated malignant melanomas and also on her cancer. We were sitting upstairs in my room, which

---
[47] Greer, *Extraterrestrial Contact* (1999), p. 253.

had a fireplace and a bay window. The lights were on, and we were in a state of deep spiritual consciousness together as we shared our thoughts.

Suddenly, a glowing softball-sized object of scintillating light flew in through the closed window. It turned, went over by the fireplace and elongated into an extraterrestrial being about three feet tall! The being was visible with the naked eye. Shari was looking down doing something with the laser healing machine, and I said, "Shari, look. He's here." She looked up, gasped, and an ET, maybe four or five feet from us, was radiating the most beautiful compassion and love. The ET then communicated telepathically how much they honored the work we were doing and how much our work was respected and needed. It was so beautiful that we were crying. Even with the lights on, any person could have seen this ET. He was not formed by neutrino light, was not etheric, and was not astral. Shari and I turned to each other while communicating with him. We had an encounter that lasted about fifteen minutes. It was a beautiful, spiritual coming-together. The extraterrestrial was an emissary from the ETs expressing their condolences, support, and gratitude specifically for the sacrifices we were making.

Shari and I swore that we would not discuss these events because there were no other witnesses. Publicly we were already being pilloried and vilified. Condemnation and opprobrium had come forth from the entire UFO research community for the few things we were beginning to talk about. So we had enough to deal with in terms of putting what we had just experienced out to the public. It was very personal, and we decided to keep it between the two of us. We were quite surprised the next morning when we found that we were not the only witnesses.

Unidentified Male
Last night, on the 24th, I had some down time because of a sinus infection. I was resting in a different part of the house in which Dr. Greer and Shari Adamiak were staying. The rest of the team was outside. I saw some anomalous lights penetrating into the windows and all around the house.

Linda Willits

Since it was our first night, we could not yet tell from the outside of the house which rooms people were staying in. Dr. Greer and Shari had gone upstairs, and the rest of the group was in the living room. Dr. Greer had specifically told us to be in the field by 10:30 PM, so I watched the time diligently. We were in the back yard by 10:30. I recall there were about six of us because the others had gone to bed. We were looking up at the house from the back. Promptly at 10:34 a ball about the size of a softball and brilliant white, flew in an arc from behind a tree and went right in a window. We were all exclaiming, "That ET thing flew right in that window!"

Ron Russell exclaimed, "That's Steve's room!" I felt tremendous emotion. My perception of the object was that of a loving ET energy, and that it was specifically going to commiserate with Steve and Shari. We were touched by that, and very excited. I checked the time, and it was 10:34 PM. Dr. Greer had told us to get out there by 10:30 and we would have missed it if we had not been there.

Kay Gibson

I also saw the "softball-size" object. It looked like an upside down incandescent bulb to me. It was very bright, but the light did not hurt the eyes. The ET lights that we see do not have the same quality or the same effect upon us as Earth lights. We were watching at the same moment, and it went through the window into the house. Of course we did not know that Steve and Shari had an experience until we started debriefing the next day. The incandescent bulb shape has shown up for me three times. At Desert Hot Springs one appeared, floated down and then disappeared. Then in England a fellow from San Diego and I saw it later in the week as we were setting up prior to an evening's work. The bulb appeared over the tumulus in the same arc and duration as the night it flew into the window. Dr. Greer said that the incident had specific meaning for us. If we have a particular contact, it may be something to watch for in the future. Everything we see and experience is not necessarily a separate event. As another example, before Dr. Greer had gone into the house, we were having a group hug and he saw a brilliant diamond-like, blue-white light. He said, "Oh, I saw that in Italy."

It was an image that keeps showing up for Dr. Greer.

Dr. Steven Greer
Kay's point is a good one. I did see the brilliant diamond-like, blue-white light. It was the ship from which the ET came, because it flew from the sky, over a tree, and into the house. Being inside the house with the lights on, we certainly did not see what the others saw. If they had not been out there looking at the right place at the right time, there would have been no independent confirmation of the amazing emissary sent to us for a meeting in that manor house in England. Thank God we had people there with their eyes open that did go out by the time I had asked them to.

Lights Flickering within the House

Linda Willitts[48]
The last few of us stayed outside until 2 A.M. We had many sightings of smaller objects, satellite-type lights that moved quickly across the sky, and many alleged shooting stars over the house. The house was clearly the focus of most of the activity. Lights kept going on and off in different parts of the house. The next morning I asked the group if anyone was walking around the house flicking light switches or flashlights. It turned out that everyone had gone to bed and could not have been flicking the lights.

Kay Gibson
It seemed to me that the "light-flicking" was very fast and had a specific pattern, as if it was choreographed. Since we all had jet lag, I cannot imagine any of us figuring out how to pull that off.

Ricky Butterfass
I was at the July 1997 training in England. Steve, Shari, and I went out into the back yard where there was a beautiful rose garden. Dr. Greer saw a craft and said, "They're back!" We had our arms around each other, and we began jumping like kids knowing that ETs were present. I said I needed some rest, and Steve and Shari did too, so the three of us went into the house.

---

[48] Greer, *Extraterrestrial Contact* (1999), p. 256.

I missed seeing the being go in the window, but I did notice as I was going to sleep that all the lights in the house were flashing on and off. Then I had the feeling that there was an ET presence permeating the house. I acknowledged them, and they acknowledged me, and I went back to sleep.

Kay Gibson
One of the lights that I saw in the downstairs living room was an amorphous, shimmering being perhaps four feet tall. At the time it was just one among many lights.

Diamond-white Craft

Linda Willitts
We visited several crop circles, and we did night work in some of them, but most of the nights we did our fieldwork at the house. During one evening, we were all sitting on tarps on the grass. Dr. Greer, Shari and I were looking towards the side of the house with a big tree to the left and a big tree to the right. We saw a brilliant 'star' that looked like Sirius, large, bright and flickering red, green, and white. It rose from behind the tree on the left. Over a period of an hour and a half, it moved 30 degrees until it went behind the tree on the right. During this same time all the other stars in the sky moved in the other direction. This 'alleged star' was a huge craft. Unless you had been still for over an hour, you might not have noticed it. It was moving so slowly that if you had just walked out and looked at it, it would have appeared stationary.

Dr. Steven Greer
I had seen the diamond white craft very briefly that night, and it rose in the west and moved east[49]. No star does that because the Earth turns the other way. It was a very bright object. The casual observer watching for five or ten minutes would not have noticed anything except another bright star in the sky. But having two points of reference, we observed that it moved 30 degrees from the west to the east over about an hour and a half. I have spoken to professional astronomers who have seen similar things, but they do not report such things because they are not supposed

---

[49] "It rose in the west and moved east" represents apparent movement to us on Earth. I realize that the effect occurs due to the Earth's rotation.

to see them. In my opinion, we saw a large exoatmospheric extraterrestrial vehicle carrying the ET that came through the window to communicate with Shari and me.

By 'large' extraterrestrial vehicle, I mean a diameter measured in miles. I know a military officer who had been to the NORAD facility at Cheyenne Mountain where "fast walkers" and other ET craft are tracked. There was one instance where they had tracked an object in deep space that was about 26 miles across—one single spacecraft.

It is possible that such enormous vehicles could be created to house entire civilizations from various planetary systems. I discuss these capabilities in my third book[50]. Such craft are like small planetary bodies in size. They are all artificially made and to quote my military advisor, "It was definitely moving under its own steam."

Arrow-shaped Objects

Kay Gibson
I had one unusual sighting the likes of which I have not seen since. I observed three objects that looked like stubby arrows, with one flying point and two flying in formation behind it. They flew in a split second over the Zenith.

Linda Willitts
I observed it, too. We were in the crop circle that night. It was very peaceful, and the weather was mild though damp. We saw a lot of activity in the sky, most notably a boomerang shaped alleged shooting star that was quite spectacular and observed by all of us[51]. It was the first and only time I have seen such a craft.

Ricky Butterfass
Yes. I saw it, too. It looked to me as if someone shot a golden arrow across the sky, a large javelin. It went from horizon to horizon in a split second. We also went to the tumuli and found the semi-circular grove of trees near a Saracen stone. From that position you could look down towards Silbury Hill and Long Barrow. We

---

[50] Greer, *Hidden Truth* (2006), p. 284.
[51] Greer, *Extraterrestrial Contact* (1999), p. 257.

did our night fieldwork there, and I recall several events.

One craft flew over the grove at the Zenith. It was a flying, spoon-shaped object with the spoon bowl seen as a lighted oval. The tail was like the handle of the spoon. When I pointed it out, Dr. Greer flashed the laser onto the oval part. When the laser hit the object, it would brighten up and then dim down. Dr. Greer flashed the laser several times, and it silently flew over us.

Kay Gibson
Following up on the "golden arrow" incident, I think there were five or six people who observed it and described it similarly. I saw exactly the same event but perceived it as a large, light orange-colored boomerang. It appeared at the Zenith and traveled a huge distance in a split second. I have never seen a boomerang shaped craft before or since. The event was particularly interesting to me because it demonstrated that an event could be perceived differently by different people.

Daylight Appearance of a Triangular Craft
Linda Willitts
Every year when we went to England we also went to Avebury. On one occasion, we saw a gray triangle in the daylight sky that was quite large. The triangle looked bigger than a 747 jetliner, was gray with rounded points, and instead of traveling with its point first, was traveling with its broad end first.

Kay Gibson
My notes indicate on that occasion Dr. Greer was talking to Linda and pointing at the sky. The craft showed up right at the end of his finger and was traveling with its broad end first.

Dr. Steven Greer
What an amazing event. A craft much bigger than a 747 appeared in broad daylight, and the blunt end of the triangle was the leading edge as it moved across the sky. The craft appeared at the tip of my finger as I pointed.

Revisiting Site of 1992 Event
Linda Willitts

1997 was the five-year anniversary of the 1992 incident in which Dr. Greer and only 3 others saw a large craft at Polly Carson's farm on Woodborough Hill. Rain had chased the other training members away that day. To commemorate the event, on July 26 we went to the field where the incident had occurred. Ron Russell was with us. He was there the first time as well, but left because of the rain. Colin Andrews also brought a group out, so there were many observers in the field that night, including many people we did not know.

Two Cylindrical Flashes of Light

During late July in England, it does not get dark until about 10:30 PM. From behind us came a flash of light we thought was a flashlight. We turned and asked if anyone had shown a flashlight on us, but no one had. It seemed unlike a normal flashlight and more like a distinct beam of light. We turned back and started walking, and it flashed again. We asked who had just flashed a light on us. Again no one had done it. We discussed the beam of light and similar light qualities we had seen often in trainings. The quality of ET light and ET sound is not like the light and sound here on Earth. ETs can make a beam of light in any shape. The one Dr. Greer and I saw was cylindrical, not a diffuse cone typical of a flashlight. It was like a light saber in *Star Wars*, clear, distinct, and cylindrical. The beam had both a defined starting and ending point in the air. It did not appear to come from anything and remained coherent rather than diffusing or diminishing.

We have experienced ET sound the same way. We have heard sound with distinct starting and ending points. You can hear the sounds external to your ear, as well as sound like an arrow coming in one ear, going through your head and out the other ear.

Kay Gibson

I saw the beam of light because it shot right in front of me. Linda and Dr. Greer were in the group to my right. The light beam came from my left and was at my waist level. I was on the edge of the group. The light beam, which looked blue to me, shot into the group. It happened twice, but only CSETI people seemed to notice it.

An Anointment
Kay Gibson
I would like to comment on the unusual practice of anointing. It is not an everyday occurrence for most of us. The anointing happened when we were on the tumulus during the meditation. I felt a very warm, soft-yellow light pour over my head and down around my shoulders. It was like being covered gently with melted butter and honey. That was exactly how I thought of it in terms of color and warmth, sweetness and richness. The process seemed very biblical, but what does it mean to be anointed in an everyday situation? The experience was so spiritual, that I did not tell anyone. After the meditation was over, I saw a semi-circle of sky visible through the trees that would have been exactly the shape and source of the light or energy that came down. I fully expected to see a craft, but did not. I gave profound thanks for that beautiful gift. It was a deep experience to be anointed during one of these CSETI expeditions.

Flares as a Diversionary Tactic
Linda Willitts
I remember the first time that I saw the military drop flares. We were near the Salisbury Plain, an English military area. Any time we had a major sighting, jets and helicopters swarmed in within 30 to 60 seconds. On two occasions we have seen flares dropped. Flares are dropped in sequence, individually, so they come down sequentially to light an area, and as they drop they leave large smoke streams.

Suppressive Efforts
Ricky Butterfass
What I saw that night was a large cloud. Then I saw a craft that dipped down out of the cloud and went back up into it. Right after that the military dispensed their flares. I think they were on a bivouac or some sort of maneuvers. They had tanks, and it seemed as if the whole regiment was out. It seemed evident to me that the military events were intended to produce a cover-up of the craft sightings.

Dr. Steven Greer

They were part of the suppressive efforts. We were on an 1800-acre farm, part of the Royal Trust Lands of Polly Carson and Tim Carson. It has become something of a tourist site in England since the CSETI CE-5 near landing of a spacecraft in 1992. A senior minister from the Dutch government was there, Dr. Zoeteman. He was the equivalent of the Minister for the Environment from Holland. The craft was seen by our trained team in the field and by untrained people some distance away who reported and confirmed it. The news of the event went all the way to the Ministry of Defense. I was subsequently invited to Whitehall to meet with Nick Pope, as he was the UFO officer for the Ministry of Defense. They desired of me an official debriefing on the event.

Now, five years later to the day, many incidents were still happening: the craft we had seen at the manor house, the ET being that had come into the house, and the anomalous electromagnetic events happening with the lights going on and off. We were on site for the fifth anniversary – and it just so happened that the English military were performing major maneuvers with artillery shells, bombings, tanks, and flares. It was not a coincidence. During the event, we were standing in a group of about 30 people, many of whom were not trained in the CSETI protocols, but we were doing the CSETI-CE5 protocols.

An ET Walks Through the Group

Suddenly, Ron Russell, a few others and I saw a strange "woman," appear. She was very erect, walked straight through the group, and then disappeared. It happened several times. It was strange, a non-human being, but it was flesh and blood. I wondered who else had seen the "woman." Ron Russell was speechless and did not know what to think. Many people have asked me about ETs appearing in the flesh. We have seen it many times, and this one walked right through the crowd with the Minister of the Environment of Holland standing there!

Linda Willitts[52]

Our security team saw a woman walking robotically out of the field and through our group. Ron spoke to her. He greeted her with, "Hello, how are you?" and she repeated his words back to him. Whatever he said to her, she repeated it back exactly. Ron said they recognized there was something very weird about her, but they were somehow made powerless to act on their suspicions. Kay also noticed her and thought she was very robotic.

Ricky Butterfass

She had a Macintosh on. She was a very attractive woman about 5'7" tall. She was wearing a pair of beige colored pants. I thought she was just a local walking through all these strange people out there in the field. She looked straight ahead, and walked right through us.

Kay Gibson

It was a hooded jacket that went below her hips. Her face had perfect features.

Dr. Steven Greer

Her face was very white. She moved very straightly and stiffly as she walked through the group. What really happened was that the first two passes of light that we saw move through the group were actually her. Her first two passes scanned the group and then she materialized and literally walked straight through the crowd.

Kay Gibson

We were all clumped in our group, and she came out of the crop field where no one had been. She walked quite close to me, and that is how I knew she was 5'7" or 5'8." She had a perfect Grace Kelly profile. She passed so closely that I thought she might look at me, but she did not. She just disappeared from my sight in the crowd around me. I had the immediate impressions: 'she is not a regular person' and 'who is she and where did she come from?' I have never had a similar experience in all my trainings and observations.

---

[52] Greer, *Extraterrestrial Contact* (1999), p. 256.

Trudy Guyker
Ron Russell told me she came out of the crop field and, even though it was muddy, there was no mud on her shoes.

Dr. Steven Greer
The way she moved was almost like gliding. It was not normal walking, but more like floating. It was very unusual and definitely was an extraterrestrial. The place in Alton Barnes had become quite a destination on this day for people, because of the event that happened five years previously. But during the 1997 event with the ET woman, most of the people did not realize anything at all had happened, which is fascinating and rather enigmatic.

Charlie Balogh
I think it is indicative of the way ETs interact with people who are ready to accept what they are seeing. ETs can be very selective in how they appear to people. They seem to know with whom they can interact and with whom they can not.

ET Craft Produces Dome Effect

Kay Gibson
We had an experience one night in the 1997 training in which we could feel a dome structure descend over us, and it felt suddenly as if we were in another place. There was a deep silence, and the atmosphere and temperature had changed. I could still see that we were in England, but the ambience had changed. A group that was triangulating with us at the same time later reported that all the traffic noise quieted for them.

Dr. Steven Greer
It is as if something settles around you that you really cannot see unless you are in the correct state of consciousness. Suddenly, you are protected from the elements, the temperature rises 10 to 15 degrees, and the environment is muffled. It is like being in a dome. It is actually the transposition of an ET craft over the space in which you are located, meshed into physical reality in a way that the craft is not quite materialized. The craft is present, there is a thickening of the air, the temperature often rises, and the humidity changes.

We have had similar episodes happen in Crestone, at Joshua Tree, and in England many times. We will be sitting out on a freezing night, and when the "dome-like event" happens it can get so warm that we overheat. Frequently, when it is cloudy, we are doing our meditation and the clouds directly above us open up so much we can see a clear sky and stars. We have had this happen hundreds of times from the power of the group consciousness.

Dr. Ted Loder
It is also interesting that the sound changes when you ring a Tibetan bowl during a "dome-like" event.

Dr. Steven Greer
It is similar to an echo bouncing off the wall of something you cannot "see."

Linda Willitts
During a "dome-like" event, if Dr. Greer shines his laser up into the sky, the beam stops ascending, as if it is hitting an unseen Plexiglas dome.

Dr. Steven Greer
Yes. You can see where the laser light stops. That happened in England. That is when I guide people into a meditation, saying, "In your inner sight see who is gathered here with us." They are with us, but it is not quite what people expect.

The Lion Lucid Dream

Linda Willitts
While we were in England, I remember Dr. Greer telling about a lucid dream he had as we sat in the living room of the big manor house.

Dr. Steven Greer
I have many lucid dreams but this one was very powerful. It occurred in the context of what was happening with the briefings we had done for Congress, with Shari and me having metastatic cancer, and with Bill Colby being killed when he was trying to help us. Tom Bearden and I both talk about the "lions" of the cabal

or MJ-12. We used that term to refer to some of the key people who are in the transnational, permanent government. He has told me for years that I am in the middle of the biggest catfight that the world has ever seen. Those metaphors set up the lucid dream that was as real as life and in full color.

In the dream I found myself with lions, and particularly one giant lion. It was ferocious. It was stalking me and intended to do harm and devour me. I avoided being in fear or anger or engaging it on the level of the energy that this powerful beast generated. Instead, I went into a higher state of consciousness much like in Mexico when we were seconds away from being killed by the Mexican police. As I went into that state, the lion circled me, checking me out the way an animal will do as it circles its prey before pouncing. As I engaged the lion with higher awareness and in love and peace, suddenly this huge beast became very peaceful, and we were looking right into each other's eyes and directly engaging each other. This lion and I became one, going into a state of consciousness that is beyond all fear, limitation and disunity. As I relied upon the power of divine love, the cosmic mind and the Divine Being, the lion became transfixed and peaceful. Then as we stood close to each other, it lay down and rolled over on its back. I sat down with it, rubbing its belly like one would a house cat, and we became fast friends.

There was no question in my mind what this dream symbolized. It was an expression of the situation that has been going on with the lions of MJ-12. If we stay in the appropriate state of consciousness, eventually those lions will allow us to become friends. Even though one has to be wary, as I was initially, we must not hesitate to engage. If we stay true to our spirit, to this higher state of consciousness and purpose, and to this connection to the Divine Being, those lions will allow us to become friends. We actually became friends in the dream, and an enormous love developed between the lion and me.

After this lucid dream, I knew that even though we had to be aware, the key was not to fight, hate, or attack. The key was to stay in this deeper state of consciousness. We need only call upon the powers of the Celestial and Divine Being with Love and engage our work in complete innocence. Eventually, the lion will come to us as a friend. That has actually transpired in a number of cases in the intervening ten years.

CSETI Training
Joshua Tree, California
November 1997

Dr. Steven Greer
By November of 1997 my health had stabilized, but Shari's condition had deteriorated. She had metastatic cancer in her liver, brain, and lungs. She was very weak, and limping because the cancer in her brain had affected her gait. Her indomitable spirit was such that when I suggested canceling the Joshua Tree expedition of 1997, she said, "No! If it is the last thing I do and the last breath I take, I am going to be there with you at Joshua Tree!"

Sighting of Large Luminous Object

Dr. Ted Loder
Joshua Tree was my second training, and I brought my second son, who is also a linear scientist. He did not bring enough warm clothes, and the weather got cold. During the training, I had an amazing personal sighting. We were sitting in a circle near the entrance to the Hidden Valley site. I was facing east while Dr. Greer and Ricky were to my left, facing south. About mid-evening I looked over my right shoulder at the moon. It was nearly full and 30 to 40 degrees above the horizon. To the left of the Moon appeared a light-bulb shaped object. It was a fully round object, which floated slowly underneath the Moon for three to six seconds and then winked out. It was not a speck of light. It was a round, resolved object about one third the size of the Moon. I was stunned to see something with that much resolution. I jumped up and asked if anyone else had seen it. Dr. Greer said, "Calm down, Ted, and tell us what you saw." I told him, and he asked whether anyone else saw the object. Six or seven people reported they had seen it. I would not have seen it if I had not looked over my shoulder at the time I did.

Dr. Steven Greer
I was looking at the object the whole time. It was a very bright, luminous object that was crystal clear, as was the night. The Moon was about two-thirds full, and the object appeared silently floating underneath the moon. It was about one third the size of the full Moon – a large object. It was bright and in the atmosphere very near us.

As you recall, in 1996, an enormous ship came down on the Geology Tour Plain and entered the earth, showing us the location of an ET underground facility. The object we saw this night was to the south, almost directly over the plain where the previous craft entered the earth.

The sighting was a very important event for Dr. Loder, as a scientist and a university professor who had personally never seen a CE-5 mediated event. I always felt that this event happened for him.

Dr. Ted Loder
Seeing the craft was wonderful. It was a pivotal event for me in that I was able to internalize the reality of the material we were investigating and studying.

ET Craft Moves Tree

Dr. Steven Greer
At that same site there was a tree 15 to 20 feet tall. It was totally silent there, with no wind when suddenly the tree began shaking and moving violently. I was right beside it, and the whole tree was shaking violently for a few seconds. That is when I knew that ETs were right there with us.

Ricky Butterfass
I had remote viewed a craft on the ground, and I saw that it had the same luminosity as the Moon. I saw an extraterrestrial dressed in black standing off to the side of the craft. His head was large and looked like a light bulb. The ET's head had the same luminosity as the craft. As we were looking into the sky, I received the message, "If you look straight up, you can see a lot more of the sky." I looked straight up, and I heard Dr. Loder say, "Whoa." I could see

a craft, the one I had remote viewed on the ground, about a third the size of the Moon and very close to us. Suddenly the craft lit up, flew underneath the moon, and then it was gone. I also saw the tree move and shake. I shined my million-candle-power light into the tree, but there was nothing in it. We lit up the side of the hill and saw nothing there. We knew an ET craft had been on site with us and that it had left.

Dr. Steven Greer
Actually, as the craft was moving away and phase-shifted, its movement shook the tree. There was no wind moving the tree, and we were in a protected area, Hidden Valley. It was extraordinary.

Trudy Guyker
I was sitting under the tree. The lowest branches were very close, and the tree began shaking violently. Since I was so close, I could look up into the center and there was nothing there, just the tree shaking violently. It was amazing.

ETs in the Parking Area

Ricky Butterfass
We were in Joshua Tree Park seated in the parking lot. Dr. Greer said the ambassador craft, a disc, was coming in. We all stood, walked out into the parking lot waiting for it to fly in. The craft was very stealthy. I could make it out, but it was phase shifted, and I had to remote view it as it came in. The craft moved like a "Hula Hoop" when you spin it, then it slows down and wobbles back and forth. The craft was dark, circular, and dome-shaped. I could see inside the dome and saw three ET beings dressed in black. I could also see inside the craft spinning hoops, which I saw oscillating back and forth, and seemed to be the power plant of the craft. Two of the beings came outside of the dome, walked across the disc part of it, dropped down to the ground and came across the parking lot in front of us. Many people saw that, too.

Trudy Guyker
There was a young man, Frank, who was part of our group, but had never seen anything. As we were sitting at the Hidden Valley site we looked to the north and observed gray forms not far away.

Frank saw them, and from that time on he was changed.

Dr. Steven Greer
The forms were ETs moving around. I wanted to go down to the parking area because I could see a shimmering disc-shaped craft at that location with scintillating beings in it. As we approached, the ETs were waiting for us in the area by the cars. The craft was a very distinct, celestial light.

Trudy Guyker
The dark forms that we saw were probably people from the craft. They were dark gray. There was nothing subtle; it was very visible.

ETs Say Goodbye to Shari
Linda Willitts
It was very cold, and Shari did the fieldwork from inside the vehicle that night. Riding back in the car with Shari, Dr. Greer and his daughter, my radar detector went off. The site is so remote, only an ET craft can trigger a radar detector there. I knew the event was for Shari.

Dr. Steven Greer
That was the last night of the training. We sent out our recorded tones as part of our contact protocols, and then we heard high pitched electronic tones coming back to us and through the circle. Leaving Joshua Tree Park we knew it was Shari's last expedition. Across the valley of Palm Springs, coming from the north, an object very similar to the one in 1996 flew right overhead. We actually heard this one whistling. It came over the valley moving from north to south and low. It was at the edge of the crossing point of light. If you can imagine, the front of the craft would get ahead of the back and then the back would catch up, somewhat like an accordion. It proceeded in this manner, moving across the entire valley. It was Shari's send-off – the ET's way of saying goodbye – and we all knew it.

The first night of our fieldwork when Shari got out of the car, she stumbled, fell, and skinned her knee. I was very concerned, but she just smiled and said, "No, I am fine." She did not mind a little help, but she would not allow anyone to give her too much attention. She wanted the focus to be on our work, not her disease. Her courage was poignant and so beautiful. She was so completely dedicated to doing the work of CSETI in heart, mind, and soul. She was strong in so many ways, and no force on Earth could have kept her from being there in November of 1997. She was a truly amazing person. Within a few weeks of this expedition, she lapsed into a coma and passed away about two months later on January 20, 1998.

Accessing Any Conversation
Dr. Ted Loder

One topic from the lecture stuck with me because it provided a very good lesson. Dr. Greer mentioned that people with certain technology or training could access any conversation in our room. It was early in my CSETI education, and I was thinking, "Really? I don't know, Steve." Dr. Greer often puts out to the group an idea and lets them think about it. So, I let that comment sit in my brain awhile, mulling it over. After the training my youngest son and I drove up to Santa Barbara. One day we went to a bookstore and picked up David Morehouse's book, *Psychic Warrior*. After reading the first five pages, I realized, "Oh, my God, this is exactly what Dr. Greer was talking about."

Night Vision Sighting at Santa Barbara

One evening at Tony and Pat Craddock's stunning house overlooking the Santa Barbara Channel, Dr. Greer, Tony, and I were standing outside. Jupiter was up about 10 degrees above the horizon. We had two expensive, high quality pairs of night vision binoculars. As Tony and I lifted the binoculars to look at Jupiter, both of us simultaneously saw a triangular-shaped craft roaring down the Santa Barbara Channel, about 20 miles off shore. It was far enough away that we could not see it with our naked eyes. It was there for about seven seconds before it went behind a big gum tree at the limit of our vision. We were astounded and went inside where each of us drew what we had seen. What we drew independently was one dot, two dots and another two dots behind in a triangular form. Tony had the better quality binoculars, and he put a light at the center of the back end. I did not see that.

I calculated it to be traveling 4,000 to 8,000 miles per hour down the coast. The question that has always remained with me is "Was it an ARV (Alien Reproduction Vehicle) coming out of Edwards AFB or was it an ET craft?

Chapter 6

1998

Shari's Passing
Denver, Colorado
January 1998

Dr. Steven Greer
Shari passed away January 20, 1998. That night I wrote a memorial tribute to her and an account of that spiritual event[53]. She wasted no time in answering.

Introduction to Kindness

That night I went into a very deep lucid dream-state. I saw Shari, very luminous and happy, wearing a long dress. She gave me a hug and then disappeared, but not before somehow introducing me to an extraterrestrial woman. This woman, beautiful in her own way, had a perfectly round head and was hairless with almond-shaped eyes, and diminutive nose and mouth. I do not recall any ear flaps, just openings on the side of the head. She was wearing a one-piece, silvery suit. She was, and is, a senior extraterrestrial ambassador and spiritual elder representing many star civilizations, not just her own. She was very much biological and physical, but in a state of God-consciousness, emanating an energy of perfect compassion and kindness. So I have called her "Kindness." At almost every one of our CSETI gatherings, Kindness has appeared in the sky in her craft and often in the building as an orb. The first thing Shari did for us after she passed over was to bring about this important introduction. Shari felt so terrible about leaving me alone in this work, and I had told her to let go because she could do wonderful things for us from the worlds of light - and she has!

---

[53] Greer, *Hidden Truth* (2006), pp. 170-172.

Dream Involving Bill Clinton

In that same dream I visited Bill Clinton at the White House. It was 1998 and he had been re-elected in '96. He had backed away from the disclosure issues because he was afraid of the powers that were keeping this information secret. This dream was a very real meeting with him. One of his good friends told me that he did, in fact, also have this type of lucid dream.

Since November of 1992 when he was elected, I had been going in the lucid dream state first to the Governor's mansion in Arkansas and then to the White House, having these meetings. In a sense, they were tutorials. I was attempting to teach Clinton about these issues. I do not talk much about this, but it was very real. The night that Shari passed away was my last meeting with Clinton on the astral level. I looked at him and said, "It is time for this matter to be disclosed and it is time to move on to the next era in human history."

He looked at me with a rather sardonic smile and said, "Well, I cannot do it, but you can. So go ahead if you can."

Green-light for Disclosure

I then went to Kindness, and asked her if she thought that we should work for Disclosure. She looked at me and said, "If it is possible, please do it." So it was a senior extraterrestrial who asked me to continue with the Disclosure Project, just when I was going to pull the plug on it. This is the true story of what happened...

When people ask me who blessed the Disclosure Project, I tell them the President of the United States in an astral meeting, the Head of Intelligence for the Joint Staff, a very senior extraterrestrial elder introduced to me the night that Shari passed away and, of course, my own conscience. That was all I needed. In 1998 I began to write letters to key officials in the government saying that unless otherwise directed, we were going to move forward with Disclosure. We explained that since these projects were being managed outside of the rule of law and the Constitution, they were rogue and therefore the laws regarding secrecy were inapplicable. No government official ever disagreed with this assessment.

We were going to bring out top-secret military and intelligence people's testimony and documents, some of which had not been declassified through official channels. The rest is history, and you know what we did.

Photo of ET Elder's Ship

Kindness, the senior extraterrestrial elder, has been with us continuously since 1998. We will often see that Shari is there, as well. In photographs we see a wash of rose/coral/pink colored light, which is Shari's energy. In one case at Joshua Tree we took a photograph of Kindness' deep cobalt blue ship, in a plasma form in broad daylight. The ship is not quite materialized, but it is very visible. Beside it is a hint of this beautiful coral/pink color that is Shari's essence and astral energy. They are in that photo together on a hill at Joshua Tree above a Native American cave where we initiate Ambassadors to the Universe.

Setting Up the Disclosure Project
1998-2001

Dr. Steven Greer
From 1998 on, we were doing the research and identifying military, corporate and intelligence witnesses and documents for the Disclosure Project. Once it was clear to me that neither the President, nor Congress, nor the United Nations nor any other country was going to hold hearings to bring about disclosure, I knew that we needed to be the ones to move this forward. We had been making contact with extraterrestrial civilizations using the CSETI protocols, and the process was progressing at a very rapid rate. We had many close encounters and mass witnessed events. We were committed to getting this information out in an organized way, and so we completed the Disclosure Project. It was a huge amount of work, and this process is recorded in my book, Hidden Truth – Forbidden Knowledge[54].

---

[54] Greer, *Hidden Truth* (2006), pp. 10, 15, 60, 96, 135, 146, 157, 184, 201, 205, 232, 237.

CSETI Expedition with Joan Ocean and Dolphins
Kona, Hawaii
February 1998

Dr. Steven Greer

The next major event was an expedition to the Big Island, near Kona, Hawaii, at the request of Joan Ocean. Joan is well known as a dolphin communicator who also teaches people to connect with wild spinner dolphins in Hawaii. The expedition took place the month following Shari's passing and was very difficult for me personally. I felt I could not let anyone get too close to me, worrying that if they did they might get killed, and I had enough survivor guilt already. I was in post-traumatic stress with survivor's guilt, and although I held myself together, I was still devastated. I was reluctant to go to Hawaii, but I went. The CSETI group gathered and we did the training. Joan Ocean found a contact site in a pasture up in the mountains above the ocean. It was there that I first met Dr. Jan Bravo.

Dr. Jan Bravo

My first training was in February 1998. I had initially scheduled that week to swim with the dolphins, and when I heard about the CSETI training I added it just three weeks before the trip. I did not have a lot of warm clothes because I am from California. That element is part of this tale.

We were at a high elevation on the Big Island, in our circle, and I was wrapped up in my sleeping bag. I was seeing and hearing absolutely nothing except the good stories people were sharing. About halfway through the week, it was still very cold and I was buried deep in my sleeping bag. At one point, my buddy stuck her finger right in the middle of my back, poked me and said, "Jan, wake up!" I was not snoring and not asleep. I promptly informed her that I was cold but okay.

Later that night I was again poked in the back. This time I got up and spun around. I was going to let this woman know in no uncertain terms that I was not sleeping. But this woman and the person next to her were not there because they had gone off on a restroom break. My left-brain tried to convince me that I had imagined the poke. What had happened was very clear. The poke was an exact duplicate of when I had been poked in the back earlier. I finally realized and accepted much later that poke was my first contact. It was a kinesthetic contact. It was wonderful, and I was very glad for it. So contact comes in many different ways. Since I am a very kinesthetic person and understand things in that form, the communication to me was presented that way-as if they were thinking "Maybe she'll get it this way."

On the last night it was cold, and I saw nothing around us. I did hear others saying, "I see this light, I see this, I see that." Some horses had come to visit us, an alpha male, a female and a mule. I was paying attention to the mule because it was close to my size, and I liked that. The alpha male stood off, but finally the female warmed up to us. The male horse warmed up to me, and I recall he let me approach. As I walked up, I looked him in the eyes and said, "Where are the ETs?" At that very moment, he turned and ran toward a group of trees about a half-mile away. He could have gone anywhere, but he headed toward that clump of trees. He ran out about 50 feet, turned around and looked first at me, then at the trees, and then back at me. I was trying to send a mental message, "I can't go there. I have a buddy. We are not supposed to stray away. Those are the rules." He looked back at the trees once more, looked at me, and then the three of them ran away.

I was transfixed on that area for the rest of the night. And later that night I had my first visual sighting of a beautiful amber orb, right over the clump of trees the horse had shown me. I was thinking to myself as people talked about the light, "Wow. There was an anomalous light with nothing else around, right over those trees." I think the important point of the experience was the communication of consciousness on all levels, with the animals, the humans and the ET. I was really happy with all of it!

Linda Willitts
Most of the events that we saw in the field were quite subtle. But Jan's experience was more overt. When those horses came and sniffed the backs of our necks as we sat in the circle, I was

wondering if they knew about the ETs.

Communicating and Connecting with Dolphins
Dr. Steven Greer

One focus of the Hawaii expedition was creating an integrated experience with the dolphins. They are very intelligent, and we wanted to be able to bridge the concept of communication and connection with them. That is also what we do with the extraterrestrial intelligence. So we went out to swim with the spinner dolphins that are known for jumping out of the water and spinning around in the air. They are smaller than the Atlantic bottlenose dolphins, and their dispositions are very sweet, but still they are wild dolphins, not captive or trained.

At one point, as we were swimming, a huge tiger shark appeared underneath us. All the dolphins had left, and we quickly figured it was time to leave the water, so we went to another area to look for the dolphins. As always, we assigned buddies to be sure no one is alone in the contact work. Linda was my buddy on the dolphin expedition. I went into the water for my last opportunity because it was getting very late in the day. I went into a state of Cosmic consciousness, as I do with my dogs, with babies, and with other animals, and then become one with them. I went into this universal state of mind and connected with dolphin consciousness.

It is a state of childlike innocence. And then suddenly the dolphins came! Four of them adopted me into their pod. There was one on my right, one on my left, one in front and one beneath, just like a star formation of flying planes. I was so close to the ones on my left and right that their eyes were within arm's reach, and I could have easily touched them. As we looked eye to eye, we connected, and I started moving with them. I am a strong swimmer, but I am not a dolphin! They would dive down, and I would go with them as far as I could. When I ran out of air and had to come up, they would come up with me. If they got too far ahead of me and I could not keep up, I would see them looking at me, eye-to-eye, and they would slow down so I could keep up. Linda could not keep up, and I knew that they were taking me out into the deep ocean to be with them. I was one of the dolphins now; I was one of their fellow pod members. I could not go, of course, and was already in breach of the safety protocols by being so far away from the boat and from my buddy, so I had to say goodbye. I could feel them going away, and still they were connecting with me. What a beautiful, sweet experience I had with those dolphins.

Consciousness Necessary for Contact
Dr. Steven Greer

The dolphin experience illustrates the state of consciousness and the state of intent I call "psychological non-violence," which is required in ET contact work.

There is a certain level of gentleness and state of oneness that must be attained before a deep level of contact will happen. Doing this exercise with the dolphins was a good way of practicing that state of consciousness. You can also do it with wild animals. Back in college when I was 18, I was learning meditation after the near death experience. I would go up behind the dorm and sit against the ancient hemlock trees and meditate. Upon opening my eyes there would be a semi-circle of wild animals – a raccoon, a bird, a squirrel, a chipmunk – all gathered to partake of that consciousness.

Calming the Coyotes

One year in Colorado there was much ET activity in the sky above us that everyone was seeing. A group of coyotes were carrying on with constant yipping and howling. I stood up and demonstrated the communication and connection concept to the group. Closing my eyes, I connected to coyote consciousness, and held my hands up. I use my hands to send energy, and I conveyed a calming energy to the coyotes. As soon as I did that the coyotes became silent. The entire group witnessed this effect. I do this often with wild animals. I love animals and children because they are pure-hearted, innocent and without guile. I am like that to a large extent, to both my credit and misfortune in this world. These animal experiences epitomize the contact experience and are a good illustration of the state of mind required for contacting the ETs.

Other Experiences in Hawaii

Linda Willitts

After swimming with the dolphins, we went to Volcano National Park before dark. We ended up at the lava tube you can walk into. We left the car, closed the doors, and left no lights on. When we came out of the lava tube, the dome light inside the car was on. Later we were going to the restaurant at a lodge near a dormant caldera. We were standing on a deck behind the hotel waiting to have dinner. No one else was on the deck. Suddenly there was a blinding, brilliant flash as though someone had taken a flash photo of us from three feet away, but there was absolutely no one around. We knew this flash was an ET object that had come in within a few feet of us.

Kay Gibson

One difference I noticed on this trip was that I sensed that the ground was multidimensional. At our site there were lava tubes below ground, which is why you could hear a vibration or echo when the horses were running. Looking with soft eyes, the ground started rippling almost like water. I had never seen such a phenomenon. The ground was rippling like the ocean when the wind blows it, and this happened every time that I looked with soft eyes. Yet if I looked with normal vision, I could not see it. It took relaxed eyes to see the ground rippling.

I decided to remote view and my consciousness went into the ground. I found a very large gold and black mandala[55] with a huge, scintillating star in the center, and from that central star emanated many spokes of golden light with a scattering of tiny stars on them. It was mesmerizing. As I looked at the central star, I felt it was drawing me into it, and I think I went into that star. It was a constantly scintillating, three-dimensional mandala, and I felt that I could leave through it, as if it was a portal. I did not leave, but it was the first time I had experienced anything like that. I made a sketch, and Dr. Greer said that it reminded him of a mandala that he was familiar with.

---

[55] mandala: http://www.mandalaproject.org/What/Index.html

Also, I experienced a strange golden cone of light and had the sense that it was affecting my senses. Cones of light went out into space from my ears. Light was also affecting my eyes. I do not know exactly what was going on, but I felt as if I was being tuned somehow. Dr. Greer said it was an augmentation of my senses. I have experienced these augmentations at other expeditions and times since then.

One of the strangest things was a sound like that of wild turkeys. I live in the foothills of northern California around wild turkeys and am very familiar with that sound. What I heard was similar to an electronic turkey gobble. That happened several different times, but everyone did not hear it. Only about a third of the group heard these sounds.

Linda Willitts
I had one of the clearest remote views that I have ever had on this expedition. I saw a surveillance vehicle exploring our site before we arrived one day.

Kay Gibson
One night as we were driving to the site, we saw small, black, sharp shapes, almost like bats, flying up out of the trees high into the sky. They were not bats because they did not move the way bats do.

Appearance by Kindness in her Ship
Dr. Steven Greer
On that trip we saw the beautiful ship that carries the senior ET ambassador, whom I call Kindness because of her countenance of perfect kindness. The ship is very distinct and blue-white, although some people may see it as amber. Her ship comes into the atmosphere, frequently from the northeast. A brilliant light will flash the group, and then the craft will turn and go back out into space. This has happened dozens of times since 1998 when Shari passed away.

ETs Welcome 1998 Move
Asheville, North Carolina to Albemarle County, Virginia

Dr. Steven Greer

Extraterrestrial expressions of intelligence can include enigmatic events, such as letters in clouds to give you an indication in some way, or they may use a symbol, such as the CSETI triangle appearing in a field. When we decided to move from North Carolina to Charlottesville, Virginia, an agent showed us various properties in Albemarle County. We finally found the one we wanted and went back to Asheville NC. Later we came back to close on the Virginia property, and the day that we closed, a crop circle appeared in Virginia near Charlottesville (see DVD). The crop circle occurred on the land of our agent's family. The figure involved was the CSETI triangle, actually a triple CSETI triangle in the sense that there were three smaller triangles around the line going into the center circle. A photo of it was on the cover of "The C-Ville Weekly[56]." Someone who noticed the photo notified me. What an astonishing thing to see! Not only was it very near the home we were buying, the circle occurred on the land of the family of the man who showed us and sold us the house!

The crop circle represented an extraterrestrial welcome mat. It was as if they were saying, "Welcome to your new home." This is the sort of expression that happens to many people in many ways. Coincidence? I doubt it.

CSETI Expedition
Crestone, Colorado
June 1998

Al Dunaway

This was my first training, and I wanted to have a first-hand contact experience. I had many years of spiritual seeking and was trying to improve my meditation skills. We were meditating in a circle, and some ETs were moving around us. I desired to see an ET and experience a contact and was concentrating so hard that I missed the interaction as an ET was pulling my scarf out from around my

---

[56] C-Ville Weekly: http://www.c-ville.com/ (Archives current only to 2002)

neck under my coat. Tucking the scarf back in and continuing my myopic quest, I later realized what was going on and that they were trying to get my attention.

RV of Grasshopper Type ETs
Kay Gibson

We had done several remote viewings, and it was the first time that my consciousness traveled far out into space. I looked back and saw the Earth. Then I turned around and kept going and could see other star systems. Suddenly, I was inside a craft with grasshopper-type beings. I made a drawing of them later. I seemed to be in a freeze-frame photograph. I observed two beings that were fairly large, probably five feet tall. They had funny little sharp points on their forearms. I stared at the being closest to me because I wanted to remember as much as possible. I could not move or speak, but I could move my eyes around to see what was in my immediate field of vision. There was a small console in the center with three workstations, and around the perimeter there was a long console with several workstations but no beings. I have not experienced anything like that before or since, so it was rather amazing.

As our group stood in a circle holding hands prior to leaving late one night, I looked around with soft eyes at our circle. We had our eyes closed and our heads bowed, and all our faces were grasshopper-like. This experience made me feel that I should share my experience of having popped into the craft with the grasshopper-looking ETs. Prior to that I felt it was such a strange experience that I was not comfortable sharing it, but seeing all of us look like that made me feel our sameness and universality and gave me the impetus to share my experience.

RV of Manatee Type ET
Al Dunaway

I also had my first successful remote view. I entered a craft and met my first ET. The occupant was standing with his back towards me when I entered the craft and appeared to be humanoid in appearance. When he turned around, however, he was that way only from the neck down. His head and face were that of a manatee, with graceful features and such a peaceful countenance that I was quickly at peace within myself relating to him.

I invited him to meet with our group and showed him how to find and interface with us. He led me over to a console and asked me to think how to get to where we were. As I did this the console morphed and moved like a series of tiles flipping up and down. I later discovered this was the craft's navigational computer. That evening the craft overflew our group as we sat out in the field. This would not be the only encounter that our training groups would have with this particular ET, as he has shown up several times on other trainings and a strong friendship has developed between us.

Invitation to a private site on Mount Blanca
Jan Brook
One night at Zapata Falls Dr. Greer and Dr. Loder were standing and chatting about field sites. Dr. Greer said, "Wouldn't it be nice if someone would offer us their private property?" The very next morning Al and I went to breakfast and a man named Roger walked in, went to the manager and said, "Where is Steven Greer? I have to meet Steven Greer." Roger, a shaman who lived in the area, said that he had a medicine wheel that had never been used on his property. He had just consecrated the medicine wheel[57], and he invited us onto that land. We had some amazing experiences there.

Experiences at the Medicine Wheel Site
Linda Willitts
I remember going to the medicine wheel. It was quite a trip up a very rocky trail lugging our equipment. We had some older people in our group, but we all got up there and tucked ourselves around the periphery of the medicine wheel. We were in a meditation when Donna Hare interrupted the meditation to point out that straight ahead of us was a beautiful, bright, pink light, very large and brilliant. It was getting brighter the way an iridium satellite does, but this light was pink.

---

[57] Medicine wheel: http://en.wikipedia.org/wiki/Medicine_wheel

Dr. Steven Greer
It was a beautiful jewel-like object in the sky and it was definitely ET. It came closer to us in the atmosphere, and it was so bright that you could feel the light.

Jan Brook
That night Bob Selover and I both remote viewed the same craft coming in. We did not know it until we described it later, but we were both describing the same thing. I think Bob saw it come in at a 45-degree angle. In my remote view, the craft appeared to have a triangular face, and when I first saw it, it was inverted. My thought was "somebody is upside down". The craft immediately went blank and then came back as right side up. Within the golden triangular faced craft were three senior ET people. One was in the front and two lieutenants were on each side. They were coming in to meet with us.

Box Communication Device Appears
Dr. Steven Greer
I had gone a short distance from our circle. A blue box-like object appeared, and I sensed that it was an unusual communication device. Before this box appeared, we had seen golden doorways open high upon the mountain. My first response was that these Beings had come through this doorway. At some point the box appeared on the ground. I went over to it, as several people witnessed this. In the next moment the box was above the ground. The box was a communication device that these extraterrestrials had placed before us.

Al Dunaway
I noticed what appeared to be a green telephone box about two feet tall, three feet long and one foot across. It was very dark as there was no moon, so I tapped the lady standing next to me, pointed to the box, and asked her what she saw. She looked for a few moments and said that she saw a box there. I had not recalled any structures there earlier when we first entered the medicine wheel. We then asked a gentleman standing next to her what he saw. This man, an engineer, also stated that he was seeing a box. As we stared at the box, Donna later confessed that she started thinking she would like to sit down on it to rest. As she was thinking this,

the box started to move away from us. We were surrounded by sagebrush, and we clearly heard the box move between the sagebrush plants.

Dr. Steven Greer
The box was visible and it was a very physical object - and it definitely moved. A strong extraterrestrial presence exists in the area of this site as evidenced by the bright pink object, the golden doorways and the strange communication box that moved around. The whole time we were there, a connection also seemed to exist with ancient Native American elders. I felt they were the same ones who had been up at the contact site the year before, in 1997. If you were very quiet, you could sense, hear and feel them above the white noise of the space/time continuum.

Trudy Guyker
The box went toward Dr. Greer, and he had become harder to see.

Dr. Steven Greer
Several people saw that I completely dematerialized. Even though there were no objects to block the view of my body, I appeared to be transparent.

Kay Gibson
I saw Dr. Greer disappear in a golden haze of light. I felt like we were all in a "golden scene" and, I felt very light. I could not feel my heavy Earth body. I saw translucent golden beings in a vaguely triangular shape with indistinct edges. They were even more indistinct at the bottom, which was also the widest part. The beings were inside our circle. I saw many golden sparkles everywhere.

Trudy Guyker
A very loving encounter happened here. There were ET beings and earth Devas[58]. I saw several little people about a foot and a half or

---
[58] Devas: http://www.soul-guidance.com/houseofthesun/devas.htm

two feet tall with cream-colored, very smooth skin, no real facial features, but two arms and legs and a head. Several of them were following Dr. Greer. There were also several other kinds of little beings that were of the Earth and seemed to impart a tremendous amount of love to the area.

Ricky Butterfass
On top of Blanca Peak I saw a golden light that seemed to be encased in emerald light. It was as if someone poured honey, and it flowed down with that consistency. It was like little golden fireflies flying down the mountain, closer and closer. We were all standing there watching it move in on us almost like lava. It moved closer, circulated around our feet, moved right up my legs and covered me up, and it felt so good. I felt as if the whole molecular structure of my body had been realigned and reoriented. That was my experience!

Dr. Steven Greer
I remember that and you hit the nail on the head! That light flowed down from the mountain and wrapped all around us.

Contact at Zapata Falls

Trudy Guyker
The contact at Zapata Falls was one of the most incredible things that ever happened to me. We went to the site, and there were hordes of mosquitoes. They were terrible, but as soon as I got into Universal consciousness, I could not believe what I was seeing. The site and our circle with the trees around it disappeared. We were in a craft, and it was immense, like an auditorium. I saw our group come up the path and form a semi-circle. An aisle went from the path straight up and forward. On each side of this aisle were hundreds of seats filled with beings representing all civilizations. These were very high officials, high ambassador types. Native Americans were in front of our semi-circle, and they went all around both sides of the seated people, apparently an honor guard. They were Indians from the San Luis Valley, called "the bloodless valley." No war has ever taken place there; no blood has ever

been shed. The area is very sacred. The sky was solid with angelic beings. I know that this sounds over the edge, but it is what I saw.

Dr. Greer stepped out of the semi-circle and talked with the first group of beings. Then he went to the next group, and so on around the auditorium and finally came back. I was watching this and seeing all of it happen. Dr. Greer was about seven feet in front of me, and then about seven feet in front of him, facing Dr. Greer, was an incredibly old ascended master dressed in elaborate tapestry type robes with a hood. I did not know who this man was. In back of him was a high arched window with a frame, and beside the window were white, puffy clouds. I was looking down at this, and all the other things were still going on at the same time.

I was behind Dr. Greer when suddenly, out of my heart area, came a tube of pure, golden light. It went from me into Dr. Greer, through his heart to the wise man, and then came back through Dr. Greer, and to me again. The light kept circulating through us faster and faster until it was solid, absolutely pure love. They were communicating, and I was a witness to it all. This went on a long while, and then it stopped, and that scene was gone. I briefly saw the auditorium, and then it was gone. Then I saw the rocky area, and Dr. Greer came back.

The experience was fantastic and incredible, but I wondered if I should say anything. I told about the auditorium and all the people, but I thought the meeting with the ascended master was really over the edge and did not speak of it.

Dr. Steven Greer
I was at the site, and the whole area lit up. A veil lifted, and on the astral and etheric levels, yet visible to anyone, were rank upon rank of extraterrestrial beings. The Native America guardians were there, and so was the Concourse on High[59] of angelic beings at the celestial level. I went from group to group greeting and welcoming

---

[59] Concourse on High: http://en.wikipedia.org/wiki/Concourse_on_High

them with my hands out, and I could clearly see them both with my physical eyes and in my mind's eye. It was crystal clear. There was a being known in the mystic tradition as the Ancient One, an over-soul avatar for the next 500,000 years for every planet in the Cosmos. It was a supernal and celestial gathering on that mountain, and it was made clear to me that there is still much work to do. Some people saw some of what happened, and Trudy saw all of it. To me it was clear that Shari was there in the celestial realm. At the time of her passing, she became a celestial bridge builder, helping to raise the world and move it forward.

Jan Brook
I saw that there was a being between each and every one of us in the circle, and behind us all as well. These beings were right there in the group with all of us.

Dr. Steven Greer
I told people that there would be an extraterrestrial being assigned to each person and that happened. On many of our trainings, beings are assigned to individuals in this way.

Linda Willitts
I saw the Casper-like figures. I saw them as many different heights, including really tall ones, but mostly I felt their incredible love and the holiness of the experience.

Dr. Ted Loder
I could feel something incredibly important was going on, but I could not see any of the action with my eyes. I am saying this for people who might be out in the field someday and for some reason do not see anything. Do not give up. Just feel with your heart and your hands. Open your inner sight and let it happen. It will evolve.

Linda Willitts
My feeling was that Dr. Greer was being asked to help. This year the feeling was that these beings were not only thanking him and giving gratitude to him for all the work he was doing, but were also giving him support and encouraging him to continue.

Dr. Steven Greer

I had a vision exactly seven days before the moment of Shari's passing in January 1998. In that vision Shari and I were in a state of God-Consciousness, and she was ahead of me going into the Cosmic Egg[60], as it is traditionally called. It was sombrero shaped, a representation of the entire relative cosmos, the material, astral, celestial, causal, thought, vibration etc. The unbelievable beauty and peace of it is hard to describe, and as we drew near, suddenly I heard an infinite number of voices singing in the most exquisite melody, which I cannot reproduce: "We are all one in spirit, we are all one in spirit, we are all one in spirit," echoed through eternity, forever. On this trip instead of just hearing all the voices, I actually saw all the people who were behind the voices. This is certain; we are all one in spirit.

Kay Gibson

On our last night at Crestone, I saw a moving mesh or grid that was made up of black lines at times and golden at others. It passed over the Zenith in slow waves. Al Dunaway reported seeing golden waves cross the sky, and I saw one like an ocean wave gathers, crests, and flows. It was transparent, wide, and crossed the Zenith.

Trudy Guyker

About three months after that event, I was at home, and late one night I saw the Ancient One again. He talked to me for about four hours. I remember very little, but it is in my consciousness somewhere. One of the things that I do remember was that he told me, "I am going to be with Steven, and I am going to be giving him advice and guidance concerning the energy devices to help him make the correct choices."

I thought, "Wow, what a strange thing to hear." Then I saw the Concourse on High, like a staircase going up, up, up, forever, with every level of cosmic life. I knew what it was. I realized the importance of what was happening. The universe was watching and is involved one way or another, in every aspect of what we are

---

[60] Cosmic Egg: http://en.wikipedia.org/wiki/Cosmic_egg

doing. All the cosmos is involved, and while it is hard to believe, it is absolutely real, and it is vitally important.

Rocky Mountain UFO Conference
University of Wyoming
Laramie, Wyoming
Fieldwork at McGuire Ranch
18-21 June 1998

Debbie Foch
Right after the Crestone training, Dr. Greer conducted a workshop, received an award (shared posthumously with Shari Adamiak) and gave the keynote address at the Rocky Mountain UFO Conference at the University of Wyoming in Laramie, Wyoming. As part of the workshop we did nighttime contact work at the McGuire Ranch, which was about an hour's drive from Laramie.

Trudy Guyker
When Dr. Greer gave his keynote speech at the conference, I suddenly became aware of two dark forms, dark gray shapes. They appeared as eight or nine feet tall. They were on the stage to Dr. Greer's left, and they were with him the entire time he was on the stage. They did not move, and I felt they were there guarding him. A woman in the crowd also saw them and commented about them to Dr. Greer after his presentation.

As we arrived at the ranch, a classic thunderstorm occurred. Dr. Greer was scheduled to lead the CSETI fieldwork for conference attendees who had attended his workshop. There were 80 or more people, including the "classic UFO researchers" talking about abductions, so what happened was even more amazing. We had to wait in the cars until the storm let up. We finally got out and settled into a circle of people in their chairs. After a short time we saw what looked like an airplane flying fairly low. Suddenly it shone a bright light on our group and flew off into space. Dr. Greer followed it with his night vision binoculars.

Kindness' Craft Illuminates Ranch

Dr. Steven Greer

Shari introduced me to Kindness in January 1998, and then we saw her briefly in Hawaii in February. We had seen her ship come in and shine a light on us on other trips, but this night was one of the clearest and closest contacts we have had. I have no doubt that extraterrestrial intelligence mediated and delivered this storm to help "wash away" the negative influences and attitudes prior to Kindness' arrival.

The storm whittled the field group from 80 to 40. The sky became crystal clear, and suddenly to the north an object flew in. It was blue-white and low in the atmosphere. The object came over us and literally stopped! I saw it the whole time and tried to get people to pay attention to it because I knew it was going to come. It was Kindness' ship, a disc with a low dome that had four beings in it. Kindness, the senior ambassador, is actually from a larger ET craft out in deep space, far outside the reach of military weapons systems. The ship came remarkably close, and it was crystal clear. Visualize the scene if you can: It came over, stopped, and a majestic bluish light unfurled, illuminating the ranch and the entire area. The blue-white light then retracted back into the ship, which took off straight into deep space and vanished. With the night scope binoculars I could clearly see it go straight up and out into deep space. It was breathtaking!

Trudy Guyker

A bit later another object was seen. It was huge. At arm's length, it was the size of an orange, and it appeared like a blue fireball behind the hill. The object landed and lit up the area.

Dr. Steven Greer

I told everyone that a craft had landed and that the ETs were going to be careful with us. Humans have to be in a state of coherence for interaction to proceed, and I tried to get the group into that state. A number of people saw and heard beings moving in the grasslands around us. The ET presence was unmistakable. I could see them in the night scopes. A group of them had come from the enormous craft, which had landed very majestically on the Ranch to the northeast.

Crestone Box Reappears

Trudy Guyker

During this time people kept leaving, and soon there were only about fifteen people left. There was a young man in his twenties who was quite receptive and sensitive. He kept saying, "I really need to go out in the field; I really feel like I need to go out there." Dr. Greer and the young man started into the field. The rest of us followed behind. AND guess what else was there; the very same box we had seen at Crestone at the medicine wheel! There was nothing astral about that box; it was absolutely solid. It was moving right along with us.

Elements of the cabal monitor our work and often place sensors in the field. So we were delighted when the huge storm occurred, knocking out space and ground sensors and deterring opponents. The storm caused enough electromagnetic atmospheric disturbance that ETs were able to arrive in stealth mode. So we had not only Kindness' ship flying in and bathing us in a light that 40 people saw, but later the other ship that came straight down onto the grasslands. That was followed by these ET beings and by the communication probe.

CSETI Trip
England
July 1998

Bilocation

Linda Willitts

During the 1998 England trip we had many incredible experiences. We bi-located on the Carson's farm in the very same field where the big craft was seen in 1992. We were sitting in a circle while Dr. Greer was leading us in a meditation. I distinctly remember the event because we were sitting in the circle meditating, but at the same time we were high above the Earth in a craft with different types of ETs among us. The craft had a glass bottom, and we could see the Earth below. We could see ourselves sitting in our circle on the Earth below at the same time we were inside the craft. We were giving healing energy to the Earth, and the ETs were helping us.

Dr. Steven Greer
We were sitting in the field, and it was cold and damp. Suddenly the temperature rose ten or fifteen degrees. It became so warm that we had to remove clothing. I could see a craft around us that was not fully materialized, but could see its scintillating light. As the temperature rose, the sounds around us became muffled. We have experienced these changes when in a ship many times before.

I saw there were various extraterrestrial civilizations represented in the huge astral ship we were in. In the center of the craft was a holographic projection of the Earth. We were in a state of cosmic awareness putting our energy on the healing, guidance and transformation of Earth. The event was very powerful, as we could literally see the Earth. The purpose of our being there at that place and time was to begin a protocol which culminated at Mt. Shasta when a massive craft flew across the sky on three different nights. We filmed the event which was seen by thousands of people up and down the west coast of America.

Kay Gibson
An astonishing encounter happened the very first night. We were barely settled when Dr. Greer said, "Oh, look, there's a red light." As I turned around, a disc larger than a harvest Moon popped up over the ridge. It went down, popped back up again, and then was gone. Dr. Greer asked if I had seen it and I said I had. He told me to explain what I had seen because Dr. Greer prefers to have people report their observations. I described what I had just seen. The object's motion was strange, like a "peek-a-boo" game. The episode was incredible, and I call it "Harvest Moon" because it was a pale, silvery-gold with sharp edges but no corona. Almost immediately, military helicopters began flying all over the ridge.

Dr. Steven Greer
To get a sense of the size of the object, imagine something four or five times bigger than the sun when it sets on the horizon. There was a hill not far from us and the large orb emerged, bobbed up and down, and then vanished. It was certainly something actually in the environment and near to us on a ridge. It was the largest ship that I had ever seen in my whole life doing the CSETI work, up

to that point. It had to be thousands of feet across, and it was very much physically present.

Multiple Channels of Consciousness

Kay Gibson

The only time I have bi-located consciously was during the "Harvest Moon" ET Craft sighting. When I closed my eyes I was in the craft. When I opened my eyes I was in our group, and I could be in either place simply by opening or closing my eyes. When I was inside the craft, there were twenty-seven representatives of different races. I was doing a ceremony with them, and another aspect of me knew each of them. I put my index fingers on each side of their temples and kissed them on top of their heads. There were several kinds of insect-looking beings, fully sentient beings. Grasshopper, praying mantis, bee, and ant were four that I remember. There were several versions of what might be called grays, but not the way we have been shown them by the media.

Dr. Greer was very taken by the fact that there were twenty-seven ET representatives, given what that number represents in cosmic knowledge. It was one of the strangest and most interesting experiences of my life. I think that we are probably partly ET, and if we allow ourselves to open up to that possibility, we can recognize it when we are with ETs. The part of me that is more cosmic than my personality knew the ETs and was quite comfortable with them.

Dr. Steven Greer

What Kay is talking about is the ability to see and be on one channel, and be on another channel in consciousness at the same time. Just as dolphins have the ability to be asleep while swimming with one side of their brain awake, humans can develop the ability to see in the inner and outer states of consciousness. Instead of going back and forth, we learn to perceive multiple realities. I can be in the field aware of everyone around me, while being on a craft or vectoring at the same time. That is something you can do on two channels, three, ten, thirty, or more. You develop that ability, and it is a very interesting development in human capabilities.

Dr. Ted Loder
It seems like the ultimate in multi-tasking.

Dr. Steven Greer
Yes, but it is not linear. It is a holism, and it is breathtakingly beautiful and very peaceful. Similarly, you can develop the ability to bi-locate the physical body materially and be in multiple places at once, which is well described in the Vedas.

Linda Willitts
The next time we saw the craft, we were on Woodborough Hill. Once again we had just settled in. As we formed our circle, some trespassers came up from behind the hill. They asked, "Are you the CSETI group?"

As I looked at them, I saw an object. Everyone who was looking in that direction saw it. The object was a deeper orange color than before. It was the size of a silver dollar at arms' length. It bobbed up above the ridge and went down. It bobbed up again and dissolved like a Power Point frame dissolves. We had many sightings that night, but the military was doing heavy surveillance on us. Within thirty seconds of seeing the object, there were jets and helicopters dropping flares!

Dr. Steven Greer
I have to say that the first time we saw the enormous globe-shaped craft, it looked bigger than this time. The second time on Woodborough Hill, everyone there saw it, and it had a bobbing motion. The most astonishing part was that instead of going down into the Earth again, it dissolved like a picture in a Power Point presentation, and you could actually see it dissolve. It was a de-materialization of an enormous object crossing the veil of light. I think it was emerging from the Earth or materializing, because extraterrestrial vehicles can go through solid matter right into the Earth. We have seen it happen many times, like at Joshua Tree when the teal-colored object came straight in from the sky and went directly into the Earth. It was one of the most astonishing things I have ever seen.

Kay Gibson

During one of our remote viewings, I perceived a strange shape with three sets of three circles. The shape was similar to a pollywog or a white soupspoon that you'd find in a Chinese restaurant. I had no frame of reference for identifying the shape. Within a day, someone came with news of a new crop circle that had formed in a field across the road and down from the tumulus where we had been doing our fieldwork. The night before, Ricky had said he had a feeling that there was going to be a crop circle formed there. It is called "the Kite," and what I had viewed was the tail end of that Kite formation. It was exciting because it was the first time that I had had a 'precognitive remote view,' for lack of a better term. The glyph appeared just one field down from where Ricky had suggested that it might show up. When we were on the tumulus in 1997, we had meditated there with Shari sitting between Ricky, Dr. Greer, and me. I was now sitting to Ricky's left and a pink light appeared between us. We each knew that the pink light was Shari, and that she was still there with us. Shari's astral spirit appeared with us.

Linda Willitts

We visited quite a few crop circles and were under surveillance by helicopters almost every time we walked into a crop circle. Dr. Greer had a meditation that suggested whenever the helicopters flew over us, we would reflect love back to them to equalize their negative energy, and sending love back through the chain of command.

Kay Gibson

Another time, we went down to the Avon River at the end of the evening's work and Dr. Greer's laser bounced off some object that didn't appear to be there.

Dr. Steven Greer

Yes. We went down across the bridge, and there was a craft. I could sense it, and when I put my laser on it, the light bounced off it even though you could not see the craft as materialized!

Kay Gibson
I have one other incident to report. We were at the Barge Inn outside having something to eat. Dr. Greer and Colin Andrews were sitting across from several others and me. The sky was still blue, but the Sun had just set. Right above Dr. Greer and Colin in the blue sky were two perfectly white equal circles touching each other.

Dr. Steven Greer
Colin and I are spirit brothers. We have an enormous, loving, brother-bond from the first time we worked together in 1992. Those rings were two craft in the sky.
Every day on our expeditions people have astonishing contact experiences. These are difficult to explain. Each night we have conviviality and get together to share what happened that night. It can take two or three hours to share what we experienced. These are just a few such experiences.

Once you move into a state of consciousness and intent, there is a non-stop progression of extraterrestrial contact and communication via an infinite number of experiences. Some come through nature, the environment, animals, altered consciousness, etc. The occurrences happen on multiple levels and dimensions. People experience a huge variety of manifestations that often differ from what others experience. Their complexity represents the reality of interstellar extraterrestrial life. Usually we reside in our physical bodies consciously while our astral bodies and soul are within a higher energy plane. Travelling faster than the speed of light, the physical dissolves, and you leap up energetically. You disappear from the physical three-dimensional plane and arrive in the etheric and astral, skimming along the underbelly of the material cosmos in a non-local way. Adhering closely to that underbelly are layer upon layer of worlds associated with that extraterrestrial capacity. There is the astral realm, the worlds occupied by astral beings. Beyond lie the celestial realm and its layers. Life evolves until eventually every civilization and planet is able to shift into the highest celestial God-consciousness while still being in physical form. Their bodies, minds, and technologies are empowered by that celestial light and energy. This is what we are encountering on these expeditions. But the world is as you are, so unless you understand, see and experience that, it cannot become so.

CSETI Workshop
University of California at Santa Barbara
Santa Barbara, California
August 1998[61]

Alice Sleight
We were in Santa Barbara at a two-day workshop Dr. Greer gave at the University of California. This was my first training with him so I did not know exactly what I was looking at, but we saw lights in the ocean, and we saw lights down below the cliffs. Dr. Greer told us they were called USOs – unidentified submerged objects. I did not know there was any such thing, let alone that I would see one on my first time out with CSETI.

Dr. Steven Greer
The USO was very brilliant. It had a rhythmic pulsing with a blue-white strobe light.

Linda Willitts
A local woman named Karen had remote viewed or had a lucid dream in which she had an experience with beings right at the base of the cliff where we were observing the USOs.

Dr. Steven Greer
Since that time Tony Craddock has filmed hundreds of vehicles, some of which we think are Alien Reproduction Vehicles, known as ARVs. These are man made craft that are often mistaken for actual ET craft by many people. What we saw could have been ET in origin or some mix of ET and ARV.

CSETI Training
Sedona, Arizona
November 1998

---

[61] UCSB Lecture Video: "Extraterrestrial Intelligence – The Evidence" http://www.cseti.org/member/video.htm

Dr. Ted Loder
We used several different field sites in Sedona. One was the Bradshaw Ranch, and the nights were quite cold there.

Coherent Thought Sequencing

Ricky Butterfass
I remote viewed a craft coming in from the west. It dropped straight down out of the sky and at the horizon stopped and broke into three craft. The three craft took positions over the ridgeline and remained there. My buddy saw it too. Then we did CTS (Coherent Thought Sequencing) and visualized our surroundings. I went up higher and higher for an aerial view. I could see the outline of North America and the coastlines, and, as I got higher, I saw the cloud layers, the whole planet as well as the Moon. Then I went out further into space and saw the whole solar system and beyond that, I saw into the galaxy.

I did an astral projection out onto the galactic arm. I could see the central sun of the galaxy, and at the same time I could look over to the side and see our solar system. It was not laid out flat as I learned in school, but was actually perpendicular to the plane of rotation of the galaxy. I looked around to see if there were any ET craft in the area, but I could not sense any. I looked back toward the Earth because I thought it was about time to come out of the CTS. Suddenly, behind me I felt something bump into my astral body. It bumped me and locked onto me, and I thought it must be an ET craft. Unexpectedly, it began pushing me rapidly in towards our solar system. It was similar to the scene in the movie *Titanic*, where they stand on the bow of the ship, but I was on the bow of an extraterrestrial spacecraft.

I could see the Earth, and I could see the cloud masses and the ocean. We came in on a curve, I adjusted to the landmass, the craft leveled out, and I could see our group of people on the ground in a circle. Suddenly, I left the connection I had with the ET craft, and was back in my body opening my eyes. I could see the craft and the three other ones that had been waiting near the ridge. It stopped right in front of me and was the size of a small dinner plate.

Dr. Ted Loder

The perpendicular nature of our solar system is accurate. Finishing Ricky's story, we had been meditating, and I opened my eyes and saw the craft that he was talking about come in from the west. It was a neat thing to see.

Earth's Geophysical Stability

Ricky Butterfass

One night we went out in the field and nothing was happening. Everyone noted that on the first and second nights we had spectacular sightings and then no activity. We sensed the ETs were busy. I looked up into the sky and saw three stars had formed an isosceles triangle with the base of the triangle tipped about 30 degrees from the horizon. At the midpoint of the base of the triangle was another star, with a reddish-orange color. Every once in a while I saw an emission of blue plasma-like light. About five minutes later the emission repeated, followed by a fifteen or twenty minute lag. I got a communiqué from the ETs saying that they were shooting these plasma balls into the plate in the Sea of Cortez. The ETs told me that there was a rift and they were actually welding it shut because the volcanoes outside Mexico City were erupting. They told me that from November 18, until Christmas, the volcanoes outside Mexico City would be erupting.

The ETs said that if they did not fuse the rift together, a fissure would open up and there would be a crack from the floor of the Sea of Cortez up through Baja California to the Grand Canyon. I thought it was an amazing communiqué. Bob Hairgrove and I were roommates and buddies. After the fieldwork that night, we went back to our room and turned on the TV to learn the authorities were evacuating towns outside Mexico City in a 70-mile radius. It was a confirmation of the communiqué.

Tony Craddock was also there, and about six months later he sent me an email with a link to EarthMatters. I went to the site and looked up the reports on volcanic activity from November 18th to December 23rd for three volcanoes, Popo, Ferio, and Izta. I discovered that they had been erupting constantly during that time. It was a major confirmation. The ETs were actually repairing the plate tectonics, and that is why they were so busy.

In Joshua Tree, just before the 1997 trip to England, an ET craft also penetrated into the ground. The ETs told me they were relieving the stress in the San Bernardino fault system. They said if they did not relieve the pressure, a volcano in the Caribbean was going to erupt and cause earthquakes from San Diego to San Francisco. After the trip I turned on the TV to learn that a volcano had erupted on Montserrat, an island in the Caribbean. So the ETs have been using their craft and technology to stabilize the Earth for a very long time.

Dr. Steven Greer
One of the things we have been told directly by the ETs for all these years is that they are very concerned about the Earth's geo-physical stability. The Earth is very unstable and becoming more so. Billions of tons of ice are being displaced and melting from the poles, becoming water. Earth is basically a huge fluid dynamic spinning sphere. The magma is fluid, the water is fluid, and the whole planet has a tremendous amount of plasticity and flexibility. The extraterrestrial civilizations that have been involved with the Earth for millennia, if not longer, are concerned about its geo-physical stability. One of their missions – but not their sole mission – is to monitor the geo-physical activity and to prevent a worst-case scenario when possible.

I briefed the head of the Defense Intelligence Agency back in the late 1990s (General Patrick Hughes) with our military advisor. We had learned that space-based and earth-based weapons were targeting and destroying extraterrestrial vehicles. We knew that these ET vehicles were actually guardian ships and were protecting the Earth, not only from near-Earth objects such as asteroids and comets, but also from other potentially unstable tectonic plate changes. These foolish actions of targeting ET craft were, therefore, a danger to the security not only of the United States, but to the planet. One of the items on the agenda was to discuss this situation with the General since shooting at our guardians made no sense!

Al Dunaway

Jan Brooks and I had occasion to be sitting outside the circle with our backs to Dr. Greer since we were part of the security function. On this evening we observed several ETs come up over the hillside where we were setting up and enter into our group. The ETs joined and sat with our group as we were observing meteors showering around us lighting up the night sky. We had several interactions where we were able to pass our hands through our visitors and see a luminescence of sparkles as that happened.

Dr. Steven Greer

One evening we were doing fieldwork. A craft moved in directly overhead, and I saw it with my night scopes. I took my laser and signaled it, hitting the underside of the disc-shaped ship as it was hovering right above us. The laser light hit the craft, reflected, and bounced right back to the group!

Dr. Ted Loder

One evening we saw an ARV (Alien Reproduction Vehicle) accompanied by a military jet.

Dr. Steven Greer

They both flew near us; an alien reproduction vehicle flying saucer, man-made, floating along silently and escorted by a military jet. They were probably headed back to the Utah range. One of their prime locations exists near Provo, Utah. The Dugway Proving Grounds[62], with highly restricted air space, is a state of the art facility, all underground.

We were under constant surveillance. You understand by now that there are a number of things going on simultaneously when we are on these expeditions. There is the CSETI group contacting extraterrestrial intelligence with spacecraft that appear and often materialize. There are cosmic and celestial beings present. There are other human bystanders who sometimes get involved, and there is a classified military presence. The classified paramilitary effort

---

[62] Wikipedia: http://en.wikipedia.org/wiki/Dugway_Proving_Ground

is a rogue project that monitors us and often sends out aircraft and other technologies to suppress the ET activity. It is a very dynamic situation...

Example of Psychotronic Attack

Classified human projects have 'trans-dimensional' devices and technologies. The paramilitary rogue group has developed these since the 1940s and 1950s. Some of these devices have been used to monitor our activities and we have experienced such monitoring more than once.

We were staying in small apartments, and I had a roommate. One morning a monitoring device suddenly came into our room. My roommate and I both saw the device come in, materialize briefly, and then dematerialize. I was in a higher state of consciousness, but my roommate was terrified. The energy from the object was ominous. There was no doubt this device originated from the paramilitary rogue group that has some very advanced technologies. I went into an even higher state of consciousness that has a powerful electromagnetic burst associated with it. People can often see the aura of someone in that state of consciousness. The device went into the bathroom, spun out of control, hit the light fixture over the sink, and disintegrated with a huge explosion as the device was destroyed. *The light fixture was shattered into many tiny pieces all over the bathroom!*

We have had similar episodes happen before, and I know other people who have had the same objects come right into their homes. Being in a higher state of consciousness is very important. Man-made technologies that are at the crossing point of light frequency have no power over higher states of consciousness. This is why at trainings we often erect a huge golden dome in our minds. We empower the dome with protection and security covering the entire area we are in, so nothing but extraterrestrial and good can enter. The process has been amazingly effective.

Jan Brook
I can verify some of the apartment incident. I shared a room on the end of that section of the hotel. At the time the event was

happening, about 5:00 AM, I was closest to the window. I heard what sounded like a woman's voice speaking a foreign language into a microphone outside my window at that moment.

Dr. Ted Loder
Sometime that morning I was awakened by a sound, whistling or some sort of strange sound not normal to where we were.

Trudy Guyker
I was sleeping facing the wall of my room, and I just woke up. I was awake, but my eyes were closed. I turned over, opened my eyes, and immediately two pea-sized lights, one red and one white, shot out from the corner of my eye, and whisked out through the ceiling. I thought they must have been communicating with me so they woke me up.

Dr. Steven Greer
There was no plausible explanation for the explosion that destroyed the light fixture. My roommate woke me up early in the wee hours of the morning. He was under some type of radionic or psychotronic attack. He knew there was something in the room that was being sent by these rogue human projects. I seem to be protected from these attacks, but he was terrified. We tried some things to protect him, but the attack persisted. Then the inter-dimensional probe came in. It was not extraterrestrial, but very human. I moved into a state of consciousness and called upon the power of protection. The device then went out of control and broke the light.

Interaction with Beings

Linda Willitts
Many people in the group at the CSETI plateau site also experienced the little beings – those scintillating light or cloudy gray beings. They were visible enough that people could see them and put their hands inside them to feel their natural heat. These little beings were sitting on peoples' laps and interacting with everyone in a very friendly manner.

Dr. Steven Greer
Yes, everyone experienced some element of interaction with the

beings. A number of people were touched and could feel themselves being touched. There were forms moving through the group and sitting on people's knees or sitting beside them. It was a dear and charming experience...

Jan Brook
During the break Dr. Greer came back and said one of the forms was sitting right between two of us. Then he walked around in the middle of the gravel parking area. Several of the beings were walking with him, and he played games with them.

Echo Manifestations

Dr. Steven Greer
There was a sound like an echo. I would walk, and there would be an echo walk, and for each of my steps, there would be an echo of each step. People asked what was happening. It was as if the beings were playing a game and mimicking my walk. Several people heard these sounds.

Tapping and Clicking Manifestations

Jan Brook
This next event happened on November 14th. I have a detailed log beginning that afternoon at the mesa. Trudy, Debbie, Kay, Al and I went out to find a field site and had just about given up when someone said, "Let's try that road," and we found a place. We decided the place was a good site, big enough for 50 people.

Al and I came back at dusk. We were the first to arrive and the only two humans there. We heard a metallic cricket sound that was very prominent in the garden area just to the right. I felt an inclination to investigate the source of the noise and walked to the edge of the garden where a big boulder delineated the walking path. I was munching on some French fries. I got an amusing flash of what it must be like from an ET's perspective as an intergalactic 'Jane Goodall'. Here were a couple of primates grazing on the mesa.

Al and I both continued to notice the unusual tapping and clicking sounds, and I went to investigate them further. Then I got another flash, "That's far enough." So I stopped and was looking east where there was low shrubbery. Overlaid on this backdrop I saw a whitish outline of consoles and people moving around, the little scintillating, grey-white people. We observed each other for a time and then other beings arrived.

Dr. Steven Greer
Some beings were waiting for us at this site.

Jan Brook
The beings had set this up. Al and I were in a 'gatekeeper position' outside of the circle and actually saw the other beings come up and join the group.

"Touch" Manifestations

Trudy Guyker
There have been several mentions of people being touched. At one point, after we had been in meditation, there was a break in our circle as people walked to go to the cars. I was sitting by myself. I was still meditating when suddenly I was touched on my right shoulder by a finger. The touch was a hard one; it went through all my layers of clothing.

Dr. Steven Greer
Trudy was touched on the right shoulder. That is where I was touched back in 1973 when I was on the mountain during my encounter[63].

Trudy Guyker
The touch was strong, and I thought it was Debbie, who was my buddy and was next to me. I thought she touched me to get my attention so I looked over and Debbie was in her sleeping bag. I looked around and no one else was there. It was the first time I experienced such a touch, and it got my attention!

Dr. Ted Loder
The last night was the night of the meteor shower. It was the most incredible meteor shower I have ever witnessed. Precisely at midnight, one huge alleged meteor came screaming over the top

---

[63] Greer, *Hidden Truth* (2006), p. 24.

of us. We could hear it, and for the next hour there must have been at least a dozen or more meteors that we could either hear or see a stream of sparks and smoke trailing behind them. At the end of an hour a pair of them went overhead simultaneously.

Kay Gibson
The meteor shower was the Leonides. They peak about every 33 years.

Trudy Guyker
The hissing meteor that went over us had a tail visible for over thirty minutes.

Ricky Butterfass
I saw the hissing meteor, too. After we cleared the site and went back to our rooms, I went outside and watched for another twenty minutes. The meteors were coming in as big balls of fire with big smoke trails behind them.

Linda Willitts
They were colorful meteors — magenta and green and white.

Dr. Steven Greer
What a cosmic display it was. We had the extraterrestrials, the ARVs (Alien Reproduction Vehicles), the inter-dimensional object, and the Leonides—all in our five- or six-day expedition in Sedona!

Kay Gibson
Another strange event at Sedona was a screeching sound the likes of which I have never heard before or since. We were on the Bradshaw Ranch when it happened, and there were horses in a barn some distance away. The screeching set them off. They began whinnying and kicking the sides of their stalls. The screeching made the hair on my body stand up.

Linda Willitts
Dr. Greer thought it might be an ET in pain. It gave me the 'heebie jeebies.' It was no animal we could possibly think of. It was creepy,

and it sounded like something was in pain, and the horses seemed tormented.

Jan Brook
I got chills too. Art Bell had an interview in which he talked about the doctor who supposedly captured an ET, and it was screaming. When they played the tape of the screaming, it sounded just like what Linda and Kay described.

Dr. Steven Greer
Space/time being as plastic and flexible as it is, we were experiencing a "sound event." The purpose of the experience was to evoke compassion for the suffering our visitors have endured at the hands of humans who have done unspeakably horrible things to them.

Triangular Craft

Jan Brook
It was also the night we had the triangular craft come right into the center of the circle.

Debbie Foch
I saw an object that flew low over our circle about 15 feet above it.

Dr. Steven Greer
Yes, a craft flew right overhead a few feet above our circle. We have had similar objects float into rooms where we were staying or come right over our group. We say, "It was this shape or it was this sort of light object," but it actually could be a craft larger than our neighborhood because we are not dealing with normal space/time proportions.

Trudy Guyker
Dr. Greer's laser light hit the bottom of a craft. Afterward there were flashing lights above us for about an hour.

Dr. Steven Greer
A flotilla of ET craft appeared overhead moving and flashing. They seemed to be at a high altitude, but you could see the one I hit, so it was in the atmosphere.

Jan Brook
On the meteor shower night there was a dome, an invisible craft above us. You could see that, as the meteors were coming in, they were bouncing off the top of the object since it was so high. They would skim off and move sideways.

Trudy Guyker
On several nights we sensed many kinds of flower scents – roses, violets, carnations.

Energy Emissions

Dr. Ted Loder
On several evenings, we noticed that the ground in the center of the circle had changed color and there were visible patterns. It was not just gravel and dirt, but colorful patterns as part of the ground on which we stood.

The last night I had just come out of the group meditation. My perception was the ground had gone from black to rose, magenta, and brown. It stayed that way for a half hour or more. In fact, when the group broke up, I was still standing there looking at it and seeing people walking around on a translucent glowing ground. The persistence of the effect was amazing.

Dr. Steven Greer
There was a craft there, and Dr. Loder was seeing aspects of its energy emissions and light.

Dr. Ted Loder
I kept blinking my eyes, and pinching myself, but there it was, people walking around on glowing ground.

Trudy Guyker
That night we experienced a craft coming up from under the earth.

Dr. Steven Greer
The event happened right under us. We had had that experience before, at Crestone when Trudy and I were standing near each other at a break. A craft was emerging from underneath, and we felt a small discrete area under our feet shake. It was like a tap from underneath, and we could actually feel it. It was a very sharp, distinct movement. It was a craft moving in the earth beneath us and they wanted us to know this. Why not? They go straight through mountains as we have explained previously.

Background on the Bradshaw Ranch
Charlie Balogh
The area of the Bradshaw Ranch in which our Sedona training took place has a history of anomalous activities. An underground military installation supposedly runs from just south of Flagstaff, underneath Sedona near the Enchantment Resort. One trail snakes alongside the Enchantment Resort. At one point there is an apparent power station with a sign saying 'Do not leave the trail. There are armed guards present. What are armed guards doing around a resort? There is really something strange taking place in the area, and it is probably the source of the probe that was sent through the hotel.

Debbie Foch
Our field site was Boynton Canyon, not too far from the Enchantment Resort.

Alice Sleight
I have read a book by Tom Dongo about Sedona[64]. He writes about the very strange creatures that have been seen around the Bradshaw Ranch. What you heard screaming may have been one of them.

Charlie Balogh
I think some of the strange things occurring in the area may be related to the military. Someone is fooling with things they should not be fooling with.

---

[64] Dongo has written numerous books on Sedona. His comments in a 2005 interview seem to indicate some of what he reports as ET encounters are actually paramilitary and PLFs (programmed lifeforms). http://www.mysterious-america.net/tomdongointervie.html

Dr. Steven Greer
We know from Disclosure Project witnesses who have worked in some of the black projects that very high tech inter-dimensional electronics have been developed. These include devices that enable people to go into a state where they can visualize some kind of creature – and the device will actually materialize it.

Kay Gibson
Reminds me of Montauk[65].

Dr. Steven Greer
Exactly. This is not science fiction. The technology described absolutely has been developed. We never shy away from an area where that type of activity has taken place. In fact, we often say that what we are bringing to such an area is another level of consciousness, and a celestial level of connection. We are also inviting the extraterrestrial beings to the area, and causing a shift in consciousness. In addition, if we sense a classified operation in the area that is trying to suppress what we are doing, we always say, "Let's connect to whatever that is and go back to the source. Bathe the source in pure, divine love and cosmic awareness. Help them find their way to a path that is peaceful and that moves the Earth forward in a peaceful and enlightened way." This is our approach to classified operations that try to suppress our activities. The practice produces a powerful, transformative effect in ways we might never fully understand.

---

[65] Wikipedia: http://en.wikipedia.org/wiki/Montauk_Project

Chapter 7

1999

University of New Hampshire
Durham, New Hampshire
Spring 1999

Dr. Ted Loder
In the Spring of 1999 I decided to come out of the closet regarding UFOs at my university. I announced to various people that I was going to give a lecture on the topic. I had waited to do it until I had met people who had seen craft and until I had my own confirmation sighting in Joshua Tree the previous Fall. The local newspaper was there, and there were people from Maine, Massachusetts, and New Hampshire, a standing room only crowd of about 160 people.

At that time I was living with a woman who had been to several of the trainings with me, and she was a very good remote viewer. She had good celestial vision, or soft eye vision. Several days after I had given that big lecture at the University, Joyce and I walked outside our house one evening at dusk, each with a pair of binoculars, just to look at the sky and to reminisce about the trainings.

We looked up at the sky and an aircraft went right over the house. We were in the aircraft traffic area for what used to be an airbase, so sometimes aircraft fly over. It looked like a big, lumbering cargo plane, but made no noise. It was completely silent, and we both remarked about this. There were other planes above it whose engines we could hear.

We watched this aircraft heading toward the west. Suddenly we both saw what looked like a meteor going right through the field of vision. We said, "Wow! What was that?" Suddenly the large aircraft that had just flown over our house was gone. We remarked on this and how strange it seemed. We went into the house, but

I kept looking out the windows to see if that plane came back around. When I suddenly saw a plane outside I went back out, looked to the north-northeast and I saw a craft, which turned out to be a low-flying airplane. Meanwhile Joyce was watching me from the door, and about a minute or so after this plane went by she came out and joined me in the middle of the yard. Suddenly, right over the trees at 500 to 1000 feet, came an incredibly bright ET craft. It flew right over the house and us, did a sharp turn to the right, then zipped out of sight and vanished!

We were both standing there shaking and I asked her why she had not come out. She said she did not want to disturb me when I was signaling with our big light. When I told her I never used the big light, she said she saw a golden light come out of the sky from right where the ET craft came over the trees. The golden light came down, shined right through my chest and up into the sky. I could not see it, but she saw it clearly, a rich golden light coming from that craft right to my chest. Two years later Dr. Greer and I were talking about this at Joshua Tree, and I finally realized that it had been Kindness and her ship, and that she was thanking me for giving the lecture, coming out and trying to help the cause.

Dr. Steven Greer
The senior extraterrestrial ambassador that I call Kindness has exactly that kind of ship with that kind of movement. She is very aware of what we are doing, is deeply appreciative of our work and will make these kinds of appearances.

CSETI Training
Albemarle County, Virginia
May 1999

The Clicking Sound in Dr. Greer's Woods

Trudy Guyker
This training was at Dr. Greer's home in Virginia. One of the incidents I remember occurred when we were in the woods. We had been seeing many different kinds of flashing lights and bars of light so we were thinking there was a craft in these woods. Several groups decided to go out into the woods and one group came upon

a clicking noise on the ground. We went to investigate it and heard this clicking coming out of the ground, but we could not find any mechanical source for it. It was very anomalous.

D. Steven Greer
Yes. The clicking sound was actually prolonged and right at ground level. We made a circle around it, and the clicking continued for at least twenty minutes. It was very unusual. You could not see anything except some subtle light in that area of the woods, but you could hear this continuous electronic clicking. It was very specific. We could locate exactly where it was, and yet there was seemingly nothing there. It was almost as if an electronic device was there but was invisible to the eye.

Debbie Foch
We went down in the woods to investigate the clicking. I had seen a band of lights shining. Besides seeing the lights shining, someone remote viewed beings down there, and he even drew pictures. His pictures showed bird-like beings with beaks. We went down there to check out his remote viewing as well. We heard the clicking and formed a circle, and then we did some chanting. When we were chanting, it was echoing and no one up the hill from us heard us. We had an energy field distortion around us, and I could see where the field ended about fifteen feet above us.

Dr. Steven Greer
It's important to point out that there was a group of us undergoing this experience. We had seen lights, objects and probes coming in. We also saw a scintillating craft that was down at that same edge of the woods. We started chanting and singing very loudly in the woods around the area of the clicking sound. It was as if we were in a craft, but there was nothing visible to the naked eye. It seemed as if we were in an enclosed sound-proofed room, because it was echoing. The temperature altered and the sound altered. The echo sounded as if we were in a 15 or 20-foot diameter chamber.

Sound normally travels up, and we were below the other people who were near the house. As we were speaking and chanting, even though you normally could hear conversation on the patio of the house, the people near the house could not hear a thing. We were astonished when we went back and they did not even know that we had been chanting.

This episode could conceivably be a space/time distortion. I am fairly certain an etheric craft was there, and the clicking sound was meant to get our attention and draw us into it.

Superimposition of Dr. Greer's Hand and ET Hand

Debbie Foch
We also heard footsteps in the woods. We were being very quiet, yet we could hear steps. We initially wondered if it could be the cows, but ruled this out. We felt it likely the ETs were there with us.

Dr. Steven Greer
There were footsteps that sounded like people walking, not like a four-legged animal, and they were very distinct. As part of our protocol we will have something beautiful from Earth like a gem or a polished crystal. In this case, it was a beautiful, perfectly round ball of polished rose quartz crystal. I offered it to the extraterrestrial, who was shorter than I was, and as I did so, my hand and the quartz took on a strange glow. My hand became a three-fingered hand. My hand was transposed on the ET hand, and it became an extraterrestrial hand! Everyone saw this. Every person was standing there with mouths wide open. They were completely shocked, as was I! I said, "My God, what's happened to my hand?" I had three fingers, and it was elongated, with a different skin tone, more pale white than my hand, which is more fleshy and pink. It was an extraterrestrial hand that received this offering, and even though they did not completely materialize their whole body, they caused my hand to change form and color.

Trudy Guyker
I was standing directly to Dr. Greer's right. When I saw this happening with his hand, I could not believe it, so I practically stuck my nose in. I wanted to get as close as I could to see this event that was unfolding. There were three elongated fingers, and it was another hand, it was not Dr. Greer's hand. It was remarkable.

Debbie Foch

I was right there too. I was next to Trudy, but I walked over to stick my nose in there, too. There were four of us out there after the rest of the group had left; Dr. Greer, Trudy, I, and another person. My experience was that there was an area with a great deal of energy, and that area must have been where the beings were. We walked up to the energy, and we were in it. That is when Dr. Greer held out his hand with the quartz ball, and that is when the incident took place.

The Firefly Craft

Trudy Guyker

Springtime was beautiful there in Virginia, and the fireflies were out. On one particular night, they were all over the place, and it was magnificent. Dr. Greer, Debbie and I were standing to one side, and we were amazed at the fireflies. Suddenly one firefly that was four or five times bigger than any of the other fireflies flew right by us. We said, "That was no fire fly." because it was enormous. I feel that it was a craft disguised like a firefly, and that it wanted us to see and notice it.

Debbie Foch

Adding to that, one of the evenings Dr. Greer was reaching into his backpack in front of him and a light flashed out of it. I do not know where the light came from but it was not a flashlight.

Dr. Steven Greer

It was a brilliant flash of light. Also, an enormous orb came and hovered towards the Shenandoah National Park, the ridge that you see from our house in the Blue Ridge Mountains. We had orbs in the woods to the south-southwest of our location, and no houses or anything else is located at the spot where they appeared. We also had a very wonderful sighting of Kindness' ship that flew in.

Trudy Guyker

Another incident occurred on the patio during a break. Dr. Greer, Debbie, and I were standing there talking when suddenly we heard a noise near us. It sounded like a tape recorder being played backwards. There was nothing there, but the sound was very loud, and there was nothing subtle about it. It was loud, noisy and garbled like a tape recorder being played backwards.

One night I saw a craft for a second or two. It looked like an acorn without the cap on it. This craft was materialized just for a short time, and I reported it. Later on Dr. Greer showed some videos of craft that had been recorded previously, and he said, "Here is Trudy's acorn," and there was the ship. So I had seen a craft that had been recorded before.

CSETI Training
Crestone, Colorado
July 1999

The Right Person

Linda Willitts
We occasionally have strangers come to training and want to join the group. We discourage this because they haven't been trained, and we have group protocols. In 1999 we were on Mount Blanca in the Zapata Falls parking lot when a woman appeared and said, "Are you Dr. Greer? Are you the CSETI group?" She said that Ron Russell had told her that we were going to be there. She dropped the right name and we let her join the group circle, but I remember being worried that it was going to disturb our group cohesion and coherence. She was apparently the right woman since Kindness flashed us that night in her ship.

Kindness Appearance

Dr. Steven Greer
That was the night that Kindness flew in from the northeast. Her ship came in, made a turn and flashed a brilliant blue-white light right into the group. The light was so bright it almost hurt our eyes. It was that beautiful, disc-shaped ship that we have seen on virtually every one of these expeditions since 1998.

Protection from a Cloud

Linda Willitts
We often experience flyovers by military jets because we are near a NORAD (North American Aerospace Defense Command) base.

One night, one of these jets flew over and into a very small cloud. We sat watching, expecting the jet to emerge from the cloud, but it didn't. When the jet did emerge, it flew with a wobble, and a tiny blue disc followed it. Dr. Greer remote viewed that the plane had some electronic warfare equipment.

Dr. Steven Greer
The plane was a highly classified electronic warfare plane that had radionic disrupters[66] in it. As it came from due east over the Sangre de Cristo Mountains, the plane went into a tiny cloud. The plane should only have been in the cloud for one or two seconds at its rate of speed, but it seemed to linger in time or space there. A small bluish-white disc had intercepted the plane, and when the jet came out you could see it wobbling erratically. Behind it was the disc, and the plane high-tailed it out of there. We had no ill effect from the radionics, but it was very interesting that we were protected. Everyone looking toward that part of the sky saw the event. This was a mass-witnessed event.

Protection for Kindness
Debbie Foch
Donna, who owned a crystal shop, had some land and allowed us to do fieldwork there. The land was marshy and full of mosquitoes, but we set up our circle, and that night the ET craft came in. It was cobalt blue, and was about thirty feet in diameter from our vantage point. You could clearly see the disc shape and in the center of it was a blue light. The blue light lit the whole underside of the disc. The craft flew over and then flew out into space. When Kindness left the area, a jet interceptor vectored in right behind her craft. Behind the interceptor jet was another ET craft that was tracking the interceptor. We thought the second ET craft to be her guard ship. The interceptor never got close to Kindness' craft at all. Later in the week when we were up on Mount Blanca, her ship came in again at a very low level and did an S-turn up in the mountains! Then one other night, just as we were breaking up, she came over again.

---

[66] Radionic disrupters refer to longitudinal or scalar wave weapons that can target places, biological systems, or mind systems and disrupt the normal operation of those systems. Bearden, *Oblivion* (2005), pg. 210-220.

Arrows of Sound

Linda Willitts

This was the year we had "arrows of sound" that came through our ears. During our fieldwork, I always sit next to Dr. Greer in the circle. I heard a high-pitched electronic sound in the shape of an arrow. The sound went in my right ear, inside my head and out my left ear. Dr. Greer and a few people around us felt something similar.

Al Dunaway

I was sitting at the Sand Dunes National Park as others were climbing the dunes. I began to meditate and soon in the sand before me a small ET face the size of a silver dollar appeared. After forming, the face began communicating with me, telling me I had a real problem. I asked the entity what he was referring to, and he informed me that I had the habit of equating intelligence with the size of a being, believing that the larger the ET types were the more intelligent than the smaller ones. In retrospect I could see his point. I began to realign my thinking and it led to many interesting encounters with smaller ET types.

At this training I experienced a remote viewing override for the first time. I was sitting with the group in the Baca, remote viewing under the sand dunes in the National Park by Mt. Blanca. I was noting a parking garage type facility under the sand dunes when I felt taken away at a rapid rate out into space. When I was able to identify what was around me, I noticed I was standing before a large crystal triangular structure. Not knowing what else to do, I did the CSETI protocol of introducing myself and saying that I was from Earth and desired peaceful contact. With that, many entities appeared in the form of lighted clouds of energy. They merged around me, and we started praying for the Earth and for peaceful contact. I had the feeling there was a very senior entity at the top of the crystal structure, but I never actually communicated with or saw him.

I did notice a pinkish cloud or mist on the right hand side of the crystal structure at its base. It was communicating with me, saying "Joy, joy, joy." After returning from this remote view I shared it with the group. Dr. Greer noted that during the meditation he saw what appeared to be a launch of something coming from the sand dunes and heading out into space. Dr. Greer shared that the pink mist was typical of manifestations associated with Shari Adamiak.

CSETI Instructor Training
Crestone, Colorado
July 1999

Jan Brook
One night we broke up into three teams and did the coordinated CSETI protocols through the radios. Debbie and I were both remote viewing, and I saw the golden light in each of our three circles connecting to each other to form the CSETI triangle. Debbie saw a tetrahedron that went straight up into space. Our three teams together formed a perfect CSETI triangle of golden light.

Debbie Foch
Yes. Together we formed the apex out in space.

Dr. Ted Loder
We went to the contact site on the Baca. We had done the protocol there, and Dr. Greer walked forward away from the group. I was standing right next to Joyce, who was almost jumping with glee. She whispered to me, "Do you see them, do you see them? They're right in front of you. Do you see? I was looking, but felt ambivalent about whether I could see some gray shapes. When we came down from the group, I talked to Dr. Greer independently and asked him what he saw. He described a tall elder and some three-foot tall, child-like ETs.

On the way back in the car later in the evening, I asked Joyce what she had seen. She described to me in detail a tall elder and some short ETs. What confirmation! Dr. Greer confirmed it. If I am correct, she and he were the only two who saw the ETs with that degree of clarity that night.

Dr. Steven Greer
We saw exactly the same features and the same number of ETs. It was a precise match. I felt a tremendous bond with her because she was independently able to perceive with her subtle vision these extraterrestrial beings as well as the spacecraft that were out in the Baca with us.

Dr. Ted Loder
She had always been able to remote view well. She was so determined to open her sight and be able to see these things that she said her own prayer the evening before we went out to the site.

Dr. Steven Greer
Every night before I go to sleep I say a prayer to open my inner sight so that I can see the lights and continue to learn. I've done this since 1974. So for over 35 years I've said this prayer before I go to sleep. A prayer is powerful. It shows the power of turning to this cosmic aspect of each of us, and to the Great Being and asking for those gifts and abilities. Ask, and it will open. However, it must be desired and asked for.

A Control Group of Sorts

Dr. Ted Loder
After the training was over, several of us went back up to the contact site. Dr. Greer was not with us and we wondered if any events could happen without him. We meditated down in the parking lot, and then the four of us walked up to the contact site late in the evening. As we walked into that area where Dr. Greer walks forward, it was like walking into a hot shower. There was a palpable change in the air quality and the overall feeling. It was as if we had stepped into a craft. I think three out of the four of us saw the small ETs who were around us. This experience made the point to us that Dr. Greer does not necessarily have to be there to make things happen.

Purpose of Book and Trainings

Dr. Steven Greer
That is absolutely correct. The whole purpose of this book and the

purpose of all these training expeditions can be summed up quite easily. The purpose has been to empower people to understand the nature of their own conscious awareness, to learn the techniques to develop it further, and then to use this knowledge to independently make contact with extraterrestrial civilizations and to sponsor CE-5s.

An additional purpose is to appreciate and understand the fullness of the cosmology that is involved with this effort, because if you just want to kick the tires of a UFO, you're missing about 99.9% of what contact is all about.

I also feel that our experiences are vitally important to share with each other, because then people will say, "Well, he did it, why can't I?" I have always resisted the idea that somehow I am special or gifted. Every single human can do what I do. Everybody can become aware of the mind, then be aware of the infinite reality of the mind, remote view, reach all these states of consciousness, and develop these abilities to make contact with the ETs.

When the time is appropriate and safe, extraordinary things will happen; and they will happen whether or not I am there. Often it is actually better if I am not around because I am under a tremendous amount of scrutiny. Often people find that events can be more fully materialized if I'm not there because there is less monitoring and it is safer for all concerned...

Conference
Port Townsend, Washington
27-29 August 1999

Linda Willitts
Dr. Greer was one of the speakers at a Conference in Port Townsend, Washington in August 1999. It was held, and we were housed, at an abandoned military installation. There was a place with concrete bunkers and cannons that had been installed during World War II to protect the coast of Washington state. Dr. Greer and I went up to that spot and did fieldwork with about eleven people. We were standing in a circle when the ground shifted and nearly dumped us over. Dr. Greer said it was the ETs showing the

earth changes that were going to come.

Dr. Steven Greer
This was an involuntary tilting of the Earth, so much so that the person next to me was almost knocked over and I almost fell down. The shift was very, very real. I was told that future changes would happen along the tectonic plate, the Pacific ring of fire, and the volcanoes. ETs would be involved in the stabilization of the Earth during all those events. I have known about ET involvement in these types of operations since my childhood. Exact dates are unknown, as time and space are not as fixed as we think.

CSETI Training
Mount Shasta, California
First Training at Mount Shasta
September 1999

Black Helicopter Buzzes Restaurant

Linda Willitts
The training at Mt. Shasta was CSETI's first at that site. We had driven from Berkeley to Mt. Shasta in my truck. The first thing we did when we arrived was go to a restaurant for lunch. A very low-flying black helicopter with an electronic platform on its bottom buzzed us. We asked the people at the workshop if they had seen any black helicopters in the area, and they said never. It was another example of the kind of surveillance that Dr. Greer is always under.

Fly-in by Kindness

Dr. Steven Greer
The first night we went up to the top parking area on Mount Shasta. While there, an amazingly close fly-in by Kindness' ship occurred. The ship came in, arced, made a turn, and went back out into space. After that, towards the south, a brilliant ruby red orb appeared that Trudy, several other people, and I saw. It came back later that night. I knew then we were going to have an extraordinary night on the mountain.

Every night there were fully materialized craft in the atmosphere. Astonishing things kept occurring, and often aggressive electronic warfare events occurred. The townspeople were upset by the black helicopters because they had never seen such "goings on." Of course, they knew the CSETI group was in town. Some of them may have mistakenly thought the bizarre activities were part of what we were doing. Despite attempts at interference, we consistently used elevated states of consciousness to create complete peace and cosmic awareness. No one was harmed, no one was delayed, and everything happened seamlessly and peacefully.

Transition in Meditation Coverage
Dr. Steven Greer

At this training I decided it was very important in our guided meditations to do what I had been doing silently for thirty years, to go into a state of God Consciousness and connect with extraterrestrial and celestial beings. The steps included expansion of awareness, going into space and then inviting the visitors from various star systems to join us. The final step of the process was to look at the Earth from space and pray for the healing and transformation of the Earth. It was something I had been reluctant to do because it seemed too spiritual, but it was something that the group at Shasta was ready to do.

Huge Triangular Craft Appears During Meditation

We were at the site below the peak of Mt. Shasta. I was leading the guided meditation, which went deeper and deeper. I reached a state where I saw the celestial and God-Conscious Being, the Avatar or Godhead state. I then joined with all the extraterrestrial people in holding the Earth in golden light for its transformation and for universal peace. At the very instant we reached this deep state of consciousness, Al Dunaway was told to open his eyes and look up.

Al Dunaway

As Dr. Greer was leading the meditation I heard a familiar voice telling me to look up. It was the same manatee-type ET that I had met in Crestone the previous year. As I looked up I saw a massive triangular craft slowly coming into view overhead. I interrupted the group meditation and told everyone to look up.

Dr. Steven Greer
Al interrupted our meditation, and instantly a massive interstellar spacecraft the size of the triangle in Pegasus appeared. It was unmistakable. Every single person there saw it. Al filmed it and we have the video. (see DVD). The object was seen from southern Canada and the Pacific Northwest all the way down the West Coast.

CE-5 with Huge Triangular Craft
The huge triangular craft appeared, turned and came over us. It was so majestic. It appeared to be three points in a triangle. In the middle was the star field of the sky except it was distorted, as if you were looking through an enormous heat wave. As it moved, the whole object came over and turned on its axis. It was not three separate craft, but one enormous ship. It turned and went over toward the constellation Pegasus. As it started to leave, I signaled to it with my laser. A brilliant light flashed from the craft back to us, and we were utterly stunned.

We know the craft was exoatmospheric, and it had to be several hundred to a thousand miles across on each side of the triangle. It was a massive tetrahedral craft out in very deep space and was just showing three of its points, or one face. It appeared just then in order to confirm and affirm the cohesive state of consciousness our group had entered. One person being in that specific state of consciousness has some effect, but forty people being in that state has an exponential effect[67]. The ETs were saying, "Yes!" and the craft appeared absolutely on cue, the instant we reached the correct state of consciousness, in deep prayer and meditation for the healing of the Earth. From then on I knew that entering that state of consciousness is what they want us to do. We are beginning a 500,000-year cycle, the culmination of which will be that our planet and every single person on it will be in a state of pure cosmic awareness and God Consciousness... Our spacecraft,

---

[67] For example, if two people produce twice the effect of one, then three people would produce twice the effect of two, four people would produce twice the effect of three, etc. Twenty people would produce a million-fold effect. Forty people, at this doubling rate, would produce over a trillion-fold increase.

like theirs, will be empowered with consciousness itself, with a full state of enlightenment embracing even the technology.

Kay Gibson
The craft was so big it was taking up all of my field of vision. I believe it came out of a dark area of the Milky Way. What I had been watching was almost like the ocean boiling in that area of the night sky. I had been watching it for some time. When I put my head down everybody said "Oh!" and the craft was there. When I looked, I was looking for something moving in a small area, and instead it was huge. I didn't realize until the second time it showed up, when I saw the lights at the tips of the triangle at huge distances apart, how large the craft was. I could see the star field rippling through it like a heat wave, and I could see the triangular shape when I expanded my field of vision. I also saw it was moving rather slowly, and then it started turning. Its lights went out one at a time, and I didn't see the ship any longer.

Dr. Steven Greer
Kay is right. There was a field distortion in the part of the sky where the massive ship appeared, and as it moved through the sky, the whole area in the interior of the triangle that was outlined by those three bright points was always in a field distortion. Col. Philip Corso described this type of effect when the craft he saw in the desert was hovering there and would then disappear. It looked like a heat wave distortion. It was very clear and I knew that it was not three objects flying in formation, but rather one massive ship.

Dr. Ted Loder
Unlike many of the objects we have seen, this large triangle craft was not a flash-by. The craft stayed in the sky for minutes. It moved slowly and majestically across the sky until it turned, moved and finally disappeared. It followed the same pattern each night, but particularly the second and third nights. If you listen to the video of the occurrence, everyone is giggling and so excited and happy about it.

Dr. Steven Greer
Yes. The joy and emotion were overwhelming. We knew we were

witnessing something of epic importance. The event happened as punctuation, exactly when we reached the appropriate, deep state of consciousness.

Trudy Guyker
We were witnessing the event take place, and at the same time the beings on the craft were able to "know" us on the ground. They knew us at that very time, and it was an extremely profound realization that added to the excitement.

Oklahoma Vortex Synchronicity
Jan Brook
I didn't get to go to the 1999 Shasta training, but at the exact moment the "enormous triangular craft" event was happening, something woke me up in Oklahoma. I got up and went into my living room. In the northwest corner of my room, a vortex opened up. I received a flash that the ETs were connecting my home and other places, other CSETI members, and other enlightened people all over the globe, in a network – a grid of energy. I emailed Debbie and she answered me the next morning. She told me my experience occurred at the exact time, real time, that the craft flew over.

Unusual to Observe Such a Huge Craft
Linda Willitts
When Al said, "Look up," I looked up. Being so accustomed to seeing fairly small objects in the sky, my eyes took a minute to see something so huge moving across the sky. As Dr. Greer said, the craft moved with a distinct sense of majesty. Every time we've seen it since, we recognize that majestic manner of movement. It was so incredibly awesome when it turned and all three of its lights were on one plane. When it went back out into space, the first point had disappeared before Dr. Greer signaled it and it returned his signal with a flash of its backlights. The object was probably up in the sky crossing the Zenith for two or three minutes. Everyone in the group had plenty of time to see it.

Dr. Ted Loder
Two nights later, as dusk approached, we saw an area in the sky where some "flash bulbs" were flashing at us trying to get our

attention. It went on for ten to twenty minutes. The triangle-shaped craft appeared again, moving across the sky.

Second Appearance of Craft at Same Point in Meditation
Linda Willitts
It appeared at the *exact* same point in Dr. Greer's meditation to confirm that reaching that state of consciousness is what it wanted us to do. There was one more night later in the week when the craft appeared again.

Al Dunaway
We were sitting with our cameras mounted on tripods the first evening and we were unable to get photos of the craft, but the craft came over three of five nights that week as we reached the same point of the meditation. We were able to get video on the subsequent two nights.

Trudy Guyker
I was awestruck at these sightings, of course. I started laughing, and I almost started dancing. I reacted to the triangular craft in an extremely joyful manner because it was so incredible.

Celestial Joy and Celebration
Dr. Steven Greer
Trudy felt a celestial celebration like Jan Brook was just talking about. Trudy sensed that there was a celebration and joy on countless planets. It is hard to describe the effect it had on everyone there. It was a celestial state of consciousness, very joyous and beautiful. We could feel that it was emanating from space and from the people on the enormous craft. It was on multiple levels, not just the physical and extraterrestrial, but on the celestial, the very High Concourse of beings, masters, and the level of the avatar. It was truly transformative. We could feel the Earth being affected, which is why I think Jan Brook was awakened and could feel the event happening in her home.

Jan Brook
I could actually see it with my real eyes; it was so clear.

Sightings Up and Down Pacific Coast of USA
Debbie Foch
Other people had seen it up and down the Coast as well. The amazing thing was the feeling of having the triangle craft come over during a meditation and finding out about it through a communication to Al to "look up." The event confirmed our connection with the ETs. They were present and obviously connecting with us. It's part of the joy of our sightings and our work.

Significance of Three Appearances of the Huge Triangular Craft
Dr. Steven Greer
The craft signaled bright light as it disappeared and left. For something of its size to appear three times in a six day training is astounding and unprecedented. This is how I knew that I had made the right decision to introduce a celestial level of consciousness and request the transformation of the Earth to a world of peace and enlightenment. That is why the ETs are here. They are watching and waiting for it. They made that very clear by appearing at the same point in the meditation and prayer each time in the week.

Chaotic Day in Mount Shasta City
Linda Willitts
The rest of the week was very chaotic in between these peaceful sightings. One day in particular, when Dr. Greer gave a talk in town, was unbelievably chaotic.

Debbie Foch
9/9/9 was the chaotic day.

Linda Willitts
One afternoon Debbie, Trudy, Dr. Greer and I had gone out to dinner. While we were sitting in the restaurant, there was a raucous person outside on the street. Then a black helicopter buzzed us. Next, someone got angry and started pounding on the windows trying to intimidate people inside the restaurant. Dr. Greer quickly told the waitress to lock the door. Dr. Greer said, "I'm an ER doctor. You should call the police. This could be a dangerous situation." The episode coincided with the black helicopter buzzing us.

Details of Chaotic Behavior

Trudy Guyker

When we were sitting in the restaurant we were buzzed more than once. I think the helicopter went over us at least three times. The berserk man was putting his face against the window. His arms were up like a bear and he was growling. It was scary, and it was very weird.

Dr. Steven Greer

The helicopter came very low over the restaurant that was on a side street. We learned the helicopter landed right outside town. The berserk man wasn't just crazy; he was also violent and dangerous. He was already in the restaurant, and they had to make him leave. I was going to give a lecture after dinner at a bookstore, but there were too many people for the bookstore, so they moved the lecture to a meeting room in a restaurant.

The afternoon of 9/9/99, after the disruptive forces entered the city of Mt. Shasta, the entire town seemed to become unhinged. There were trashcans overturned in the street and people pouring out of stores in fights. There were people walking down the street who were drunk and apparently psychotic. There was talk of someone coming to the lecture with a gun to kill me. It was as if there had been a massive psychotronic weapons system released over the area to suppress what we were doing, and to create mass chaos in the city.

Al Dunaway had a remote view that an attack on me was going to be attempted. He remote viewed it prior to people hearing the threat. So we were debating what to do. I wasn't planning to cancel the event, so I decided we needed to all go into a deep state of consciousness. While in this deep state, we put the orderliness and coherence of cosmic light and peace over the city and over us. Then we orchestrated it so I had a security detail. We waited for everything to be set up at the restaurant where the lecture was going to be held. I was ushered in, did the presentation, a book signing, and met with people. Nothing adverse happened. We got into the vehicles that were waiting right outside and left. The event was without incident...

Animals Taking on Human Karma

After the talk, we departed for our field site. Someone also named Steve was going up before I was. As he was driving to our site, a deer leapt in front of his vehicle. He hit and killed it. It was tragic, and he was very upset. Animals occasionally take the karmic repercussions so the humans will be protected. We have had this happen before. I think the deer gave its life so that the negative energy in the area would dissipate through its death; we were preserved and safe.

This is a real and profound mystery upon which you should meditate. Another example was 1996 when several of us were getting metastatic cancer. At the time I had a golden retriever named Yami who was very bonded to me, and I was his master. He was a dog of enormous nobility, intelligence and sweetness. To this day if I meet someone who is a really fantastic, standup, wonderful person I call him a 'Yami' guy. It is my highest compliment to a male. At the same instant when I got a metastatic malignant melanoma on my left shoulder, Yami got a big sarcoma, a type of aggressive cancer, in his left triceps muscle near his left shoulder.

The world's expert on melanoma said my cancer was metastatic and had arisen from somewhere else in my body. But I didn't have a primary site, and that was the clue for what we suspected. The 'primary' was in a Petri dish in an underground base being radionically transferred onto me. (I recently had a CIA operative confirm to me that this can absolutely be done!) At the same time, I had the surgery to remove my melanoma, Yami had to have his front left leg removed, and he had the exact same number of staples at the same angle in the same place I did. It was a total match, and no coincidence! I looked at my dog, and I thought, "He took on that cancer for me through his non-local mind and bioelectric field to save my life." I believe that to this day, and I think the deer at Mt. Shasta did the same thing. It is beautiful – and yet tragic. I know this sounds bizarre to some people, but you will learn it is a profound truth about how nature and the animals can be with us and do things for us in mysterious ways.

ET Craft Distortion Field on Ground

Charlie Balogh

Early in the week Dr. Greer, Debbie, Trudy and I had gone out during the day to Sand Flat. We wanted to make sure there weren't too many campers who might interfere with our fieldwork. Debbie once again spotted one of the "heat mirage" objects. There's a medicine wheel up by Sand Flat near a big bowl, and the heat mirage was in a little group of trees near the medicine wheel. We went over to the mirage, and it was distinctly warmer in there.

The night we were doing our fieldwork in the bowl at Sand Flat, Dr. Greer left the circle. He had his green laser and went off into the distance. We could not see him anymore, and then he called to us, "Come." We thought he flashed his green laser. It looked like a green laser flashed in the direction of his voice. We followed, thinking he was showing us where to go with his laser light. It turned out that he could see us perfectly clearly, but that he never flashed his green laser.

Dr. Steven Greer

I never took the laser out of my coat. People saw the "distortion field" and thought I had dematerialized. I was there in an ET ship, which appeared to them as a distortion field, and what they saw was not my light at all. I was there in a state where I could see with my inner sight, feel with my hands, and see a shimmering with my outer sight. The shimmering was the extraterrestrial beings in the very discretely shaped ET craft that was there hovering above the ground. It was exactly in the area where we saw the field distortion during the day. It was not like a vague heat wave that you would see on the road. It was circular and had a definite size to it, some fifteen or twenty feet across.

Kay Gibson

I saw the mirage-looking field at the same place but at a different time. It appeared to me as a disc standing up on its edge. It was about twenty or thirty feet across and had rough edges. When I saw it, it seemed to be a scintillating but solid bright yellow color, similar to the chrome yellow that artists use. It was quite amazing. I have not seen anything like it before or since.

Linda Willitts
We played with it by walking from the cold area as if through a curtain into the distinctly warm area. Then we would walk back out, and it would be cold. We could walk back in and it would be hot. It was a very distinct temperature difference inside the craft.

Interaction with Entities on the Ground

Trudy Guyker
When the group got up to follow Dr. Greer, the night was pitch black, and we were stumbling along. I was walking next to Dr. Loder. He tugged on the right shoulder of my jacket to get my attention. I looked over and saw him point. He had his hand in front of my face and pointed to our left. I looked there and saw a light about the size of a flashlight. It looked like a light I had seen in Sedona earlier in 1998. I acknowledged it and said, "Yes, I saw it." We continued walking.

The next morning when we were debriefing, I was telling about what Dr. Loder had done and how it looked like a light I had seen before. Dr. Loder said, "I didn't pull your jacket." It turned out Dr. Loder had not pulled my jacket to get my attention. There had definitely been a hand in front of my face pointing toward the edge of the forest. I suspect an ET was present and pointing to the light in the forest to remind me that it was the craft I had seen in Sedona.

Kay Gibson
During the group experience on the night of September 5th, the area to our south was full of manifestations. Al told me that a 5'6" entity was moving toward me. I turned to see a vertical shape about 4'5" tall which seemed to stay about 2' away from me. Debbie saw the same entity. I had been standing with my hands down and palms forward. I felt a soft warmth on the back of my left hand and turned to see a small, rectangular entity about 2' tall. Al saw it too. He, Debbie and I ran our hands over and through its silvery-gold, wavy energy. When my hand passed through the entity, my hand seemed to be covered with a layer of mesh. I tried to make myself receptive to the beings and resonate with love and brotherhood.

Al Dunaway

Dr. Greer encouraged us to get to know the ETs that were interfacing with us on a more personal level, so I introduced myself to a particular entity. He was only about two and a half feet tall. We wandered over to a grove of trees and sat down to communicate with each other. Not really knowing what to expect or at what level this communication would take place, I just relaxed and we started to share our desires for open contact between Earth and Extraterrestrial peoples.

The entity had us place our hands in front of us palms down. He produced a crystal pyramid six inches tall having a smoke essence within it. As we sat with our hands over it, it seemed we sere soaking up knowledge from it. The pyramid disappeared after releasing the smoky substance, and the entity repeated the process with another pyramid. I lost track of how long the process lasted. We eventually went back to our circle, and the ETs returned to their business. I will never forget the ease and simplicity of communication with them. Not all conversations are earth-shattering in importance. Sometimes it is enough to meet and relate as friends.

Kay Gibson

Sitting facing where Dr. Greer had "disappeared", I saw multiple lights in the trees to our left, and then a large, yellow, plasma-like craft. I saw a green light in the trees to our right that traveled to the right. Then, in rapid succession, I saw a mix of ETs, Native Americans, devas, ghosts, and other entities.

The large triangular craft was sighted the next day. Dr. Greer said the event had been set up for nine years. When we got to the site, the energy field was already there, along with the many beings. The actual event could be considered outside the normal time/space continuum. Dr. Greer had sensed the gathering was a completion/ fulfillment, a closing of one period and the opening of another.

Arizona Sighting of Triangular Craft in August 1999
Charlie Balogh

I was not at Shasta during the triangle craft event. However, the previous month in August, we had a meteor shower party at our home. An active meteor shower was waning at 1:30 in the morning. It was summer in Phoenix, and the weather was beautiful. About 2:30 in the morning, I was lying flat on my back looking straight up. I was in a meditation when I opened my eyes and saw three points of light in a triangle. The huge triangle appeared directly over my head and started moving off toward the Superstition Mountains to the northeast. I watched it and was speechless. I finally called to my wife, who came running out and saw it. Her friend saw it just as it passed over the mountains to the northeast. The next day, I made a report on Peter Davenport's website[68].

CSETI Training
Joshua Tree, California
November 1999

Pseudo Moonlight Envelops Group

Dr. Steven Greer
We were sitting at the site we had been shown to us by a craft in 1996 when a brilliant light flashed in the sky, not just one but multiple lights, and everyone could see them. There was an energy source from a craft in the quadrant of the sky where Orion is located. We had been meditating and were in a deep state of quiet awareness, inviting the extraterrestrial visitors to come in. They were scanning us and evaluating the whole group. I pointed out that we were suffused in a silvery white light. Just as I called everyone's attention to it, they turned this light off, and the area became pitch black. Everyone gasped. This sort of thing happens very often.

Everyone saw the light but no one could explain it. I think we were actually in contact non-locally with a craft that was in the sector of Orion. They were beaming an energy field around us that was both consciousness and light. The light was silvery, almost like the reflected light from the Moon, but the Moon wasn't up. As soon as we became aware of and acknowledged this light and contact, it ended.

---

[68] http://www.ufocenter.com/

Linda Willitts

We were seeing our shadows and suddenly realized there was no moon by which to see a shadow! As soon as we got the message, it became pitch dark again. It was the first time that we saw such light, but we have seen it happen often since.

Dr. Steven Greer

Yes, we have seen this hundreds of times since. This event began a series of expressions of higher intelligence that bridge extraterrestrial and what I call cosmic consciousness or God-conscious civilizations. These expressions have been increasing regularly since this trip.

Trudy Guyker

When I started, learning was simple – but it accelerates with each training. We learn, and they put out a challenge to us to learn more and to use our senses more. It just keeps growing and growing – to this day.

Dr. Steven Greer

Yes. It's all recapitulating the experiences I had in 1973, but now, instead of just one person having the experience, dozens and hundreds and thousands of people are having the experiences. That is one way the morphogenic field[69] is growing. All of humanity is learning and growing through the effect of nonlocal awareness...

The Orange Disc and the Teal Globe

Ricky Butterfass

The next night while we were doing the CTS (Coherent Thought Sequencing) I told Dr. Greer I thought something would be coming out of the northeast, and he agreed. Both of our heads turned, as if someone reached out and turned our heads simultaneously. We saw a teal globe the size of a grapefruit. This globe tracked along the mountain ridgeline, reached a saddle gap, went behind the peaks and stopped. Then it changed course, remained in the middle of that gap and lit up the whole group with a turquoise light. The globe stayed there the rest of the night.

---

69 Morphogenic field: http://www.experiencefestival.com/a/Morphogenic_Fields/id/4781

Later, looking through my binoculars, I could see a large orange disc spinning with sparks flying out the sides and a trail of orange sparks two miles behind. The disc came right over us and just as it reached the Zenith, it instantly stopped spinning, turned into a golden teardrop, and silently floated off. There was a contrail from the cloud of sparks that dissipated. It sounded like hair being singed.

Dr. Steven Greer
And this was only about 300 feet above ground level. This disc was very close, and you could hear it as well as see it.

Trudy's Alert
Trudy Guyker
An incident happened in which the people in Dr. Greer's car saw a craft as they entered the park. Before we went to the site I had a communication that said: "Be very alert approaching the park." Sure enough, as we were approaching the park, Dr. Greer and Linda saw a craft come out of those hills. I was sitting behind Dr. Greer. His vehicle had tinted glass, and I didn't see anything. I received the message to 'be aware' but then I didn't get to see this craft.

Campfire-like Plasma Craft
Linda Willitts
I was in the truck with Trudy, Debbie, and Dr. Greer. As we drove in and parked, there was a 'campfire' in the sky to the south. This 'campfire' was directly behind a Joshua Tree and twenty to thirty degrees above the horizon. This object, which resembled a plasma craft, was orange and looked like a campfire. The rest of the group then started arriving, and they were filming the 'campfire' in the sky. Trudy, Debbie, and Dr. Greer saw some things about the 'campfire' that I didn't see because I was directing traffic.

Dr. Steven Greer
For one thing, the 'campfire' object was interactive. I was signaling to it, and it was pulsing and signaling back. The object was out over the plain where a big craft had come down. The object was about fifteen degrees above the horizon, and remained there a long

time. I think Al Dunaway got a videotape of it. (See DVD)

Linda Willitts
This craft was brilliant and was there the instant we got on site. Smaller craft came off of this object. The object itself was the size of a nickel held at arms length.

Dr. Steven Greer
Yes, there were other objects that were coming out of the 'campfire' craft. The event continued for at least ten minutes.

Trudy Guyker
The object kept changing. At times the craft was like a campfire because it had flames radiating out like fire. Then the object would change into more of a diamond shape.

Dr. Steven Greer
Yes, the object was big and was lighting up the sky in that area. It was like a welcoming party. We've seen this happen dozens of times where we arrive on site and within minutes, there is an ET craft hanging in the sky or directly on site.

Interactions with the Plasma Craft

Trudy Guyker
Other incidents took place besides the plasma object. Two craft came toward the plasma ball from each side. The objects were at the same level, and they came together toward the plasma object. Then three lights appeared to the right of the plasma ball, and they were stacked on each other, one above the other.

Dr. Steven Greer
That's right. The two other craft seemed to be docking with the plasma object. This object was fully materialized in the atmosphere. This incident was quite astonishing and continued for a long time, and there were a number of craft.

Trudy Guyker
Later, as we were walking around the circle, I suddenly saw two

more of these lights in the east—a red one, and a white one.

Radar Detector Anomaly
Linda Willitts
We always had a radar detector, and we had put it on the hood of the truck. In Joshua Tree, the detector would sound as we just parked on the road site. Nothing is there that could make the detector go off other than ET craft in the area.

Dr. Steven Greer
We also had magnetometers sounding off as well.

Ricky's Daytime Sighting and the Akashic Record
Ricky Butterfass
Before we went to the Hidden Valley site, I remote viewed a chocolate chip cookie rock formation and a daytime craft. We broke up into two teams, walked back into Hidden Valley and did a meditation. When I opened my eyes and looked out in the distance I saw a chocolate chip cookie-shaped rock formation. The formation was circular and had rocks and tree branches that made it look like a chocolate chip cookie. Right above that formation was a silvery shaped craft, which was about 1,200 feet away. The bottom of this craft looked like an egg carton and was silver. Attached to the side of this ship was a silver globe. The craft was just hanging over the rocks. A team member said it had been there about five minutes. I asked why he didn't wake us. He said he didn't want to disturb the meditation. I told him that interacting with a craft is what we are here for, to get his camera out and take a picture. He was fooling around getting his camera out as the craft took off and went to the western horizon. I notified the other team, but they did not arrive in time to see the craft.

When I do this fieldwork, I often contact and work with my spirit guides and guardian angels. One, whom I call Running Elk, is an American Indian who has crossed over to the other side. I have another guide called Gray Eagle. I saw Running Elk on his pinto horse, and he was against some rocks. I asked him what he was doing, and he said, "I'm listening to the rocks. They're telling me their story." I thought the ETs might have the capability to listen to what's recorded in the crystalline structure of these rocks, like extracting the Akashic Record[70] right out of the rocks.

Fog-like Heavy Atmosphere Anomaly
Trudy Guyker
At the Joshua Tree site, when I was sitting on the south side of the circle the atmosphere started to get very strange, very heavy and fog-like. The inside of our circle became fuzzy. I had almost a hypnotic feeling, as if I was in an altered state and things were not quite sharp. I never had an experience like this before in the group. As I looked at the north side of our circle, I saw some lights in the group.

At the next day's debriefing I explained that I saw lights by the people on the north side. They explained there were no vehicles behind them. I recalled there were no cars in that area, but did see the lights there.

Linda Willitts
Trudy's story reminded me of similar episodes where during the evening we can see the people in front of us on the other side of the circle. But at other times of the evening, the circle will be filled, like Trudy said, with a thick atmosphere. And if we're standing, sometimes we can only see the other side of the circle from the waist up but we can't see their hips, legs or feet. At other times, we can't really see them at all, even though we should be able to.

---

[70] Akashic Record— theosophical term denoting a kind of central filing system of all events, thoughts, and actions impressed upon an astral plane, which may be consulted in certain conditions of consciousness. [http://www.answers.com/topic/akashic-records-1]

Chapter 8

2000

CSETI Training
Wilcox, Arizona
March 2000

Linda Willitts
After meeting a man who reported that he had been having experiences with fully materialized craft in Wilcox, AZ, we decided to go there. Wilcox is southeast of Tucson, near the Mexican border. It borders Fort Huachuca[71], the Army Intelligence headquarters base. White Sands[72] is to the east, and Davis-Monthan Air Force Base[73] is in Tucson, so Wilcox is surrounded by military installations.

Cigar-Shaped Craft by Mt Graham
Debbie Foch
We were near the Vatican Observatory[74] on top of Mt. Graham, and we saw amber objects flying just below the observatory, which meant astronomers could not see them. I also remember a cylinder-shaped craft that was flying slowly over the mountains. It was not fully materialized, but fuzzy.

Rosy, Fog-Like Craft on Ground
Linda Willitts
Near the Observatory we also saw multiple fog-like craft nestled at the base of some small mountains. We had been seeing a brilliant, rosy glow from the other side of the mountain. When we left that evening, Dr. Greer, Debbie, Trudy and I were all in one vehicle and stopped on the other side of the mountain where we had seen that rosy glow. We saw a disc-shaped alleged cloud that was glowing a rosy color. It was pulsing, and it was quite bright. Whenever a car

---
[71] Fort Huachuca: http://en.wikipedia.org/wiki/Fort_Huachuca
[72] White Sands: http://en.wikipedia.org/wiki/White_Sands_Missile_Range
[73] Davis-Monthan AFB: http://www.dm.af.mil/

went by on the highway, which was infrequent, the 'cloud' would dim down.

A Lesson in How Craft May Appear

Dr. Steven Greer

The glow was just above the ground. This occurred in the desert where the climate was very dry, not conducive to low cloud formation. There were four of the 'rosy glowing clouds.' We stopped on a road by the highway, and saw two craft on one side and two on the other. They were distinct, disc-shaped, domed, and they would lift up and begin to pulse. When a car came along the highway, these 'clouds' would dim down considerably. We stayed there for at least thirty to forty minutes, interacting with these spacecraft. They were etheric plasma, not totally materialized, but they were completely visible with the naked eye. The light pulsing in and out of them was not subtle. It was very clear. The light emitted was so bright it would light up the sky when we were on the other side of the mountain.

Trudy Guyker

Dr. Greer would outline each one of the craft with his laser. The craft were all the same shape, and they were large. They were sitting close to the ground right on the edge of the hill.

Dr. Steven Greer

They were very large craft. The casual person driving by would never have noticed. This is an important lesson in how the extraterrestrial people and craft can appear. They can be hidden in plain sight. You have to know what to look for, and you have to be aware of these possibilities, or you'll fly right by it. In point of fact, the rest of the group did.

Trudy Sees Angels Surrounding Dr. Greer

Trudy Guyker

I remember Dr. Greer giving his cosmology talk when we were at the retreat site. It was beautiful because the words he was using were all so profound, so spiritual and so beautiful. There were angels – I can't prove it to anyone – but there were angels all

---

[74] The Vatican Observatory Research Group is hosted by Steward Observatory at the University of Arizona, Tucson, USA. [http://clavius.as.arizona.edu/vo/R1024/VO.html]

around Dr. Greer. It was beautiful.

God-Consciousness Dream of Enormous Craft
Dr. Steven Greer
One of our sites was located on a big plain that was very dark at night. I'd never been in a place that was so dark. That night, when I went to sleep, I awakened in the dream and was out in that area of the desert. It appeared to be daytime in the desert. There was an enormous ET craft filled with extraterrestrial people from various planets who were in a state of perfect God-consciousness. This craft was of the most beautiful light and color, ruby red and jewel-like. It had a high dome and a big, flat skirt around the base. The craft was floating along, and I was in a state of God-consciousness. I was having a lucid, crystal clear, full color astral experience. I realized the spacecraft itself was conscious. I knew the spacecraft was of such purity and a technology so advanced that it was of a celestial light, that even the space ship was God-conscious! This is very hard to explain. There is a technological level of celestial consciousness that enables a civilization to be one with the actual vehicle—and the ET craft itself is imbued with that level of consciousness...

This entire ship and its beings were the highest possible manifestation that intelligence can take in a relative form, coming out of a mountain and interacting with us in the most profound way. I saw that it was our future as well. Humans will become so developed over the next several thousand years that everyone who dwells on Earth will be in a state of God-consciousness with the capacity for celestial perception. Every manifestation of our technologies will have that level of awareness associated with it. And yet we will still be on this physical planet. There are entire worlds at that level, hundreds of thousands to millions of years more developed than we are now. It is beautiful, astonishing...

Green Laser-like Light
Debbie Foch
We had some anomalous laser light-like phenomena shooting through our group the same night that we saw the cylinder craft. I

think on the same night on a break we were walking down in the grass when we saw a red light shoot along in the grass. At another time, we saw it up in the sky. We went looking for this light, and we saw it again.

Trudy Guyker
The green light appeared during a break while Debbie, Dr. Greer, another man, and I were standing together talking. Suddenly, a green light about the width of a nickel came straight out of the ground. It came right to me, and it was heading for my face. I threw my head back because I was afraid it was going to hit me and then it was gone. Debbie saw it. It was very strange.

Dr. Steven Greer
I saw the light, and we did not have any lasers then. We were below a major flight path, and there were countless military planes. We were only at that place for one night because of the interference.

Linda Willitts
We suspect the overt ET activity seen in the area was being curtailed by military surveillance. Jets 'strafed' us often. We were right next to Fort Huachuca with White Sands right around the corner. In meditation I could sense interference, and I knew it was from the electronics in that plane.

Hudson Valley CSETI Training
Pine Bush, New York
April 2000

Massive Triangular Craft: Two Looks

Dr. Steven Greer
We went to Pine Bush at the end of April because we had heard of events occurring there. Remarkably, in September of 1999 on three different nights at Mt. Shasta we saw an enormous triangle that came over during meditation and prayer. When we went to Pine Bush, the triangle followed us there.

Dr. Ted Loder
It was a very clear night, and the triangle appeared low on the

horizon and sat there for a while. It sat there while the star field moved behind it slowly. We didn't see the triangle initially. We thought at first it was a star.

Linda Willitts
I remember there were some broken clouds. Each of us knows that sometimes when clouds move, it appears the stars are moving. In fact, the triangular craft was moving, but we thought it was the clouds moving that made us think the stars were moving. That is why we missed the craft at first.

Dr. Ted Loder
The craft had been there quite a while before we finally figured it out. Then it showed up in another part of the sky overhead.

Linda Willitts
It was as if the ETs were thinking, "Hey you guys, you were kind of slow on our first fly by, so we'll give you another chance."

Dr. Steven Greer
The triangle appeared twice in one night. The second time, everyone saw it. It was the same enormous triangle majestically moving across the sky. We knew that they were connected to us just as they had been at Mt. Shasta.

Kindness Appears at Pinebush

Linda Willitts
One night as we were driving in at dusk, Kindness flashed us spectacularly – a bright flash like a diamond.

Dr. Steven Greer
Yes. The beautiful blue-white ship came in and shone an intensely bright light toward us as we were coming in.

The Crackling Antenna

The first night we set up on the lawn of a house, and something very unusual happened. Some energy appeared and began to interface with the antenna on the house. The antenna began crackling and moving. The incident was extraordinary. It was clear that some type of energy field entered after we started meditating. You could hear it crackling on the antenna of the house like loud static electricity.

Linda Willitts

I remember that crackling. There were lights on in the house, even though it was unoccupied. A very low-flying helicopter then buzzed us and shone a giant light beacon on us.

Debbie Foch

I remember the crackling with the antenna and the helicopter that flew in.

Dr. Steven Greer

Yes. We're out in the middle of nowhere, and here comes a helicopter doing surveillance on us. It put a bright searchlight right into our group. It was an extremely aggressive act by the helicopter.

Interactive Walkie-Talkies and Magnetometers

Linda Willitts

Dr. Greer has often mentioned the concept 'expressions of ET intelligence.' One of the expressions of ET intelligence at the Pine Bush training was ETs creating interactive chirping with our walkie-talkies.

Dr. Steven Greer

It isn't an isolated occurrence. It happened in England, in Pine Bush and at Crestone. We were transmitting the CSETI beeping tones through a radio transceiver. Then the radio started receiving, which is not possible under normal operating conditions. The tones came back through the electronics in an altered state. They sounded spacey, no pun intended, and began chirping. It happened at Pine Bush repeatedly. Eventually it began to happen in a way that fit a clear pattern, as if a code was coming through. We've also had magnetometers behave this way on various expeditions. There would be a series of three tones and a pause, then two tones. The tone numbers were definitely not random. We would hear a repeating, electronic pattern. Our electronic devices have not only detected the magnetic flux field, or an electromagnetic release of energy in the case of laser radar detectors or magnetic magnetometers, but they have also acted as communication devices. It would go on for half an hour, forty-five minutes at a time, as signaling would come through the electronic equipment.

Linda Willitts
Yes, the chirping was coming through our walkie-talkies and continued all night. It was clearly a communication. In class, when Dr. Greer talked, it would react by punctuating things he said. The ETs were communicating with us through this machine, and when Dr. Greer said something really profound that the ETs wanted to emphasize, it would chirp once, twice or three times. When he said something humorous it chirped, indicating they had a sense of humor.

Dr. Steven Greer
It was very interactive behavior. We experienced this dozens of times with these magnetic field flux meters. These devices go off when the magnetic field moves or is altered. We began to find that the ETs would literally punctuate certain statements or comments through the magnetometers or the walkie-talkies as an affirmation. There was a period when it happened frequently on these expeditions.

Debbie Foch
At Pine Bush the walkie-talkies were responding to us laughing. Every time we had a break and we were more joyous, they would start beeping, responding to our laughter.

The Alleged Star that Looked like Sirius
Trudy Guyker
I remember coming onto the farm site at dusk and seeing a beautiful, 'alleged' star. It was similar to Sirius and low on the horizon. We were thinking, "Could that be Sirius?" It was so big, diamond-like, colorful and shimmering. We said, "We'll just keep our eye on it." We got out of the car and looked over a few minutes later to see that it was gone.

MRA Conference
Caux, Switzerland
July 2000

Dr. Steven Greer
In July 2000 I was invited to Caux, Switzerland. There was a group called MRA, Moral Rearmament Association[75], that Phillips Electronics[76] and some other folks had funded. Many business people attended, but I was invited to share CSETI information. I was introduced to the leaders of Canon, Medtronics and other corporations.

An Impromptu Session
Word got out that "Doctor Greer" was there. A number of folks were quite curious, so I did an impromptu salon. After that a group of them who had heard about remote viewing approached me. So we sat in a circle of about twenty people. There were vice presidents of software companies and a chartered accountant from Sheffield, England, and the Lord Mayor of London. We were sitting in a circle and we went into meditation. I led them into a deep state of consciousness and went into the vast ocean of unbounded mind. I had put a box in the center of the floor into which was placed a bottle of cologne. No one knew what was in this box. I took people into a deep guided meditation into unbounded silent mind. Then I told people to allow themselves to open the box with their inner vision and see what was inside. They tried that for ten minutes, and then we ended it. We went around the circle, and I let people share what they had viewed.

One woman, who was very skeptical, was a computer engineer from Boston and the vice president of a big software company. She said, "I got the sense of a fragrance of the woods and saw this black object shaped like this." Another person said, "I saw a black container, and there was a nozzle with a sprayer."

The Shock of Success
When I opened the box – I'll never forget this as long as I live

---

[75] Renamed "Initiatives of Change" (IofC) in 2001.
[76] Wikipedia: http://en.wikipedia.org/wiki/Philips

– the chartered accountant from Sheffield said, "Oh, no. It can't be. This is ridiculous. I don't believe this. It can't happen. This is the end of my life!" He got very upset, because it was completely outside of his operating paradigm. Later, the woman vice president approached me privately and said, "You know, you've ruined my life. I never thought this could be possible. But I absolutely saw what was in the box. The implications are that this conscious mind is not what I thought it was. The conscious mind is not just the result of the firing of some neurons that follows a reductionist mechanistic view." She added, "I don't know what to do with this. We talked at great length, and it was quite a heartfelt discussion about how the remote viewing exercise had completely changed her entire worldview. I told her, "You can use your capability for a lot of good in the world if you develop it. This is the nature of reality. It's the nature of who you are."

Changing Flawed Realities

I like to share this story because an experience like that can become a doorway. It opens us to the fact that our entire compilation of knowledge, experience and reality can be flawed. What we never entertain as being possible is often the true reality. Paradigm changes represent a big part of what we are doing. We are introducing new concepts, not only through this book, but through our CSETI trainings and expeditions. Experiences outside one's worldview can initially be disturbing, as the examples of the chartered accountant and the software company vice president illustrate. But ultimately, such experiences lead to growth…

CSETI Group
England
July 2000

Hide and Seek with ETs

Dr. Steven Greer
We took a small group to England in 2000. England was having one of the longest stretches of hard rain that they had ever had until the day we arrived.

Linda Willitts

There were a few showers, but we got sunburned in the crop circles that year. We had a number of profound experiences associated with magnetometers[77]. One of the fellows helping with Disclosure had some Raytheon Brazilian-made magnetometers that detected ET energy. We started using them in the field, and we had one of them in England. It was extremely interactive in the field.

Several nights we did fieldwork in a magnetic grid crop circle, a dipole crop circle. The picture of it shows 'tractor trails' called tramlines running through the crop circles. These tramlines are where the tractor tires go when they spray the wheat. We walk in on the tramlines to avoid damaging the crop. Dr. Greer and I were always in the lead, and he had the magnetometer. We walked into the crop circle, and at some point the magnetometer would activate. The beeping was our signal to make our circle. There were only about fifteen of us.

We had the most fun one night watching the small luminous ET beings who were highly visible. We could see their diminutive scintillating shapes. Dr. Greer was showing us how the magnetometer beeped when placed in the middle of one of those scintillating beings. The ET would respond by scooting away, and the magnetometer would stop beeping. Then Dr. Greer would follow the being, reinsert the magnetometer, and it would start beeping again. It quickly became a game of hide and seek. Dr. Greer would begin the game by putting the magnetometer into an ET scintillating shape, then scamper after it and reinsert the magnetometer. He ended up chasing ETs around the field as they played hide and seek with him. We took turns with the magnetometer, enjoying hide and seek with the ETs in the crop circle that night.

A Learning Tool

Dr. Steven Greer

Yes. This lasted about an hour. I've learned to see the neutrino light emissions where there is a scintillating area, but not everyone

---

[77] magnetometer—a scientific instrument used to measure the strength and/or direction of the magnetic field in the vicinity of the instrument [http://en.wikipedia.org/wiki/Magnetometer]

can see it. I would see a scintillating area, walk over to it with the magnetometer, and the magnetometer would go off. This apparatus was a very helpful learning tool because other people then learned to see or sense the neutrino light emissions of the ET beings. I know these beings were also playing this game so that people would get engaged and be able to see them in their subtle form. Everyone in the group learned to see the beings, and they would take turns.

Trudy Guyker
I especially remember the ETs loved Dr. Bravo. I felt that the ETs thought that Jan was a distant cousin, since she's a very diminutive, sweet little person.

Dr. Jan Bravo
This 'hide and seek' interaction was wonderful because often I can feel but don't see these beings. Even though I can feel these ETs, I have yet to see many of them except as scintillating light or astral energy. These beings taught our group not to fear them, an important lesson for all people on earth. It was a marvelous, sharing experience.

I am not usually one to yell or interrupt, but Trudy was talking about Dr. Greer's work. It was very insightful and heart-felt, a manifestation of love for what Dr. Greer is doing. At that moment, I was across from Trudy. I looked over her shoulder and yelled, "Kindness!" People often see her as blue light, but I see her as a magnificent golden, pure light traveling in an arc. She came in above Trudy's head as if to punctuate what Trudy was saying. Kindness' appearance was profound and wonderful.

Significance of Magnetic Dipole Crop Circle
Linda Willitts
This magnetic dipole crop circle was especially meaningful to us because we were starting to do the major work for Disclosure. We felt that this magnetic dipole crop circle was for us, since it formed the night Dr. Greer landed in England and magnetics are an integral part of the energy systems on which he is working.

Dr. Steven Greer

Yes, this crop circle literally appeared that night, as we were landing in England. This event was probably not a coincidence. We had a number of sightings of ET craft and orbs on that trip, including Kindness. I saw this craft also; it was astonishingly bright. I agree with Jan that this entire event was a response to, an acknowledgement of, and punctuation for the thoughts being shared by Trudy.

An Enigma for the "Scientists"

Dr. Steven Greer

Earlier we had been at Marconi's Hill with our group. Some British researchers were present who were very skeptical. Their attitude was, "We know everything because we're scientists." We were sitting there with clear weather and we all saw a "satellite." I said, "Well, maybe. Let's just say it's an object. But let's ask it to do something that a satellite couldn't do." I was remote viewing and I knew it was not a satellite, but actually an extraterrestrial disc. I asked this object "to do something that a satellite can't do," and as soon as those words left my lips it exploded in a burst of light, made a right hand turn, sped off across the horizon and into space! Everyone's mouth dropped open. There were fifteen to twenty witnesses to this event.

Coining the Term, "Alleged"

That is when I coined the term, 'alleged satellite,' or an alleged object. So many times people casually looking up will say, "Oh, it's a satellite," and look away instead of sticking with it. They should follow it and go into an expanded state of mind to connect with the object. Then they should send the object a thought and ask it to do something unusual and see what happens for confirmation of a CE-5.

This episode was very exciting, but it was mystifying to the British scientists. First, they didn't think the interactive part of a CE-5 was possible – especially using mind and thought. Secondly, they were convinced the object was a satellite. Finally they knew it couldn't be a satellite because satellites don't make right hand turns and change directions at such speeds! However the most enigmatic part of this incident was that it happened exactly when we sent the thought asking this object to do something that a satellite couldn't do to prove that it wasn't a satellite. This was mediated through thought and consciousness. This was too much information for them, so they left.

Creating Events from Mind

Alice Sleight

Dr. Greer and Linda were talking about this being the place where he had seen the alleged satellite. No sooner had he done that than it happened again. So as Dr. Greer was explaining the first event, the same thing happened again. Dr. Greer commented at the time something about how we can create reality.

Dr. Steven Greer

Yes, I was talking about it and a craft appeared again in broad daylight. And right behind it, a fighter jet in pursuit. We were almost at the same place in Avebury. Someone said that CSETI is creating these events from our minds, which is true, but not in the way they think. They don't understand that conscious mind is a singularity. There is only *one* conscious mind and, therefore in reality everything is consciousness resonating as that thing. This concept in the Vedic tradition says: "All This is That[78]." In reality, whether we're talking about matter as a star or a plant or our bodies, all of it is consciousness resonating as that object. On one level you can see it as a discrete object, and it is. On another level, it is actually conscious "stuff" manifesting as body, stars, plants, wood, minerals etc. So from the point of view of a cosmically awake person in touch with the Cosmic Being, everything is emanating continuously from mind. And so it is true.

Golden Lights on Kay Gibson's Eyelids

Kay Gibson

We had many different experiences on this trip to England. During one incident, I was sitting next to Dr. Greer as we were in a quiet, meditative state. He said, "There are golden lights on your eyelids." He said he believed that these lights were working on my eyes in

---

[78] See IV-11: http://www.shiningworld.com/Home%20Page%20Links/Mundaka%20Upanishad.html

some way. This sort of occurrence may be another example of the way that ETs are tuning and preparing us. I wouldn't have known this without Dr. Greer's telling me.

Crop Circle Photograph by Japanese Woman
Linda Willitts
We did four nights of fieldwork in the magnetic grid crop circle. One late afternoon as the sun was setting, we were sitting in a crop circle that overlooked a field with cattle. It was the crop circle where we had seen vortices of energy in the field. The next day we went to the Barge Inn where all the crop circle researchers gather. We met a Japanese woman who had taken a digital photo of one of the vortices in that very crop circle where our group was working.

Dr. Steven Greer
We were in this crop circle with this Japanese woman, and we were doing our vectoring and our meditation. It was daytime, but I could see this vortex. It was like a small tornado of energy that was very powerful and present. If you relaxed your eyes so that you weren't staring, you could see this energy field, like a heat wave in the shape of a tiny tornado. The Japanese woman actually had a good digital camera and captured the vortex. We have that photo (see DVD).

Kay Gibson
I have the information that this crop circle is called 'White Hill' and is near Lockeridge.

Old Sarum[79] and the Re-enactors
Dr. Jan Bravo
One night as we approached our site, we noticed that there was a large group of people doing a re-enactment at Old Sarum It was a gathering to commemorate different battles throughout history. We could see people with spears and shields, people dressed as Nazi Brownshirts, and many other military costumes. As we walked through them going to our site, none of these re-enactors noticed

---

[79] Old Sarum—the site of the earliest settlement of Salisbury, in England [http://en.wikipedia.org/wiki/Old_Sarum]

Metaphor for CSETI Work

Linda Willitts

The events of this evening were profound as a metaphor for the work CSETI is doing. We were doing cosmic work with all this war and chaos going on around us, and the re-enactors were utterly oblivious to anything our group was doing. We were having the most peaceful, loving interactions with the ETs while they were reenacting war. You could hear them drinking, singing songs and the re-enactors were wearing all manner of different military uniforms from various eras.

As we left our cars and walked through the entry gate, there were five men walking towards us in full Nazis uniform. We all thought, "What kind of a time warp are we in?" These people didn't appear to notice us. It was surreal. None of these re-enactors ever acknowledged our presence, and we walked past their tents out to a quiet corner of the field and made our circle. At one point we had a half-hour long interaction with an ET craft that was glowing behind a cloud.

CE-5 with Orb in Cloud

Dr. Steven Greer

Let me set the stage. The location is England, and this puffy cloud is low and very discrete. Within this cloud is a glowing orb and luminous light that is pulsing up and down. As we signal this ship, it signals back to us. If we move the laser left or right, it moves. This craft is connecting to our group, and we are remote viewing the interior of the ET craft. This craft is silent and nearby. It is low altitude and very distinct, not neutrino light or scintillations. Everyone sees this ET craft. We are signaling with the laser and connecting with this ship, and not even one of these re-enactors is aware of this ship. We are making contact and actively signaling and filming, yet it seems as if we have been made invisible. All these other people a few yards away never looked up and never saw us.

When we walked by these re-enactors it was as if they were in some sort of fugue state. They never saw us, never blinked, and never looked at us. This incident was quite extraordinary, and it is a metaphor for moving through the world doing this work. Every major war that had happened in Europe was being reenacted all around our CSETI group. The entire scene was almost poetic.

Kay Gibson

My notes indicate that on that evening the sky was totally clear. This totally clear sky made an isolated cloud even more interesting.

Trudy Guyker

At least an hour before this event, I noticed another cloud to the left of the cloud containing the ET craft. This second, stationary cloud resembled a hand with a finger pointing, and I felt we needed to pay close attention. We later learned that it was pointing to the cloud where the craft was.

Debbie Foch

We also saw Kindness that night. It was our last night in England for fieldwork, and we saw Kindness in the direction of Salisbury. What an amazing ending.

Event Q&A

Chuck Schnibben

Is it possible you were involved in a time/space distortion event where you could see these re-enactors but they couldn't see you, and their 'performance' was being replayed for your group?

Dr. Steven Greer

No. The re-enactors were really there and our CSETI group was really there. It was similar to situations where I enter a state of consciousness and just float by like a cloud, as if in stealth mode. It's a consciousness event.

Arnie Arneson

For your information, when I was attending communication school in the 60s, I knew a Cambodian Air Force captain. Before he became an officer in the Air Force, he was a Buddhist monk and he told me of cases where the Buddhists could actually enter such a 'stealth mode' state of consciousness. These monks could appear invisible to the people that they were fighting.

Dr. Steven Greer
This state of consciousness is actually called a Siddhi – a Vedic Siddhi. Each member of our CSETI group was in that state of consciousness powerfully all week. I think that's why we were able to move in and move out without being noticed by the re-enactors. I think we could have stomped right through one of their campfires and still not been noticed.

Other Reports

Alice Sleight
I remember that we saw many twinkles. My daughter, especially, saw a number of what seemed to be tiny fireflies everywhere. This was the first night. Sarum is a very, very old site with quite a history, so any number of things would have been possible there. It was very exciting to be there.

Trudy Guyker
I like to tell this story about our stay in the Salisbury Bed and Breakfast. It happened the first morning, when I came out of my room to go down to the meeting. I had to lock my door manually with one of those big old skeleton keys. As I turned around, I distinctly heard, "Hi Trudy." But there was no one in the hallway or nearby. It was a man's voice, and I could not tell its location. I wondered, "Who are you?" and I said, "Hello." Then I went down and joined the group but didn't mention this incident.

The next day, I again left to go to our CSETI discussion. There was an Englishman named Phillip from Manchester staying in the room next to mine and our doors were adjoining. We left at the same time and turned to leave. Just as we did that, I heard a voice say, "Hello, Trudy." Phillip heard it too, and he said it sounded like a female voice.

Phillip and I then went down and joined the group. Later that night I related this occurrence to our group when we were in the crop circle. I told them that the only reason I shared this incident was because Phillip heard it too. We discussed whom I might have heard. I said that I thought it was two angels, because I had had encounters with angels years and years before.

I'm reporting this incident with the two angels to show that we are not just experiencing ETs in our work. We are also experiencing celestial, cosmic, and many other beings. They, too, are involved in this. These two angels wanted me to know that they were there, involved in this and interested in what was going on.

The Cosmology of Creation
Dr. Steven Greer
I love that Trudy shared the point that our work involved more than just extraterrestrials. I think it is important to note that western culture has trained us to view the world via separation and reductionism.

If you look at Aboriginal people in their dreamtime, there are no notions of separation and division. These ideas have only recently been "accepted" ways of understanding the world. But that doesn't necessarily mean that they are true. In reality there is no separation. The reality is that this effulgent, conscious Being is omnipresent and is manifesting as all things. And we are that conscious being.

When you go through the crossing point of light, you have entered into the residence of angelic beings, astral beings and others. This is a very important point about the operating paradigm we use, because all those beings are actually involved in the work we're doing. They are supporting us in seen and unseen ways. This is all part of the operating system to understand. We are involved in cosmic and celestial process with many levels of the cosmic creation.

Meditations at Stonehenge[80]
Trudy Guyker
I was excited to go to Stonehenge because it is truly beautiful, and

---

[80] Stonehenge: http://witcombe.sbc.edu/earthmysteries/EMStonehenge.html

the stones are incredible. It is a very small area. We sat down to do a meditation led by Dr. Greer, a beautiful meditation and prayer for the Earth.

Suddenly I started to get depressed. What seemed to be happening to me was that all the centuries of activity that had taken place in that spot was coming out into me. It was horrible, and I experienced the vast amount of pain, suffering and horror that have taken place there. Centuries and centuries of that came up through me, and I almost burst out in tears.

Akashic Record
Dr. Steven Greer
Some archeologists believe that there were human sacrifices made there, just as in ancient Mayan, Aztec and other societies. So the possibility Trudy mentions is quite likely. Such events can be encoded within the structure of space/time and what has been called the white noise of space/time. Within that is recorded everything that has ever happened in any given point in space. That encoding is called the Akashic Record in some traditions.

In 1974 a military witness who works very closely with us learned of a program in which a technology had been developed at the White Oaks Naval Facility[81] in Maryland (now closed). An electronic system enabled extraction from the white noise of space any event that had ever happened. People say it sounds like science fiction, but it is not. The man reporting this has the utmost credibility. And that was thirty-two years ago!

Crop Circle Researchers
Kay Gibson
While working in the crop circles, we met two important English crop circle researchers, Michael Green and David Kingston. Dr. Greer told them that he would be speaking at the Glastonbury Crop Circle Symposium, where they would also be speaking. He also informed them about the upcoming Disclosure event. It was

---

[81] White Oaks Naval facility: http://www.globalsecurity.org/military/facility/white-oak.htm

all quite connected and synchronous.

Inside the crop circle near Avebury Trusloe[82], the magnetic dipole, the heads of the wheat were a golden color. I saw what looked like goldfish jumping in the crop. The tops of the wheat were flickering like flames of energy but weren't moving physically. There was no wind. The next day Trudy reported that she also saw shapes jumping but referred to them as elbow macaroni.

CSETI Training
Crestone, Colorado
July 2000

Linda Willitts
Prior to the Crestone Training we had a meeting at Dr. Greer's house in June about starting Disclosure. We used to see the amber orbs hopping around close to the horizon in Crestone. We saw that for a period of years, and we also saw the amber fuzz balls quite often.

Alleged Clouds

Trudy Guyker
One time we were in the Zapata Falls parking lot waiting for it to get dark. There was a cloud to the east that was shaped like an equilateral triangle. It just stayed there and stayed there, perfectly still, until everyone saw it, and then it was gone.

Dr. Steven Greer
This particular alleged cloud was extremely unusual because it was just hanging there. Other clouds were moving around it and by it. Also, we saw a rectangular cloud toward the sunset. It was a perfect rectangle and did the same thing. It was very unusual and hard to believe that it was a natural cloud formation.

Magnetometers

Debbie Foch
We were out in the Baca, and there was moonlight. We were seeing

---

[82] Avebury Trusloe 2000: http://www.zefdamen.nl/CropCircles/Reconstructions/2000/AveburyTrusloe00/Reconstruction2000AveburyTrusloe.htm

many craft flying to and from the Moon. There was much activity and our three magnetometers were being triggered simultaneously that night.

Ricky Butterfass
I was sitting in a circle when suddenly a colored light showed up on my left thigh. I thought it was pretty strange. During that session someone had a magnetometer in the middle of the circle. What really caught my attention that session was seeing a craft that came in from the southwest. It was about 700 feet AGL (above ground level), and it was going about 350 knots. Suddenly, a light came out of the craft, hit the magnetometer dead on and set it off. The beam of light came down like an arm reaching out and touching the magnetometer. Then it retracted right back up into that craft. It wasn't like a laser that you turn on and off in an instant. The light extended itself, touched the magnetometer on the fly, and then retracted. It was a pretty amazing experience to see that type of light technology.

Appearance by Kindness

Linda Willitts
I only remember one distinct ET event that Dr. Greer, Dr. Loder and I experienced. The very last night of the training, after everyone else had left, we took our chairs to the field adjoining the townhouse where Dr. Greer was staying. As we sat talking, we had a major fly-in by Kindness. There was no doubt it was Kindness. Kindness has a distinctive "comma-shape." No satellites look like that. This was the lowest we had ever seen her.

Dr. Steven Greer
Kindness flew in from the northeast over the Sangre de Cristo Mountains, at low altitude, on the west side of the mountain peaks. As she flew in, her ship came down and an enormous blue-white light came out that shone right towards us. I was facing that direction. The light was bright enough that it fully illuminated the area! We all saw it clearly.

The ship then made a curved turn, made a loop and back up into space. This was Kindness' way of acknowledging the work we are doing. Her appearance came during a period of time when we were putting together and discussing the Disclosure Project witnesses, the filming, and the strategy for the project.

CSETI Training
Mount Shasta, California
September 2000

Debbie Foch
One night we had over an hour of flashing lights toward the east that Al Dunaway video taped. Tiny flashes occurred, like fireflies up in the sky moving along slowly. They were moving toward the north for a long time. The weather was very cold. Suddenly there was a flashing and we were flashing back at it.

Dr. Ted Loder
The flashing lights remained in the same section of the sky while the star field kept its normal motion. It went on for almost an hour.

Dr. Steven Greer
It was like a little strobe light bulb that was going off and was in that area of space for an hour. It was very unusual and definitely not a satellite or aircraft.

Trudy Guyker
At one point there were at least seven of them, and then some would disappear. Frequently three or four would come back.

Tall Beings Seen by Some

Kay Gibson
On September 4th several people reported seeing 6-feet tall beings. Trudy said a tall form passed in front of her quickly and startled her. One night I saw a golden "screen" mesh between me and everything else. I also saw a grid pattern on the ground and three tall beings behind the chair of a trainee who felt "pushed." In meditation, I saw a human-looking man in a white, shimmering, form-fitting suit walk into our circle. He was a scout.

I resonated with Dr. Greer saying that even as things seem hopeless on earth, transformation is ready to emerge and is coming. We are midwives to this transformation, and our consciousness must be transformed. The process only takes a small amount of energy to shift the whole reality. Focusing on this picture keeps you on track with your dharma[83] – path or purpose. I further perceived that the CSETI Disclosure Project is driving the time line and agenda for the whole disclosure event. This was told to Dr. Greer by an MJ-12 insider in England. For me, that message was vitally important.

---

[83] dharma—an Indian spiritual or religious term, that means one's righteous duty, or any virtuous path in the common sense of the term. [http://en.wikipedia.org/wiki/Dharma]

Chapter 9

2001

CSETI Retreat
Joshua Tree, California
April 2001

Dr. Steven Greer
In the spring of 2001, Dr. Loder and I were very busy working on the Disclosure Scientific Briefing Document. Still, I felt guided to come to Joshua Tree for a group retreat a few weeks before the May 9th National Press Club event. In April 2001 we came to Yucca Valley and went into Joshua Tree National Park. We did this primarily to recharge our batteries on a spiritual level, to connect to the ETs for guidance, and to potentiate and protect the upcoming May 9 event.

Pink Alleged Aurora Borealis[84]

Linda Willitts
We took a picture of Kindness, Shari and the mountain in Joshua Tree on April 18th, which was Shari's birthday. In the wee hours of April 18 we saw what looked like an aurora borealis in the northeast area of the sky. It was Shari's color of pink and incredible.

Charlie Balogh
2001 Joshua Tree was my first training. A number of things happened to me. During one of the meditations someone had seen a precise time. We made a note of it. At the break we had taken a walk out the path into an open area. As we came back, that specified time occurred, and Shari's pink aurora borealis-type light started. It looked like it was coming out of the ground. Everyone saw it. It was absolutely beautiful.

---

[84] Aurora Borealis: http://en.wikipedia.org/wiki/Aurora_(astronomy)

Linda Willitts
It is very unlikely for an aurora borealis to occur in southern California. Although it looked like the aurora—an 'alleged' aurora—I think it was an ET expression. The light was a beautiful pink and had very tall white columns in it.

Ricky Butterfass
Just before the magenta-colored aurora borealis emerged, I had meditated about some light work I had done in 1987. At that time I projected a magenta light into the core of the planet. I related to the ETs that the light was there and if they wanted it, I was going to release it to them. Right after that, a huge magenta cloud came in, about ten feet across. The cloud either was an aurora borealis or resembled one. It looked as if four trap doors opened in the ground. When the doors opened, shafts of white light came up into the magenta cloud. I could see a gold glitter. The white light was moving into the magenta cloud, and I could see the scintillating gold from the four trap doors. Suddenly the doors closed, and the cloud dissipated. It was as if a huge ET craft was present and absorbed the light.

Dr. Steven Greer
Yes. It was beautiful. I remember how beautiful that was.

Being Stimulates Radar Detector

Trudy Guyker
I was sitting on the south side with Dr. Greer sitting on the east side. Suddenly I saw a light form 7 to 8 feet tall that looked like a lightning bolt. I estimated it at four inches wide. It was not bright, just a light gray white. The light form appeared toward the center of the group and started moving toward Dr. Greer. It stood in front of him. I said, "Dr. Greer, there's something standing right in front of you." As I spoke, the light being started moving west, away from Dr. Greer to the center of the circle. The being disappeared when it got to the west side. In the time that I watched it, the radar detector had sounded. Kevin had the radar beneath his chair. Just when that light form reached the west side, it went off.

Jan Brook
I can confirm that. I was sitting on the west side of the circle almost directly opposite Dr. Greer. It happened almost exactly when Trudy told Dr. Greer, "There's a being in front of you." The words were hardly out of her mouth when the ET moved and the detector sounded; the sequence was that quick!

Dr. Greer's Vision in the Shaman Cave
Dr. Raven Nabulsi
I had been to a shaman's cave in Joshua Tree a year before this training. I had gone with friends who showed me an initiation cave for shamans, an ancient spot. There were markings in the cave that tracked how many people were initiated as shamans in that place. I felt that Dr. Greer had to go there, that something important was there. I told him about it, and we went as a small group. Dr. Greer received a profound message during the meditation there.

Dr. Steven Greer
I was sitting in the Shaman's Cave for the first time, and we were meditating. The date was three weeks before the Disclosure Project news conference. I received a very clear message as part of the meditation in which I was seeing the Earth transformed, moved into a wonderful future as a result of her transformation.

The phrase I received was: "This vision must guide the world." It was crystal clear. The information in the message explained that the cosmology we teach helps move the world and set the pathway for Earth's future. The detail was breathtaking; it was very clear, very moving.

Within that context I thought, "This is a place where I should bring the whole group" so we returned there. We went into the cave in groups of nine and sat in a meditation to transform the world. Each person was made an ambassador to the universe in the cave. We have done this initiation every year since at Joshua Tree.

A Photo of Kindness' Ship and Shari
As we were leaving I stopped to look at a mountainside, and I

sensed a powerful presence there. I could sense that the ETs, Shari and other beings were present. I honestly did not see anything with the naked eye.

A few minutes later, some group members were walking along the path behind us. They didn't hear me say anything about the presence on the mountain. Deanna took a digital photograph of the beautiful area. When she returned and examined the picture, she found a cobalt blue, plasma craft sitting on the top of the mountain with a wash of peach/pink colored light, which was Shari. Kindness' ship and Shari were present, and it was captured in that photograph (see DVD). It was the first time we had used that initiation cave. I think the photo was an important confirmation that we were being guided and protected there. We were certainly not alone as we sat in the cave!

Linda Willitts
That very day was Shari's birthday, which made the entire experience even more meaningful. She was helping from the other side, as was Kindness. Both were with us.

Jan Brook
Dr. Loder and I had a very profound experience while the other two groups were inside the cave. We were in the first group to be initiated in the cave. While the other groups went in for their initiation ritual, Dr. Loder and I climbed up the mountain and found rocks on which to sit. We ended up exactly opposite each other, framing the cave itself.

During the meditation, Dr. Loder raised his arms, I raised my arms and we could literally feel the energy. I felt like we needed to hold the energy, and we did. We spread our arms out and held the ball of energy in that area during the entire time the other two groups were in the initiation cave. Members of our initiation group, who were down below and didn't know what we were doing, also started doing the energy work that Dr. Loder and I were doing, spontaneously.

Dr. Greer completed the initiation with the final group by playing the singing bowl. As the last note from the bowl dissipated we all stopped our energy work. The energy emanated wherever it needed to go.

Trudy Aided by Shari

Trudy Guyker

One night, on the day the group was going to the Shaman's cave, I had a medical problem and had to find a doctor. My husband and I then went to meet the group in the parking lot. When we arrived we couldn't find the group, only one other group member. The group was not there because they had gone to the Shaman's cave. The three of us stayed there and did our work. During that time a raven kept flying around us. The man we met said that when he had reached the site, he had walked up the path to the east, and the raven stayed just in front of him, keeping him company.

The next night, while packing to go out into the field, I could not find my warm gloves. I looked everywhere in the room, and Fred was helping me. We looked in the car and could not find my gloves. We went to another site, a very isolated site where the wind was blowing fiercely. During a quiet period, I reached down to get something out of my bag, and right on top of the open bag were my gloves! Now I have to say that while we were at the first site, I could feel Shari's presence. In fact, I heard her call my name. My medical problem was that I had an inflamed breast. All night long, she was standing beside me on that side.

I think that when we left the Geology Tour Road site, my gloves fell out of the car. The raven had been there flying around, and it was Shari's totem. Shari was present there and the next night, all night long. She brought those gloves back, and she was with me. She was with me because of her breast cancer, and she was sympathizing with me, although I didn't have cancer.

Dr. Steven Greer

I think Trudy is exactly right. It is interesting because last night as I was getting ready to lie down and read, about 3:00 in the morning, I heard very clearly, "Steven." It was Shari saying, "Steven"— crystal clear.

Dr. Bravo's Interaction with ET Craft

Dr. Jan Bravo

I had several personal, delightful interactions that showed me how we can interact with ET craft. I was shining my green laser light into the sky. Often I look for equilateral triangles and will flash on each point. Eventually I found one such triangle just above us and flashed on each point three times. When I reached the third star at the bottom right, the star flared. I flashed three times again on that star, and it flared up again. I was having so much fun. The experience was very nice, and it was unmistakable. I knew we were interacting. I flashed three more times, it flared up, went out, and then I saw an arc of light. A ship had been in front of that star and had gotten my attention. It was very simple and very sweet.

Jan Brook

I was standing right next to Dr. Bravo and saw every bit of the interaction.

What "ETs" Prefer to be Called

Charlie Balogh

A similar interaction took place later in the week. We were sitting and sharing. It was my first training, and I had many questions. I asked Dr. Greer if he knew what the ETs like to be called. He replied they really do actually like to be called ETs. At that very moment, all the magnetometers went off. I said, "Well then, they do actually like to be called ETs," and again the magnetometers sounded. It was a great interaction.

Underground Craft Sounds

Another incident happened earlier that night at the site when we had just come out of a meditation. We were sharing, and at one point it felt like there was a huge electric generator underneath us making the humming noise. To my knowledge, there are no electric generating stations in that area. I felt it in the ground, like an electrical surge, and then we saw a light fly overhead. Immediately afterwards Dr. Greer pointed out that a craft had flown overhead and made a ninety-degree turn.

Dr. Steven Greer
The light was definitely an ET vehicle that had been underground, and moved out. We were in a very remote area, far from any possibility of a man-made system capable of triggering our magnetometers or making that sound.

Event in Circle During Break
Charlie Balogh
One other incident took place that Jan Brook and I experienced. The group had gone on break. It was really cold and windy. Jan and I had just gotten wrapped up in our sleeping bags and were not about to extricate ourselves just for a break. We sat there, just the two of us. A bright sapphire blue streak went right through the center of the circle. The streak was physical; we both saw it.

Jan Brook
I remember a blue white flashlight bulb that flashed in the center of the circle. I thought Dr. Greer was sitting there, too, forming a three-point CSETI triangle at the time.

Charlie's Experience with the CSETI Tones
Charlie Balogh
In a morning meditation, I saw the CSETI logo and heard the sounds it was making. From that experience I created the CSETI tones we play in the field. When I got home I sat down at my keyboard and tried to recreate what I had heard. If you listen to the tape we made of the sound, especially with headphones, you'll notice that it will pass from left to right because that was exactly what the sound I heard was doing. It was turning counterclockwise as each globe passed in front of my perception.

I heard the sounds and saw the image. The first globe had soft pulses of light, like the zero point field. The second globe had a very bright crystalline structure that was glittery inside. The third one was also crystalline but had tiny crystalline gears moving in all directions. The three connecting tubes had an electric blue light traveling back and forth between three globes.

Dr. Steven Greer
Wow! From that meditation experience, you created the music, the CSETI sounds.

Charlie Balogh
Yes. I remember that I was extremely excited to get to the afternoon session to tell everyone about my experience. I'd like to share another aspect of that entire experience. It was the first time I had spent that much time in meditation. I have meditated off and on over the years, but a great deal of meditation takes place during CSETI expeditions, as any participant well knows. When I returned home, things looked different to me. I walked into the house and things were bright. Everything was more clear and vibrant than I had ever noticed before.

A few days later, I met a friend who was an experienced meditator, and I told him about my experiences. He said, "That's very interesting, because I attended a very intensive meditation training and one of their strict protocols was that the room be kept at the same temperature, the same light level and the same ambience every time they meditated." That was a control. After two or three days of meditating in the same room with all the same factors in place, my friend experienced the room as brighter. His Master explained the room was the same, but he was brighter!
Suddenly, it made sense to me. My perceptions had changed completely. My whole first training was a life-changing event for me.

Washington, D.C.
April 2001
Meeting with Shadowy Figures Near Pentagon

Jan Brook
Two days before we left for the Joshua Tree retreat in April, I had a very clear, lucid dream in which I saw that dark influences would not be allowed to interfere with the Disclosure Project.

Dr. Steven Greer
At that April 2001 Joshua Tree retreat, Jan Brook related the

lucid dream above, and in fact they did not interfere. Jan had her dream about the time that I was in Washington, D.C. meeting with a group of shadowy figures near the Pentagon. There were just three of them present. We were in a conference room where all the walls were glass and video. Other people whom I couldn't see or hear were watching us – that's how it works. At a certain point, one gentleman asked, "Just what do you think you're doing with this?"

I replied, "You know what we're doing." I had a witness with me, and I said, "Know this. If you do not assist us, I understand. But if you threaten or harm one hair on the head of any of these witnesses or anyone associated with this project from this point forward, you will face serious consequences. And that's been authorized and it's in place. Stand down." You could have heard a pin drop in the room. They knew I was not bluffing. It was very clear to me that they understood my message. There are many powers within Majestic who want Disclosure and real change – and they have our backs...

To this day with all the conspiracy mongering and all the rumors on the internet – over 8 years later – not a single one of the people associated with the Disclosure Project has been harmed. I think that is a very good sign, and that we are going to be able to continue to do the CSETI Trainings, the Disclosure Project, the Orion Project and AERO. There will be challenges we know, but what Jan Brook was told in her lucid dream was exactly right.

Neighbor Sees Craft over Greer House
Albemarle County, Virginia
April 2001

Dr. Steven Greer
I want to share a story that occurred in April of 2001, right before the National Press Club conference event. I live on sixty-two acres in Albemarle County, just west of Charlottesville, Virginia. We have a large Georgian Manor house on a knoll. It is not far from Monticello, Thomas Jefferson's home site and location of the

University of Virginia. Our nearest neighbor, the only neighbor we can actually see from our house, lives due west of us. Their parents, Ralph and Betty, come to see the grandkids and stay a few months at a time.

Betty got up about 4:00 A.M. When Betty looked out towards our house she couldn't believe her eyes. She saw a cobalt electric blue craft sitting on our house and partially enveloping it. The craft was disc-shaped, came up into a dome, and was a gorgeous translucent blue color. Ralph and Betty didn't know who I was. They had no idea I was the director of CSETI and the Disclosure Project and they had no interest in those subjects. Betty just looked out – and there it was! Later, when we became better acquainted, she shared the story I'm relating to you now.

Betty perceived the craft to be emanating the most perfect peace and protection. She used those two words, peace and protection, over and over again. The experience was one of unbelievable peace and protection, and she knew the craft was something deeply peaceful protecting whomever lived in that house. Betty said the ship stayed there for as long as she watched it, and then she went back to bed. The description seemed exactly like the photograph of Kindness on the mountain at Joshua Tree, but larger. The craft was not hovering above, but was partially enveloping the house. That was Kindness and her ship, visible to a person who knew nothing of me or CSETI.

Fast forward to the 2001 Christmas party at our neighbor's house where this time their daughter saw the craft. She is a nice woman, but also a direct, no-nonsense, investment banker. She told me "A couple of weeks ago I got up to check on the baby, and I looked out the window. Above your house in the sky there was a lit object. I thought it was a very low helicopter or airplane except it was stationary. Then it started moving up and down, undulating up and down in the space over your house. It was just the most amazing thing I have ever seen."

This is a continuation of the theme of the ETs telling Burl Ives' wife, Dorothy Ives, "We are always with you. You will be protected, and you are never alone." The initial event with the cobalt blue craft was in April 2001, and obviously the ET craft was assigned for peace and protection. That's what the investment banker, our neighbor, felt. She wasn't aware of anything we were doing, but she intuitively knew it.

Library of Congress Visit
Washington, D.C.
May 2001

Linda Willitts
I have something else to add about the day of the National Press Club Conference in Washington, D.C., May 9, 2001. When the event ended, groups of us went to the Congressional buildings. We visited senators and representatives to talk with them about the Disclosure Project, which most of them had actually heard about. Later that afternoon, Bob Salas, one of our witnesses, wanted to go to the Library of Congress to look up the transcripts of a Congressional hearing on UFOs held in 1968. I went with him to the Library, which is similar to a warehouse. We found the Congressional hearings on microfiche, and read that the Congressman from Illinois, Donald Rumsfeld, did indeed introduce the speakers on the UFO subject at the 1968 hearings. The presentation consisted of everyone's experiences with the craft, and the conclusion was that we should look more deeply into the subject. That was 1968. The Disclosure event was the first time since 1968 that someone pressed Congress on the UFO/ET subject. The man was Dr. Greer.

Dr. Steven Greer
Dennis Kucinich was very supportive and interested but, by and large, no one really wanted to deal with the subject of extraterrestrials. Fast forward from April 2001 to the January 2007 meeting with Paul Hellyer, former Canadian Minister of Defense. He told me about meeting with the chairman of a major committee in the Senate of Canada who echoed what the senators and congressmen with whom we met said – that this is too big a thing for them to deal with. The chairman didn't deny that he thought it was real, but he just didn't want to deal with it. This is

why CSETI had to launch the Disclosure Project, and continues with that work. CSETI has done the CE-5 Initiative to establish contact because the governments of the world are 'missing in action.'

Dr. Bill Clendenin
The world governments don't see any political relevancy, I suppose.

Dr. Steven Greer
The leaders actually <u>do</u> see the relevancy. They're just terrified of how big an issue it is – that is my point. It is not that they think it is unreal, trivial, or irrelevant. The problem to them is the global implication of the subject. Laurance Rockefeller said to me that the implications are so vast and so profound that no aspect of life on Earth will be unchanged by disclosure of this information. It is true, and these apparatchiks[85], bureaucrats and politicians, are afraid to take it on. That is, of course, what happened with Bill Clinton after I briefed his team and his CIA Director. Clinton was terrified of the implications of disclosure. He was convinced that if he did what was recommended, which was to issue an Executive Order to look into this subject, that he would end up like Jack Kennedy. Most of these political people do not want to take on something this controversial – or something that would really change the status quo. It has been kept secret not because the issue is silly, but because it's so enormously powerful. The interests that would be affected are so powerful – big oil, energy, orthodox religious beliefs, geo-political power, world banking and financial interests, etc. – that it is easier to just let things stay as they are. Since many congressmen are invested in these aspects of society, they do not want to upset the apple cart.

The day after the Disclosure press conference, one of the witnesses went to the White House as a tourist, and he was wearing his Disclosure Project Witness identification. Andy Card, chief of staff of the President, saw the badge and said, "We've been reading about this in the *Washington Times*. Good luck with what you're

---

[85] apparatchik— a subordinate who is unquestioningly loyal to a powerful political leader or organization
[Taken from the 'Microsoft Word 2004 for Macintosh' Thesaurus]

doing." The witness put the briefing documents that we had been giving members of Congress in the hands of Andy Card and saw him walk back into the White House West Wing with it. This was 2001 when George W. Bush was President.

Arnie Arnesson
A comment: there is an old television commercial from years ago that said something like this, "You can change your oil now, before the transmission goes. You know, pay me now or pay me later." Later has come.

Dr. Steven Greer
Right. Later has arrived.

Norm Fletcher
I work in an operating room. Since the Disclosure event what I have done in my spare time has completely changed. I think it has changed because the CSETI effort is a mission whose time has come. Dr. Greer has greatly affected the lives of many people just by defining the issues that need to be addressed. I have been working on energy matters most of my life. Dr. Greer has initiated the investigations into 'zero point' energies and developed an organization for disclosing the existence of extraterrestrials. It takes many people to change direction. Eventually we'll get the 'powers that be' to help change our government.

Dr. Steven Greer
Yes, if the people lead— the leaders will follow.

Disclosure Press Conference
National Press Club
Washington, D.C.
9 May 2001

Arnie Arnesson
It was mentioned that the first hour of the May 9th conference was being jammed. Did they ever find out what caused the jamming?

Dr. Steven Greer

Yes, it was NSA (National Security Agency). Interestingly, after the initial flurry of activity from the Disclosure Project press event, the President of 'Connect Live' called me into Washington[86]. 'Connect Live' was the contract host for all the web-casting and satellite broadcasting for the National Press Club and at the time it hosted the Pentagon's website web-casting, as well as CNN's.

He said that the first hour of the event was externally jammed by something they had never seen. He reported the number of people wanting to see it live on the internet was the largest up to that time in history. He told me personally that Larry Ellison of Oracle and Bill Gates of Microsoft were watching the event[87,88]. He also said that we used up every available T-1 line in Washington, and that the existing lines were not enough for the demand. The executive then showed me a graph in his conference room showing the most-watched live Pentagon conference and the most-watched CNN event on the internet. Those two events were like half an inch on the chart compared to four inches for our event. He added it was absolutely stunning, and his entire staff was amazed.

We did not have large funding for this endeavor. The funding we did have was thanks to Dr. Jan Bravo and a few other people. We had one 'PR' person, who worked out of her home in Georgetown, and she was all we could afford. I remember our 'PR' expert said, "Let's get the little Holloman Room." I told her we would need the main ballroom of the National Press Club.

She said, "You don't need something this size for what you're doing. The last time they filled the ballroom was when Ronald Reagan was in there." I replied, "Yes, we need this size." They laughed, and said it was ridiculous to expect so many people.

We did get the big room and it turned out there were twenty-two network cameras at the back of the room and the whole place was jammed with media people. The more our event got on line, the more the media were calling their headquarters saying things like

---

86 Connect Live: http://www.connectlive.com/
87 Lawrence Ellison, CEO of Oracle: http://www.oracle.com/corporate/lje_content.html
88 Bill Gates, Microsoft Chairman: http://www.microsoft.com/presspass/exec/billg/default.mspx

"This is the real X-files[89]."

The covert operatives also were calling the networks trying to take us down. It was a battle. It is true that the first hour that was being web-cast was externally jammed. Ultimately it did get up and running and had an enormous audience.

Linda Willitts
I was going in and out of the National Press Club. The people at the front desk asked me, "What is going on in there? We never have this many people attend, and when they do attend, they never stay. They just run in and out. These people are crowding the room."

Dr. Steven Greer
The media and camera people were actually applauding the witnesses when they were making their comments. It was unprecedented – an amazing event.

CSETI Training
Crestone, Colorado
June 2001

Pseudo-Fog

Linda Willitts
Crestone is a dry high-desert climate, yet there was a bank of fog shaped like a very large saucer in the field to the northeast of us. The fog was about four feet above the ground, not on the ground, and you could see underneath it clearly. We recognized it as a craft.

Dr. Steven Greer
Right. This craft appeared as a pseudo-fog. It glowed. When a car came by, the craft would dim down. As we watched it and connected to it, it would start glowing from within. Everyone saw the pale white and sometimes greenish-blue glow that would get bigger and bigger. Even though there was wind, the "fog" did not

89 Wikipedia: http://en.wikipedia.org/wiki/The_X-Files

move. It was hundreds of feet across. When military aircraft flew over, the "fog" would almost instantly dissipate to nothing, and then would reemerge. It wasn't far from us – just a few hundred yards. We watched for almost an hour.

Golden Dome of Protection
Ricky Butterfass
We started out to erect a dome of protection around us. We began with a golden light and passed it around from our heart ckakras. The golden light sped up and turned into a solid ring of light. We just let it rise and form a golden vortex above us. Then we sent it straight out into space to connect with our Sun and the central Sun of the galaxy. We dispersed it into the cosmic consciousness, then brought it down and formed a dome of golden light around us for protection. The dome protects the both ETs and us.

White Eagle Inn Observers Spot the Dome
Debbie Foch
There had been many thunderstorms during the week. One night we had to stay in the cars for a while, and when we finally got out, we did the exercise of putting the dome up.

The cook at the kitchen at the White Eagle Inn and his assistant were out smoking cigarettes late at night. They were looking toward our site out in the Baca. There was a farmhouse located very near our site. Whenever the lightning would flash, the cook and his assistant looked for the farmhouse, but they would see our dome instead. They could see the lights circling around the bottom of the dome as we were in our circle. When we are creating the dome, we send the energy, a golden light, around the circle, and they were amazed to be seeing it.

Dr. Jan Bravo
The next morning the people from our group who were staying at the White Eagle Inn were having breakfasts. They were telling the cook and his assistant about their experience from the previous night. In fact, the two workers came to our group that day and told us what they saw. We then informed them that we had erected a dome. They just thought it was an interesting phenomenon. They

ended up moving away and really didn't understand that we had constructed a dome with circling, golden light. But they told us what they saw. What they saw was exactly what we had erected. In other words, it was a confirmation. The electrical storm magnified the dome for them and helped make it more visible for them.

Dr. Steven Greer
The lightning made the dome more visible by silhouetting it. As the storm moved away, there was a lot of electrical activity. When the lightning flashed, it lit up the entire area near our site. So the two White Eagle workers could see the dome with red and white lights going counterclockwise around the base. Now, as we were sitting in the dome, we felt the temperature go up, and there was a wealth of unusual scintillating light. I pointed out to people that we were in a craft with red and white lights going around counterclockwise. I could see them, and other people saw some aspects of it. But the two workers, who had no idea what we were doing, described exactly what we had seen and felt. I think many people in our group, who were experiencing something like this for the first time, were thinking, "My god, we thought this was imaginary." I think the realization that the event was not imaginary really changed many people's lives.

People realized that we were making contact in an ET craft. It was a craft that was slightly shifted resonantly, and so was not totally materialized. It was present in a very dense way, but not visible. They also realized that we were seeing the lights of the craft going around, and that the ETs were present. They comprehended that we had constructed the dome using our collective powers of consciousness. They now understood that the golden dome of protective energy was visible to people outside the hotel. The event and these distant witnesses represented an extraordinary confirmation.

Ricky Butterfass
What really astounded the cook and his assistant was that the farmhouse disappeared. They could see the dunes in the background but the buildings and the landscape that had been inside the dome had disappeared. When I was inside the dome, I could actually see

the support arcs that made the dome. The arcs went clear across and I could see a number of them radiating out from the center of the dome. I thought it was really unique, and I was fascinated by it.

As I was sitting there looking up, a door opened and we could see golden light come out of the opening. Al Dunaway confirmed it at the time. We could feel that ETs were walking around.

NORAD Responses
Dr. Jan Bravo
I have noticed over the years that whenever a manifestation occurs, often some incident will follow that serves as a confirmation. As Dr. Greer pointed out, we were on the backside of NORAD) and military jets converged at the very place immediately after this anomalous event occurred there. It is a major confirmation.

Ricky Butterfass
Another group of jets will fly over and replace the ones running low on fuel. Then they go back, refuel and continue fly-overs all night long.

Dr. Ted Loder
As we've gone back to Crestone in subsequent years, the story is out, and the people in town know that we are the ones making domes.

Electrical Storm Effect on Sensors
Dr. Steven Greer
There is a motif here: A huge craft comes in after an electrical storm. We have found these enormous electrical storms to cause considerable alteration in the ability of sensors to pick up whether something is ET, electromagnetic energy, or an electrical storm. In that context, the storms cloak the craft and enable many events to take place. We have found that it is often the case that extraordinary encounters and materialized craft are able to come further into linear space/time with the massive electromagnetic discharge from a storm.

Ricky Butterfass

I recall a time when two major electrical storm systems were moving in. One was coming down from the north and the other was coming up from the south. They produced massive amounts of lightning, thunder, and rain. The two storms merged right over us. I thought to myself, "When these two cells merge, all hell's going to break loose." But when they did meet, they just dissipated, evaporated, and the sky cleared. It was one of the most incredible things I'd ever seen. Following the storms we had all types of ET craft going over. It was amazing!

Emerald Column of Light

Dr. Steven Greer

As we drove into the San Luis Valley from the north, we came over a pass and into an enormous valley visible from space. In the distance we could see Blanca Peak with the Great Sand Dunes at the base. Everyone in my vehicle saw an emerald green column of light coming up from the Great Sand Dunes. It shot up to the sky as far as you could see, in broad daylight. We knew that it was going to be an "amazing encounter". It was spectacular, and the weather was crystal clear without any rainbows. It was a beautiful emerald green, translucent column going straight up into the blue sky.

Anti-gravity Effects

Linda Willitts

We enjoy doing our fieldwork in the rain. One of the things we do is sit in our cars and meditate. We have walkie-talkies so we can communicate between cars.

Once, while working from our cars, Dr. Greer imaged an anti-gravity device consisting of counter-rotating magnetic fields. He did the imaging in his mind during one of our meditations. As a result, he moved our car while we were sitting in it, and he moved the car next to us also!

Dr. Steven Greer

I will expand on the incident Linda was describing. By now you understand that we've spent thousands of hours doing this work. At this event, after some time in deep meditation in the car, I decided to practice a technique that I had discovered. From deep quiet awareness, I visualized two energetic discs, one rotating clockwise, and the other counter-clockwise, slightly separated spatially. I empowered these energetic discs from a deep, unbounded state of consciousness with enormous mental focus and intent, while the mind and body are very energized and yet calm.

With a counter-rotating field, a magnetic flux is created in consciousness. I did not move my body at all, but the whole vehicle lifted up and hopped. The vehicle next to us did the same. It was embarrassing for me because I was really just playing around. Of course, it is exactly the technology of the ARVs and ET craft. In the interior of the ARVs there are counter-rotating magnetic flux fields and there are coils. Over the last few thousand years there are accounts of people who have had these sorts of experiences of lifting up or levitating in a consciousness state. There are techniques, Siddhis, used to do this[90]. It was a very interesting experiment. It was also a bit disconcerting, because I remember people saying, "What was that?"

But I explained it, and people thought it was fascinating. I said, "Well, you can do all kinds of things if you put your mind to it!"

Jan Brook
I did not realize Dr. Greer was performing the technique he discovered. For some reason, when our car hopped like that next to his car, I said, "Steve, what are you doing?"

Alleged Star

Alice Sleight
When we were in the area of the Stupa[91], I stepped away from the group for a moment. The moon was shining and it was almost full. I looked up and there was a huge light, one-third the size of the Moon, just hanging *there*. It was an orb that suddenly appeared. I yelled to everyone to look at the moon, so I know a lot of people saw it. It was there for quite a long time. Then it quickly became

---
[90] Wikipedia: http://en.wikipedia.org/wiki/Siddhi
[91] Wikipedia: http://en.wikipedia.org/wiki/Stupa

just a tiny star. It was still there, and it was there all evening. It didn't move like the other stars did, but stayed right next to the moon.

Chapter 10

2002

CSETI Training
Crestone, Colorado
June 2002

Charlie's Remote View of Zen Dome
Charlie Balogh
The 2002 training was my first visit to Crestone. About six weeks before we went to Crestone, I decided to remote view the area because I had never been there. I wanted to see if I could get a mental picture of what the area was like. During meditation, I found myself floating over a dome structure with a little ring of windows on its top. I floated around the front, went in through the entrance and immediately noticed many multi-colored tiles on the floor. As I looked up at the interior of the dome I saw it had a latticework construction. I could tell it was an all-wood structure. Something that looked like two chunks of wood in a V-formation was on a pedestal in the center of the dome. It appeared to be sitting in a pool of blue, purplish water. It was a lucid remote view, and I could see everything in colors. I could tell the outside had a greenish blue color to it.

I emailed Debbie about my remote viewing experience. She just about fainted when she heard the story. I related what I had seen in my remote view.

Debbie Foch
It is true that I nearly fainted when Charlie told me his remote view, but I did not want to say too much to him about what was there in Crestone.

Charlie Balogh
I got to the Crestone training, but did not know that we would go to a Zen Buddhist retreat for many of the sessions during the course of

the week. At the Buddhist retreat is a wonderful meditation dome about sixty feet across in the center. I had a feeling up the back of my spine, and I said, "This is it." It was exactly what I had seen. It was blue-green on the outside. I could see the windows around the top, for venting and to let light in. I walked inside and there on the floor were multi-colored tiles in a pattern spiraling out from the center. The interior of the dome was latticework wood with huge arches. Debbie told me that normally there is nothing in the center of the room except for a large stone. But they had had some sort of a ceremony in the center of the room and a set of elk antlers was sitting in the center with a purple-blue scarf. The realization of what I had seen just hit me like a brick. I broke down into tears; it was such a powerful experience. Not only had I remote viewed the dome, but I did it at the correct point in time, because the antlers are not always there. It was a transformative experience for me.

Meditations at the Zen Dome
Dr. Steven Greer
These techniques and protocols really do work for consciousness development and remote sensing. It is interesting that of all the places Charlie could key in on, it would be the Zen Dome. We go there every year, and we do a deep group meditation together. I do a speaking meditation of what I'm experiencing as I share the unfolding of the cosmology. It takes forty-five minutes to an hour, and it is where there have been an enormous number of peak experiences for our groups.

Guided Meditations
Linda Willitts
Dr. Greer does the most beautiful meditations. One year in Stonehenge, after a meditation, I asked him, "Can you meditate while you are thinking of all those beautiful words to say to us?" He answered, "Oh, yes, I'm describing what I am seeing." It's awesome.

Dr. Steven Greer
I actually describe what I experience from a level of cosmic awareness, so it is a simultaneous process. You have to first go into the experience deeply enough to know and understand what it

is – and then have the language to articulate it. Once that happens it's very powerful. I think this is a gift given to me at the time of my near death experience in 1973...

A Column of Light
Charlie Balogh
I do not recall what happened earlier that week because I was having problems seeing anything except for the Zen dome experience. I was getting a bit frustrated. Toward the end of the week we were sitting in our circle, and Dr. Greer was sitting on the side looking toward the mountains facing east while I was facing west. At one point he yelled out, "Oh, my God, did everybody see that?" He described a vertical wide column of light that had appeared on one end of the ridge. The column moved horizontally across the ridge and shortly afterward, military jets flew in right over that spot. As the jets passed over the mountain ridge, everyone was focused on the area, and we saw the light again. However, this time it was horizontal. It was visible to everybody.

Lucid Dreaming and Its Powers
Dr. Steven Greer
At Blanca Peak there was a gentleman who seemed to always be looking in the wrong direction when an event would unfold. He was missing most of the sightings and was frustrated, which he had voiced. We were sitting in meditation on the last night, and afterward he shared something that was quite remarkable. In the meditation a fog lifted. He recalled a lucid dream that he had many years ago, in which he was on an extraterrestrial spacecraft with ETs and me. It was before he had ever heard of what we were doing or had ever met me. He realized that it was not just a "dream," but rather that he had actually been there.

Many people have had that experience. You have to understand the nature of the dream state, the lucid dream, where you are awake in the dream. These types of experiences are crystal clear, and in full, living color. In that state, you are experiencing a real state of mind, as well as a place. You can go to places, and people have precognitive dreams by doing so. What the man was actually experiencing was that his astral body of light was on an extraterrestrial spacecraft where we were all learning and sharing together in the Cosmic School. He realized that it was real because he remembered it, complete with me and the other people. It was an amazing experience for him and also for the whole group because it showed what the possibilities are in consciousness. Many times when we go to sleep, with intention we can remember such experiences, learn and actually do specific things in the dream state just as we do in the physical body.

Dream State and the After-Life State
David Alfassi
Is there a difference between the dream state and the after-life state?

Dr. Steven Greer
It depends on the state of consciousness of the person having the dream. These two states can be the same and certainly the lucid dream and flying dream gives us a hint of what is to come. The lucid dream is essentially the astral body experiencing and traveling. I relate a story in my last book, *Hidden Truth – Forbidden Knowledge*, where I had an experience of flying along the coast of Costa Rica in a super-lucid dream. It was beautiful, and my wife woke up just as I was leaving my body. She saw a silvery gray form sit up and fly out the window. She thought I had passed away and she was thinking, "Oh, my God, I have four kids, and here I am stuck down in Costa Rica with a dead man!"

I was having one of many very lucid, awake dreams. I had a beautiful experience of seeing the Earth in astral/celestial perception: you see the light shining from within all things. The water was a gorgeous aquamarine and deep blue, the forest was emerald green, and the light was a beautiful celestial light. When it was over, and I was back in my body, I felt as if I was being watched. I looked over and saw Emily; her eyes were enormous and she said, "You're back."

I said, "Back? Where have I gone? I haven't gone anywhere." She replied, "You did! I saw you leave!"

That is when I realized that in many lucid flying dreams, we are actually traveling and can visit places and people. You can do it intentionally, even without sensing the separation of the astral body, by going into a deep state of consciousness. The universe really is folded within you for the entirety of the cosmos is folded within the structure of mind. We all have our own minds and are awake. You can become super awake and see anything or anyplace you intend...

CSETI Expedition to Mount Adams
Trout Lake, Washington
September 2002

Mount Adams Events

Dr. Steven Greer
Similar to Mount Shasta, Mount Adams is a mountain in the Pacific volcanic range. Numerous lit objects came off the mountain and signaled with us. They interacted for extended periods of time and we also had a very profound sighting of Kindness' ship. Her bright ship flew in over the mountain and was seen by virtually everyone.

Dr. Ted Loder
The first night, we saw lights on the mountain that were coalescing, and then separating. These were not flashes that disappeared quickly. They were there for an hour. The lights were blooming all over the mountain at about 12,000 feet or higher. They were far above the tree line, and above anything on the mountain. It was then that I decided I needed a telescope, because with binoculars all I could see were little lights, which was very frustrating. We saw triangles a couple of nights. They were not similar to the Shasta triangle but a set of triangular lights flew over.

Linda Willitts
The lights that we saw flashing on the mountain were quite significant. The mountain was twelve miles away from us. At that distance we have determined that we could not have seen even one of those million-candle-power flash lights which have a beam six to eight inches in diameter. The lights also appeared on the

rocky face of the mountain. Absolutely no person could have been traveling along the mountain face with an enormous spot light. The lights were interacting with Dr. Greer for about a half hour while he was flashing his laser. He would flash the laser at them, and they would flash back. It was totally interactive, and it was amazing. It was the same kind of thing that we saw on Mt. Shasta and it was thrilling. The triangles in the sky were about half an inch apart, not nearly the size of the big triangles we saw at Shasta and New York.

These triangles at Mt. Adams did not move with the same majesty. They were nothing like the huge triangular craft. When Kindness came, I captured her spacecraft on film just because I already had the camera aimed at that part of the sky.

Dr. Ted Loder
During one of our breaks, Trudy and I went out to the east side of the field, because we thought there was something out in the field. We stood and watched for awhile. Then we recalled that Dr. Greer often says we can see more with our eyes closed than with our eyes open. So we decided to close our eyes, and we could actually see a glowing object in the field.

ET Craft in Field

The second incident occurred a night or two later. It involved many ETs on the ground, as well as many higher evolved spiritual beings. Dr. Greer had gone forward, and he seemed to fade in and out. Everyone was standing quietly watching and wondering what was happening because he seemed to be disappearing. I closed my eyes and saw a very bright glowing light. I saw silhouetted beings that I surmise were ETs.

Debbie Foch
Yes. We actually saw the object land in the field. The object appeared as an amber light to the left of Mt. Adams, but then it landed in the field, which is why Dr. Greer went to it.

Interaction of Consciousness and Magnetic Flux Field
Dr. Steven Greer
We saw the craft fly in and land in the field, lighting it up. I went

over, and many ETs were present. I walked into the ship, and some people saw me dematerialize enough that, amazingly, they could see right through me. When consciousness and the magnetic flux field interact on these extraterrestrial craft, both the craft and all the beings in it shift to a resonant frequency beyond the speed of light. I have told people you can sometimes see more with your eyes closed than open because instead of using your physical eyes, you sense and see with your mind and your astral vision. We have our own astral infrared camera in our mind with which we can see. It is a profound capability anyone can develop. With the naked eye, there may be just certain aspects of your astral vision that will confirm it to you.

Charlie Balogh
Is that the third eye?

Dr. Steven Greer
Inner sight has been called the third eye in the mystic tradition. It involves seeing with astral vision combined with intention. You can open your eyes and see nothing then close your eyes and sometimes see something very clearly. You wonder if you are imagining what you see. Just ask for some kind of confirmation and accept it when it comes. People do not trust themselves enough. I think many people have the ability, and they shut it down. They neutralize their ability. CSETI training helps people develop this capacity. It is an innate capacity of every human being and opens us to new worlds and new information.

Small Floating Orbs
Trudy Guyker
I saw orbs floating all around the craft. Hundreds of them were just floating around. I didn't see them with my physical eyes open, but they were there in my inner vision.

Ricky Butterfass
I have a digital camera, and I took a flash of the orbs that Trudy saw. I took a picture of her with the orbs. One picture shows an orb on every chakra on her body. They start on her crown chakra and go right down her spine, following the Kundalini[92]. I have the

picture at home. I took photographs of other orbs also.

Ping-Pong Satellites

There were some other interesting sightings too. We saw multiple lit objects flying over. We would signal to some, and they would signal back. On one occasion, I saw two objects that came in one behind the other. When they hit the Zenith, they dropped down out of orbit. They came straight down to about 500 feet above us, and then bounced just like a ping-pong ball hitting a table. The first one came straight down, did one bounce and went back into orbit. Then the second one came right behind it, bounced once, and went back into orbit.

Appearance of Kindness' Craft

Ricky Butterfass

Kindness' craft also came down. Her craft stopped about 500 feet above us, then went right back up into orbit. It all happened within a matter of three seconds. It is an indication of the performance capacity ET craft have.

Another time we were doing CTS (Coherent Thought Sequencing), and an object came in. Dr. Bravo also saw it, took her laser out, and sent a flash back just in front of it.

Dr. Jan Bravo

The event Ricky described occurred during a meditation. Often I have my eyes open, and I love it because I'm scanning the sky. I'm just looking while Dr. Greer is saying beautiful words in the meditation. Ricky and I were sitting next to each other. Straight ahead of us at about thirty-five degrees above the horizon, I saw a brilliant flash bulb in the sky. Ricky pointed it out, so we both saw it. I took my laser and flashed three times. The mountain was to our right. We saw a flash bulb to the right of where I flashed, so I flashed to the right of it three times. The object flashed again. We did that about five or six times as a game before it stopped. It was extremely interactive and a wonderful experience!

[92] Wikipedia: http://en.wikipedia.org/wiki/Kundalini

Ricky Butterfass
I saw the craft come in as one solid light over the trees, and it was right behind Dr. Greer. Dr. Bravo used her laser to lead it a bit by flashing three times in front of it. The craft would move to the right of where she flashed the laser, and then it would signal her three times. Then she'd flash the laser in front of it again, and it would flash back three times. I was hoping she would flash her laser three times on the ground so it would land, but the craft flew out of sight.

Q&A on Orbs

Terry Underwood
Besides a craft, what else might an 'orb' be?

Dr. Steven Greer
An orb could be several things. The orbs we have seen float through the group can be an entire spacecraft manifesting, but the orb represents only a portion of the spacecraft we are seeing in linear time/space. An orb could also be an extraterrestrial probe or it could be an actual extraterrestrial being. For example, in England one specific orb came out of space over the trees, flew right into my bay window, went over by the fireplace and elongated. It was an extraterrestrial life form, very much ET, shimmering and communicating with us. Our task is to determine the nature of each orb we encounter. Is it a craft? Is it a probe assessing us? Is it an extraterrestrial conscious representation that is under intelligent control? Is it an intelligent being itself? It can be any of these. It may also be a spirit being, not ET.

Development of deep consciousness helps you discern what an orb is, so you can discern what is within what your physical eye perceives. For example, your physical eye may only see a blue ball of light, but your inner vision may show you what it is. Of course, you can also ask the orb to do something to show you what it is. In the case of the ball of light that flew through the window in England, it clearly became a shimmering humanoid form. I previously mentioned the famous case in Belgium where the gendarme in town saw an enormous triangular ship 800 feet on each side. The ship collapsed instantly into an orb – a ball of light

– that was a pulsing reddish-orange light. It hovered for a second, and then shot straight up into space, and vanished.

Chapter 11

2003

CSETI Training
Joshua Tree, California
February 2003

Linda Willitts
During the 2003 Joshua Tree training it rained most of the week. Dr. Greer had the experience with the Godhead and the God-consciousness. We spent one night at Alice's house, and Kindness came to the corner of Alice's living room.

Dr. Ted Loder
Yes, I saw Kindness. While I was sitting next to Dr. Greer I said, "Is that a craft up in the corner – the blue sort of area?" He nodded affirmatively. It was wonderful.

ET Craft as Orb in Living Room
Dr. Steven Greer
Alice's home has a big living room. We were in group meditation and discussions when I saw an orb – an area of scintillating light – fly in. The orb took up position near the ceiling in one of the corners of the living room. I do not know how many people saw this orb, but it was absolutely visible with the naked eye. We were seeing a scintillating, bluish-white orb. It was an extraterrestrial vehicle with Kindness in it. There were probably thirty people in the room. Many of them saw it, and it was beautiful.

ET Communication Device
Dr. Warren Wittekind
One night at Hidden Valley people saw two extraterrestrials standing next to Dr. Greer and one standing behind each of us. The next day a box appeared in the center of our circle. It was some kind of universal translator. The scenario involved a craft that came up underneath us, bringing its deck up to the level of the ground. One person said the ETs were probing us as to our capacities.

Dr. Steven Greer
Warren is right. In the center of the group you could see the object. It was a communications device.

Dr. Warren Wittekind
Tuesday night as it rained we were all in our cars. We got called together for a description of two beings, one of which touched Dr. Greer's hand. They were with an ascended master who had lived in the 1800s.

Linda Willitts
The night it rained Dr. Greer, Dr. Bravo and I were standing under some rocks that were protecting us from the rain. We continued our meditation silently in the truck, where Dr. Greer had an experience that he related once we were back in the circle. His entire body was vibrating as if he was being electrocuted. We were holding hands with my hand resting against his leg, and it was vibrating strongly. Raven was on the other side of him and had the same experience.

Meeting with Ascended Masters
Linda Willitts
Dr. Greer could barely talk as he tried to relate his experience. He had gone out into space to the Godhead. There he met the two Ascended Masters from his near-death experience. One Master actually touched him. An enormous, holy being touched Dr. Greer in the center of his left palm. Dr. Greer said his body could not have physiologically withstood that energy if he had not been so physically fit. Some people have actually died from such an experience. He saw that these beings were us in the far future. Dr. Greer saw that eventually all of humanity on Earth is going to be in God-consciousness. He said we would have the ability to materialize and to become light beings. He said we are like drops of water merging back into the ocean. We can reemerge from the ocean as drops of water and so on, infinitely. Many ET civilizations exist in this state now. Eventually all of humanity will be in the state of God-consciousness.

Levels of Consciousness
Dr. Steven Greer

There are extraterrestrial civilizations with which we are in contact that have already attained a level of God-consciousness evolution. These people have physical bodies, physical craft, and a physical world, and yet they are in a state of God-consciousness. Even the manifestations of their technologies are celestial; the light is celestial. They are empowered with consciousness at the level of the Most Great Light of the Center of the Universe.

The experience I had that night remains very difficult to explain. It was a soul-shaking experience. The levels of consciousness we typically conceptualize include the waking state, the dream or sleeping state, cosmic awareness, cosmic consciousness, God-consciousness and unity consciousness. I moved into the next level, called "Brahman consciousness" in the Vedic tradition[93].

Bridge to the Future

My physical body became an electromagnetic recipient. The Master was a humanoid-looking being, but it was not an extraterrestrial or a human. The Master was an expression of the Godhead— – amazing, powerful, enormous. He put his finger in my palm, and my whole body became a circuit. My other hand was pouring all that energy into the Earth and through humanity. It was like forming a positive and negative pole, but it also formed a bridge across time.

What I was being shown was present-day humanity and the Earth now being carried forward with Earth as a spaceship and with human life evolving in the future to that level where everyone on the planet would be in God-consciousness. The Earth itself would be a God-conscious place. I do not mean a religious awareness of God per se. I mean a place in the state of the Godhead, at that level of enlightenment and high state of consciousness. With the connection made and flowing through me, I became a bridge from now to the end of a cycle about 500,000 years from now. All of that was flowing through me.

---

[93] http://www.atmavedi.org/Public/BrahmanConsciousness/index.cfm?requesttimeout=100

I thought I was going to vaporize and disappear. Such a powerful experience left me unable to speak very well. I have heard of other people in the past having similar experiences. My near-death experience was like that, but I didn't have to worry about my body then. The experience had an amazing effect on me physically as well. I realized the reason I was in Hidden Valley in the rain was for this experience to happen. A circuit was created that was conscious and spanned half a million years of time. This circuit was both spiritual and physical. Since our bodies are of the Earth, we are wired into the Earth and her bioelectric magnetic field. I was simply a step-down transformer through time, space and matter. What was shown to me and what I experienced is much more than I have ever discussed. We discussed some of it on the way back down to the valley, but some of it I did not want discussed, even after I pass away.

A Change in Cycles

Dr. Steven Greer

We are in a completely different cycle now, so sitting in a cave to experience these things alone does not help. Being in the world does help. My whole life I have felt that we are in the closure of one Earth cycle and another cycle is opening. Indeed, we are the bridge generations, with one foot in the previous era and the other in the new era.

I left Joshua Tree in a state of enormous excitement and joy.

Vision for Meditation Training

In these retreats, I teach meditation and remote viewing techniques. We schedule extensive time for people to be in their rooms to meditate. After I had the near-death experience as a young man, I wanted to expand my capabilities. I wanted to be able to be in a meditative state and understand it while living in the world in my body. I found that I needed prolonged and intensive experience in meditation and spent six to eight hours a day in that meditative state for months. That experience has informed everything I have done since. We are not oriented in our society to retreat and take time to meditate, but it is very important to do so.

Newcomer Perspective

Greg Heller

I had just joined CSETI, and it was the second night in Joshua Tree. It was raining, thirty degrees; the wind was blowing; it was miserable. The group had split up and was hard to get back together. We were all trying to stay warm and dry. When I went back to the circle, a woman from Aspen told me she had just remote viewed the strangest spacecraft shaped like a golden golf key.

Dr. Greer was out of his car and trying to form the circle. He is a powerfully built individual and a very capable speaker. However, at that time he was shaking, barely able to stand, and barely able to speak. When the group did not convene he waited patiently, returning to the car when he couldn't continue to stand. He kept saying, "This is meant for everyone," and would not speak until the whole group was there. Dr. Greer looked as if he had been electrocuted!

As he began to talk about his experience – the past, present and future he saw – a counterclockwise vortex of golden light started lighting up around the circle. Not only did it go around the circle, but the light was also emerging from people's heads. I could sense the light forming a golden vortex going straight up and encircling the globe. It was so bright that it lit up the entire area. It had a permanent effect on me and when I left the training, I made a promise to commit myself to service to CSETI for rest of my life. I have never experienced anything so powerful before. The truth of it was revealed to me about three weeks later. We can talk about that some other time.

Energy Transfer

Kay Gibson

Dr. Greer wanted to pass the energy in a circle, so he was trying to get us back together. I was one of the sheep that was out in a valley up and over the hills. There were several of us. There was a big fog bowl that I went to explore. It was probably a craft. We kept approaching it, but it kept moving away. We kept getting closer but we never did get to it. It was very strange. We finally came back, and Dr. Greer had us sit in a circle. We held hands and Dr.

Contact: Countdown to Transformation

Greer passed that knowledge, information and energy to us.

Dr. Steven Greer
I was still in that state, connected to that state of God-consciousness. I wanted the energy of that state to go through everyone there and into the Earth and into space. What Greg saw was correct. When I was in the vehicle with this event happening I knew that I was supposed to be simply a vehicle for the energy of that experience. That is why I wanted everyone to be there.

Greg Heller
What happened to Dr. Greer amazed me. There was so much depth in it, in the touching and in the energy, that it can't be communicated in words.

It was the first time for me at the site. We had gone to the parking lot at Hidden Valley. It was not yet completely dark yet, but the rocks were flashing light and I was wondering if Dr. Greer was flashing his laser. We went into our meditation and within moments an orange orb appeared right in front of my foot. That is how it started. I was communing with it and knew it was alive, but I did not know what it was. Five minutes later Dr Greer, who didn't know me at the time, said "There's an ET at your foot."

ET Asks for Permission to Scan

I was trying not to break out of meditation, but finally I opened my eyes, and Dr. Greer had shined his laser right where the ET was. I couldn't tell that it was an ET at that point. As time went on, my vision improved until I clearly saw two humanoid ETs. One ET had a device with which he was taking readings. There was another ET at a control panel with his hands on it. He never lifted his head and was absolutely tuned to making sure that the ship stayed perfectly around us. The ET who went around the group spent three to five minutes with each of us, and there were at least thirty-three of us. On the second pass, which was probably an hour, he said subliminally, but very clearly and politely, "I'd like to scan you; is it OK?"

I looked at him and this time I was able to see him clearly. He was still orange, but I could see his clothing. I said to him, "Go for it. Yes, you have my permission. I have no more to hide than any other human. You can see it all." I felt the scan, which was a nice feeling. He continued around the group again. The next time he came to me, he did something with the device. I saw everyone in the group turn into a fountain with light shooting out of their heads. Then there was literally a fountain around them. I'd never seen anything like it in my life. I was opening my eyes, closing my eyes, and I could not believe what I was seeing.

I was so amazed that I walked out into the dark desert. In front of me, having the same color as the spacecraft, a rosebud appeared. It blossomed before my eyes. Actually it scared me a little, and I wondered what I was doing in the desert in the middle of the night. I came back in and told Dr. Greer. He said the ET had followed me into the desert. I will never forget the event as my initiation.

Dr. Steven Greer
This particular avatar that has a connection with the Godhead has as his favorite essence, the oil, the essence of red roses, which we've often smelled during these experiences...

Sombrero-shaped Craft
Ricky Butterfass
I did remote view a large disc, a sombrero-shaped craft. There was about an acre of land in front of a parking lot and a large sombrero-shaped craft came over. It parked about thirty feet above us.

Dr. Steven Greer
That sombrero craft is the one I saw in Wilcox in 2000. It was exactly that shape, and it was filled with God-consciousness people. It would be there and then phase to become one with the most great light of the Godhead. Then it would reconstitute from the Unbounded and be visible again. Eventually, humans will evolve to be able to the same. We are both the Unbounded Being and our individuality. It becomes such a perfect state of oneness that you can phase in and out from the Unbounded Being back to relative existence...

Kay Gibson

I saw the sombrero craft with my physical eyes. It was frosty white, unlike the clear light that I usually see. I have never seen that shape before nor seen that quality of light. It came rather slowly and passed behind boulders. Then it reappeared and came around our way. That craft was one of the most amazing things. I still have a picture of it imprinted in my mind.

Dr. Steven Greer

You should draw it. It is a celestial light.

Kay Gibson

The quality of light would be difficult to show!

Probe of Capacities

Dr. Warren Wittekind

Three weeks before I came to Joshua Tree in 2003, I was in my bedroom. I looked up at the ceiling, and I was suddenly out on a CSETI expedition. I looked "up" in the "sky" and there was the Earth; I could see it very clearly. I could see the North American continent, the South American continent, the Atlantic and Pacific Oceans – the whole Earth! Then the Earth melted into a swirl like a whirlpool and disappeared into a point of light, and there was a smaller one off to the side. I thought we were being probed for our capacities and abilities, and we are going to have to develop them – that was the whole point.

I went to Joshua Tree and, as situations played out over the week, I could see very clearly that we were being probed as to our capacities. I felt that the lucid dream I had three weeks previously had, in essence, played out.

Chapter 12

2004

CSETI Training
Crestone, Colorado
June 2004

Shari's Tree
Linda Willitts
Every year we go to Crestone, Dr. Greer and those of us who knew Shari go out to Shari's tree. Her ashes are scattered around the base of her tree on property that Dr. Greer owns. We often take pictures in that area. Debbie took a photo of some of us standing around Shari's tree, and Shari's pink mist is in the photo.

Dr. Steven Greer
We have had it happen several times. Shari's tree is a beautifully shaped cedar on the land that we own along Magic Creek. The locals call the stream Magic Creek because it passes by the Tibetan Stupa the Dalai Lama asked Ambassador Jim George to build in Crestone. When Shari passed away, we went there after her service. We took part of her ashes and put them in a circle around the cedar tree. Every year we go there to remember her and say a prayer. More than once someone has taken a picture of us gathered at Shari's tree, showing an amorphous wash of peach, coral-pink, and salmon colored light around or between us. That wash of colors is Shari's astral essence.

Rose Fragrance on Mount Blanca
Charlie Balogh
At the contact site I saw Dr. Greer phasing in and out. As we walked back down, several other people and I smelled the distinct fragrance of rose. Here we were on top of Blanca, which is nothing but scrub brush and pine, and we were smelling roses! That was an extraordinary experience.

Ant or Termite-like ETs

Ricky Butterfass

The first night, I contacted a new group of ETs that looked like ant people. When I saw them more closely I could tell they could have evolved from a termite. They were white and had a head. They looked like a character on Stargate[94].

I recall that when I contacted them, I asked if they would help us with some of the new technology – with the new technologies on which we are working. I also asked for support when we started other contacts. They said they would give us support for the new energy devices. They added that if the ones we were working on did not work, they would support us later on. I asked them if they would come closer, and they said no. They had heard of us and when I made contact, they came in. But when I asked them to come closer, they could not because their home planet directed them only to observe. I asked them to make their presence known to us on the ground and they said they would. I asked the beings to track in behind the iridium satellite and to do a flare up right behind it. They did. That was my confirmation that we were actually in contact with these beings.

Jan Brook

I had a profound experience at the contact site at dusk. I went up and did a little meditation by myself in the center of the contact site. I actually connected with one of these ant people that Ricky described. I did not know he had contacted them at that time. I thought to myself, "This is an ant person; this is new." I opened my eyes just in time to see three black chevrons come up from the trees to the west of me and fly overhead. Right after that, it was as if the entire clearing shifted slightly counterclockwise. I sensed that the trees were closing a door and I had better come down because I was beginning to get disoriented. I came back to the site. Lisa said that she saw a vortex or portal, open up where I had been. That was a confirmation for me. It was also confirmation for Lisa.

---

[94] Wikipedia: http://en.wikipedia.org/wiki/Stargate_SG-1

Precognitive Remote View of Craft in Front of Moon
Ricky Butterfass
I remote viewed the moon. It was crescent shaped at the time and I saw that three ET craft were going to bisect it right at the terminator. About three days later, they did exactly that. I was amazed because they gave me the memory of the encounter before it happened. It was as if they downloaded the whole video scenario in my head. I described it as a sliver of the Moon and three craft flew across the Moon in succession. They bisected right through the moon's terminator, just as in my remote viewing. I was blown away!

Fred Guyker' "Sees" an ET Craft
Trudy Guyker
That was the year when my husband Fred saw the craft. That was the beginning of a remarkable event for me. We were up at the contact site. Fred and I were walking around together. He stopped and said he saw a craft. It was twenty feet away. I saw something but it was not very clear to me. Fred was using his inner vision to see it. He was moving his head like a spotlight. He had to move his head like that because he could not move his eyes to see the craft. I got Dr. Greer to come over and he confirmed a large craft by outlining it with his laser.

Debbie Foch
Fred said when he put his attention on the craft it brightened up. Also, when we all put our attention on the craft it was brightening up.

Dr. Steven Greer
From Fred's viewpoint, as he looked at the craft and as he placed his awareness on it, the craft became very clear. This is the Siddhi that I have been talking about. He could absolutely see the shape of an extraterrestrial vehicle there, not very far away down the road.

Linda Willitts
I was standing next to Fred as he was standing next to that craft and it began lighting up. I could see the beam coming from Fred's focus. Fred could light it up.

Dr. Steven Greer
I could see it, too. It was a real and an amazing ability that manifested through Fred.

Trudy Guyker
Fred says that it was not his eyes, but rather some sense beyond that.

Dr. Steven Greer
Yes, it was the stream of consciousness plus the intention coming from Fred's mind in a directed way. It is a real Siddhi. It is like a laser, coherent light that we use to vector ETs and use with CTS (Coherent Thought Sequencing). Extraterrestrial vehicles in deep space see CTS as strongly as if we were sending up a trillion candle power light or a mega laser into space. With their sensing systems, their reconnaissance and their imaging systems, they see that kind of coherent conscious light, and it is physical as well as consciousness.

ET Thanks Trudy and Group for Feelings of "Joy"

Trudy Guyker
During a meditation before the event started, I couldn't even get out into space because I was overcome with an incredible sense of joy. I felt like I was going to burst. I told everyone about my feelings of joy, and then we went to see the craft. Jan Brook told me a person had come out of the craft and was walking toward me, but I could not see anything. I could sense someone standing there, but not see anyone. I put my hands out because an extremely sensitive, wonderful lady behind the crowd told me the person wanted to give me something. Still I did not see the being, but I did sense it. When I extended my hands to the being, it came halfway into me, paused, and then continued on through me. It was thanking me for the incredible joy and returning its joy to me. It was returning the feeling of joy, and went to every single person in the group.

Jan Brook
During Trudy's encounter the clouds north of us spelled out the word "joy."

Debbie Foch
Yes, I do remember that.

Ricky Butterfass
Yes, I remember that, too.

Celebration of Astral Blueprint of Future
Trudy Guyker
After the "joy clouds", we went up to the contact site on Mount Blanca, and I saw a large room filled with ETs and celestial beings. Dr. Greer entered the room and carried on his diplomatic work, moving around and talking to different groups. I saw a group of celestial beings there, and I was dancing with one of the beings. The feeling of the gathering was pure celebration and created great joyfulness.

We learned that it was the celebration of the current cycle coming to an end. Everything that we were working for in the CSETI project, contact and being ambassadors and becoming knowledgeable with the ETs, was coming to an end. It had already happened in the energetic realm and would soon be happening in the material. It had already "happened" within the realm of consciousness, and there was a huge celebration.

Dr. Steven Greer
Exactly. This was the celestial and astral architectural blueprint of the future. All the elements are in place, and it is *done*. It is going to manifest. There was an enormous celebratory joy felt by so many of us. Trudy described exactly what I was feeling and sensing from the beings – not just extraterrestrials, but many celestial beings too. Shari was there as well.

An Avatar
Ricky Butterfass
That was the first time I could see the Avatar. Sometimes I do not see him and I suspect I am being tested to see if I will speak from my ego saying I see him when I do not. This time I saw him, so I told everyone what I saw. The Avatar looked as if he was sitting. He was about eight feet tall and like a Buddha. His head was twice

the size of mine, and he had broad shoulders. I had the sense that there were other beings present as his honor guard. Around the Avatar was a group of smaller ETs that were sitting down.

ET Emotional Themes

Linda Willitts

Often during our sessions there is a theme, an emotional theme. We have had celebration and joy, utter, beautiful peace, a very solemn feeling, and very serious feelings. Sometimes we sense the ETs are busy somewhere else. The feeling of love has happened many times, especially in Crestone. I experience very loving ETs there. Sometimes there is a Native American motif. The lesson is that our "emotional sensing" is just as important as our celestial vision and other physical senses.

Importance of Sharing

Dr. Steven Greer

Yes, sensing and feeling with the heart are as important as seeing with the remote viewing mind or the physical eyes. The heart chakra picks up a texture and meaning that the conscious mind often does not. It is about opening up those avenues of perception from the very physical to the very etheric. We seek to integrate all those capacities in our work. Everyone has different ways of knowing. We all have all of them, but some may develop at different times or in different situations. Certain people have an especially strong ability in one area. So it is important when we are dealing with multi-dimensional and celestial events, that we share what we sense, feel, see, think and remote view. That way we get the most complete perception we can.

Importance of Group Coherency to ETs

A very important thing to remember as we go out together and do our work is that extraterrestrial civilizations observe us to see if we function in a coherent way where manner. They want to see if people are truly contributing and not holding back. It is difficult because people take a risk going out on a limb when they say they sense, feel or see something unusual. That is why a certain amount of trust has to be developed in a team. There needs to be a sense that you can really share what you are feeling and seeing and sensing without fear of any ridicule, condemnation or judgment. When we are sharing, there is a respect for what everyone is reporting.

Concern for Dr. Greer's Safety
Dr. Ted Loder
I always feel incredible excitement, thrill, joy and love in what is happening during our events. One year those feelings were present along with a feeling of concern for Dr. Greer. My point is both feelings can be present. One year there was major concern for Dr. Greer's safety because of what he was doing.

Getting to the Next Level
Charlie Balogh
In 2004 my brother David came with us. He is more sensitive than I am and told me he had been trying to recapture the ability to astral travel. One night, after breaking into smaller groups, we went to the Tibetan Stupa. We arrived before sunset, sat and watched the sunset. After doing a short meditation, we got up. However, David stayed in the chair as we all walked away.

I was twenty feet behind him when suddenly I heard him say, "Whoa." I asked him what happened. He said that while sitting in his chair a mist 3 feet high had started to materialize next to him. It looked like the swirling affect you see when you pour milk into water. The "mist-like swirling" started to coalesce into humanoid figures. When he saw that, he panicked, and the beings disappeared.

Shortly after David's incident, we did another meditation and had a break afterwards. David wandered off to the edge of the small parking lot near the Stupa, and he was looking up at the mountain. I was behind him. I saw three tall columns of light, two in front of him and one behind him. The columns were about eight feet high. David could not see the columns, but I told him they were there. Since that time, he is aware of three forms of consciousness each time that he goes into meditation. He calls them sentinels which stand by him while he is in meditation.

Dr. Steven Greer
People will receive what they *need* in order to get to the next

level of understanding. We grow only as we are ready and ask for that growth, and no further. Also, the assignment of entities like David's sentinels is a leitmotif that has occurred over the last 18 years. People will come to these expeditions and find that they have an extraterrestrial biological being assigned to them. Often, when we are in our circle, we will ask that people see that they do have a being assigned to them. Participants will begin to become aware of and see the beings. The association continues after they leave, and it manifests some powerful experiences for people.

Etheric Light at Zapata Falls
Dr. Warren Wittekind
At Zapata Falls I found it quite interesting that it could be so bright when there was no moon out. The rocks were bright even though the bushes were not. It was strange because the temperature changed and the sounds were muffled. We continued, and Dr. Greer described that he was being instructed to take two steps forward since he was the leader. Then afterward, each of us was instructed to take two steps forward because we would become leaders.

Dr. Steven Greer
Warren's story is representative of several very unusual incidents we've had at the Zapata Falls site. The brightness Warren refers to is an etheric/astral light. The rocks and the path seemed to have a glowing light within them. That is the effect of an ET craft phasing in the astral, nearly materializing. It is palpably still, warm and muffled with an echo chamber effect.

Sensing Individual Protection
Trudy Guyker
At Zapata Falls as we were coming down from the contact site, I was behind a lovely man in his 80s and afraid for him because he seemed frail. I felt there was something incredibly important about this frail-appearing fellow. We linked arms to support one another as we continued, but he was not as frail as he appeared. Suddenly from behind, I felt the presence of an enormous person who seemed to envelope/surround us. I sensed that he was being protected in order that he could do something regarding the CSETI and Disclosure Project. Although I cannot prove it, I have had enough experience to know the event represented the presence of tremendous protection.

Using Knowledge

Debbie Foch

The whole theme on Blanca Peak was the importance of what we do with the knowledge we gain. We were in the process of stepping forward as leaders. We were supposed to do something to help and change the world. It was up to us.

Phoenix CSETI Training Group
Sedona, Arizona
July 2004

Anomalous Lights (Alleged Headlights)

Trudy Guyker

One night, I was riding back from the training site to the hotel with Charlie. We were on a dirt road late at night, and I noticed two lights in the southeast. I first thought they were car headlights on a road near us. But from where the lights came there was no car, just these lights. The lights were not making illumination, they were simply shining, not bright and not dull. They were like a car light, with a yellowish tinge, but they were not illuminating the dirt in front of our car. They came closer and suddenly zoomed down directly in front of us. There was no road, no dust, nothing – just the object that came right in front of us.

Charlie Balogh

We were coming back from the training site and nothing extraordinary had been happening. When we saw the lights, I recall them coming down on the passenger side at an angle in front of us. I thought they were headlights because we were approaching the main highway. I realized the next morning that they could not have been headlights because we were not close to the main highway. The incident unfolded just as Trudy said. The lights descended from a southwesterly direction, and moved in front of us before bursting into the ground and disappearing.

They were not illuminating the area in front of us. They were globes of light that I remember being pale blue, and not terribly bright.

ET Technology in Lights that Do Not Illuminate
Dr. Steven Greer
The episode reported by Trudy and Charlie is a classic description of the ET technologies. When there is such a light, it will be contained, and it does not shine or reflect off anything. It is very unusual technology.

Teleportation Technology
There are also experiments with simultaneous teleportation of particles where we have the ability to teleport a particle to another point in space instantly. Teleportation has been accomplished on the particle level in laboratories, and we know that it was accomplished on a larger scale in 1953 classified projects. The *Disclosure* Book mentions a witness, Fred Threfeld, who was in Canada at an air base when they did an experiment with an electronic device[95]. The experimenters had a glass object on the device, and it vanished from that point, teleported and appeared in another room in another part of the air base. The object teleported back and forth under controlled circumstances.

We know there are strange electromagnetic effects involved with these extraterrestrial spacecraft. The difference is that ETs have mastered these sciences and are light years beyond our experiments. That is why the manifestations of extraterrestrial technologies seem "out of this world." When people see them, they know they are not looking at normal incandescent light.

Alleged Satellite Course Reversal
Charlie Balogh
Something also happened on the last night that we were there. We saw a satellite traveling across the sky in front of us that suddenly turned and moved in the opposite direction. We knew it could not be a satellite. Toward the end of the night both Trudy and I received a message at the same time to look at the same spot in the sky. The second that we both looked, there was a bright flash. We think it was an acknowledgement.

---

[95] Steven M. Greer, *Disclosure: Military and Government Witnesses Reveal the Greatest Secrets in Modern History* (Crozet, VA: Crossing Point, 2001), p. 553.

CSETI Training
Mount Shasta, California
August 2004

Lights on the Mountain

Linda Willitts
The very first night on Mt. Shasta Dr. Greer was signaling some flashing lights that were moving around the face of the mountain. No one could possibly have been walking there, as it was too steep. The lights were interacting with his laser and moving around the mountain. Since Dr. Greer had an interview on the Art Bell Show[96] that night, we had to prematurely conclude the encounter.

Dr. Steven Greer
Everyone was seeing a number of lights that were in impossibly high and steep areas on Mt. Shasta. The lights were moving on the mountain and were interacting with the laser. The encounter went on for at least an hour.

Art Bell Show of August 8, 2004

We had to leave because they wanted me on the Art Bell Show. ABC News was filming him while they were interviewing me for the Peter Jennings' ABC News special on UFOs. The producers of the ABC special had approached me because they learned that we had a great deal of testimony and documents from various government witnesses.

More Disclosure Witnesses

We also had quite a few people who had never come forward, but were waiting for the right opportunity – some three star generals and folks like that. I met with the producers a few months before the 2004 expedition to Mt. Shasta, and they were thrilled. They said they wanted to do something that would make history.

Series of Specials Planned for "20/20"

Rather skeptically, I said that ABC had wanted to do a "Primetime Live" and "20/20" series of specials[97] with the witnesses. Although

---

[96] http://www.coasttocoastam.com/shows/2004/08/08.html
[97] "PrimeTime Live" ran on ABC from August 1989 until 1999, when it merged with "20/20."

they wanted to get the story out, they were not allowed to. An executive producer at ABC news called me after the Disclosure Project Event. He came to my home and I gave him thirty-five hours of digital interviews with military and intelligence witnesses. I also gave him several thousand pages of government documents, which are "smoking guns" by any standards. While sitting in my home he stated that it was the biggest story in history.

After the Disclosure Project news conference, the producer finally called me and said they would not be able to air the story. When I asked the reason, he said that THEY wouldn't let him do the show. I asked, "Who are THEY?"
He said, "Dr. Greer, you know who THEY are!" And that was the end of that.

ABC News Debacle

Next came the chance to do a television special produced by Peter Jennings' main producer. Peter Jennings had his own production company, and he was also the anchor of ABC News with, allegedly, a lot of clout. Jennings' producer had won Emmys for documentary work, and they wanted to make an earthshaking show that would "blow the lid off of this."

I thought to myself, "I have heard this before a half dozen times or more by major media players, and they were not able to deliver, but nothing ventured, nothing gained." The ABC production company was going to meet us at Mt. Shasta, to interview people, to see what they could, and to make a two hour ABC News Special.

The unique aspect of the situation was that the news department of ABC was making the show, rather than the entertainment department. The ET subject is usually red-lined[98] in the news divisions. I felt it was an enormous opportunity if it was not a hoax. Having been burned many times before, I was still skeptical. We went along with it, and they interviewed us at Mt. Shasta. I did the interview with Art Bell so they could have that for their news special.

---

[98] Redline means to remove from broadcast status.

The ABC special aired in February of '05. ABC interviewed people like John Callahan, the senior FAA official who had all the digital radar tracings of an airline-UFO event[99]. Then we started to receive phone calls from some low-level executive at ABC. The executive said they were not going to be able to use the testimony we provided due to "time constraints."

When the piece finally aired it was "fluff" that featured ABC interviewing media people like Art Bell, people in trailer parks, and debunkers rather than the military witnesses we had supplied. They only showed interviews of one or two credible low-level pilots. Not one of the high caliber witnesses we provided was used – not a single second of footage! ABC News cannot claim they did not have the material, because I gave it to them on a silver platter.

Afterwards, I wrote an expose of the ABC incident which appears on our website[100]. It is just another example of how Big Media operates. From the very beginning I had a bad feeling about Jennings' award-winning producer. I sensed he had his mind made up, and was not going to do what Peter Jennings and others wanted him to do. I felt he took his marching orders from someone else and intended to do another brain-dead, media fluff piece. In fact, there are B-rated documentaries on the History Channel that are much better and more accurate than what ABC News produced with all its billions of dollars and resources.

Corruption of Big Media

People need to know that the only thing more corrupt than big government is Big Media. They are absolutely the most corrupt because they portray themselves as the keepers of the flame of truth. Bob Schwartz, who had been on the board of Time-Life, told me that in reality Big Media had become scribes taking dictation at the right hand of the king[101]. I have had intimate involvement with multiple major networks. I have seen projects where the networks had positive proof and strong evidence, but they will not put it out to the public. You could have an ET craft land on the White

---

[99] Greer, *Disclosure* (2001), John Callahan testimony and documents, pp. 79-93.
[100] http://www.disclosureproject.org/abcnewsdefrauding.htm
[101] http://www.disclosureproject.org/mediaplay.htm

House lawn, and no one would ever know about it. I am convinced the major media outlets centered in Washington, D.C. would be ordered to ignore it or make up a false story about it.

Many Americans have a certain naiveté about all of this and still believe that we are living in a free country today. In reality, secretive interests have infiltrated our corporations, and corporate media have overtaken 'the fourth estate'. Ironically, the appearance of an ET craft will be reported more honestly and openly in Pravda and the Chinese news agency than in the *New York Times*. The most culpable and corrupt element in America is the media, because the public believes them. Everyone knows government is corrupt, knows there are secret projects and knows many of the politicians are on the take. The media is an essential part of a democracy, and serve as one of the great checks and balances so that the people get accurate information. They portray themselves as investigators, but in reality they are cover-up artists.

CBS "48 Hours" Fiasco

For example, in the 1990s, there was a show on CBS News called "48 Hours[102]." They wanted to do a program about the ET craft seen around Popo, a volcano in Mexico. We went there with the CBS news crew to engage the CSETI protocols and have the events documented. Before I left, I signed an agreement with their producer, Kathleen Kennedy, agreeing that they would share any footage they got from the expedition with us. The CBS production is a multi-million dollar undertaking, but we had to pay our own costs for transportation and lodging. The quid pro quo was that they would share the footage unedited with us.

One of the CBS chief correspondents was on site, and Dan Rather was hosting 48 Hours back in the New York studios. CBS had their top-of-the-line cameras on location and a key correspondent with us. One evening, an ET craft suddenly emerged from the mouth of the volcano, circled the volcano and shot over toward us, and flew out into space. The CBS cameras filmed this and the correspondent came running down the hill exclaiming "Anyone who sees this will know that this is REAL!!" They also filmed a

---

[102] http://www.tv.com/48-hours/show/8236/summary.html

massive triangular craft that appeared and was clearly interacting with us.

The CBS crew returned to their studio with all this film evidence and their correspondent's response to it. But what they actually showed was a fuzzy image of a triangular-looking object with a debunker saying it was an airplane missing its aviation lights! Dan Rather made some acerbic remarks, and "Ha-ha-ha." And that was the end of the piece.

So I called Kathleen Kennedy and said, "I'm not sure what your people are doing, but I did not get a copy of this footage as we had agreed upon in writing. Please send me a copy so we will have it as evidence of the event." She told me she would not give it to me, despite our signed agreement. She ended with "Go try to enforce it. We're a multi-billion dollar company, and you don't have anything. We'll outlast you in court."
We never got the film. That is what you are dealing with at CBS, ABC, NBC, CNN—the whole gamut...

Trudy Guyker
Debbie, Dr. Greer and I were the last to be interviewed for the Peter Jennings Show. Afterwards one of the cameramen said, "My God, these people are smart. This is extraordinary." It seemed to indicate the interviews would be good for their show.

Dr. Warren Wittekind
I had a strange sense about ABC and the Peter Jennings crew. When they came to the field site they told us to bring our cars and shine our lights on our group to get better lighting. It seemed strange because they never did use the car lights to illuminate the circle. The people I knew in the media tended to be left wing, very loose, loose clothes, long hair, and had animals in their house—very left-wing people. The news crew that came had very short hair. They walked with a military bearing, and they were very proper. It was not what I expected from an ABC News crew. My sense was they were not really a news crew.

ABC Production Had Wrong Equipment
Dr. Steven Greer
Other evidence for Warren's point is that a multi-million dollar ABC production team arrived on our site for night filming, but they came with no night scopes, no night shot cameras, and no night vision cameras. We did have an object come out of the volcano. Everyone saw it, even the ABC producers. They said they could not film it because the cameras they had were cameras for close range that needed huge floodlights. You could have had the mother ship come down and land, and they would not have been able to film it because they had the wrong equipment. They did not want to film it. The whole thing was a hoax perpetrated on the American public. It was a very interesting experience that further cemented my low opinion of the big media.

Open Door Incident
Linda Willitts
Dr. Bravo, Dr. Greer, and I were staying in a condo. After arriving back from our fieldwork, Dr. Bravo and I got to the condo door first. It was wide open and every single light was on in the downstairs. We had neither turned any lights on nor left any on. I first checked the doorknob and it was still locked, but the door was wide open. Nothing was taken. Nothing was disturbed. Dr. Greer's computer was out in the open in the living room. There was no evidence that anyone had been upstairs; everything was dark upstairs.

Dr. Bill Clendenin
Someone wanted the three of you to know they were in the condo.

Cigar-shaped Craft with Inchworm Motion
Trudy Guyker
During a break, in my peripheral vision, I saw a craft nearby and to the south. We decided it was about 2 miles away. The craft was on the way to becoming totally materialized. I have never seen a craft quite so solid. It was large and rectangular; somewhat cigar-shaped with slightly rounded ends. It was dark gray and just on the verge of becoming material.

Dr. Steven Greer
It was flat on the top and bottom with rounded ends. It was very close to becoming fully materialized...

Trudy Guyker
I realized that the craft was moving with an "inch worm effect" that Dr. Greer has described many times. The craft had been moving along slowly when suddenly it went out. The left side bottom section leapt forward, and then it moved along slowly again. The duration of the sighting was between five and ten seconds.

Synchronicity of Sightings Common
Trudy Guyker
After I returned to Phoenix from the CSETI training, I learned about a sighting made by my son-in-law, who is very perceptive. He told me that at 5:00 PM on the same day that I had my sighting (thus, his sighting would have preceded mine), he was in North Phoenix driving north. Directly in his line of sight he saw a craft moving exactly as the craft I saw later that evening at our Shasta site. The craft he saw was moving with the inchworm effect and fully materialized.

Often, as our trainings are coming up, events will start happening for some people a couple of weeks prior to the training. Similarly, people will continue to have experiences, visions, and sightings for a few weeks after the training.

Rust-reddish Craft
Dr. Steven Greer
I saw a large craft with a rust-red color, and from my viewpoint it was 99% materialized. I don't believe it was very far out—a few thousand feet.

Trudy Guyker
I saw the craft below the mountain line in front of the mountain.

Four Questions Asked
Dr. Warren Wittekind
Another incident occurred at our secluded Shasta site after our

meditation. Upon returning from a break, Dr. Greer told us to walk very quietly to a certain spot and return. When we reached the spot, it was as if we were being taken onto a stage with an audience watching us from many rows of balconies. Each of us was asked four questions. We were tapped on our right shoulder. Some people remembered the four questions that were asked.

Greg Heller

During Dr. Greer's meditation a tremendous dome came over us. As Dr. Greer was delivering his meditation, his words began to echo even though we were in an area that doesn't echo. Interestingly, it seemed to me that Dr. Greer was somehow directed to change his meditation slightly. I saw that celestial beings, the actual avatars, were located at many points of the circle around us. It seemed as if we were in an echo chamber and the laser light was bouncing off its walls. A huge protective field surrounded us, and all the bushes were scintillating.

Dr. Steven Greer

We kept seeing a ruby red light in the trees to the northwest.

Greg Heller

Dr. Greer, Ricky, others and I saw the bushes were scintillating. Dr. Greer said we had been asked to go to a very sacred meeting spot, and we were to go silently, following him. We walked up to the sacred area. The largest field of scintillating light seemed to be in front of the sacred area. As we went into the scintillating light, everything unexpectedly went dark for me. We gathered and formed a circle, holding hands. Suddenly I realized I was not in a normal state of consciousness, I was in a meditative state that was quite shifted from normal. Suddenly, as if from a portal, the stage that Warren mentioned in his account appeared and overlapped the rocks at Shasta. For a moment I saw a V-shaped auditorium with empty seats in it. Next, it seemed as if a violet-blue light flew out of my eyes and filled up every seat in the auditorium. The auditorium contained 800 people who seemed to have blue faces.

I clearly saw four or five emissaries that walked around to each member of our group. They touched the members who could not see them. Everyone nodded solemnly as if in prayer. When they reached me, the first question they very politely asked was, "Are you comfortable?" I replied, "Yes, I am." The second question was something like, "Why are you doing this with the group? This could be dangerous, and why do you feel this is so important?" The third question was, "Are you willing to come back?" They listened very carefully, touching me the whole time, as they did with the others in the group. I answered, "Absolutely." I don't remember the fourth question. After the ceremony finished, I walked out in tears. I had never seen anything like it!

Dr. Warren Wittekind
After we left the stage and were returning to the circle, it was as if we were all anointed with a beautiful fragrance. We were treated with the utmost honor and utmost respect for our efforts. It was a very beautiful situation.

Dr. Steven Greer
We were being invited to be ambassadors to the universe. These beings were asking us to be their emissaries from Earth and to carry on the work on this planet. They were deeply honoring people's willingness to commit. It is important to realize that you do have to be willing put yourself at service or it does not happen.

Ricky Butterfass
The night of the ceremony I saw a tree about 150 feet from me, towards the mountain, with a large blue light the size of a large pizza pan in it. I returned to the circle and asked if anyone had a blue light or laser that they were shining up in the tree. People said no, and I told them that I had just seen a blue light. I sat in the circle, and everyone else started seeing the blue light. That was about the time the craft came around us and the dome appeared.

Linda Willitts
As Greg and Warren described, we experienced a beautiful ceremony. Its purpose was to allow us to commit ourselves to service in the contact program. It was quite moving and similar to the rite at the contact site at Blanca Peak. It had the feeling of reverence and sacredness. Our contact site at Shasta is not very

far from where we usually make our circle, and it is only slightly higher in elevation. But when we are there, it seems like we are much higher and in a totally different space. We have had so many amazing experiences at that spot.

Electromagnetic Field Weapon Fired
Dr. Steven Greer
Late one night we were at Sand Flats doing our CSETI protocols. There were campers 100 yards away in the woods, but we still used our usual site there. Suddenly we saw a luminous orb emerge, as if from the side of the volcano. We were signaling the orb as it approached us, and it was signaling back. Some trees blocked our view, so we moved to see more clearly.

We also noticed a very high aircraft coming into the area. Suddenly we heard a sound like lightning ripping through the air. An invisible, electromagnetic field weapon had been fired from the plane overhead, and we could hear it tearing down through the atmosphere. We heard a crash in the forest, and we could hear the enormous tree limbs and trees breaking as they were struck. The impact was so loud and powerful the Earth shook beneath our feet, and the impact zone was just a few hundred yards in front of us!
That was a shot across our bow, and my hackles went up. I had twenty or thirty people up there on a training team with me, and I was responsible for them. I went into high alert because I have a very good instinct for when real danger exists. What happened on Mt. Shasta was a real wake-up call. Warren was there, and he immediately recalled the aircraft and saw something had come from it, but later he could not remember it. It was as if his perception was erased or his memory scrambled.

Dr. Warren Wittekind
What I presently remember is that I had a very bad feeling about the airplane that was coming up. The normal flight paths were to the east and west sides of Mt. Shasta, but this path was coming right over us. Another car in Sand Flats had its lights on in the middle of the night, driving forward and back, forward and back. I thought, "Oh my goodness, they're going to fire at the top of Mt. Shasta!"

Dr. Steven Greer
I was very concerned that one of the ET vehicles could be destroyed even if it was only in a plasma form, or that there could be loss of life. Those possibilities are real with this kind of classified energy weapon. The violence of the impact was breathtaking.

Greg Heller
Dr. Greer took the group close to the trees. Just before midnight the jet was flying in. It was visible in the moonlight. It was high, and it looked to me like an unmarked 747. I sensed Dr. Greer's hackles go up. I do not know if he had seen the jet, but he called out, "Is everybody here?" Ed was still lying down in his chair back in the circle, and Dr. Greer said, "Go get him, now!" I saw Dr. Greer's hair rise straight up, and I knew something was going on. My first impression when the noise came over was that it was an eighteen-wheeler coming down the logging road. Then it was like an atomic bomb echoing back and forth. The group seemed very calm for what was going on.

Dr. Steven Greer
We were all stunned for a moment. It was shocking.

Linda Willitts
We had been up on that hill watching the lights, and I had been recording. I always have my recorder on, and if anything happens I first look at my watch and record the time. I had turned the recorder off because the lights had stopped. Suddenly, an explosion occurred, and you could hear wood splitting. When that died down, you could hear the rumbling of rocks, a continual rumbling, and the Earth shook. The first thing I did was look at my watch—12:04 AM. The second thing I did was look up because I had the sense that a plane had dropped a bomb. I saw a plane, big like a 747, flying over. Next I looked for a mushroom cloud because the sound was that loud. I also expected emergency vehicles or campers to be driving around, but there was just utter silence and peace after that.

Ricky Butterfass
I saw the aircraft flying over. I could hear the sound of the tree

branches cracking and breaking, and soon after I heard something big hitting the ground. I thought it might be one of the big trees coming down.

People were camped in the Sand Flats area, and the next day we talked to some of them. We asked a husband and wife if they heard anything, and they said they hadn't heard a thing. There were also people in the other direction. We asked them, and they didn't hear anything either. We thought it was quite amazing.

Time Reversal with Scalar Weapons

Dr. Steven Greer

One interesting feature about longitudinal, or scalar, high frequency weapons is that they are very directional. They are not normal occurrences in space/time. Precisely one hour later, at 1:04 AM, we heard a "time echo" of the same event, which happened again, but softer.

Greg Heller

But it sounded in reverse, like trees were being put back together.

Dr. Steven Greer

Yes, exactly. It was as if the event was happening in reverse, which is interesting because our teams searching the woods the next day to look for damage found none. One should understand that we are not dealing with normal systems here. It is not like dropping a metal bomb with explosives or even an atomic bomb. It is a whole new type of weapon system.

We have consulted with experts on these systems, and we believe from what happened that such a weapon was fired. One wonders: Was it a shot across the bow? Was it diverted by the ET craft so it did not kill us? Was it inaccurately aimed? All I know is that no one was hurt, and we were protected. We were calm. We were not thrown off track from our purpose – but it was a serious event. You could actually hear whatever it was cracking through the air before it hit the forest. It was like a lightning bolt splitting or cracking the air and it moved very fast.

Linda Willitts

None of the regular campers heard a thing when the enormous explosion went off. The clincher was a lady and her dog on top of the hill. She watched us standing on the road at the moment the event happened, but she did not hear a thing, and her skittish dog showed no reaction!

One of the fellows in our group lived in Mt. Shasta, and I asked him to interview any authorities in the area, like the forest service. He learned that there had been no report. We were the only ones who heard it.

Dr. Jan Bravo

Another physical manifestation of that event occurred. Dr. Greer had my green laser and was pointing it at the area where the beam came down. The glass lens broke at precisely the moment we heard the explosion. I now have a split beam, and it remains that way.

Greg Heller

Another interesting point is that three to five seconds before the blast, the orange orb or ship we had been watching suddenly phased out.

Dr. Warren Wittekind

Immediately after the crack, the car that had been driving back and forth with its lights on turned its lights out and stopped. Someone got out of one side and slammed the door. Then someone else got out and slammed their door.

Trudy Guyker

I heard Warren say that he saw a light come out of the aircraft. Later he did not remember saying that. A huge lightning bolt type of thing came from the plane, followed by a boom that sounded like a huge tree cracking and falling over. It was interesting to me that the boom did not stop, but went on and on. I think it went on for fifteen seconds. It sounded like a gigantic bulldozer kept pushing tress over.

Linda Willitts
The whole incident lasted at least fifteen seconds. We were all astounded. It sounded as if the Earth was being ripped open over a long distance.

Dr. Steven Greer
Something was burrowing and impacting into the ground. I could feel the Earth moving and shudder. The sound was not just coming from the trees, it was coming from the Earth. Trudy is correct in that after the impact into the Earth, and after the trees were ripped, a roar continued.

Debbie Foch
I thought something had crashed, either a craft or a weapon. I thought the craft we had been watching had crashed.

Dr. Steven Greer
We were concerned initially that the continuing sound was of a craft impacting the Earth, as if it had been hit and was burrowing into the ground as it crashed. We were concerned that an ET craft had been hit right in front of us!

Greg Heller
I was locked onto the consciousness in the craft the whole time, even before the event. I felt surprise myself and from the people in the craft, as well as concern. They were not to be hit. Exactly an hour later, when everything reversed, I felt the craft south of Shasta and received the message that they were OK.

Dr. Steven Greer
So time is not what we think it is. Space is not what we think it is…

Spoiled Nature of Sand Flats

Dr. Jan Bravo
Every time we have gone back to Sand Flats since the "EM weapon" event, the energy there has been chaotic. There have been unwelcoming people there, and something has been wrong with that area, so we have not done our contact work there since (as of 2007 – see later events)

Dr. Steven Greer
We have not been allowed to work on that site, even though we have tried. A weird series of events happens to direct us to another site where a better energy is present. Once the destructive energy of that Sand Flats event violated that point in space/time, the Universal Being /Consciousness apparently does not want us doing our work there any more. It is very interesting.

Chapter 13

2005

CSETI Training
Crestone, Colorado
June 2005

Linda Willitts
The big impression that Crestone 2005 had on me was the abundance of contact with Avatars and celestials wherever we went. At the contact site, I saw Dr. Greer walk into an arch of scintillating golden light. There were more Avatars and celestials at the site than ETs, and I had the direct feeling all were giving Dr. Greer help. They were empowering him, assuring him that everything would be okay. It was emotionally meaningful. Kindness flashed us twice that year. Whenever Dr. Greer is feeling down, she gives him support.

Dr. Steven Greer
Twice that week we saw a beautiful blue-white disc fly in, shine light into the group, and fly back out into space. It was very beautiful. Kindness is so kind and compassionate.

Charlie Balogh
At the contact site, I physically saw a huge object with very bright lights around it. The object appeared and re-appeared three times. I did not realize what I was seeing until Dr. Greer started talking about that great cathedral-like space he was in and it became clear to me. Also, I encountered an Avatar during my meditation before we went up to the contact site. The Avatar rose up in front of me. He was wearing a crimson-red, wide, V-shaped tunic with long, flowing robes. I could see all aspects of the dress, but not his face. When Dr. Greer heard that, he told me that I was not ready to see the Avatar's face. It was very compelling.

Linda Willitts
Dr. Greer always waits for a sign that it is time to go to the Mount Blanca contact site. We were having a break when he saw a bright flash on a vacant seat.

Dr. Steven Greer
Actually it was an explosion of white light on the east and south part of our circle. Rather than a flash in from outside, the explosion of light appeared right in the circle and radiated out. It was brilliant—like something you would read in a mythological story. I knew the beings had come through the crossing point of light and were ready to escort us to a meeting. Extraterrestrials from very advanced star systems, and celestials and the over-soul Avatar for the next half million years for the entire cosmos were at the meeting.

Charlie Balogh
That evening on Mount Blanca was extremely warm. It got colder as we went down. It was warmer on the mountain than it was in the valley.

Dr. Steven Greer
It was almost hot on Blanca – unusually so. People saw objects flying overhead very quickly. I saw a crimson red orb up against the eastern mountains for several seconds, and then it vanished. The orb was the same color Charlie saw on the being.

Debbie Foch
When we got back from the contact site some people reported that there was another explosion of light when they left.

Dr. Steven Greer
It was as if the signal we saw when we arrived – left. We often have a book-end event like this.

Dr. Raven Nabulsi
That night there were a number of planes flying back and forth over our circle. After we saw the explosion of light and went to the contact site, a cloud covering arose and encapsulated the area.

It became dead quiet, and we could no longer hear the waterfall. Dr. Greer walked ahead of us, and I saw the archway some of the others mentioned. I saw a being much taller than Dr. Greer who touched him on his right shoulder. When we finally did come down, the clouds had dissipated, and it was a crystal clear night, quite a contrast from what we had seen up there.

Linda Willitts
It was the year that Karen Ong from Australia was with us[103]. She received a message, which Debbie includes in the CSETI training materials, called *Wisdom from the ETs*.

Dr. Warren Wittekind
I saw the bright explosion of light before we went up to the meeting place. It was very close to the edge of our circle, and it was very dramatic. A light appeared and was bright but it did not shine onto anything around it; it was not normal.

Dr. Steven Greer
The light we have been discussing is extraterrestrial light. The light appears and unfurls from their craft, then stops in space. It can emerge from a point in space and be incredibly bright, without flashing like normal light. Still, everyone saw that blinding explosion of light 9,000 feet up on Blanca Peak.

Dr. Raven Nabulsi
Every time I have gone on a training, it seems that some new civilization introduces itself to me. On the 2005 Crestone training I saw a being that looked like an owl, except that it was humanoid. I had mentioned it to Dr. Greer. When the four of us were at the hot springs, four enormous owls flew past us. They flew by at eye level, and they landed in the field outside of the hot springs.

Dr. Steven Greer
The four gigantic owls hung around us for quite some time, which is unusual.

---

[103] http://media.www.harbus.org/media/storage/paper343/news/2007/10/15/News/Karen.Ong.oj.Founder.Of.Myhappyplanet.Shares.Her.Entrepreneurial.Experience-3028114.shtml

Dr. Ted Loder
I was there, and I remember that.

Dr. Warren Wittekind
While we were in the Baca, we were told that an extraterrestrial being and a celestial being were standing behind each of us. We could ask the beings questions. I wondered something, and received a strange response. I could hear myself thinking with a certain quality. Then there was another thought having the same quality, but it was not constructed with words that I would have used.

CSETI Training
Mount Shasta, California
September 2005

Ball of Flashing Light

Trudy Guyker
Five or six of us had just gathered at the sacred site and were setting up our equipment. Out of nowhere appeared a brilliant ball of flashing light about the size of a basketball. It had a most magnificent brilliance. The light remained for a second or two. It was intelligent and totally different than other objects I have seen. When I went home after the training I asked my husband if he had any experiences while I was gone. He said that he had an incredible, lucid dream. At one point in the dream a flashing ball of light about the size of a basketball appeared. He said it had been a small light but grew into a magnificent, "brilliant" light. Fred asked the light, "Are you spirit?" The light responded, "Yes."

Dr. Ted Loder
On at least one evening we watched "flash bulbs" in the sky. Some of them appeared in the southwest, and everyone saw them.

Extraterrestrial Sound with Form

Linda Willitts
Shortly into one of Dr. Greer's meditations, he paused and we heard the distinctive sound of an ET tone. We heard the tone about twenty-five feet to the left of Dr. Greer and me. I was taping the

meditation and my recorder caught the sound faintly. I sent the tape to Charlie for analysis. Everyone agreed it was an ET sound, and we each had a picture in our minds of its form. For me, its form was a vertical string of dark pearls.

Charlie Balogh
Linda, Trudy, and I had a long discussion about what that observation represented. I think what Linda saw was a visual representation of the harmonic structure of the sound she heard. Just as the harmonic structure is a blueprint for the sound of whatever you perceive, so the vibration level is also a blueprint in sound with its individual harmonic structure. As such it defines what the physical mass is going to be or how it appears in physical space. Each expression of mass is simply an expression of the harmonics of the vibration. It goes into string theory – vibrating string theory; everything is vibration.

An electronic synthesizer takes a fundamental sound and adds harmonics to it. Then electronically it can create the sound of a trumpet or a violin simply by manipulating the harmonic structure of the waveform. When Linda mentioned that the sound's form looked like a string of pearls, it was an example of the harmonic structure of sound. Each pearl represented a different harmonic of the sound she was hearing. It was both a visual and an aural representation.

Trudy Guyker
It was the first time for each of us that we *saw sound*. It started with the very first tone. I saw it as light gray pearls, and Linda saw it as pearls also.

Dr. Steven Greer
We knew the sound Linda heard was extraterrestrial. You could see and feel the form of the sound. It was a fascinating experience for everyone. Everyone heard the sound. It was neither metaphysical nor subtle, but was auditory. We did get some of it on the tape recorder.

Benefits of Visual and Auditory Monitoring in the Field
Hopefully, we will soon get the necessary funding to buy sophisticated equipment to record the sights and sounds we observe during our trainings. With the appropriate devices running continuously we would have astonishing results. When we obtain substantial funding for this work, we can hire the personnel needed to analyze these amazing sights and sounds.

Greg Heller
Some of the events we see or hear happen so quickly it is difficult to record them without hi-tech recording devices operating continuously. Proper recording equipment would capture each incident as it occurs during our sessions.

Debbie Foch
With the sound that Linda reported, the form that I saw in my head was similar to the volume bars on a stereo or cell phone. It was in packets; I think it was red.

Greg Heller
I saw the form of the sound as a column of vertical triangles moving downward.
The first night I saw a beautiful, cream-colored orb or a ship up on the hill. I could feel the consciousness pouring from it. I put my night vision on the object. Suddenly, a plasma beam came from the ship as a perfectly formed cylinder and shot out to a big tree about 100 yards from us, returning within half a second.
Millions of sparkles streamed down that Pine tree. They slowly moved toward our group, and formed an actual humanoid being that walked around the group during the break. After returning from the break, the being was still present. The being went around to each member of our group. I believe it was a conscious, remote sensing device made out of light.

Dr. Steven Greer
It is actually consciousness, light, spirit, and technology. It defies categorization; it's truly trans-dimensional.

Linda Willitts

I saw the light that Greg was discussing. I saw a waterfall of sparkles come out of the tree, slide down the tree and into the circle. It was very bright.

Double Flyover of ET Craft

Linda Willitts

Perhaps the most awesome event I've experienced in my years of trainings occurred at Shasta 2005. The general routine at the end of each evening is for Dr. Greer to have all of us hold hands as we stand in a circle while he says some closing remarks. This particular night Dr. Greer and I were at the south end of the circle and I was looking due east. We could not see the ground horizon because of trees around the periphery. While he was making his closing remarks, two large, white craft resembling balls of light riding side by side, came from behind the trees east of us. The balls of light shot up from behind the trees like a fountain, and they arced over our group. They left a trail which made a white, double arc over our whole group, and they went down in the west. It was incredible.

Dr. Steven Greer

The movement of the two balls of light was precisely east to west, and it was in tandem. It was at a moment when I was saying something very spiritual to everyone, and at that moment, the lights punctuated my statement. They flew in, horizon to horizon, and everyone saw it. The incident lasted several seconds and was breathtakingly beautiful. It conveyed a certain joy and acknowledgement. These two, side-by-side objects were not meteors or jets or satellites. The event had an interesting synchronicity because earlier I had been talking with someone about ancient twin avatars, and then the two objects came across. I'm a twin and I have a twin motif in my life; then the twin, brilliant objects lit up the whole sky and sailed across the star field with Mt. Shasta in the background. It was one of the most spectacular things we have ever seen.

Dr. Raven Nabulsi

Some prominent astronomical features were in the sky at the time. Mars was in the Pleiades to the east; Jupiter and Venus were in the west. This male/female duality meta-theme kept appearing, as with the twin ships and the twin avatars.

Dr. Steven Greer
The fly-over by the twin craft was perfectly orchestrated, as in a movie. The theme of the balancing of the male and female energies and the polarity of the male and female energies was running throughout the evening. The fly-over was the perfect energetic climax of the evening, and it happened just as we were making our circle to say good night. They originated at that point on the horizon with Mars and the Pleiades, came straight over the Zenith, and ended with Jupiter and Venus. It was so beautiful—like cosmic poetry.

Ricky Butterfass
Before the training my mother predicted we were going to see something we had never seen before. I told the people in the group what my mom had said and I felt like a major event was going to occur.

Figures Dancing in the Circle
Trudy Guyker
While we were in the circle, I had seen a rock with picto-glyphs similar to Kokopelli[104]. They were ancient figures resembling the fertility deity, Kokopelli. I became aware of figures dancing around the circle near our feet, counterclockwise. They danced for quite a while and there was a green glow around our feet.

An Avatar's Appearance
After that Dr. Greer stepped back and said, "Oh, there is an avatar that has just come into the circle." I saw the Avatar, and he followed us as we went back down to our chairs. The Avatar walked toward me and came close enough that I could have reached out and touched him. He was a normal sized man with a porcelain type of complexion and dark, human eyes. His cheeks were naturally rouge colored. He had a full beard with thick curls. He wore a garment like a blanket over his head. This garment was made from

---
[104] Wikipedia: http://en.wikipedia.org/wiki/Kokopelli

a magnificent fabric and resembled a brocade tapestry. The Avatar came and stood in front of me. He looked at me, but not directly in my eyes. Rather, he looked through me – into me. Then the Avatar went around the whole group and stood in front of each person, while he studied each one.

Dr. Steven Greer
The tone we heard earlier prepared people. It had such power that it affected the structure of consciousness, and that is the power of pure, harmonic tones. True Mantras have this effect. They affect the mind and consciousness and can elevate and open us. I agree that this harmonic tone was preparatory to the cosmic, celestial being who visited us.

Tuning Fork Tones

Charlie Balogh
Something told me to bring two of my tuning forks that are tuned to a very unique interval. You strike them and place one on each ear, letting them ring for a while. When you then take away the tuning forks, you can still hear that tone in your head for fifteen to twenty minutes. It has a very direct affect on the mind.

They are in the keys of middle D and A sharp, but not quite. The interval is very pure. Western music has a tempered musical scale which allows different intervals to be played without harsh-sounding chords. But these are pure intervals, and there is no interference pattern – no wave beat – between the two tones. It is a very pure and pleasing sound that helps one transcend.

Dr. Steven Greer
The Tibetan prayer bowls and certain types of chanting also have an effect on consciousness. The sound we heard was not just a consciously perceived tone, it was auditory. It demonstrated the interface between extraterrestrial advanced civilizations, the celestial, cosmic awareness and humanity.

Many people want to separate all these levels of consciousness. We live in a time of separation where everything has to be compartmented so we can easily understand it. But in reality it is like the Tower of Babel[105]. We cannot understand the whole by looking at one part. Many people are comfortable in mental boxes. But those boxes are simply constructs of our own intellect and have no more resemblance to reality than a map of the United States has to the actual land mass of the United States.

I think that understanding the interface is an important lesson. Some people become uncomfortable with the implications, while other people are thrilled. We are trying to present a paradigm of holism, bringing all these elements together.

The Cathedral: Shasta Contact Site
Linda Willitts
My perception of that experience began with us standing in our circle. Initially we could see each other. Then the circle filled with a gray fog, and I could not see the people on the other side of the circle. I did not see the Kokopelli, but I had a definite sense of Native American ceremony with circular movement taking place around us. We call the site of the event "the cathedral," as it feels both protected amongst the tall trees and it is slightly elevated. A perfectly framed view of the volcano peak of Mt. Shasta is visible. I have the strong sense the land has been an ancient Native American sacred ceremony site for millennia.

Site Found First Year at Shasta (1999)
Dr. Steven Greer
I got the sense of sacredness at the site, too. In fact, I got that sense when we originally found the site the first year at Shasta. I was in one of my flow consciousness modes driving on difficult roads coming down Mt. Shasta, and I just remote viewed/ felt my way to that site. It was very intuitive. It is like operating on several channels at one time. On Channel 1 I am driving the truck. On Channel 2 I am looking at a distance, sensing, feeling, being pulled in heart and mind, and remote viewing. As I came into the site I said, "This is it." Nearby was a tall stand of beautiful evergreens making a cathedral.-like space. It is a protected, beautiful spot

---

[105] Wikipedia: http://en.wikipedia.org/wiki/Tower_of_Babel

where all these events have taken place.

Trudy Guyker
Dr. Greer refers to beings like the man I saw as avatars. The man I saw looked like he was in his late '30s. The thing that was so striking was that he looked Young, but he was very old. He is known as 'the Ancient One.' Another occurrence that night was someone seeing a black pyramid that contained living beings.

Black Pyramid-shaped Craft
Dr. Steven Greer
It was a pyramid-shaped craft, not a pyramid like at Giza[106]. It was a very black ebony craft that we have seen repeatedly. It is the same description of the vehicle that landed at Rendlesham Forest in England, United Kingdom[107]. The beings in the craft are very highly evolved. The craft that came down in Rendlesham Forest near the air force base broke off tree limbs and left an indentation on the ground. The indentation was later analyzed, and we have received the results from the Ministry of Defense of the United Kingdom.

Trudy Guyker
The incident with the Kokopelli showed us that the site was sacred, and that the Indian people of the Mt. Shasta area had used the sacred site for as long as they had been there. The Kokopelli were there representing the ancients. Our CSETI group was representing the present. The pyramid craft was an indication of the future, and the people in the pyramid were representing future man. The Avatar – the Ancient One – and the Kokopelli ancient people were all assembled. He was the Avatar for that area from the past, the present and the future.

"The Ancient One" Avatar
Dr. Steven Greer
The "Ancient One" is the over-soul Avatar for the next 500,000 years. The beings that landed at Rendlesham Forest communicated to the military officers there that they (the beings) were humanity

---
[106] http://www.geocities.com/athens/delphi/3499/gp1.htm
[107] http://www.ufos-aliens.co.uk/cosmicrend.html

from half a million years in the future! That message content is not widely known, but it is true. At that point in our future we are extraterrestrial – as well as terrestrial. Our origins are Earth, but we have traveled to the stars. It takes me back to the experience in the rain at Hidden Valley at Joshua Tree in 2003...

CSETI Mission as a Bridge

Some of the events at Mt Shasta 2005 seem to confirm the concept that came to light at Joshua Tree 2003. We in CSETI represent humans today and act as "bridge" people. On the one hand, we are in the "now" and a part of all the history of humanity. On the other hand we are seeing and being shown everything for the next 5,000 centuries, or 500,000 years. The doorway from now to the past and the doorway from now to the future are fully open, and the CSETI purpose is to bridge the span between those eras.

Weather Event: Temperature Change
Dr. Raven Nabulsi

We had an interesting weather event at the Sand Flats. The sky was clear except for one little cloud drifting along. The cloud expanded until it became a cover illuminating our location. A large, nearly physical disc landed in the field, and people disappeared into a large clouded area as they entered it. When the sky cleared, the temperature was warmer than it was when we went down to the city. On the way back, while driving down the hill I looked into the woods. I saw on the floor of the forest a large, electric blue, disc that looked like a hockey puck.

Complexity of Expressions
Dr. Ted Loder

On the same evening as the weather event, I saw either a big flash or light in the woods as we were returning to town.

Dr. Steven Greer

We saw the same light that Dr. Loder, who was in our car, saw. It was definitely an ET *and* celestial craft. We have seen a progression in which expressions of extraterrestrial civilizations and the ancient human presence have come together. The theme seems to involve the present state of humanity and the future state of humanity interacting with the celestial and cosmic beings.

This paradigm of combining extraterrestrial and celestial involvement represents the key to understanding what we are really doing in CSETI. It is also a key to understanding the events on site when we are in a state of cosmic consciousness. By spending many hours each week in group meditation together and going into a state of cosmic and celestial awareness out under the stars, we are creating the foundation for the next whole level of our civilization on Earth.

The next level of civilization already exists in its perfected form within the celestial realm. The celebration that we shared on Blanca Peak signified that the next level of civilization already exists in the empyrean and celestial realm as a crystalline architecture blueprint. It is all *here*, at that resonance level, and is now coming into manifestation. This manifestation is really what the CSETI project is about.

Alleged Star Responds to Fighter Jets

Greg Heller
Another event from this training involved a supposed star that should not have been there. Suddenly three fighter jets flew in and at this star. The star jumped across to the other side of the mountain, traveled forty miles, and then shot off into space.
I asked Dr. Greer, "Why would they do that?"

Dr. Steven Greer
This incident demonstrates suppressive tactics used to keep CE-5s from going too far. The Cabal does not want CE-5 encounters reaching a point where they become too well known. That would blow the lid off the secrecy. It is obvious to me that suppressive activities have been strong since 1992. We have seen it repeatedly and at close range. A few nights ago at Joshua Tree some of you saw the jet loaded with electronics. It is typical of this cosmic cat and mouse game, but ultimately we know that the outcome will be very favorable.

Consciousness Training
Joshua Tree, California
November 2005

Focus on Consciousness

Dr. Steven Greer
I decided that it was important to have a retreat where we focused primarily on higher states of consciousness and the development of cosmic consciousness. I felt a retreat with this focus would help prepare people for being cosmic ambassadors. Many people view the state of Samadhi[108] as the endpoint of one's development. For what we are doing, it is the beginning point. I taught people meditation techniques and I did a Puja[109] at this retreat.

Linda Willitts
We took a path to the Shaman Cave, which Raven had located. Dr. Greer led meditations in groups inside the cave. As we were leaving I took a photo of the sunset and Venus, which was sparkling like a diamond. I actually took two photos in quick succession. The first one is a normal shot of Venus, a Joshua tree and the sunset. In the second photo some orbs appeared with Venus at the top of the photo. Zooming in digitally on the computer you can also see a small craft. Every year that we go to Joshua Tree, I take photos on this path but have never seen an orb except for November 2005.

Greg Heller
After the ceremony, I was meditating while looking at the cave and saw a vortex of light surrounding the cave and flowing from it. I saw a golden yellow craft that flew over fast in an arch towards our dome of light.

Dr. Steven Greer
A golden ET craft did fly in. It was late afternoon, the sun had just set, and it was not a meteor, nor a satellite nor an aircraft Many of us saw it. It made an arc across the sky and framed the whole area as we were leaving the meditation and initiation cave. It was very beautiful.

---

[108] Samahdi—is a Hindu and Buddhist technical term that usually denotes higher levels of concentrated meditation [http://en.wikipedia.org/wiki/Samadhi]
[109] Puja—is a ceremony that is performed on a variety of occasions to pray or show respect.

Kay Gibson

As Jan Brook and I were driving into the park, a big black bird with a wingspan similar to what Dr. Greer mentioned in his account flew down over the hood of the car and flapped as if it was leading us on. It was remarkable – huge.

Dr. Steven Greer

I could not identify this stunningly huge, alleged bird. It was silent, and it tracked exactly above and around our circle. It felt like a harbinger of peace.

Crop Circle Sounds

Dr. Jan Bravo

During another incident we heard the crop circle tones reproduced for us outside and above our circle. Many people gave descriptions. It was the first time I had heard them. No one in our group was playing those tones at that time.

Sentries Appear

Dr. Warren Wittekind

At one break, someone located a warm spot. We put our hands into the place, and it was very warm. Dr. Greer said there were five sentries located around our position and that we had located one.

Kay Gibson

I found myself standing inside a being as I extended my arms as far as possible. I have no idea how big the being was; it seemed to be everywhere. I have had training in sensing energy, and the being emanated a pale salmon-gold energy. When I put my hands in it, they took on a mottled pattern. I walked around the area but could not feel that energy anywhere else. Dr. Greer mentioned that he felt the being was a sentinel.

Greg Heller

My recollection was that the being was warm and the light inside was a swirling golden, silver and red. When I put my hand into it I felt the warmth; it was very visible as it spun around.

Military Show of Force and Suppression

Dr. Steven Greer

We went into an area where we felt an energy shift. We looked around and saw a very large circular craft, similar to a plasma field. It was a foggy white area filled with scintillations that were extraterrestrial. We saw extraterrestrial life forms of varying heights. When we walked up to them, they would light up so brightly that their presence was unmistakable. The beings were nearly fully materialized flesh and blood. It was not subtle, and continued for at least thirty minutes. As the event continued to unfold, a military jet flew in menacingly from the east-northeast, dead-on towards us, and shined a light right into our location. I urged everyone to get down as it flew a couple hundred feet above us. It flew very slowly, then turned and left the area. I think they were aware the craft was about to materialize and the military craft was making a very strong suppressive effort.

Group of Beings Interact

Dr. Raven Nabulsi

We decided to find that place where Dr. Greer saw a ship go into the desert floor in 1996. As I was walking back with my hand out, I clearly felt a little finger poke the palm of my hand. Greg was behind me, and he saw the little being that poked my hand.

Greg Heller

I was following Linda, Raven and Dr. Greer and saw vortices, flashes of light, and little beings on either side of them. We continued walking in the energy of that one area, and when we turned around, two whitish beings suddenly appeared as Raven was walking with extended hands. They looked like the cartoon character Casper the Ghost. They were almost materialized and were walking behind Raven with their hands out. They started to imitate human walking. They were rocking. I decided not to say anything, and I had to put my hands over my mouth to stop from laughing. When I returned I invited them to come into the group, but they faded out just before joining us.

Linda Willitts

Dr. Greer invited the beings to come with us. As we walked with extended hands, the beings trailed along with us. You could see their Casper-like shapes. There were many of them, and they were glowing brightly. Then the huge military plane appeared. Prior to the arrival of this military jet these beings and the craft were glowing a bright, white color. When the jet came with its spot light, the beings dimmed down to almost nothing. After the plane left and the danger had past, they brightened up again.

Greg Heller
On the earlier walk the two beings were materialized, very close, and bright. I felt the warmth, love and happiness that the beings emitted. They were having fun and enjoying being with the group.

Dr. Steven Greer
They were very playful, pure-hearted, and innocent, emitting a sweet feeling. It was exactly the feeling that came from the being that was in the house in England when Shari was dying. They were very pure-hearted and compassionate. You never forget it when you feel that from a person or one of these ET Beings.

Silent Black Bird and Craft Making Unusual Sound
Dr. Raven Nabulsi
Once an enormous, silent black bird flew around the group and disappeared. Immediately after that, the craft came over that made a very unusual sound.

Dr. Steven Greer
That night some people stayed in town and about sixteen came out for fieldwork. We were in meditation, and an alleged bird flew out of the northwest, in complete darkness. Rather than fly in, it just appeared at a certain point in the sky, and silently circled our group. It was huge and had a wing span of at least six feet. It circled the group just feet above our heads, making no sound, then went to the point of its origination and vanished into thin air!

Moments later an ET craft came out of the east making an unusually complex harmonic sound – "Wha, wha, wha, wha" – that everyone heard. The craft was definitely fully materialized and was only ten to twenty feet above our heads!! I think that if I had been on my chair and jumped up, I would have touched the underside of it. Then, it passed over our circle and vanished in complete silence again. This ET craft originated from the area of the landing site, where the large craft went into the desert floor in 1996. It was the closest a fully materialized ET craft has ever been over a group…

Close Approach and Scan

Greg Heller
When Jan was sitting right next to me, she opened her eyes and saw a craft go over the Joshua Tree.

Dr. Steven Greer
I saw it, felt it and heard it too.

Jan Brook
I said if it had gotten any closer, it would have brushed the top of the tree!

Linda Willitts
It was over us and had the weirdest sound; it reminded me of a Rain Bird sprinkler[110], "Chua, chua, chua."

Dr. Steven Greer
The resonance of the sound was another omni-directional sound, like nothing you hear on Earth. The sound was manifesting the shape and vice versa.

Jan Brook
The craft looked like an inverted convex mirror to me. When the sound first started, I had been tuning into the cricket sounds out in the field. The cricket sounds became super intense, metallic and almost physical. I opened my eyes a little, still looking down, and at the very top of my peripheral vision, I could see the Joshua Tree. At the top of the Joshua Tree, I saw an object that looked like

---

[110] http://www.rainbird.com/

an inverted, convex mirror. The object was floating very slowly, and brushed the top of the tree. It lit up Dr. Greer's car and then went on around.

Dr. Steven Greer
It was so close and the sound was unmistakable.

Demonstration of ET Compassion

Greg Heller
I was actually in contact with that ship, and the beings onboard wanted to scan us. They asked me and I told them I thought it would be fine. The close sighting happened just five seconds later.

Dr. Steven Greer
What Greg just shared has <u>profound</u> significance. Greg had shared that he has had anxiety stemming from childhood experiences. Greg shared with everyone that five seconds before the craft appeared, the ETs asked him in a mental request, "Is it OK for us to come?" He was the only one who received that message because the ETs were concerned about provoking anxiety in him. I am giving some insight here. Of all the people in the circle, these beings went to Greg because they knew if their attendance was fine for Greg, it would be fine for all.

This is a key point. The actual extraterrestrial people are amazingly compassionate. They do not want to induce fear, anxiety or trepidation. This behavior is very different from the "stagecraft" operations of the counterintelligence alien reproduction vehicles (ARVs) and the pseudo-abductions and pseudo-mutilations used to scare people.

Incident at Alton Barnes 1992

Recall the incident at Alton Barnes in 1992 when the woman psychologist was with me. She was fine initially. The ship was at ground level in the field and fully materialized. You could hear its transformer-like hum and see its lights going around. Our hair was literally standing on end from the electrostatic effect generated. When I signaled to the craft and it began to approach us, the psychologist became so upset that the ship stopped instantly. At the moment her anxiety and fear became uncomfortable the craft backed off ever so gently. Then it rose up into the mist to a safe distance for her and remained there for an hour. The magnetic needle on my compass was moving counterclockwise around the dial, ever so slowly, and in the same direction that the craft was spinning. There was an opening in the cloud cover, and the ship appeared as a beautiful amber-golden orb. When I signaled to it, it signaled back, and then vanished into space.

Real vs. Pseudo Contact

One can clearly see the kind of compassion, kindness and gentleness that takes place in actual extraterrestrial contact as opposed to the counterintelligence pseudo contact. This pseudo contact is the main phenomena recorded in UFO literature, movies, books, magazines, radio shows, and UFO conferences. Greg may not have even realized the importance of his story when he shared it, so I want to emphasize that importance now. Greg knew that issues existed within him, and the ETs wanted clearance from him, not from me, in order to proceed. They went to Greg to be sure that he would know they were coming. They made certain he was prepared for this ship to enter in such extreme close proximity to the group. The extraterrestrials wanted the experience to be positive for Greg, and not something that would invoke anxiety, fear or distress. I think this shows the true nature of these visitors.

Greg Heller

I want to confirm what Dr. Greer is saying. The true nature of these visitors is warm and loving. These beings are always careful in approaching us. If there is fear involved, it is not an ET visit. Frankly, I can communicate with ETs better than I can communicate with humans. These beings can communicate a whole chapter of information at once.

Myths of the "Evil ETs"

Dr. Steven Greer

The ETs are clear in their intent and their actions. When I give a lecture I am often challenged about the "evil ET" paradigm. People ask if they are here to eat us for lunch and if they are snatching babies out of our wombs and have them floating in incubators – on and on ad nauseam. This issue runs deep into counterintelligence capabilities and psychological warfare stagecraft. These classified human capabilities are extremely complex, but well-known and documented.

The CSETI Experience

On the other hand, we have the CSETI experience – the theme of this book. We have gone all over the world with thousands of people and have had close encounters of all types. We have had bizarre longitudinal weapons fired at us at Mt. Shasta. We've had federales[111] rob us at gunpoint of our passports and money in Mexico. We have had all manner of problems with various human elements. But we have never had a scintilla of threat, harm, fear or danger from ETs. I take that as a body of experience and knowledge that speaks against all the third-hand mythology and rumor mongering. Because there is so much deliberately false information imbedded into the public consciousness, a real-time diplomatic effort to make contact is vital. The false information is designed to invoke fear, hatred and anxiety. Our direct experiences confirm that people have not been zapped, dragged on board a craft, mutilated, tortured, sexually abused, or harmed in any way as the UFO subculture so frequently suggests.

You have to ask, "What's going on here?" A huge counterintelligence and propaganda operation exists, and it is designed to invoke fear to lay the foundation for conflict. The "negative ET perspective" is extremely well orchestrated. One of the main abduction researchers turned clients away if they appeared in his group but did not have a negative story to tell about an encounter with a UFO or ET. Thus he included only negative and frightening stories in his database. I later learned the name of the covert cell that was funding him.

So an effort to demonize ETs is going on and the great majority of the public is not aware of it. The disinformation specialists have perpetrated a fraud on the public that is designed to evoke a very specific conditioned response. Fear of ETs is a very dangerous conditioned response, so it is important that you know the truth

---

[111] federales—slang term for Mexican federal police [http://en.wikipedia.org/wiki/Federales]

about the encounters we have had. These extraterrestrials were extremely considerate and clear in asking permission before approaching us. This episode was a very close encounter, and yet they showed such consideration.

Greg Heller
I have had experiences with ETs since I was three years old. I can tell you that not only have I never been harmed, but also that if I felt frightened in an experience, it would stop. I actually have had to talk to the ETs and tell them to let me get over my own propensity for being startled or having fears. They have gone out of their way to make sure I felt no fear. People I have met who have had true ET experiences look forward to it. Unfortunately the *Independence Day* movie image usually prevails, and I have to spend half an hour explaining that this is just not the way it is.

Dr. Steven Greer
In conclusion I think that the real extraterrestrial contact is universally very enlightened, peaceful and compassionate. It is juxtaposed to the dominant myth that is prevalent in our society today. This dominant myth is the product of a very well thought out psychological warfare campaign and counterintelligence operation. This fact needs to be stated just that clearly. There is no need to fear ETs, and we do not need to prepare for or conduct a war against them.

Wide Range of Events and Intelligence Happening

Kay Gibson
We walked out from the Geology Tour Road site into the plain where we heard Native American chanting and drumming. My consciousness was in a fire-lit circle dancing with Native American drummers. It was so uplifting to my heart.

Dr. Steven Greer
This happens very often. The layers of intelligence and events that take place range from human activity to extraterrestrial, astral, ancestral, Native American, and angelic/celestial/avatar/God-head presence. While this seems bizarre to many people, I tell them it is happening everywhere. Our group is simply talking about it and

opening up to it. We are interacting consciously and sharing our experiences.

Sound and Anechoic Chambers

Trudy Guyker

During the meditation I could hear my heart beat for a long time and feel the blood pulsing through my body. After returning to Phoenix following the training, Linda and I had a discussion with Charlie about what might have been occurring.

Charlie Balogh

In music there is a harmonic structure of sound. There is the fundamental frequency and then first, second, third, fourth, fifth, etc. harmonics of it. These are created by halving, doubling, tripling, etc. the original frequencies. When you hear any one sound, every one of those harmonics is present at successively lower volume levels. If you start with a fundamental sound and start to add harmonics electronically, you can create any sound that you wish simply by varying the harmonics. I think you were hearing all the harmonics and feeling them.

In sound engineering, when they test sound equipment, they put it into an anechoic chamber. An anechoic chamber is a chamber in which the ceiling, floor, walls, are lined with baffles that reduce all sound reflection. When you walk into an anechoic chamber, you can hear your heart beat, you can feel the blood rushing through your veins. The only sound you hear is what is being generated within you. So Trudy was in a situation where there was no sound reflection whatsoever; she had to be within a space that allowed that to happen.

Dr. Steven Greer

I had the same experience. We were in an anechoic chamber created by the extraterrestrials. The sound was permeating and profound.

Chapter 14

2006

CSETI Training
Crestone, Colorado
June 2006

Debbie Foch
Early that week a huge thunder storm came through the town of Crestone flooding many of the roads on the side of the mountain. It was like an energy field that came through and affected events for the rest of the week.

Linda Willitts
We had to find a new site for our fieldwork in 2006. Eventually we found a site resembling a huge circle of beach sand. It was lovely doing work out there and it was very close to the town houses. We had a panoramic view of the whole valley. I remember one night after most people had left the site. Those people who came with Dr. Greer and Dr. Loder remained on site – a total of seven of us. After everyone else left, we were sitting out there in a mini-circle when a huge spotlight of Kindness' blue light shone down over us.

Debbie Foch
Yes, that was when Trudy and I were returning late after dropping off the rest of the people in our small car-group. We were walking on the road and saw the huge spotlight coming in from the east over the mountains.

Dr. Ted Loder
I can confirm the whole thing. I did not see where it came from, but I was looking into the circle and saw shadows it cast. It was the biggest light or flash-type object I had ever seen until Joshua Tree 2007. It was really "Wow! Wonderful."

Dr. Steven Greer

The weather was absolutely beautiful. I was aware that Kindness was locked onto us in a geo-synchronous location. Often she flies in, flashes us, then curves away and flies back out into space. Her ship was east of our location over the Sangre de Cristos. As we were sitting as friends in a very high state of cosmic awareness and love, we were bathed in cosmic light. It was not ethereal or astral, though it had that component. The light was very visible, to the point that you could see shadows from it. Beautiful!

Trudy Guyker

One of the most spectacular events happened when we were in our circle and became aware of a large craft just south of us. We all walked over and saw a brilliant, almost fully materialized craft. I recall several of us could see beings walking in the craft and outside of it. My sense was that there were only a few ET people outside the craft. I could see inside the craft and the majority of the ETs were still in there doing their work. I remember that while standing there, I got so warm I had to take my coat off. I was sweating just standing there. The ET craft seemed to be emitting immense heat.

Dr. Steven Greer

Trudy's account is a very important confirmation of something that otherwise could be dismissed. We're there with an ET craft and it is so visible to some of us that it was really just one notch from being materialized. It was like a plasma light, and you could see extraterrestrial life forms inside and some ETs moving outside and coming near us. As we entered the craft, the temperature went up twenty degrees. This is not an exaggeration. We were all hot, not just warm.

The next day I discovered a bubble in my compass, although there was no leak or breakage. The fluid used in compasses is usually alcohol or glycerin. You can't get an air bubble unless it is broken or certain electromagnetic fields are present. When others looked at their compasses, virtually everyone who was in the group that came close to that craft had a bubble. The meta-theme of that night was 'oneness.' We were in a 'bubble of oneness,' and a perfectly round bubble had formed in each of our compasses. A few days later, the bubbles disappeared. It was phenomenal, an expression of an actual encounter via magnetic compasses.

Charlie Balogh
This was also the first year that Dr. Greer led meditation based on counter-rotating fields out in that same area.

Dr. Steven Greer
Just imagine magnetic discs, rotating in opposite directions at infinite velocity. We formed two groups, an A group and a B group, one doing the rotation mentally in one direction and the other group in the other direction. At that moment a craft appeared and these effects happened with our compasses...

Dr. Warren Wittekind
My notes show an event occurred toward the end of our silent meditation, when Dr. Greer stood up. He said a number of beings were walking around us. They started coming into our circle. There was a lot of activity in the middle of the circle – a consecration ceremony – and we smelled a perfume odor. This marked another time we were treated with the utmost honor and respect.

Dr. Steven Greer
It was like being anointed. This fragrance was beautiful.

Charlie Balogh
I remember that night clearly because as we were sitting in meditation I definitely felt movement behind me, as if a circle of beings was moving around behind us. I also had the impression that they were rather tall beings.

Linda Willitts
Kindness flashed us with a rectangle of blue-white light about a foot long and three feet above the ground, just two feet in front of us. Dr. Bravo and I both saw it, as did Dr. Greer.

Dr. Ted Loder
I'd like to mention a wonderful, personal event the day we went

to Blanca. Peak. We had done our usual meditation in the circle followed by our short hike up to the contact site. Dr. Greer had moved forward from the rest of the group and quasi-disappeared. Generally I do not see as much as others do, but that night I was very close. I noticed the beginning of a gray area and a whitish type amorphous being, and a lit area about four feet in front of me. I watched it for a long time, and it stayed right there. As we continued our observations, I sent this ET love and thanked it for coming and being with us. Later, I mentioned this to Dr. Greer and he told me something thrilling. He said that this ET was the same one that had been in the room with Shari and him in England during an earlier expedition. I felt that the meta-message, which many of us know, was that certain ETs are with us and continue to be with us throughout these trainings. This experience brought that fact home for me. It was very wonderful for me because it was confirmation that we had made the contact there and I had witnessed it first hand.

Dr. Steven Greer

We see many of these extraterrestrial beings, and some of them are so fully materialized that at times they touch us. Other times they are shifted beyond the crossing point of light. Often you become aware that it is the same being from past encounters. They have personalities and feelings just as we do. The being Dr. Loder saw was the same being with us in England in 1997. This contact at Crestone happened nine years later almost to the week – nine being the number of fulfillment and a very holy number. The square root of nine is three, and the CSETI triangle has three circles at its corners. It seems these other themes involving numbers, geometry and patterns of events come into play and are quite interesting. This ET was very sweet and about three feet tall.

Deep friendship is another theme and characteristic that we see. Interestingly, this Ancient One has an appellation. He is known as "The Friend."

CSETI Training
Mount Shasta, California
September 2006

Craft from Mount Shasta

Dr. Steven Greer

While at the Mt. Shasta cathedral contact site we had a number of sightings as craft came out of the volcano, moved around and signaled us. People also saw brilliant red and blue lights in the trees nearby. One particular night we gave people the task of going to find their own sites. We returned to the main site around 10:00 PM. A dozen or so people had already returned to the main site so the total number of people was sixteen or seventeen.

We were doing our protocol in consciousness when suddenly very high celestial, pure-white beings appeared from the mountain as physical God-consciousness craft. They were totally visible with the naked eye and amazing in the night scope. They were expressions of the most powerful intelligence, consciousness and celestial light.

I saw eight of these 'beings' during half an hour. They came down the mountain towards us and were shining brightly! The unusual characteristic of the light was that it didn't shine out like an incandescent light. This light could only be described as celestial – not of this world. The beings were connecting with our group on a profound and deep level of God-consciousness.

I knew that they represented a civilization several hundred thousand years – or more – beyond where we are now in evolution. They had evolved to the point where their spacecraft and their consciousness were one. I knew that the whole expression of their being and their technology was at the celestial level of intelligence – a combination of consciousness, love and this type of light energy. It penetrates your soul and your entire being. It was an astonishing experience for everyone present. I knew then that a major opening had happened that would continue with multiple people, and that the CSETI experience would continue to evolve on a mass level.

Digital Photo

Two members of the CSETI group, were camping near our contact site that night. After our fieldwork ended, they were told by some super high intelligence to go out, look up in the tree and take a digital photograph. They captured an image, and the love they felt prompted them to name this ET "The Loved One of Mt. Shasta".

Trudy Guyker
I happened to be looking through my stabilizing binoculars when I saw one flash and then another flash. I saw the light shine down and flash out like a funnel, with black in its center. To me, it had the brilliance of a million diamonds – like diamonds under lights that were alive and brilliant. The closest I have come to seeing anything like them were the big basketball size balls of light that appeared in the very same spot in an earlier year.

I was fortunate to be looking through the stabilizing binoculars when I saw the lights; I really saw them well. It took me a few seconds to comprehend what I had just seen. The craft itself was alive. It was made up of life. The craft was the being intertwined in the craft, this brilliant light that was alive.

I felt emotion coming from it and could feel personality. It had a very human feeling about it. The being and I were talking back and forth. I finally reached the conclusion that it was ET. It was an ET craft as ET and celestial together.

Later, I was thinking about it and determined it was ET but it was also human, because I was feeling the human element – the personality from this being. My conclusion was that it was the human civilization that will evolve from present day humans. What we saw is the way humans are going to be thousands and thousands of years from now. They were time travelers, and I could feel the human personality. They were ET, and human. We will evolve to the point where we will be in that celestial state.

Dr Steven Greer
It is not a case of 'either or,' but both. Remember the Zen saying 'Neither this nor that.' The transcendent combination of extraterrestrial, human and celestial appears now and in the future.

Trudy Guyker
This realization affected my soul; the awareness of the potential totally changed me. There is a part of me that has been transformed. I will never look at life the same way. The meaning of life, mind and consciousness has become sharper.

Dr. Steven Greer
This manifestation was physically visible with the naked eye to the people present. Real light was floating and moving. This was not an astral vision. There was a technological component present at the level of celestial technology. That is the point I keep writing and talking about – where manifestation combines extraterrestrial and celestial technology. It was very powerful, and the intelligence was extremely advanced. We were dumbstruck, absolutely thunderstruck by the high level of the intelligence that was present.

Earlier Preview of ET/Celestials

Debbie Foch
The first time we saw them was earlier in the week when we were up at the cathedral site. We had formed our circle and I happened to be facing the mountain when I saw the brilliant, brilliant light.

Dr. Steven Greer
It was near the top of the mountain. The light emerged and though it lasted only a few seconds, it seemed like an eternity. It is hard to explain; time stood still. It was transcendent. Debbie and I were the only ones that saw it. It was the same craft of beings and intelligence.

Trudy Guyker
The light went outward, stayed there, and then it dimmed back. It was exactly as Dr. Greer said; the incredible intelligence that was emanating from this thing was extraordinary. It just boggled the mind. The energy was of the very finest celestial quality – so refined. It was incredible.

Debbie Foch
When we were up at the cathedral we were feeling love but Trudy

saw the word 'love.' That was all part of it – the love coming to us. Trudy was feeling it and seeing it.

Greg Heller

I was not feeling well that night, and I decided to go back to my motel room. I do not know the exact time, but I remember going into the bathroom and seeing Mt. Shasta from the higher window. I was leaning on the back wall of the bathroom and went into a deep meditation for almost two hours. I did not see the light, but the energy coming from the mountain was exactly what Debbie described. I watched for two hours, feeling a download and a love that I cannot believe. It was an amazing experience for me and I wasn't even there.

Owls and Ancient Being at Cathedral Site

Debbie Foch

Remember? The reason we went to the cathedral when we first saw that flash was because we were hearing sounds like owls to the east in the woods.

Dr. Steven Greer

The important point was that an ancient, pre-homo-sapiens being was close to the site. It was extraordinarily atavistic, truly a return to the primitive and primordial. This was an ancient being – a representative of an intelligent life form that lived on Earth pre-homo-sapiens. He manifested, and was walking through the woods when we heard him. He let out a cry/shout when we were in a meditation that everyone heard. The shout was stunning, as it moved and was directional. Owls were communicating with him and with our group. They went in a circle moving from east to south and ended up at our contact site. That was the sign, which we always look for, that it was time to go as a group and stand together at the contact site.

Trudy Guyker

The previous year I had seen the Kokopelli[112] dancers and the Avatar at that spot. He had been there from the very beginning

---

[112] Kokopelli—a fertility deity, usually depicted as a humpbacked flute player [http://en.wikipedia.org/wiki/Kokopelli]

when people were in that area. So this night we witnessed an even earlier person than the Kokopelli.

Dr. Steven Greer
Yes, it was truly ancient – it could have been millions of years ago. This being was a keeper of the energy of that area and had a profound connection with the mountain, the Earth, and with the extraterrestrial beings. He made it clear that he was going to be with us that night. His presence was not subtle; everyone heard this being walking and heard his cry. We had an audio system working and recorded the cry.

Greg Heller
I felt this year at Shasta was a continuation of some of the events that had happened the last time – the changing of the age, the Kokopelli dancers, the Ancient One. Now we had the animals. I left the group on the first night. The location was considerably past the sacred site where we normally meet. I went into meditation at that spot and the first thing I heard were Tibetan bowl tones.

I began my meditation, and I heard it again. The next thing I knew there were 'alleged' owls, big owls. They buzzed me. They were in my face, looking right in my eyes, literally inches away. I had my hand out, and I thought one was going to land on it. They circled, looking directly at me six times. It was six exactly, and I think there were three owls. I was stunned; the owls were very loving.

Then across the dirt in the forest, I saw two beings. I had my night vision and was finding the incident unbelievable. One of the beings walked away and then came back. I invited them down but instead sparkles came at me by the millions. I invited the sparkles up on me. They covered my body with love and that is how they interacted with me. I started walking back in amazement. I was so far out that I thought for a moment I might get lost. But the group had put up a golden dome, and I could literally see it over the trees. The dome guided me back to the group. I listened to the group for a while from a distance before coming back in. It was an amazing week of the ancient ones communicating through the animals.

Dr. Steven Greer

I think it's very important to recap the sequence. The night before we had been at the cathedral grove where Trudy and others had this profound feeling of sacred, divine love. Then Debbie and I saw the brilliant light that emerged and shone its light right into us, right into everyone. The ancient being and the owls were present. Then the next night these celestial ETs appeared.

Fog Effect

Linda Willitts

The same night we felt the intense love we also saw a ten-foot diameter, circular cloud. It was at ground level near a tree and so fully materialized that some people thought it was a bush. This 'cloud' was an opaque gray, distinct, ten-foot diameter ball and was sitting on the ground! It became more translucent at one point. You could see through it and eventually it dissipated.

Dr. Steven Greer

The 'cloud' was very dense, though, and I think virtually everyone who looked in that direction saw it. It was an almost unbelievable object to see because it was so close to us. It was no more than fifteen feet away. The object was an extraterrestrial vehicle that has been described many times by others as an astral fog effect.

Trudy Guyker

When I saw the 'cloud,' I was standing next to a person who was at his first training. He saw it as clearly as everyone else. He asked if it was a bush and kept looking at it, wondering if it could be something else.

Dr. Steven Greer

I think a good description would be a dense etheric object as opposed to finely etheric. It was very dense, to the point that it was very close to being fully materialized.

Points of Light and Owls

Dr. Raven Nabulsi

During that week we saw two points of light that looked exoatmospheric and were moving together. It happened two nights in a row at about the same time. There were no satellites at that time.

On the night that we had the encounter with the owls and the Ancient Being, we had been signaling to lights on the mountain for almost twenty minutes. I have a couple of minutes of it on video. It was almost at the glacier area on the mountain. People would not be hiking there. The light that was coming back to us must have been a very strong beam since we were able to see it at that distance.

The whole encounter with the owls was an amazing orchestration of events. The owls were calling back and forth to each other, while we were all standing silently, listening to them. It was as if each of us was in an altered state. Everything was surreal; moonlight on the mountain, stars sparkling, and immense beauty. Many people experienced being touched, some on the back of their calf or on their shoulders. When it was over, the owls stopped their activity.

Dr. Steven Greer
There were two points of light that looked like two stars that we had seen on multiple nights. Initially, everyone thought they were two satellites on the same trajectory moving together across the sky. But it happened again and again the same night, and in various directions. This fact would completely dismiss satellites. It also happened multiple nights.

I had a remote view override that the lights we were seeing were the two tips of a massive double-tetrahedral ship.

Triangular Craft from Different Aspect
In 1999 at Mt. Shasta we saw a massive majestic triangular ship that was out in deep space. These points of light had the same kind of majestic movement and feeling, and I came to realize that it was the same craft. I recognized that these two points of light were the two tips of the massive tetrahedron because I had seen the other one as a tetrahedron also. It was the same huge ship, an interstellar spacecraft that we have estimated to be hundreds of miles across on each end.

Randy Tielking
I was sitting on the north side of the circle, and I was looking straight up with my binoculars and picked up the two lights moving together. One was in front of the other, and it looked like it was extremely high. The distance between the two lights was miles and miles. I watched the first light track across the sky. It maintained the same distance the entire time. It was always at the same orientation, with one leading the other; I probably tracked it for a minute.

Bi-location onto the Triangular Craft
Greg Heller
One night, Dr. Greer did a meditation based on that ship. It was the most profound experience for me because I literally bi-located. I was on the ground and simultaneously, I was in the beautiful ship. I was looking through a tube pointed down at the Earth. Behind me were ETs telling me here is something that can amplify your consciousness, your love, as humans. This is something we are offering you to use as a group to project peace and amplify it over the Earth.

I think Dr. Greer spoke about that in his meditation. I could see it, but at the same time I was sitting and could feel it. The next day Dr. Greer told about a dream he had in which he saw me standing in that ship. Everything that Dr. Greer said was true. It is exactly what they want us to do.

Dr. Steven Greer
I felt the entire group of thirty people was ready to go into a meditative state in which their conscious and astral bodies could bi-locate onto the tetrahedron extraterrestrial spacecraft. This craft was hundreds of miles in diameter. We went into it, and many people had a very clear and profound experience of being there. From there we were seeing the Earth and joining with many extraterrestrial and celestial beings who are very much involved in this project.

Dr. Greer's Mandala and Pictures

Dr. Steven Greer
The last morning for conviviality we went to the 'Has Bean,' a coffee house in Mt. Shasta. Honey and her sister, Mickey, came rushing into the coffee shop and showed us a photograph of the beautiful, luminous being called "The Loved One." It appeared in the picture about twenty feet above a tree. We were all excited. She had the barista[113] take a picture of the five of us – Dr. Bravo, Linda Willitts, Honey, Mickey and myself. The picture showed a beautiful mandala orb that appeared to be emanating from the center of my chest, probably as a result of the boundless joy, friendship, and love I was feeling for these people, the extraterrestrial and celestial beings and the experience of contact.

Debbie Foch
Honey and Mickey came to my room at 2:00 in the morning to show me the picture they took of "Loved One" at their campground...

Linda Willitts
I have another photo of our circle in the secluded site. Before it got dark I took two pictures in close succession. One of the pictures is normal and the other picture shows a ball of light on the ground. The ball of light is right between Jan and Debbie. When you zoom in using the computer, you can see the ball is made of light and is translucent; you can even see the flowers behind it.

Randy's Decision

Randy Tielking
While we were at the site during the day, Dr. Greer asked for anyone who had any technical experience to please volunteer to do some work to develop new energy devices. I had been thinking for several weeks about what I could do to help. When Dr. Greer said that, I immediately thought it might be a possibility for me, so that evening I talked to him about it.

Dr. Greer and I were standing in the center of the circle discussing this work. While we were talking and while I was feeling that this

---

[113] barista—a professional who is highly skilled in coffee preparation [http://en.wikipedia.org/wiki/Barista]

is what I should do, I was also thinking about how I could possibly describe to my wife why I should be doing this. How could I tell her why it is important, and how could I answer all those questions she might ask. I had some doubts as to whether I should be doing this.

Just as I was thinking about all this, a light object flew over from east to west. It was streaming sparkles behind it. As I looked up and started to follow the object across the sky, it split into two parts. One part of the object branched off to the north and one part branched off to the south, just for a brief moment. When I saw it split like that, I thought that it was a message to me. I thought that it represented a decision that I needed to make; it was an expression for me to see.

ETs and Military Surveillance on Woman's Property
Linda Willitts

On the last night of the training Honey related a story about an experience she had from the winter of 2004 to March 2005. She lives alone on 85 acres in the woods, and she started smelling campfire cooking every morning at 10:00 AM. When people began stealing her firewood, she started to pay attention. There was snow and she smelled cooking every evening at 6:00 PM. In March 2005 she noticed military surveillance on her property and encountered military personnel in her woods moving in a stealthy way. It was making her uncomfortable to the point that she bought night vision binoculars and went out looking in the middle of the night. At this same time, her neighbor had a fully materialized craft land in her front yard. The neighbor saw ET beings come from the craft when she awakened at night. So there had been ET activity there, and immediately the military surveillance arrived. Dr. Greer said the ETs were there to stabilize the earthquake zones as a way to help the Earth.

On the night of June 1, 2005 she was driving and her intuition told her to turn on Art Bell. She had never heard of Art Bell, but she tuned into his show on the radio. Dr. Greer was the guest speaker, and she began to put two and two together to get help with her situation. She showed up in Mt. Shasta and shared this story.

She and her sister were both at the training, and they had a real love connection. The very last night, after our training, they were staying in a tent nearby. They went back in their tent and were meditating on love. One of the sisters pointed a camera toward the sky and captured the image of a light being.

Dr. Steven Greer
The military had invaded the entire area where she lived because ET craft had been seen there going into the Earth. She was not the only one who saw the military or the ET craft, but she was at the epicenter of this activity. It was clear that it was a military operation. There were motion sensors, high tech devices in the forest and all the typical things that happen when there is a clandestine operation like this. She found out about us and came to our training at Mt. Shasta.

This particular photograph, taken in the wee hours of the morning on 9/9/2006 is important because it was taken right after we had an amazing series of encounters at our contact site on Mt. Shasta.

Reconnaissance Operations
Greg Heller
On the last day of the 2006 Shasta training, a vehicle with its parking lights on came close, not making much noise. After the group had broken up, I decided to go see who they were. I went across the road under a nearly full moon and moved to within ten feet of a man with a machine gun! I was told to remote view where these special ops came from. I stood back in the shadow of a tree and remote viewed him and his two partners for about seven minutes. He did not move an inch, and they never pointed their weapons at me. I can tell you they were sent to figure out what was going on.

Trudy Guyker
While the car was in the woods and Greg was heading there, many light flashes were occurring in a pine tree that was directly in front of the group. We have had enough experience over the years to recognize that there was a craft just barely touching, coming into material form.

Kindness Makes Her Appearance
Greg Heller
Remember Kindness' appearance? It was amazing. I know Dr. Greer saw her, but I am not sure how many others did. Kindness always makes a fly-in at some point during the trainings, but this was incredible. I saw the craft coming in from the northwest right into the top of Shasta at full speed. Dr. Greer thought it was going to hit the mountain, but it reversed direction and split into two. It was Shari's color on one part and the other part was a brilliant purple – Shari's and Kindness' ship.

CSETI Training
Charlottesville, Virginia
September 2006

Dr. Steven Greer
We had a group of twenty to thirty people in Charlottesville, Virginia, at my farm in Albemarle County. We had some amazing sightings and events that took place.

The Communications Probe
Linda Willitts
The light anchor was one of the amazing sightings and events. Thanks to Kevin we have a picture of this anchor.

Dr. Steven Greer
The extraterrestrial probe Kevin filmed was a Fibonacci based ET probe. He captured it with a Sony Super Infrared NightShot camera. The important lessons of this event were: (1) have someone with the right technology handy, (2) have someone with the consciousness to capture the event, and (3) have someone with the diligence to analyze the tape and find the object. Kevin had all three qualities and that is why I was so impressed with him. He was a wonderful, pure-hearted guy, and he went through the videotape from that evening frame by frame to find a series of frames that show this probe. That took patience because each frame is just a fraction of a second.

The event began when I sensed an object in the northeast, where

Kindness' ship is often present. I saw, felt, and actually remote viewed an extraterrestrial vehicle above and behind me. I looked up saw with my physical eyes a corkscrew shape coming in at the crossing point of light.- – it was visible but extremely fast! This object moved so fast it was at the limits of what the human eye can see. The videotape of this event is more interesting than the photograph because the tape shows me looking up and my hand tracking the probe exactly as it came down. I said, "A probe, an extraterrestrial communication probe, has just come into the center of the circle." The device was scintillating, and it was assessing and scanning everyone. This incident happened early in the week.

Some have said the image is that of a moth near the camera – but it would have been moving so that it traversed the area in 3/58ths of a second. And the image coincided with what we saw and pointed out.

Linda Willitts
The picture of the probe is just one frame from the videotape that Kevin took. Another light that 'snaked' down in an "S" shape is seen in three separate frames.

Dr. Steven Greer
This probe was at the crossing point of light, and yet the object remained in the center of the circle. A few people in the circle could see a field distortion as a or an area that was scintillating area.

Linda Willitts
Dr. Greer remote viewed it as an ET communication device. We had one of the physicists in our group analyze it and he said that could be entirely true. The device had characteristics of a Fibonacci sequence. It had points on one side of the shaft and rounded sections on the other side. The physicist said that it could possibly be duplicated in a lab but it would have to be in a vacuum. In the video it was obviously centered right in front of Dr. Greer. You can see the heads of those of us who were sitting next to him turning in unison to follow it down. We all saw it.

Contact: Countdown to Transformation

Dr. Steven Greer
Our eyes are neither IR (infrared) projection sources, nor are they IR receptive, but our minds are. My consciousness locked onto the spacecraft and felt the object coming in. Now to normal human perception, there was nothing there and nothing was seen. But this communications probe was there, and we have the proof.

Dr. John R.M. Day
The night before we saw the video of the device, I was walking about the grounds during a break and noticed small, glowing spots at several places on the ground. The spots were less than 1 centimeter wide and appeared as a bioluminescence, not unlike the glow of a lightning bug. I reached down to touch this "bio-light," and I attempted to pick up several of these spots that were integrated into the ground and the grass, but I could not pick them up. I now realize that these light spots were likely the residual that the probe left behind after it came through and penetrated the ground. The probe could not be seen with the naked eye and was caught by the camera only.

The SETI Project

Dr. Steven Greer
Probes are real and they are well documented. The problem is that we are up against the limits of current Earth technology. Most of our equipment cannot measure, detect, photograph, image or otherwise prove their presence. We need to understand that most of the resonant frequencies and activities of extraterrestrial technologies are beyond the instrumentation anything available to us can measure.

This is why the SETI project[114], the Search for Extraterrestrial Intelligence of Carl Sagan and Seth Shostack, et al, is a very anthropocentric effort. The SETI project is scanning space with radio telescopes for intelligent life forms, but their effort has two presuppositions. Presupposition 1: Other civilizations would evolve with our technology. Presupposition 2: Other civilizations would continue to use such technology for long periods of time even if

---

[114] SETI project: http://en.wikipedia.org/wiki/SETI

they did evolve it. A much higher likelihood exists that speed of light technologies would only be used for a small time during the evolution of a civilization. Most ET civilizations would already have gone beyond the current radio wave level of communications because that speed is too slow for interplanetary communication.

Kindness' Appearance

Another spectacular event happened during the week after someone had pulled a muscle. As I walked out and entered the perimeter of the circle, we saw a brilliant ET craft appear in the south, about forty degrees above the horizon. The light of this craft was shining right into the circle!

Dr. Ted Loder
I saw that brilliant craft too.

Dr. Jan Bravo
I normally see Kindness as a pure, white light. But as I came out there was a circular light, very bright, forty-five degrees above the horizon, and it just got brighter. I was transfixed. It got brighter and shone its light on us for seconds.

Dr. Steven Greer
This light was not a flash. This craft hovered very close in the atmosphere for several seconds and then vanished.

Dr. Ted Loder
I saw essentially the same thing that Dr. Greer just described. I saw a very bright object that stayed there and got brighter and brighter and then disappeared.

Dr. Steven Greer
The craft unveiled itself and hovered. I saw it from start to finish. I would say its duration was three to five seconds, and then it vanished. This craft was so close that you could feel it. My sense was that the object was in the hundreds to a few thousand feet away – not far out.

Linda Willitts
When the craft did leave, it receded into space, and you could see that happen.

Dr. Steven Greer
Yes, for people who had a straight-on view the object did seem to recede. And that is how she often comes in. I felt the craft was Kindness, who so often visits.

Green Neon Cylinder of Light
Trudy Guyker
Also during the week we saw a light green neon light appear very close. It went behind a tree and as it came from behind this tree, it turned into a cylinder of green neon light.

Dr. Steven Greer
This light was close, and I think it actually went by the Shenandoah National Park just west northwest of our site. This light was a beautiful green color.

Thunderstorm and Military Aircraft
Trudy Guyker
Another night it was raining terribly and we had to do our work inside. The thunder was incredible, and we heard a strange sound appear in the house.

Linda Willitts
One night we were breaking up our circle and people were leaving. Some of us saw a craft in the field near the woods. This craft was nestled on the ground at the base of the woods and was so close to materializing that it was shooting sparks as commas of light. Kevin came over with the camcorder, and he got some additional footage of light forms. There was a cloud cover, and I was aware of a military jet circling above us. We could not see the jet because of the cloud cover.

Dr. Loder's Flashbulb Sighting
Dr. Ted Loder
I was standing three or four people away from Dr. Greer and

looking in this field at a craft, a gray amorphous object. I could see the object's outline. As I looked at this craft, from my peripheral vision, I caught a flash of light right over Dr. Greer's head. As Dr. Greer has said many times, often you see something in your peripheral vision that you might not see if you are looking directly at the object.

Dr. Steven Greer
I saw the flash at exactly the same time Dr. Loder did. During this period, Kevin was filming and took some very good footage of this unusual object with Super NightShot. His footage shows the swirling motion of the flash as it makes almost a figure eight. The film confirmed that there was actually something there and that it was viewable with night shot. With your eyes you could see only a flash but with your consciousness, your inner sight, you could see the entire ship and the ETs that were there. This object was right in the area where we had seen a craft when we were in Charlottesville in 1999, some seven years before, when we had also done a training on the farm.

We also had a number of orbs come into the living room during the rainstorm. We were doing the fieldwork and meditation inside. I did a Puja and taught people a meditation technique. As we were sitting there, a beautiful blue-white orb hovered in the room. A number of people saw this orb.

Deer Sounds in the Woods

Linda Willitts
One night while we were in our circle, there was a huge beam of light emanating from the field adjoining Dr. Greer's property. This very distinct large beam of light came out of 600 acres of forest and grass land. As we were observing the beam, suddenly from the woods we heard a repeating noise. I cannot describe it because it was like nothing I have ever heard.

One of the people in the group said it sounded like deer when they are really afraid of something. The sound was the reaction of these deer to this craft that was right near them. You could hear them crashing around and making this noise. She said they do it when they are confused, afraid, and do not know what to do.

Dr. Steven Greer
This lit area was aglow with the beam of light, like an opening in Hollywood. The beam was two fingers' wide at arm's length, going straight up into the sky. It was very pronounced and was not far away from us—certainly within half a mile.

Stan Meyer's Appearance

Linda Willitts
Another event during this week began when Dr. Greer had a meditation one evening and saw a crouched figure that was handing him something.

Dr. Steven Greer
The meditation was very deep. Suddenly, an override occurred in which an image popped into view, and I knew it was real. I saw an older man bent over. He had something that he was desperately wanting to hand off to us. It felt like he was a human who had passed away, and was in the astral realm and had something to give us. So we went through a gate and out to the field. I could tell in the remote view that the person was over to the southwest in the field. When I reached this area that was glowing, again, there was a light form there. I knew that the form was not extraterrestrial or celestial. The form was a human that had deceased. I initially thought maybe it was someone who had once lived here years ago and had passed away on this land. I then realized that the being was Stan Meyer.

Stan Meyer was an inventor who died in the 1990s[115]. A few months prior to the Charlottesville training we had been working with an individual who claimed he was going to work with us to build a device invented by Meyer. The man working with us then got cold feet and disappeared. Meyer's device would split hydrogen and oxygen from water to create a special hydrogen-oxygen gas[116]. The gas would then essentially run a generator. The amount of energy needed to create this special resonant frequency signal was

---
[115] http://www.mail-archive.com/vortex-l@eskimo.com/msg14099.html
[116] Brown's Gas—a nonexplosive mixture of hydrogen and oxygen gas in the precise atom-to-atom ratio of two volumes of hydrogen to one volume of oxygen. [http://www.brownsgas.com/brownsgashistory.html]

only about 200 watts, but it was running a 4,000-watt generator! The result was twenty times over unity. At the time Stan Meyer died, he actually had a dune buggy running on this type of device. Meyer's invention was featured on the local news in the town in Ohio where he was living[117] Meyer came to IANS[118] with Ricky and shared this information back in the '90s. The intelligence community and the military got very interested.

Stan Meyer's invention was so advanced that the CIA was able to retrofit a Lear Jet with it. Of course, they had to add something to the water so it wouldn't freeze at high altitude. So Meyer's invention was running a Lear Jet on water, and the exhaust was nothing but water vapor. Such a device running on Brown's gas would completely transform the world. You could have a resonance frequency generator in your car and your gas tank would be filled with water. You could run your car, your house, and everything on it. This idea is not mythological; it is known and tested. The man with whom we were working (but later got cold feet) had reproduced Meyer's device in a former project. He had reproduced the device with software so you could run it on dirty water, salt water – anything. It was what the world so dearly needs to end fossil fuel use.

Stan Meyer was the being in the field that night desperately wanting us to carry his work forward. The incident was very touching because Meyer's invention had died with him in the sense that it was no longer operating anything except in the classified covert world. And I knew he wanted it to benefit humanity. Since that night I have wanted to find someone competent to reproduce his work since I do not personally have the mechanical and engineering abilities to recreate what Stan Meyer did.

Meyer's technology could transform the world into a rose garden, eliminate all pollution, all poverty, all geo-political war games, etc. If only we had the funding equivalent to one percent of what is being taken by Halliburton and other contractors in Iraq, we could have a research and development program that would come out with at least half a dozen technologies like Meyer's!

---

[117] http://waterpoweredcar.com/stanmeyer.html
[118] IANS: http://en.wikipedia.org/wiki/International_Association_for_New_Science

I felt an enormous sadness from this man in the field. He was trying to get this information to us. But of course, he is on the other side. I know this technology is something that we need to carry forward. It is a real science and a real technology that existed not that long ago...

Ricky Butterfass
Stan Meyer had many patents for the technology. He had everything from cars and trains to aircraft. He had also given the technology to the military.

Dr. Ted Loder
Conceptually, the technology is simple. But the actualization of all of his technology is a different story. Stan Meyer spent years and years developing all this, but the process is rather complex for driving the oscillations and frequency. We talked with the co-worker about it extensively and it's going to take someone with many technical skill sets in various areas of engineering. The technology is not just electrolysis as you might see in a high school lab.

CSETI Consciousness Training
Joshua Tree, California
November 2006

Trudy Guyker
Debbie, Al Dunaway and I led the group because Dr. Greer could not be there. We took the group out to the Joshua Tree site on two nights. What made it special for us was that the event happened even though Dr. Greer was not there. Since he is such a magnet for ETs, we always wondered if anything would happen on site without him.

Dr. Warren Wittekind
The pattern that had been established over the years for the CSETI protocols continued without Dr. Greer's presence. We all felt that to go on a training without him would be quite an achievement. We went into silent meditation the second night at Joshua Tree, and something in the silent meditation said to me, "Open your eyes."

When I opened my eyes two people were standing outside the group. I had not heard anyone get up. These two people standing there were very serious, and they were dressed just like we were. They were wearing dark winter hats and coats. I thought they were just two people standing outside the group, but I saw no empty chairs in our circle. I looked away, then back, and they were gone. There we were in the desert asking ETs to come join us and looking for them, and when we saw them, I did not recognize them.

Trudy Guyker
I was sitting on the south side of the group. During the silent time after the meditation, I opened my eyes and saw two tall people standing directly behind people to the south. There were two smaller people near the Joshua Tree where Dr. Greer usually parks his car. The two taller people were at least seven feet tall, and they were dressed in normal clothes. The Moon was shining so we were able to see them well. Later on I began thinking about these people, and it seemed as if they were dressed in brown leather. This leather clothing was like a flight jacket type of garment and helmet; a close helmet that kind of stood up like a winter hat. The two smaller beings were more normal sized and I thought I had better look around the area to see if there were more of them. When I looked, all the circle seats were taken. There were no other people, and when I looked back they had vanished! My husband Fred saw them as dark gray forms rather than people.

Alice Sleight
I saw these people too. I saw them wearing our kind of garb, not the kind Trudy mentioned, but with hoods or something on their heads and warm jackets. I saw four people and wondered where they would sit. They never did. We looked back again, and there were people seated in front of them. At first I thought that they were standing behind our chairs and stretching their legs. But as I looked closer, there were people in those chairs, so I realized that they were standing. I looked back later, and they were gone.

Greg Heller
I saw the scene similar to Fred's view. I noticed the darker and ET-like beings moving around. I knew they were not human. When

I looked back, they were almost in front of me, and I never took note except that I thought it was strange. It seemed they were just part of our group, but we were all in our seats. I went back into meditation, and I heard someone say they were gone.

Trudy Guyker
From all my experiences in all these years of trainings, I have never seen anything ET so materialized. They were there – solidly material. To me that was significant!

Five of us in the group saw that event. The fact that the group saw these beings without Dr. Greer present is an indication to me that the ETs are on the verge of ramping up. We have reached a point where as a group, we can see them – not just little energy sparks, but actually see them fully materialized. To me that is an indication that we are on the verge of a new level of contact with the ETs.

Chapter 15

2007

Meeting with the Hon. Paul Hellyer
Washington, D.C.
February 2007

Dr. Steven Greer
I met with Paul Hellyer, the former Minister of Defense from Canada, in February 2007 in Washington, D.C. We discussed two key issues. One was the opportunity CSETI is pursuing with a G7 government that wants us to make open contact with the ETs for them...

The citizens of Earth must put together a senior interplanetary team of the wise elders of this planet to make open contact, and move this contact to a higher level. A team of wise elders would be made up of people like Senator Claiborne Pell, Paul Hellyer, and Ambassador Jim George of Canada, who is a supporter of our work. These are people who are very enlightened, educated, have the right intentions, and have peace in their hearts and minds.

We need to assemble these people in a protected environment with the full support of space command and air traffic control, and this is exactly what we will do with this G7 government. We will have air traffic control steer all civilian and military air traffic around the site we will be using and will have space support and perimeter security. This is currently in the planning stages...

Fieldwork at The CSETI Experience
Events and Discussion about Those Events
Joshua Tree, California
February 7, 2007

The Slow, Low Military Jet

Linda Willitts

We had a huge military jet fly over nearly at stall speed. It was loaded with a framework of electronic equipment and weapons and was lit up with green lights.

Dr. Steven Greer

I got a menacing feeling from this craft. It was a jet flying too low and very slowly, loaded with electronic equipment. It originated out of Edwards AFB. I could see the interior. I knew exactly why they were here. Their presence meant they had detected ET activity and were coming to suppress it. This aircraft came in very low out of the northwest, diverted from the direction it was going, banked, turned and came across the National Park directly toward us. It moved right over the plain, and flew right by our site at low altitude, a few hundred feet above ground level, neither climbing nor descending. Then it turned back and resumed its course. I sensed that the flight was some kind of an electronic surveillance and suppression effort. At the time I asked the group to erect a golden dome over the site. The wind died down and it got very still.

Greg Heller

That plane was fully lit up, very bright, and was probably 'stealth' on radar. No one would have seen it, so it kept its lights on because this is a high traffic area.

David Alfassi

I saw lights on in the middle of the plane as though someone was inside looking at sonics; that is why the green light was on.

Dr. Steven Greer

I also think the plane was in stealth mode.

Arnie Arneson

But stealth mode is against regulation.

Dr Steven Greer

People in these projects do not follow regulations! These projects do what they want. To wit, last night an enormous military jet flew over at the limits of how low and slow one of those aircraft could fly and in a national park!

Suppression Rather than Reconnaissance
Dr Steven Greer
On the Internet today you can see the Google satellite pictures of this area – you can see the individual trees[119]. Compare that with the capabilities of the rogue elements. By 1968 with the super-classified material that was in that program, you could see from space each individual and even a necklace they were wearing, as well as hear everything being said in any remote place on the planet. That is absolutely true. I know men who have worked on those technologies. They are highly compartmentalized operations. That jet was not scrambled for reconnaissance, because they do not need to scramble one for that. The jet had electronic warfare suppression technologies on it.

ET Craft Do not Often Fully Materialize
Everyone saw the jet. It was not a subtle event. People often ask why ETs do not just completely materialize in the field. I explain how many of them have been hit with electromagnetic pulse weapon systems that destroy, disable, and even capture them. The ETs are not going to dematerialize if there is a chance that something like that might happen.

That started in 1992, after the landing in Alton Barnes. Every single time we had an encounter subsequent to that in Great Britain, within minutes, there were helicopters buzzing the field and sometimes even military people in the field. We have had this happen all over the world.

It does not matter how remote our field site is. The suppression teams can be transported via inter-dimensional transport systems or ARVs. They have the ability to move in a matter of seconds anywhere on Earth – minutes at the most. They are able to monitor what we are doing and dispatch teams to keep ETs from going too far with contact. This cat and mouse game has been going on for years.

---

[119] Google Map of Joshua Tree National Park: http://www.joshua.tree.national-park.com/map.htm

Such surveillance and suppression efforts are counter-productive to the contact results CSETI wants to achieve. I tell CSETI-trained people it is useful to do this work without me because my presence is an encumbrance in some respects. I say that completely honestly and with no false humility.

Platforms in Space Target ETs

A man I know very well designed and built the early platforms that were put into space around 1965. These platforms have high-powered longitudinal weapons systems. He worked for Hughes and virtually every other aerospace contractor you can name. Those platforms were up and fully functioning by the time I was ten years old. He excitedly told me about how great it was when they could actually get a 'kill' – that is, hit one of these ET objects and have it go down. They did bring down some of these craft, and to me it was horrifying to hear. Of course, he was programmed to think it was wonderful because his system worked. That was over forty years ago, so imagine what is operational today!

Materialization Disrupters

I emphasize to people that often the most profound contact happens in the frequency range just short of full materialization. Some would describe this non-materialized frequency range as being in another dimension of space/time. When ET craft do fully materialize, it is a potentially high-risk operation. Some people got a good look through their binoculars at this aircraft that was loaded with electronics. These aircraft involve sensing and monitoring, and they also deploy longitudinal energy weapons, that stay in an area to suppress or disrupt the materialization of the ET craft. Suppression and the potential for an attack are very significant, and that is why we ask the extraterrestrials to appear only in a way that is safe and appropriate for that time and place.

Some have asked: Why don't the ETs just disable these offensive systems? The answer is: If they did so, this could – and would – be used by hard-liners within Majestic to make the bogus case that the ETs are hostile. They are too wise to cross that trip wire and fall into that trap. It is our responsibility as humans to control our behavior and restrain the madness of Star Wars...

Positions Made Clear

I have stressed this safety factor to the ETs since the early '90s after the head of Army Intelligence and the NSA spooks took me to a hotel room and aggressively interrogated me. It was made very clear to me that they: (a) realized we had developed the Rosetta stone of contact with the ETs; (b) thought we had no right to be making such contact; (c) believed such contact was their business, not ours.

Contact Not 'Their' Business

My view has always been contact is not their business because they have lied to the President and lied to the American people. I think they have no legal jurisdiction. Who has jurisdiction for making contact with interstellar civilizations? The UN? The State Department? The Senate Foreign Affairs Committee? The military of one country?

The current Majestic operation is unconstitutional, illegal, rogue and murderous – and committing high crimes, misdemeanors and treason against the American people, as well as Earth and humanity.

Global Paradigm Needed

We need to put ET Contact in a global and universal paradigm or it will not work because the ETs are not going to open up to us unless we do. The world has been delayed in evolving into a functioning planetary society for about 100 years. Such evolution does not mean the disappearance of national interests. It does mean that all countries must be able to function for the greater good, as opposed to the dysfunctional situation in which we now live. The extraterrestrial and interstellar civilizations are very concerned about our society, because they view us as a dysfunctional family traveling into space with advanced weapons of mass destruction.

The Two Problems

Two problems continue to face the good men in this world who hold power, and I know this from having briefed them. These 'white hats' include the head of the Defense Intelligence Agency, a sitting CIA Director, Senate Intelligence Committee members who have high level clearances, the Head of Intelligence, Joint Staff and the head of the Ministry of Defense in England and many senior officials who are victims of the secrecy.

The first problem is they have never been granted access to the ET information. The second problem is that none of them know about the counter-intelligence/suppression capabilities of the rogue Majestic group.

These good people in government want Disclosure and Contact to happen and are sick of the secrecy. Behind the scenes, they are being supported by elements within the so-called 'MJ-12' or secret government group who are also weary of the secrecy. Majestic is not a homogenous group. At this point in time, I think at least half of that covert, transnational group wants Disclosure to succeed. Unfortunately, a good number of them remain ruthless and selfish, suppressing Disclosure and Contact at every opportunity.

End of the Algorithm

This secrecy will end soon. We are getting near the end of the old algorithm. But because of the Contact suppression incident that happened last night, I thought it would help to put things into perspective historically with the events that have happened in England, the United States and other countries since the early 1990s up until now.

We remain undeterred in what we are doing with our Contact and Disclosure efforts. We know that the suppression continues but we remain unaffected regarding our goals and our conscious intentions – and have no doubt of the ultimate outcome: Universal Peace – on Earth and throughout the cosmos.

Debbie Foch

Because the rogue operations are promoting Star Wars, their interaction with the ETs entails a 'shoot them down' approach. We are making only positive respectful contact as representatives – ambassadors – from our planet.

Malfunctioning Equipment

Dr. Steven Greer

Often when we have electronic interference from suppressive aircraft, our recording equipment malfunctions or fails immediately on site. I suspect this is a result of electromagnetic drain effect. Tape recorders, walkie-talkies, tri-field meters, camcorders, radar detectors, transmitters and battery operated devices usually die or malfunction. The effect is often directional and dependent on where the interference burst occurred. Shari Adamiak used to call this 'equipment shrinkage.' She sat beside me and many unexplainable electromagnetic events happened.

Dr. Bill Clendenin

I was sitting directly across from you and my cell phone battery was fine.

Terry Underwood

These peculiarities are incredible to a person from the outside looking in. It is the first time I have seen such oddities. I initially could not understand what the low, slow plane could do to us, but now I know its field effect.

Simultaneous Use of Awareness 'Channels'

Dr. Steven Greer

Remember that as we are talking and sharing in circle, you can also operate on multiple channels of awareness. On Channel 1 you are listening and sharing. On channel 2 you are in a state of cosmic mind, seeing space and remote viewing space. On channel 3 you are going beyond the crossing point of light and seeing the ethereal craft and astral manifestations. On channel 4 you are on a security reconnaissance watching for activity. On channel 5 you are getting the big picture, etc. This is all happening at the same time as an integrated function. You can train yourself to do this.

You can develop a multi-dimensional, higher state of consciousness. It is not like multi-tasking, which divides the mind. It is about being super-awake and aware from an expanded state of consciousness, and the intuition is fully functioning. It is about being able to experience, see, and sense multiple things at the same time. Affirm to yourself that you can do it, and suddenly you will find that you are doing it.

Experience with the Pulsing Joshua Tree

Pam Fletcher

When we were looking around before breaking up, I saw a shape I thought was a tree. It was black and about four or five feet tall. We went over to the car, and when I came back, the "tree" shape was gone.

Jan Brook

I had gone into the field and was feeling for the energy spot where the ETs might be. Someone shone a green laser right toward one of the objects I was approaching. Pam related the incident from the previous night where she saw a tree as a black outline. She looked later and it was not there. I was just about to ask her to take me to where she had seen it, when the Joshua Tree we were standing next to suddenly leaned sideways thirty degrees toward the west as though someone had walked up and pushed against it. First the tree tipped to the side, then moved more when we walked over to feel it. We put our hands on it, and we could feel it moving and gently rocking. We focused on the energy field and the underground ET movement as we encouraged them to rise out of the Earth. It was amazing.

Pam Fletcher

It was amazing. As Jan Brook and I were watching the tree, we could not stand it. We had to go over and touch it. It was vibrating; it was the neatest thing! Norm, Jan and Greg each touched it too.

Dr. Steven Greer

Others of us went over and touched the Joshua tree. It was pulsing, as if a heart was beating in it. It was a relatively small Joshua Tree, tall and thin. It rose up with two branches, like an antenna. It was being affected by the underground ET craft at that locale.

At one point I felt moved to lie down and put my head on the sand. I could hear multiple harmonics of a metallic tone coming into the Earth. I then had an experience where I put my forehead against it. At the same time the tree moved, tilted thirty degrees and then began vibrating. It was very strange and recapitulates the 1997 event at Hidden Valley where the tree shook vigorously.

Norm Fletcher
I am a very practical person, and I wanted to see how solid the tree was. I walked up to it and I did move it a little bit one way, and then I stopped it. But it clearly had movements of its own too. Pam and I are nurses, Steven Greer and Jan Bravo are doctors, so we know what a pulse feels like. What struck me was the pulsing through the Joshua Tree felt like it was about 120 to 130 beats a minute. It was very clear, and there was no equivocation about it. The pulse was strong.

Pam Fletcher
When we returned with Dr. Greer the tree felt happy to me. I don't know if anybody else felt that. But it felt like the Joshua Tree was happy that we were all there.

Dr. Steven Greer
Oh, very much so, the tree was very conscious, very happy.

Jan Brook
I felt when we put our hands on the Joshua Tree, we were actually sending healing energy into it and down through it into the Earth.

Linda Willitts
I felt like when we all had our hands on the tree afterwards that it really loved the touching.

Trudy Guyker
I also felt the tree and have a feeling that the tree moved in order to get our attention to go over to it. It had been waiting its entire life just to be touched.

Greg Heller
I had just walked over to the spot where Jan and Pam were looking at the tree. I objectively went through and sensed the ground warmth, light, or any vibration. I felt under the tree to determine if it was about to fall. I put my hands around it with us, without us,

even moved it a little bit and was able to stop it. I sensed energy from the ground and the life in the Joshua tree. It was spectacular and continued. I started laughing because every time the tree started to move, all I could see was the scene with the railroad trestle in the movie *Close Encounters of the Third Kind*. That's the vision that kept popping into my head.

Jan Brook
When Pam took me to the spot where she saw the tree in the road, I noticed its location was the same place where Kay and I encountered an entity a few years earlier.

Orbs

Pam Fletcher
I photographed some orbs with my Super NightShot camera after the airplane incident.

Dan Krevitsky The four of us had just walked away from the group and offered a prayer of gratitude. We also asked for any type of sighting that would be appropriate and safe for the ETs (according to Dr. Greer's earlier advice).

As we began heading back to the circle, in the southwest I saw several orbs that were very distinct, bright lights. Not just one light, but four or five, and they were right at the level of the brush. These orbs seemed to be skipping through, and I picked up an emotional element, too. The scene felt whimsical, a bit frivolous, as if the orbs were racing home. We saw these small spheres for a few seconds then they disappeared for a moment or two. We automatically sent gratitude.

They seemed fourteen to eighteen inches long and four to seven inches tall and probably four to six feet above the ground...

David Alfassi
I saw two of the orbs in the brush but did not see them with my eyes. I looked with the goggles. There were two of them in the brush and two in the sky, about five degrees above the horizon.

Greg Heller
To me the streak was either slightly rippling through the brush or just above the brush. The orbs were traveling extremely quickly, and as they disappeared out of view, the whole area lit up again.

Dr. Steven Greer
Dave, Dan and others saw transient orbs. One special moment occurred when Dan said that he was in a state of innocent consciousness and detachment. When he expressed gratitude for any way that the ETs could appear, they did.

When we connect to the ETs during meditation and vector them in, I encourage them to appear in any way that is safe and appropriate for the time and place. I also tell them that we will be grateful for their company. I explain that we understand the full range of their technologies and how their presence can manifest.

Orbs and Light Quality from Night One
Norm Fletcher
The first night we were at the fieldwork site, I saw one orb that made an impression on me. We were talking about the color quality. It was a perfectly white circle and at no point did this light get foggy at the edges. It was very clear, and it was there and gone. The quality of the light was unique in my experience. It was a myriad of colors and gradations around us and yet a perfect, white circle. When we saw the large flash in the sky, I thought its purpose was to show me that ET light is quite different.

A Probe
Randy Tielking
During the "Moving Joshua Tree" episode, Terry and I were looking at his camcorder with NightShot. We were standing on the northeast and were pointing Terry's camcorder to the southeast looking at people through the display. As we were doing that, we saw the same shape that appeared in some pictures at the Charlottesville training move very rapidly from left to right on the display. The object was about four feet above the ground. It appeared to be four feet long and about four inches in diameter. It flew very quickly; for a split second.

Terry Underwood
One eighth of a second. It was so fast!

Randy Tielking
It was very clear and looked almost exactly like the object in the Charlottesville training picture. The difference was the one we saw tonight traveled horizontally about four feet above the ground whereas the one in Charlottesville entered the ground vertically. The one tonight seemed as if it moved right over our chairs.

Terry Underwood
I thought it was wider. I thought it was more in the eight-inch range rather than four or five. It happened so fast that you almost have to have infrared in your mind to remember. I am upset that I was not recording. I had it on night vision. It was not visible to the eye.

Importance of Spiritual Consciousness

Norm Fletcher
I had a sense of urgency that we need to understand the techniques of meditation and the seriousness of the situation on earth. Also we need to know how important it is to upgrade our general consciousness for mankind.

Dr. Steven Greer
What Norm said is very important. If geo-political or geo-physical events become more prominent, it is very important for people to go into a high state of spiritual consciousness. They also need to have the protocol for contacting the ETs, because the ETs will help stabilize the situation, as they are committed to the continuity of an advanced civilization here on Earth. That is the ET's chief mission right now. They know the situation is fragile and has been for decades.

Dr. Steven Greer
During a meditation, I dove very quickly and deeply into a quiet state of consciousness and suddenly an archaic word came to me. It was "mentalis," Latin for "mind" or "mental." Next I saw cosmic mentalis. Then I saw the circular base of an ET craft shining through

some clouds above our circle. The craft was shaped like the bottom of a bowl. Its center was open with beautiful yellow-white brilliant light pouring out of it, connecting with our group. My sense was that a very large extraterrestrial vehicle was not very far above us. I was at the level of the ship, looking from the side at the group. We looked small. The ship was at an angle and had a brilliant light connecting to the group. I could see a transmission and pouring of energy beyond words. It traveled between the Earth and us. It surged, through us and from us, to this cosmic, extraterrestrial craft. The energy as light from the craft was a beautiful yellow-white color like sunshine streaming into each of us.

As we were leaving Palm Springs, we heard a high-pitched electronic tone that was very pure. It was to the right of Linda. Nothing in the car would make that noise; even the radar detector in the car was unplugged and the other one was turned off. We all heard this noise, and I knew our extraterrestrial visitors were locked on to us.

A small community of houses sits near the Park entrance at Joshua Tree National Park. As we drove in, Linda was sharing the fact that years ago we saw an ET craft appear in this area, almost like a welcoming party. As Linda recounted the earlier encounter, suddenly to the left of our vehicle, about fifty feet up, a brilliant, pure-white, round craft appeared. It was there for a few seconds. Raven was in the back on the right side of the truck while the object was on the left. As we drove along, Raven saw an arc coming toward us with a luminescent trail behind it as it disappeared into space.

Dr Raven Nabulsi
I saw something make a white, J-like arc. The object left a luminescent trail for about three seconds.

Dr. Steven Greer
When Raven described the object, I was told that it was heading over to our group site on Geology Tour Road. We proceeded to the site and set up. I was clearly told in my meditation not to back the truck into our site, but to have the car facing the other way. We had

a radar detector that we were using, and it was on the dashboard of the truck so it would be facing the group.

Linda Willitts
This radar detector is wired into the truck. Dr. Greer had flashed the headlights at Greg three times, and the ETs signaled back to him three times.

Terry Underwood
We arrived about five minutes before Dr. Greer entered the park. We had decided to go off and meditate before we came up to the site. I remember that Jim put on the meditation tape. We were just outside the Park, and we meditated for the full length of the tape. It seemed as if we paved the path for you to have the experience coming into the park.

Dr. Steven Greer
Terry may have actually already had them there. That is where we saw the brilliant white flash manifest. The flash was beyond fluorescent white. It was pure intense white, brilliant and close.

Real-time Reaction to Dematerialized ET Craft Surrounding Group

Dr. Steven Greer
The whole area around us was alive with an endless amount of electronic scintillating light. This was a ship and there were ET beings lit up in the ET vehicle. The whole area was scintillating and there were swirling vortexes of energy around us. If you looked with soft eyes, it was like the fuzziness of a black and white TV when it is on the fritz. This ship greeted us before at the entrance of the park and came over to the contact site. It is now dematerialized and is around us. I just saw a blue-white diamond light about two feet behind Trudy.

Temperature Change from Craft Enveloping Group
Dr. Steven Greer
When we first arrived on site the environment was unusual. The night was cold, but as we made the circle and sat there, it was warm, even our hands were warm. There were beautiful scintillating lights

around the circle as if a craft was enveloping us in an energy field where the environment was being controlled and made warmer.

We were in a meditation and prayer for Earth. As we were going into a deep state of God-consciousness, I began to hear an enigmatic beeping at key points during the meditation. At first I thought someone had a magnetometer or a radar detector with the sound muffled in a bag under a chair. But the noise sounded further away, and it did not sound like an extraterrestrial tone. We know what ET tones sound like. The beeping tones we heard sounded like man-made electronics. It turned out the beeping noise was the laser and radar detector in the truck going off and punctuating key points during the meditation. We could hear it even with the windows up, and everyone heard it. There is no source for a laser or radar detector in the middle of the wilderness, none whatsoever!

I made note of the radar detector and continued. I sensed that everyone was in a deep state of cosmic consciousness when suddenly a blinding starburst of light from an extraterrestrial craft appeared over us! The burst was visible just a little off zenith, just as in my preparatory remote view and meditation earlier. It appeared a few hundred feet up in the sky directly over the Joshua Tree to our south. An explosion of blue-white light came into the group, and it was not just astral. Anyone who was looking anywhere near it, even with their eyes closed, saw it.

I sensed that the starburst was not just light but it was actually a transformative cosmic energy that permeated every atom on Earth. It permeated the soul of everyone on Earth and carried with it a celestial energy undoubtedly arising from this ET craft. The craft was completely materialized when it sent out this brilliant light that we all saw. It was the brightest burst of conscious light – consciousness and light together- that we have ever had stream into us. The event was very much a recapitulation of our meditation and the remote view I had just hours earlier. This burst was a beautiful, celestial God-consciousness moment.

The Second Burst of Light

We continued in the meditation. At the end of the prayer, directly east of us was the same light except that it appeared for much longer, a little further away. Those of us who were facing due east saw this craft. It was large, almost the size of the full Moon in the sky. The edges were fuzzy, as if they were partially going out of phase or resonance. The craft was right over the desert in the east and shone the light right towards us again, as if to say, "We have been with you during your entire meditation and prayer," and then it left. It is of interest that in November 2005 several of us heard and saw a craft, twenty feet above our heads. It came over making a distinct sound in exactly the place where tonight's starburst of cosmic energy shone down upon us.

Discussion of the First Flash

Dr. Steven Greer
How many people saw that first brilliant flash overhead?

Many Voices
I did. Yes.

Dr. Steven Greer
It permeated every aspect of being. The energy it projected was consciousness, love, celestial energy, and great knowledge. All that came in a packet that is still here...

Jan Brook
At important parts of the prayer, the detector went off. It was very interactive.

Dr. Steven Greer
This kind of electronic interactivity happens quite often on these journeys in the Cosmic Mind. We were all in that deep state in which you experience the one conscious Being. That is what the ETs appreciate and want of us. When a group enters that state, the entire Earth is transformed and civilization is transformed.

Jan Brook
Dr, Greer, there was something else besides the radar. A couple of times I heard a Doppler echo.

Linda Willitts
At the beginning of the meditation, when all was really quiet, there was a chirping going on in the east.

Ricky Butterfass
I saw a big disc-shaped cloud above us. We just had a celestial event, for those of you who are new to this. This is amazing. So you are all here for a reason.

Trudy Guyker
This is the first time that I can recall on any of these outings that a flash has hit us with that intensity of communication! I was facing directly south but had my eyes closed. It was so bright that I could see the veins in my eyelids! As the light entered me, it seemed as if a white smoke filled my entire body. No emotion was involved. At one point as the smoke was coming into me, the word "Joy" seemed to appear. Later on it seemed to change to the word "Optimism." Debbie later explained to me that it was a download of information. It was business. That is why there was no emotion involved; it was strictly information.

Dr. Jan Bravo
I had my eyes open for the amazing, bright flash. After this flash, what struck me was what Trudy said about the joy. I was not feeling well at the time, and I felt like I was getting a cold. I can corroborate that something was being downloaded – some information. Suddenly I felt the joy so much that I was smiling. I felt the joy as opposed to seeing the words. When the incident ended, I was finished smiling, but the joy continued, and I was struck with feelings of calmness and intelligence.

Linda Willitts
My eyes were closed for the first burst of light, so I did not see it. But I saw the brightness *through* my eyelids. The source was directional, as the radar detector went off in the truck.

Greg Heller
I was sitting in the southwest and was in deep meditation with my eyes closed. I was already seeing bright blue and white light.

When the flash appeared and Dr. Greer spoke, I perceived a burst of light through my eyelids. The light was very apparent through my closed eyes.

Jan Brook
The flash looked as if it came right in between David, who was on my immediate left, and the two gentlemen on his left. It appeared that a beam of pure, white light shot over.

Dr. Steven Greer
There was a low cloud slightly to our south, right above the group and slightly outside the circle. It was very low, and it was from within that cloud that the discharge, this brilliant burst of cosmic light originated. I was looking directly at it when it happened.

David Alfassi
Looking through the night vision goggles, just to the east I saw flashes in the ground and the orbs that I saw the previous time. I decided to try what Dr. Greer suggested, asking the object to move to the right and the object did move to the right, very slowly.

Real-time Reactions to the Second Flash
[Spectacular Blue-White Light Appears at End of Meditation at 10:35 PM]

Dr. Steven Greer
Due east! The sacred east! The most beautiful blue-white light that I saw earlier is coming into the Park. How many people just saw it?
How many people saw the one that was above us here?

[Linda Willitts and several other people say they did]

Trudy Guyker
I had my eyes closed but it was so bright that I could practically see the veins in my eyelids. I am so glad that you spoke about joy at the end of the meditation because when that flash hit me, it blinked through my body with a feeling of joy.

Discussion of the Second Flash

Dr. Steven Greer
There was a brilliant light at the end of the meditation. It was just to our east over the landing area and very close. It was a beautiful white, round sphere, clearly visible with the naked eye, and fully materialized.

A couple of voices
Yes, I saw that.

Dr. Steven Greer
That was what came into the Park with us and now it is here overhead. It was very large. In my meditation earlier today, seeing it in its astral clarity, it was an enormous ship, and it is here now...

Linda Willitts
My eyes were closed for the first burst of light. I saw the second burst, and it was the only time I have ever seen a burst of light that came from our level, not from underground. The burst came from the Joshua Tree level. It came from the path we use to walk out to the landing site where the ET craft went into the ground in 1996.

Dr. Steven Greer
Yes. When we walked out there, it was clear to me that the location of the craft we saw tonight was exactly over the landing site of the craft we saw in 1996.

Linda Willitts
Dr. Greer said that he was told that the truck should face that direction tonight instead of backing in as we often do.

Dr. Steven Greer
The flash overhead that we have been talking about was so bright it illuminated the whole area. It was at the level of the clouds or below. It was a burst of light over the group.

Trudy Guyker
That had to be the brightest one I have ever seen, because I had my eyes closed and it came through my eyelids. I could see the veins in my eyelids.

Charlie Balogh

When I saw that second flash, I noticed it blew up very fast, then it slowly faded away. It made a noise, "Wheeew," as if it was being closed down.

Dr. Steven Greer

It seemed to unfold itself from another dimension or another level of reality, and then it folded back within itself and was gone.

Dr. Ted Loder

It was unlike electronic flashes that most people have seen. It was very different.
It was different from an electronic flash in that it had duration, expansion and contraction. I observed the flash straight on and saw a white light with a pink surrounding tint. It is interesting other people reported subtly different colors.

Dr. Jan Bravo

There was also a wonderful purity to that light in the east. As we were driving out of the park, I realized that no city lights or any other manmade lights resembled the light we saw.

Debbie Foch

I saw the second light in the east before it disappeared. Right after that, as Dr. Greer was standing up, there was an object in the south, about forty degrees up, which arced up through the clouds. I think it was connected to all that.

Pam Fletcher

I saw that.

Dr. Ted Loder

I saw the second flash, the low one over the field. When I saw it, I was thrilled the way anyone else who saw it was. About thirty seconds later, I was still sitting in my seat and could feel shivers go up and down my body. I choked up a bit from the thrill and joy of it. Kay said that she had the same kind of reaction. My reaction was after the fact. For a minute or so afterward, I was still recovering from it, and then I had a feeling right down my whole body. It was wonderful.

Kay Gibson
I was filled with an energy I cannot describe because I have not felt it before. I was completely filled with something that felt liquid. It felt like it went through me, and I am covered with goose bumps as I say this. Every pore, every cell of my body was filled with emotion, but not in a negative sense. There was so much to feel and tears started flowing. I was not sad; the tears were just streaming down my cheeks for a while. So I experienced much emotion. It was as if I had every feeling in one pack, and I was soaked in it.

Dr. Steven Greer
I felt an infinite bliss, joy, energy such that I could have levitated. I had such a high level of energy, joy and excitement that it was thrilling. The energy was there the whole night and as we were driving back to town. It took an hour after we returned to wind down to where I could begin to think of sleeping!

Charlie Balogh
I experienced a huge exhilaration, as if I had just come down the first hill of a roller coaster. The other thing I noticed about the light was it felt liquid as Kay mentioned. I felt a substance to it, as if it had mass. It was not ordinary light.

Dr. Steven Greer
That is correct – this energy was actually being poured through us.

Jan Brook
I actually felt like someone had poured a bucket of ice water down my back. It was not cold. The feeling was like a thrill or chill everywhere up and down my spine and back. It was a very physical sensation.

Dr. Steven Greer
When we ended the prayer and meditation, the ETs came and sent us this burst. It was their affirmation that they had been with us and joined us. They are a celestial, God-conscious extraterrestrial civilization, and they are always with us. We thank them for

coming to Earth to do this with us.

Summary of the Two Bursts of Light
Dr. Steven Greer
We saw materialized bursts of light. They were not etheric, and they were huge and close. They burst through the cloud and every atom of our bodies and every aspect of our souls was permeated with a packet of celestial knowledge. I am telling you this because this knowledge is going to unfold in your life over time... As we ended the prayer, it re-appeared in the east, which is a very sacred direction, the direction of the Dawn. It is also the direction of the Navaswan.

Navaswan is Sanskrit, and refers to the energy that sweeps the Earth an hour or so before dawn each day. That is why many people have amazing experiences at that time in prayer, meditation or dreams. What we experienced was a burst of the Enlightened Being at Navaswan . With this experience, you have all been initiated into this cosmic process.

Temperature drops as ET Craft Moves Off
Dr. Steven Greer
How many have noticed that the temperature has fallen?

[Several people reply affirmatively.]

Dr. Steven Greer
In the ten minutes since the ship moved off to the east, there has been at least a ten-degree drop in temperature. Those extraterrestrials are still connected to us on a deep level even though their ship has departed.

Recap of the Flow of Events
Here is the flow of what happened: The craft that came into the Park with us was a celestial, extraterrestrial, God-conscious craft, and it produced a temperature increase. As the beings on this craft settled into their presence here, they put out a warmth – like sunshine. As we went deeper into a state of consciousness where we could be receptive vehicles for cosmic enlightenment, a burst

of energy entered into each of us, and it was very warm. Because it was located near the truck and right above us, the radar detector went on and off repeatedly during the prayer and meditation. As we ended the meditation, the craft went to the east, which is the symbol of the dawning of enlightenment. The ship appeared and hovered there for a few seconds as a brilliant, round blue-white light with fuzzy edges. Then it moved further beyond the crossing point of light. It was still present, but had receded, so the temperature fell ten or fifteen degrees.

Significance of the Burst of Energy

In all the years we have been out on these trainings, this was the most important energy burst that has ever happened. Even though we have had craft fly over, this burst of energy was sent into the soul and body of each of us. I cannot explain in words what they were transmitting, but try to unravel it tonight, and in the coming days, so you will know it. It was a beautiful event. What happened tonight was not just a flash of light. It was a 'starburst' of light and cosmically aware energy that permeated everyone.

Trudy Guyker
When it went through my body, I felt not only joy but also tremendous optimism.

Dr. Steven Greer
An empowerment manifested with this energy. They are asking us to step into our power, our purpose, and our destiny because we *must*; the Earth needs all of us to be in service...

Everyone present was being brought to another level of energy and consciousness. It was also a burst of non-linear knowledge flowing into people and was affecting them in ways not easily articulated. It was at a very high and fine level of celestial knowledge. You have all been initiated in the cave and are now here with the Star People. The next step is yours - it is now up to you. These beings will always be with us. (Just as I said that, a beautiful red orb appeared in the bush behind Jan Brook and David.)

Trudy Spots Kindness

Trudy Guyker

I saw some blue lights that appeared just to the right of the Joshua tree about a foot above the truck. A little blue light came on, and it was not a flash. It was there, and then it just went out.

Dr. Steven Greer

It is Kindness. She is with our truck.

Jan Brook

Just as you said that, a little blue light flashed on and off on your chest at about chin level.

Dr. Steven Greer

In your inner sight and with your physical eyes, see Kindness, the beautiful ET with a perfectly round head and most beautiful countenance. She is beautiful in her own exotic way, with almond-shaped eyes. She is transmitting the most wonderful compassion, like an extraterrestrial version of the Buddha, with infinite kindness, infinite compassion. And as I said that, down the path there was a ten foot area that shimmered with multi-colored lights. Did everyone see those brilliant flashes of cosmic enlightenment?

(Several people respond that they saw flashes in different directions.)

An old master says, "When the mind becomes empty and pure of all distractions and is centered in this unbounded being, there will appear in the Zenith of the heaven a brilliant flash that will contain all knowledge and all sciences and all arts." I am quoting from an ancient text, and this was sent into each of us while we were in that state of consciousness via the brilliant flash. It was very, very important knowledge. That text describes precisely what just happened. The wondrous sciences that I refer to are the new energy technologies we are working on.

Dan Krevitsky

I was going to say that mystic language often conveys the wonderful experiences that cannot be described any other way once you have had them.

The Helicopter Episode

Dr. Steven Greer

We noticed a large military helicopter that moved in after the flashes of light. There was a faint smell of ozone as they flew over. We connected to it and sent peace to its crew and to its command center and all those with whom they work. We were putting the most perfect golden light of peace and enlightenment through to all of these people and invited them to join us in universal peace.

Linda Willitts

The helicopter came out of the south and flew behind us along the western perimeter before heading north.

Discussion of the Helicopter Episode

Dr. Steven Greer

After we had the two amazing encounters with the object that filled us with light and then appeared at the end of the meditation, I started hearing a very low frequency sound pattern. I knew it was a helicopter and knew it was military. It was literally vibrating the air around us.

Charlie Balogh

You could feel it in the ground.

Dr. Steven Greer

The aircraft was a huge military helicopter that came up out of the south and was moving north. It flew west of us, but it was over Joshua Tree National Park, and it was definitely surveying us. It carried some kind of electronics. My sense was the helicopter blades that you normally hear were like a carrier wave for something else that was creating an ELF[120] effect on the ground. You could feel it in the ground and through the body.

Randy Tielking

Yes and there were two helicopters. I was watching both of them through my binoculars, and one had its lights off the entire time. I could see its silhouette against the sky. I estimated it was about

---

[120] ELF— Extremely low frequency (ELF) is the band of radio frequencies from 3 to 30 Hz. [http://en.wikipedia.org/wiki/Extremely_low_frequency]

200 feet high. The one with the lights off was leading.

Trip out of the Park

Dr. Steven Greer
The four hours we were doing fieldwork seemed like an hour and a half. To book end this incident, as we were leaving, I flashed the headlights of the car on and off to let Greg know we would pass him. As I drove by and flashed three times, the laser radar detector sounded three times. A craft was electromagnetically flying with us!

We felt that there would be an event as we exited Joshua Tree, and as we came to the exit of the park, it happened again: three beeps through the laser radar detector. There were no police nearby and no sources of microwaves so it was very anomalous. On the way back, even in areas where there was nothing but desert, the radar detector squawked with a regular periodicity. Using the radar detector these beings were signaling they were still with us, and they were still with us after we reached Palm Springs during our debriefing until 3:00 AM.

The CSETI Experience
Joshua Tree, California
February 9, 2007

Starting the Whole Process

Dr. Steven Greer
I started this ET Contact process because I knew humanity needed a vanguard of people who were knowledgeable on the subject, wise in the cosmology, and skilled in the art of these techniques. I knew we needed people who could step into this ability because the world needs interplanetary ambassadors who are deeply spiritual and deeply committed. There is an enormous vacuum of leadership in this area of knowledge and experience on our planet. The lack of leadership is both dangerous and tragic.

I encourage people on our expeditions to go home, form small groups and practice the protocols. If they do, they will be amazed by the kinds of events that will transpire. I have emphasized it is not about me or about any individual. It is about a time in human evolution on our planet when we must become a universal people. It is an evolutionary step onto a higher pathway. That pathway will take us into a time when all of humanity will be enlightened, living in universal peace and openly communicating and traveling among the stars. It is very important for people to step into that place of service.

Last night at the site, I sensed that the enormous energy that came from the cosmic 'starburst' of light conveyed real empowerment to humanity so that we may make this quantum leap into the future. I felt that people have been called and empowered to be leaders. It is very important for people to understand that no matter what happens in the world, each person can become a point of leadership, enlightenment and knowledge. Each person can provide an orderly and enlightened approach to working with extraterrestrial beings who are watching and stand ready to help and support this very important stage in the evolution of Earth and humanity.

CSETI Training
Mt. Shasta, California
August/September 2007

Puja Cleansing

Linda Willitts
At Mt. Shasta in 2007 Dr. Greer did a Puja at Sand Flats to clear the Akashic record of the negativity remaining there from the explosion that occurred in 2005. After the Puja, I was sitting in the circle and heard a muted explosive sound. I believe the sound was the 2005 explosion being transmuted and cleansed. Others heard it also. Afterwards, when we were all in meditation in the circle, purifying raindrops fell briefly even though rain had not been predicted. We had very productive fieldwork that night and the next night. It was the first time we had been able to do fieldwork at that location since the night the explosion occurred. It was beautiful to see nature, spirit, and the ETs cooperating.

CSETI Fieldwork
Joshua Tree California
November 2007

The Orion Transmission
Linda Willitts

Many things happened during the three nights we did fieldwork at the Joshua Tree CSETI Consciousness Training. The most amazing and unusual event was the transmission from beyond Orion[121]. The event began as we were preparing to leave the field at 12:50 AM our first night out (Tuesday, Nov. 6, 2007).

Sensing that his rose quartz crystal ball would facilitate contact, Dr. Greer held it up in the air and the cordless radar detector under my chair started beeping chaotically. We were standing about 3-4 feet from the detector and I had my recorder on the whole time. The ETs and Celestials were transmitting through the crystal, and then through Dr. Greer's body as a bio-antenna, and we were using the radar detector to provide an audible signal of the transmissions.

Even though we were in the center of the National Park where there are <u>no</u> radar signals, the radar detector beeped in an anomalous sequence for a total of 20 minutes. Dr. Greer moved like a robotic antenna, using the strength of the sounds to lead him. He was holding the rose quartz ball up high in his left hand and using his right hand as part of his "bio-antenna," pointing it in the direction of the radar detector, but never getting closer to it than 3-4 feet away. The transmission changed depending on which way Dr. Greer (as the antenna) was pointing, and it became very strong when he pointed the quartz ball at the constellation Orion.

At first the beeping sequence was fairly gentle, increasing and decreasing in volume, with the sounds sometimes seeming to float above the chair. When Dr. Greer pointed the crystal at Orion, the beeping became louder and more urgent, and he stated several times, "They're coming from Orion!"

---

[121] Orion— a constellation often referred to as The Hunter [http://en.wikipedia.org/wiki/Orion(constellation)

The sounds from the radar detector conveyed emotion as well as sound. Some of the patterns of the beeping were repeated several times. I recorded the entire transmission and several technical people at the training have attempted to isolate and analyze the sounds.

Dr. Greer said the transmission was going beyond us to nature, the Earth, and to everyone on Earth. There were also bright white flashes in the sky, coming from right under Orion's belt before, during, and after the transmission. This series of flashes included a large one at the end of the transmission. Greg Heller's identical radar detector[122], which was also on the whole time and was about 20 feet from mine, never made a sound, indicating the specific directionality of the signal.

Interestingly, in 1999 at that same site, the whole area was illuminated as though there was a full moon, but there was no moon at all. Once we began noticing the illumination and commenting on it, the light turned off as though someone had flipped a switch! At that time, Dr. Greer had said the Interplanetary Center out beyond Orion was controlling the light, just as it controlled the transmission the night of November 6 (or technically November 7, since it happened between 12:50 AM and 1:15 AM).

Temperature Indications of Craft at Site

When we first arrived on site the night of November 6 at around 8:30 PM, Dr. Greer and I walked out on the sandy path to the east and saw sparkling ET energy for as far as we could see. A huge craft was covering the whole area. The temperature was distinctly warmer in that area and in our circle than in the surrounding desert at the same elevation. We later noticed on the thermometer in the vehicle Dr. Greer was driving that the temperature was 64°F when we left our field site at 1:56 AM and 47° on the paved road just 2-3 miles away and the same altitude!

A Pseudo Mars

As we walked out on the sandy path at the beginning of the night,

---

[122] Greg's radar detector was an Escort Solo S2 Cordless Radar Detector

we noticed amber-colored Mars shining brightly in the northeast sky. After several minutes, we noticed an even brighter "Mars" at the same elevation near the rising Orion—in the southeast! The real Mars (in the northeast) happened to be behind a cloud at that moment. Then the bright "Mars"- like object in the southeast disappeared suddenly and we realized that it was an ET craft!

Translation of the Orion Transmission

For the next few days and nights in the dream state and in meditation, Dr. Greer was able to translate some of the information that was transmitted during the Orion Transmissions. Knowledge was transmitted to all of the approximately 40 people present, but it was primarily coming through Dr. Greer. One of the things he said was that the transmission was about our stepping into our individual and collective power and becoming a transformational force. He also translated part of the message as, "Oh God, let me be of service to you." He said that during the transmission, he was serving as the step-down transformer from the Universal Being through the Celestials and the ETs – then through him – to all of us, to complete the cycle. We must all be willing to step into this position.

Energy in the Quartz Ball

After the transmission—the night it occurred and on subsequent nights—Dr. Greer walked around putting the quartz ball into the right hand of many of us with his hand on top of it. We could feel the ball was warm, energized, and throbbing. Many of us noticed that it sent light sparkles up through his hand, visible on the top of his hand and around the sides of our hands. Dr. Greer said that he put the ball in a bowl on his bedside table that night, and it kept spinning around in the bowl much longer than what was normal; in fact he had to stop it because it just kept moving under its own vibration.

Other Manifestations

Each of us was given a packet of knowledge. It's interesting that, during meditation the next two nights at the same field site, several of us received "slide shows" of ET faces morphing one into another. I was one of the people who received a "slide show" and

I received a "slide show" of landscape scenes from many different planets. Some other people also received that, and Dr. Greer was shown many different types of jewel-like ET craft. On the second night at our field site, we had many subtle ET energy sparkles and another huge craft over the whole area and over us, keeping us warm. The thermometer in our vehicle read in the 60s the second night at our field site, and 39° out on the paved road just 2-3 miles from the field site!

Flashes in Area of Orion Respond to Laser

On the second night the radar detector sounded again briefly at one point when Dr. Greer took his "bio-antenna" stance with the crystal. Later, as we were getting ready to leave the site, 8 or 9 of us were standing around looking at Orion. Dr. Greer let out a native cry, then signaled Orion with his laser, and there was a flash exactly where he had signaled that was a clear response! The same thing happened a few more times. As Dr. Greer and others were pointing their lasers into Orion, something in a distinct area seemed to truncate the laser beams – the beams were being stopped or absorbed by something invisible to the naked eye – a large craft.

We also saw many fully materialized ET lights and craft in the sky and on the ground over the next two nights. Our sightings included a few spectacular appearances from Kindness, which will be further discussed later.

Shaman Cave Puja and Meditations

On Thursday afternoon, November 8, we went to the Shaman Cave in Hidden Valley and Dr. Greer did a Puja on the rock in front of the cave. We sat inside the cave with him in groups of approximately 9 people and he did a guided meditation with each group. Many profound experiences in consciousness occurred in and around the cave. Afterwards, we drove to our Geology Tour Road site and meditated before we took a break for a picnic dinner followed by a resumption of our fieldwork.

Of the many materialized craft that we saw, one was so bright it looked like the headlight of a vehicle that was coming down the road behind me. I was sitting on the west end of the circle with the road behind me, extending to the south, which was to my right. My eyes had been closed, but the bright light caused me to open them. It happened towards the end of a quiet period of meditation, so we didn't mention it, but Dr. Bravo, Dr. Greer, and I watched it, thinking at first that it must be a vehicle. I had my image stabilizing binoculars on the light, trying to see two headlights to make sure it was a vehicle. I could only see one light, and it was going behind bushes so I kept watching to see if it would get to a clear spot. I was thinking it was strange because we should have heard the vehicle by then. Finally, it just went lower and the light spread out, became very diffuse and disappeared. Then we realized that the light or craft hadn't really been on the road at all, but was barely skimming the top of the ridge that was just above the road from our perspective. I was still watching the area through my binoculars when Dr. Bravo, who was sitting on the other side of Dr. Greer from me – so she was in my line of vision – pointed towards the east-southeast just in time for me to see Kindness make a dramatic appearance. Dr. Greer saw her too, as did others in the group.

Chapter 16

2008

CSETI Training
Outer Banks, North Carolina
April May 2008

The Hybrid Craft

Dr. Raven Nabulsi
The strange hybrid aircraft that we saw travel along the shoreline made quite an impression on me. It was totally silent and from my perspective resembled a strange-looking helicopter, not a winged aircraft. As we started putting our awareness on it, its "engines" suddenly kicked in.

Dr. Steven Greer
This bizarre ship was man-made, a classified aircraft of some type, and completely silent. At first, I thought it was a blimp but as I looked more closely, it resembled something you'd build with an Erector set. This aircraft had several angular structures floating along with bizarre, orange lights phasing through a hypnotic-like pattern of sequences. I've never seen this on a military or civilian aircraft. The craft appeared very close and moved west just a few hundred feet high when it turned on what sounded like fake jet engine sounds. It seemed like an antigravity aircraft that made a phony roaring, jet-engine-like sound. Finally it moved off to the west and joined a squadron of jet fighters that were flying in the west.

Linda Willitts
Todd's and my radar detectors went off simultaneously right at that same time that we saw that strange craft.

Dr. Steven Greer
Right. We were having contact that was so close that the radar detectors did go off together, and that's when we started having

very heavy reconnaissance from this classified antigravity military platform.

The Scientific ET Group and More Reconnaissance
Dr. Steven Greer
At another point in this training a scientific ET group with whom we've had contact was in the water monitoring the ocean. We saw an egg-shaped craft going out on the beach and we had contact with those beings. They're very sweet and very small; the adults are only about a foot-and-a-half tall. We had seen and sensed that these beings were offshore from our site on the National Seashore. We saw helicopters shining floodlights into the water and circling as if looking for something. Other aircraft flew overhead and were involved in this activity. So, we were at this place, this site, and we were in meditation. Trudy had a remote view of a craft that would tilt in flight.

Trudy Guyker
I was extremely tired that particular night, but that morning I remote viewed a small craft about that would fly right over us then turn and tilt so its occupants could see us before flying off. Lovely!

The Manta Ray Craft
Dr. Steven Greer
Another amazing event during this training occurred one evening near the end of the silent part of our meditation. Suddenly, out from over the dunes beside the ocean, came a flying 'manta ray'-like craft from the ocean. Between twenty and thirty feet wide, the craft was matte black; completely black against the sky; completely silent and tilted. It was like a living creature – it was alive. We watched the craft for several seconds before it flew over the spot where there is an old renovated building (part of the National Seashore) and it then dematerialized in clear air! It just vanished, maybe a hundred feet on the other side of our circle. The craft's manta ray shape was interesting and whether that was actually the shape of their craft in its original form, or whether that's what these ETs manifested because of their connection with the ocean, is uncertain. But the motif was that of a gigantic sea creature with

these ETs on board who were a scientific team monitoring our oceans and the Continental Shelf that humans are destroying.

Linda Willitts
Four or five people saw this manta ray craft.

Dr. Steven Greer
I felt that the ETs associated with the manta ray craft were honoring us. They manifested that way because we had achieved the coherent meditative state. We shared mutual respect and admiration for each other's work. These ETs had great reverence for the prayers and meditations for Earth's healing and for the cleansing of Earth's oceans that we were doing. I sensed they were thanking us for that work.

Trudy Guyker
As I thought about the manta ray craft I felt that it was velvety rather than metallic.

Linda Willitts
I had my eyes open during the quiet time of the meditation that night and I saw the manta ray craft fly over about twenty feet above our circle. It was so different from anything I had ever seen that I uncharacteristically blurted out "Did you see that?" When Dr. Greer asked everyone to describe what we saw I fumbled for the right words before saying, "It was shaped like a manta ray, and in fact, it looked alive like a manta ray!" It was velvety and was gliding gracefully as though it was swimming in the ocean of air above us. It appeared to look at our group as it passed over us before circling and heading towards that old building where it just vanished.

ETs in the Earth

Trudy Guyker
During one of the breaks that week, I stood on a small dune when suddenly something hit me from underneath the sand. I put my hand into the sand to feel but nothing was there!

Dr. Steven Greer

This is reminiscent of what happened at Crestone in an earlier year when we were out on the Baca. We felt, right underneath the sand, this very discrete area that went "pop." I felt it, and then Trudy felt it. I'm convinced that these sorts of things occur when the ETs are shifted, and they're in the earth. They're letting us know, so don't always just look to the sky. They can be within the earth and can materialize an effect physically. It felt like a little earthquake under our feet.

Tall ET Sentinels

Linda Willitts

We also saw during the week a group of sentinel beings. Each being appeared to be about fifteen to eighteen feet tall and they stood at the same site as the manta ray flyover. I could see maybe three or four of them as very distinct sparkling forms standing just outside of our circle. They gave me a feeling of being safe and protected.

CSETI Training
Crestone, Colorado
June-July 2008

Acquifer under the Baca

Linda Willitts

On July 2nd in Crestone in 2008, Dr. Greer did a guided meditation that revealed ETs in an aquifer underneath our field site on the Baca. A number of people who had compasses noticed that bubbles appeared.

Dr. Steven Greer

I could see in my remote view that the ETs were just under the ground, much on the order of what Ellen had seen at Blanca Peak the year before. They were in the water, and they were dematerialized, but shifted there under the ground beneath us as we were sitting on the sandy field site. As I described what I was seeing, we began experiencing beautiful, pure water dropping on all of us – coming from a crystal clear sky! However, it didn't really feel like water. It felt like silk or satin – or almost like an oil that was anointing everyone. It represented a purification, and it was the ETs' way of saying, "Yes." The other verifying feature of course, consisted of all the bubbles appearing in people's sealed compasses.

The ETs were also saying, "You're right. We are dematerialized under you and around you."

Appearance of Triangular Craft
Linda Willitts
As soon as we finished that meditation, Al Dunaway spotted the triangular craft going over us. We had not seen that craft in over eight years. Our first sightings had been at Shasta on three nights in 1999, and then we saw it at Pine Bush, New York on two occasions the same night in April 2000.

Jan Brook
I remember I was so thrilled because, having missed all the other times, I finally got to see this triangular craft. It was truly awesome.

Dr.Steven Greer
Right. It was beautiful – very majestic. Three points of light moved across overhead through the star field without obscuring the background stars.

Big Dipper Stars Disappear
Todd Goldenbaum
On the evening of July third Dr. Greer performed a Puja Ceremony at sunset and a meditation with us afterwards on Blanca Peak. The night before, I'd had some internal, personal breakthroughs with being able to go into deeper states of meditation in the field, which prior to that had been difficult for me. The night was clear and we had a good view of the Big Dipper constellation. Sitting in meditation I asked the ETs to show their presence in a way that involved the big dipper. I thought they might have two stars switch places with each other, but I realized my request might seem like I was asking them to do tricks for us. So I made it clear that was not my intention and requested they do whatever they wanted to do as a demonstration.

Twenty minutes later one of the stars in the Dipper slowly faded out, as if it was on a cosmic dimmer switch. It actually disappeared and was gone for a few minutes! With our advanced night vision equipment we could clearly see there were no clouds and that in fact the smaller stars surrounding the one that faded out were still visible. The ETs somehow produced an effect that obscured a Dipper star from our point of view.

Within a few minutes the star slowly faded back into view with its full brightness. Then a few minutes later, a different star in the Dipper did the exact same thing. It slowly faded out, was gone for a few minutes, and returned to full brightness again. This went on for 23 minutes, alternating between four of the seven stars in the Dipper! It was fascinating. The ETs had heard my sincere desire for confirmation and had responded with a display unlike any other in the CSETI experience.

Dr. Steven Greer
Sometimes two stars at once disappeared, and the process seemed to be mathematical. There seemed to be something abstract about it, and communicative about it... It was very powerful. Everyone saw this.

We were located on the Zapata Falls side of Blanca Peak, facing north with the Great Sand Dunes below us. Just before the Big Dipper event, a completely materialized golden red ET craft came from above the sand dunes and went into a cloud and vanished. Shortly later, it continued on its path and left and traversed the same part of the sky that contained the Big Dipper. I think that craft shifted beyond the frequency of light, but remained in the area and produced an energy field to absorb the light from each star in the Dipper.

Arch Portal on Mt. Blanca

Linda Willitts
Since we had gone to Mount Blanca on the night of July third, the Fourth of July began while we were up at the contact site. It's always quite incredible when Dr. Greer goes ahead while the group stays behind. This particular time, as he walked forward, I

saw him go through an arch of sparkles but the sparkles were so wild and distinct that they looked like Fourth of July fireworks. Then the coyotes in the distance started howling as he played the Tibetan prayer bowl.

Trudy Guyker
I also saw the arch, as did Charlie Balogh and Jan Brook. The arch I saw was very similar to the arch that was behind the Avatar that I mentioned recounting the out-of-body spiritual experience Dr. Greer and I had in 1998 at this site.

Dr. Steven Greer
Right. The arch is held there. If you go to that spot in the daytime you would think it to be a bunch of rocks surrounded by some bushes and trees, but it's a sacred space and there is an arch in a portal that one can enter. I can actually see it. The first time I went through, in 1997, I saw brilliant, scintillating light all above me. I knew that I'd entered the correct spot.

Events at the Contact Site

Linda Willitts
As we walked up to the contact site, I noticed a military jet coming towards us on a descent. Almost immediately a cloud made by the ETs totally obscured the contact site with us in it, so no planes could see us. I also felt another purifying rain. After most of the group had started back down to our circle, some of us stayed a little longer. The air seemed thick. Moving your arms felt like moving through water full of phytoplankton. We were sweeping our arms through the air. It appeared to me as if we were disturbing a green florescence like phytoplankton.

Dr. Steven Greer
The air seemed filled with Celestial and extraterrestrial energy so thick that you could see it moving as you moved your hands around in the golden light. It was beautiful!

Jan Brook
We seemed bathed in the sparkling, golden light. The entire site was electrified. Also, our voices were muffled when we spoke

to each other. I saw what appeared to be a shaft of sparkling moonlight arching over our heads, except that it extended from the ground up, and the moon was not visible at all, so I knew we were all standing in the portal.

Todd Goldenbaum
That marked the first night at the contact site where I really saw astral light, and later I saw the outline of some beings in the light. I was standing maybe twenty feet away from those up front, allowing my vision to blur slightly. It looked like people had flashlights and were waving them all over the place, much like a light show. When I would switch over to my peripheral vision there was nothing there but pitch-black darkness. Then I'd relax, get out of focus again, and the light would start up again. I found that amazing.

Trudy's Dive

Trudy Guyker
Earlier, before we had gone up to the site, a vehicle drove into the parking area near the site, stopped momentarily and a couple of people got out and disappeared. Then someone parked the vehicle. I thought someone might have been sent to interfere with us.

The path to and from the contact site consists of rocky, uneven ground. Dr. Greer had undergone major surgery on his knee from a mountain biking accident several months previously and had to be very cautious. I was behind him as we were returning down the path to the circle, walking along just fine. Suddenly I landed flat on my face. I did not trip. Something pushed me, and the next thing I knew I was flat on the ground with my face in the dirt! I think something was aiming for Dr. Greer because of his weak knee and got me instead.

Jan Brook
I happened to be a few feet behind Trudy when she went down. No one was near enough to touch her. I sensed at the time that she had taken a "hit" that was meant for Dr. Greer, and deflected it. I thought she'd vanished down a sinkhole or something for a second or two because she was in front of me, then suddenly she wasn't.

Dr. Steven Greer
I'd only been off crutches slightly over a month from major surgery from a mountain biking accident. We were aware of some characters around that may have had some psychotronic, radionic or other human trans-dimensional technology. So it may have been that I was protected but it happened to Trudy. It would have been quite a setback if I had a fall like that right after major surgery. Thank God Trudy was not injured at all!

Unusual Clock Patterns

Linda Willitts
The next day as people reported their experiences, several mentioned that upon returning to their rooms their digital clocks were blinking unusual numbers such as three-zero-three. Power failures usually result in a clock blinking twelve-zero-zero.

Dr. Steven Greer
Weird numerological phenomena indeed occurred. It was either a three-o-three, or a multiple of it, six-o-six. I think it related to the abstract mathematical pattern of the Big Dipper stars going in and out in some sequence. A message occurred and some type of abstract communication happened.

Orbs Seen and Photographed

Trudy Guyker
At the Baca site during a break we were out on the bridge. People were taking pictures to see if any orbs would show on the photos. Sahab was taking pictures near me and I saw a dull red globe of light that was about the size of a grapefruit. It appeared very faint, but it was definitely there. I went over to Sahab and said, "I just saw a globe of red light. Could you take a picture in the area?" He did, and it showed up in the photo!

Kindness Appears Twice

Linda Willitts
We were returning from the Stupa in our car, and we saw Kindness' ship. She came twice because not everyone saw her the first time. She came twice in close succession for us.

Dr. Steven Greer
Right. Her ET craft appeared very bright and very close in the atmosphere.

CSETI Training
Mt. Shasta
August/September 2008

Help from Night-Vision

Linda Willitts
Jan Bravo and Todd Goldenbaum had purchased a night-vision scope for our camera and this training was the first time that Todd used it. The first night of the training we had nonstop activity including an appearance by Kindness. We also saw several objects down low and close. At Shasta we use a spot we call the secluded site. It's a small bowl-shaped area surrounded by trees located no more than fifty feet from one edge of the circle. Numerous craft appeared right in front of these trees, which served as a backdrop. Raven and Todd did reconnaissance at the site in the daylight with Todd's camera and there are no structures here. We always investigate to determine that we're not seeing city lights. Todd is producing a DVD that will show these lights were clearly originating from craft in front of the trees. Todd's production shows these craft in real time and then replays them at slower speeds. The slower speeds let you see very distinctly how they're appearing.

Dr. Steven Greer
These lights were illuminating the trees. A red craft came in that actually stayed in the tree near our parked truck before several more came in to the north and west. These lights were brilliant white, fast-moving craft coming from space to our site. As Linda mentioned this was the first time we had a night scope hooked to a digital camera and the recording shows the objects actually illuminating the tree and the ground under it as they're coming in. This is normal activity for this Shasta site every night and now we're able to capture their images with the night-scope equipped camera. Several craft arrived to join in the meditation and some of them emerged from Mount Shasta, similar to those we see coming

up and out of Blanca Peak. It reminds me of a "falling star" but goes up, rather than across the sky.

A God-Consciousness ET civilization uses Mt. Shasta as some type of a base. People have reported this for years, and now we have many images of these objects originating from the mountain and coming onto our site where they then join us in meditations for Universal Peace. It is quite beautiful.

Another Example of Electromagnetic Confirmation
Linda Willitts
When we left that evening, we drove my truck, a 1999 Ford F-150 with an old-style switch. Its lights don't go on automatically when you put the key in; you have to turn the key first. My truck was parked under the tree where much of the night's activity had been occurring, and Dr. Greer was driving. As we got in the truck and closed the doors the headlights came on, and he hadn't touched the light switch! We took that as the ETs telling us, "Yeah, it really was us."

Dr. Steven Greer
We receive a lot of electromagnetic confirmation and this stood out as one of the stranger ones. The ETs seemed to be saying, "Yeah, we were right over this truck," and, as Linda mentioned, the truck was parked under one of the trees where many of these ET objects appear on video! Later we also had an orb and light illuminate inside the truck.

Jan Bravo gets a Compass Bubble
Linda Willitts
Also that first night at Shasta we had a meditation about the aquifer the previous couple of months earlier in Crestone. Jan didn't have a compass in Crestone.

Dr. Bravo
I really wanted a bubble in my compass. In past trainings I had brought a compass but found I didn't really need it. So when everyone got these bubbles in their compasses, I thought, "Oh, man, I wish I had a bubble." I had my compass in my small

bag, and I didn't think about it. At the end of the night, when we returned to the place where we were staying I was unpacking my bag. I looked at the compass and started screaming. They probably thought I'd had a heart attack or something, but I said, "Oh, my god, I have a bubble!" I had simply put out the thought that I'd really like a bubble and it was really kind of them to do that for me. The ETs had confirmed for me how important it is to ask.

Dr. Steven Greer
The ETs placed an energy field to create the compass bubbles for Jan as a confirmation for her. We've never had these occur until a couple of years ago and we have always had the same compasses and been at the same elevation, etc.

Randy "Orb"
Linda Willitts
Randy Erb is this wonderful man who has been coming to Shasta every year for many years now. We enjoy calling him Randy "Orb" because he's taken a lot of orb photos. He took some pictures and captured some again this night when we were having so much activity in front of the trees.

Debbie Foch
It happened right near sunset. Randy photographed a big, huge orb by a tree near where the vehicles were parked and where we were seeing all the amber glowing areas in the trees.

Dr. Greer's Speaking Energizes the ETs
Linda Willitts
We have an area of our secluded site that's somewhat uphill and surrounded by a semicircle of trees. We call it "The Cathedral." The second night at the Cathedral, Dr. Greer made his first tap on his singing prayer bowl to start the meditation and the God-Consciousness craft immediately appeared. They just kept coming non-stop, an armada of ET craft. It was the second day of a week of non-stop activity at Shasta.

Dr. Steven Greer
Dozens of craft came in from every angle and they were absolutely

not satellites or airplanes. This flotilla of ET ships astounded us, there were so many!

Trudy Guyker
My notes from the training say, "as long as Steven spoke out loud, craft kept appearing."

Linda Willitts
That's correct. He said his continuous talking maintained the energy and the craft kept coming while he kept talking.

Dr. Steven Greer
Yes. As I spoke I was pulling in that energy and holding that energy, and if I stopped, they would stop coming. Countless numbers of fully visible craft kept appearing.

Debbie and Connie Spot the Golden Laser Light
Debbie Foch
Connie Metcalf and I saw one of those golden laser lights coming over into the group from the east. The light dropped right into the center of the circle.

Glowing Area on Mt. Shasta
Debbie Foch
Our group also noticed a glowing area that resembled a craft, a big huge area on Mount Shasta we were videotaping for awhile.

Dr. Steven Greer
Through my night scope, you could see that area where a craft sat very close to us on the mountain. You could not see it with regular binoculars, and you could not see it with the naked eye – but you could see it clearly with a night scope. But it could not be filmed by the night scope! I found this unbelievable because it was huge, with a very visible glowing area.

Woman's ET Voice
Linda Willitts
The second night of the training Trudy, I, and several others heard a female ET voice. Trudy and I seemed to hear the voice behind

us, but others heard an omni-directional woman's voice that spoke in an ET language. Raven recognized it as Kindness.

Dr. Raven Nabulsi
Yes, and thinking back to the Outer Banks training earlier in 2008, Kindness was in the room and I heard her voice talking during the meditation. A female ET was having a deep meditation where Kindness was situated and we were on board a ship. Now, returning to our Shasta expedition, I recognized her voice again and she was present with us.

Dr. Steven Greer
Many people heard her voice as she was actually speaking in the circle.

CSETI Training
Charlottesville, Virginia
October 2008

Craft Positioned in Sky Flashing

Linda Willitts
We saw as a prominent feature a pattern that we hadn't experienced at previous trainings. From the second night on, from two to four ET craft would take up a position in the sky and periodically flash and interact with us with some regularity for long durations. We had a video camera with a fourth generation night scope attached filming these events.

Dr. Steven Greer
The various ET craft appeared as bright diamond-like flashes at about a 40 to 60 degree elevation in the southwest sky and functioned like a little flotilla. They were not constantly visible with the naked eye but would flash at different intervals. They keyed into what we were doing: When we took a break, the flashes would stop. When we resumed, they would also.

Ellen Costantino
The constellation Aquarius seemed to figure prominently. The activity began slowly and built upon itself every night. There

was a steady sense of gathering as Sirius and Orion rose. There seemed to be a remarkable ET "show of force" as an armada of ET craft appeared in the sky clearly encouraging our efforts and discouraging those "darker" forces which many of us could feel trying to shut down our advancing contact work.

Fog, Orbs and Disks

Linda Willitts

We also had fog appear the second night that seemed to happen within seconds. We had some concern for people returning to their motels but they later reported that the fog was only over the field site, not elsewhere. Fog returned subsequent nights as well. It seemed to be tuned into our energy, swooping down within seconds and then disappearing just as quickly; it was not at all like natural fog.

Dr. Steven Greer

People reported orbs in their vehicles or back in their hotel rooms, with some close range electromagnetic events such as lights turning on or off. We tell participants the training becomes a 24-hour a day event – a cosmic tutorial to introduce people to their role as ambassadors. Many begin to have experiences with the ET beings that are personal, and it continues into the dream state at night.

Ellen Costantino

On one night I clearly saw a partially materialized spherical craft emerge from the ground in the pasture and hover there before speeding off into the atmosphere.

Dr. Steven Greer

We also had daytime sightings of disks. I had a lucid dream of a craft coming out of Humpback Mountain to our west. Many historical sightings have occurred in that area.

Consciousness Training Fieldwork
Joshua Tree
November 2008

The Celestial Fragrance

Linda Willitts

The second night of the training, November fourth, occurred on Election night 2008. The whole theme of this week was the heralding of a new era, and the election symbolized that theme. That evening at the site a Celestial fragrance manifested and engulfed the whole circle of forty-two people for ten to twenty minutes.

Dr. Steven Greer

That night we had temperatures in the twenties and gusty winds when this beautiful, celestial, carnation-like fragrance graced us for twenty minutes. Everyone smelled it. This angelic fragrance seemed to emerge from 'infraspace': from within the subtle realm to physical, linear space/time. The principle is similar to how we receive the tones on the detectors.

Later, as everyone was milling around before leaving for the night, a massive burst of light above our site illuminated the entire desert – all of Joshua Tree National Park! This great light followed our earlier contact experience with multitudes of craft in the sky and luminous figures around us in the circle. This massive craft, actually a group of them, flew in directly overhead and illuminated the area before zooming off in a couple of different directions. Its close proximity and spectacular brightness across the whole desert floor created shadows of the Joshua trees.

Linda Willitts

I felt the incident with the fragrance was another orchestrated event that we often experience. Immediately before the fragrance came, Dr. Greer was talking about a meditation he had had earlier that day in which he gave an Executive Briefing to President Obama. Dr. Greer said that the President's grandmother, who had died the previous day, had come onsite with the Avatar and the Celestials. Just as Dr. Greer was explaining this, the fragrance permeated our area.

Dr. Steven Greer
Yes. President Obama's grandmother, the Avatar being and these Celestial beings all were present.

Eye of Horus Moves through the House
Dr. Raven Nabulsi
We also had an incident in which an object went through parts of the house.

Dr. Steven Greer
It is important to connect some dots here. As I was in deep meditation upstairs in this huge, geodesic dome where we stayed, adjacent to the National Park, I clearly saw an object that seemed tethered energetically to an ET craft. The craft came from the landing site within Joshua Tree and approached straight towards the house before moving between the upper part of the dome where my bedroom was, and the part of the house where Raven and Todd Goldenbaum were staying. The object was connecting us to the underground ET facility within Joshua Tree National Park.

On the last morning of the training, as everyone was beginning to check out and leave, I was meditating. In a lucid dream-type state, I saw that same object. The object was a translucent eye, the Eye of Orion, the Eye of Horus. It is both technological and extraterrestrial. The eye was not round but had a flattened front like an eyeball and then receded a bit, not sharply, but rather rounded at the back. It resembled a picture tube, and was totally transparent like clear glass. This electronic object moved from window to window, wanting someone to acknowledge it the whole time we were there. I saw it the last morning, and it moved very electronically, an example of consciousness-assisted technology. It was connected to the ETs from the Orion sector of space... The object and I experienced an interconnection of consciousness.

I was told that even though the object has a specific size, anyone can go within it mentally. It magnifies remote viewing capability and magnifies the concept "to Intend the Good." So you can use the device to amplify intent and to see. Then when you desire to see a distant place, or intend something good to happen, you can access the object and it amplifies your intent thousands of times. The device projects the power that is connected to the God-consciousness ETs from the Orion sector of space. They are in charge of the interstellar effort regarding Earth.

Orion Transmissions Continue

Linda Willitts
November fifth was declared an optional night, and people could go to whatever site they wanted at whatever times. Since we didn't meet at our Geology Tour Road site at any specific time our car group went to some other locations where we had some amazing activity. When we arrived at eleven p.m. at the Geology Tour Road site, Deb Andrews was present with her Cobra radar detector. Dr. Greer walked up to it and we started immediately receiving Orion transmissions!

Dr. Steven Greer
The radar detector had not been active prior to that.

Trudy Guyker
Before our group traveled to the Geology Tour Road site, we gathered and meditated. While we were in meditation I felt a presence – an entity. Someone said they had heard a drum beat as they entered the site and Debbie had heard a drum beat too. Raven mentioned that she saw three blue orbs right at the level of my heart, and then we went into an incredible meditation filled with love and Oneness. It was then that these three orbs penetrated me. I sensed that they were Native American entities that transformed into the three blue orbs that entered me. I felt they came into me because they knew what was going to be happening with the transmissions and they were using my ears and my eyes to witness the event. The Native American entities perceived what was happening with the transmissions as the return of the Star People. So they were witnessing the return of their ancestors!

Dr. Steven Greer
The Orion Transmissions that began in 2007 and lasted about twenty minutes, continued for five more hours and continued the next night. During those hours I sat and translated the tones and

the multi-phasic nature of it the best I could into words. Ellen Costantino graciously edited the original forty-some pages down to about seventeen pages. I acted as a step-down transformer for these transmissions. Interestingly, I don't recall much of what transpired. The transmissions happened in the center of a national park dozens of miles from any source of manmade electromagnetic energy. While the transmissions took place, an ET craft appeared in Orion. We saw this craft and I believe Todd had it in his viewfinder. Similar to the events at the Zen Dome in Crestone in 2007, the Orion Transmissions moved me and affirmed for me that there is going to be an unbroken, unstoppable force that will make transformation a reality. There is no force on earth – no cabal, no military force – capable of stopping it. We are in the final sequence, the final countdown to Transformation: The most significant change in the history of humanity...

(See The Orion Transmissions at the end of the book for the transcript of the meaning of the Transmissions)

Chapter 17

2009

CSETI Training
Outer Banks, North Carolina
April/May 2009

Linda Willitts
Shortly after dinner on the first night of training, our group of 41 gathered on the field site at the National Seashore. Twenty-seven members of the group were attending their first CSETI Training. Usually we will have something amazing happen towards the end of the week after we've been together. New people who have never done this before get a feel for the group and the group develops a degree of coherence. On this occasion amazing events began happening almost immediately!

Dr. Steven Greer
The area is a highly militarized one, with Norfolk and the Atlantic Command just a minute or so away by jet. The previous week we had been visited by an official delegation of the G7 country we have been working with to set up a contact event and move forward with open contact with that nation.

We noticed first to the north and then to the northwest two separate groups of about a dozen brilliant white objects flickering on and off repeatedly in space. Then a large bright light – large being about three inches at arm's length! – appeared in the southern sky and streaked downward at an angle towards the ocean. The object traversed the sky in a second or two in a series of interrupted materializations follow by dematerializations. When materialized, it was a lenticular-shaped object. Then it would vanish and reappear, vanish and reappear – on the same trajectory until it completely dematerialized as it reached the ocean!

About one-third of the group reported seeing the object as it streaked down. The other two-thirds were focusing on the two dozen flashing objects in space in the north and northwest section of the sky. I sensed that those objects provided a force of protection by the ETs for our group so the large craft could fly in and then manifest on the beach in a fluxing, pulsing, magnetic field form.

The craft that had dematerialized in the ocean emerged as an energetic field and manifested as a bright light signaling intermittently ninety feet from us on the beach! We filmed it and everyone on the beach saw it (See DVD). It was an extraterrestrial vehicle, manifesting as points of light about five feet above the beach and flashing at least 100 times over the course of an hour.

Linda Willitts
We paced off the distance later in daylight conditions and the dematerialized craft was ninety feet from our circle. Looking through the night scope I could see even more light flashes than with the naked eye. There were at least two and possibly three lights. One was amber-orange and the other was bluish-teal in color. With the naked eye you would see an intermittent flash but with the delay between flashes you couldn't tell that it came from more than one spot.

Dr. Steven Greer
Our camera with night-scope had difficulty imaging the mostly dematerialized craft but no trouble picking up the flashes it was emitting to us.

Linda Willitts
The flashes often seemed to occur in the context of what Dr. Greer would say or share with the group, so it seemed to be interactive in that sense rather than random.

Dr. Steven Greer
We gathered at the edge of the circle and then I walked into the area of the dematerialized craft. As I approached, I experienced a huge white light appear to my right. Some people reported I seemed to disappear or become indistinct but from my perspective I experienced an almost overwhelming love and emotion, so much so that I wept.

Linda Willitts

To me you were engulfed by the beings. They seemed to cluster around you. Some people reported seeing an aura around you.

Dr. Steven Greer

Interstellar beings at a level of God-consciousness were present as well as celestial beings. I received clearly a communication that the visitors are not going to push the contact envelope beyond what we're ready for. They're operating in a cautious way until the time comes when contact can be more open. The appearance and manifestation of an ET craft at close range with a light phenomenon that could be seen by everyone on the first night of our training was no coincidence. We had been meeting only days before with the official delegation of a major world power that wants to do a contact event in an officially recognized capacity, with backup from their military (rather than the usual harassment we receive in the US and UK). Our ET visitors were demonstrating they are ready to do such an event even with people who haven't had 20 years of experience with contact! They were saying: "We can do this even though it's a brand new group of people that has never been together previously." It was a very encouraging sign to me personally because they were saying, "Yes, we are ready if you are."

I believe this event and the others we have related represent an affirmation that we are in the final countdown for contact and disclosure. The era of living on this planet with a zero-sum game of oil and poverty is going to be vanquished forever. We're heading toward a transformation into an entirely new civilization with not only a future of abundance and dignity but also zero pollution.

Chapter 18

Orion Transmissions

Joshua Tree National Park, Geology Tour Road
November 5, 2008 CSETI Training

Background Information
This is the second Orion transmission, almost exactly one year after the first Orion Transmission at Joshua Tree National Park in 2007. The transmissions are streams of electromagnetic energy flowing from Orion through the various electronic detectors on site. We are in a very remote area, with *no* man-made source of microwaves or anything that would set off the radar detectors. The emissions began once Dr. Greer entered the circle and then they became continuous. They are being transmitted from an area of space around Orion, through non-local Consciousness interfacing with Dr. Greer's mind and then his bio-electromagnetic field and then into the detectors. They are, therefore, emerging from 'infra-space' – from ET consciousness technologies interfacing with non-locality within space/time and self. It confirms that Conscious Intelligence is omnipresent, and fully integrated into every point in space/time in its fullness. Dr. Greer's words are *interpretations* of the energy being transmitted, which are confirmed by the electronic beeps of the detectors.

This year's transmissions were longer, more intense and more detailed. They were witnessed by the entire group, as were the first transmissions. The exact events, times and number of radar detector beeps have been recorded precisely, but for ease of reading, the following narrative describes the experience.

Linda Willitts
The moment we arrived on site we noticed that the temperature had risen 15 degrees, and that the radar detectors began to chirp immediately even though there were no conventional radar emission sources for at least 25 miles.

Dr. Steven Greer

Now, what this means is we are getting a real lock-on by ETs vectoring from Orion. We are having more Orion Transmissions and there is a ship coming in. Notice this began just as I started flashing the sky with the laser inviting them here in peace. Be very still. **This is a real electromagnetic contact.** This is coming out of Orion and is a continuation of the Orion Transmissions that began in 2007.

This is a very mathematical electromagnetic event happening. As you look around us, we are in a ship; there is a scintillation surrounding us from all directions; there is an astral, etheric ship that immediately enveloped us as we arrived on site, and there are ET beings standing amongst us. Look with your inner eyes. If you need to shut your eyes briefly, see them. Now visualize us working with all these star people, in the Celestial realm, and our fellow humans in creating a completely new civilization on earth. The changes we will be witnessing in the coming months and years are beyond what you can imagine: The Quickening is happening.

I am serving as a step-down transformer – an electromagnetic antenna vectoring this energy through awareness, mind and body to the electronic detectors. There is a tremendous amount of telepathic information being transmitted to each of us, so open up and receive it. Open your heart and your mind and receive it. There is an enormous amount of energy pouring in tonight from Orion. As long as I stay in proximity to the detectors, I am downloading electromagnetic data and energy from Orion. Now, these are the beings that originated the human race; they are the Oversoul Guardians of the planet, and they are with us. There is a beautiful, God Conscious Advanced ET Being standing right here between Jan and me.

Todd Goldenbaum

I have been seeing several fast moving objects in Orion with the night scope…

Dr. Steven Greer

The Deep Space Coordinating Center of an ancient civilization millions of years old is communicating with us and through us.

And Sirius is involved with this. Do you feel the joy of what is happening? The earth is being bathed in energy. This electronic device is just affirming what we know on a more profound level. I see a constant stream of Celestial energy coming into the earth, and from this spot, permeating the earth and the human race, and there is a new energy, a new spirit – a new world emerging. This is a transmission that is affecting the entire planet. A new spirit, a new consciousness is being born.

This is the God Consciousness civilization that is connecting with us. See in your inner sight the Cosmic Egg that has a magenta, peach, rose color, where the entire Creation is represented, surrounded and held by the Divine Being – we are in it with an infinite number of other souls, All One in Spirit. Our entire civilization is going to be transformed before our eyes, within our lives, through all of us on Earth now. All of you present here are acting as a step-down transformer. God Bless you all. It is faster now, coming in and having a Kundalini effect up my spine. We are getting lighter, and the possibility for dematerialization is high.

We are within a massive ship that is resonating around us, beyond the crossing point of light... It is enormous and has enveloped us in this area, doing energy work on everyone. Open your heart chakra and mind and feel the Celestial energy that is being sent to all of us here right now. Bring in the other civilizations that are within this interstellar order. They are coming. There are thousands of civilizations approaching – several thousand civilizations. Orion's Belt and Sirius are lined up almost equidistant. I feel energy pouring into my heart chakra. Fill your hearts with this energy, and your hearts will be transformed. The entire bio-electromagnetic spiritual field is being bathed in Celestial energy. Everyone who should be here is here. No one who should not be here is here. We are all bound up together in this forever. There are several thousand extraterrestrial spacecraft encircling the earth, shifted faster than the speed of light. The force is gathering...

Any human agency that resists this change is neutralized and transformed because the time has arrived. Everybody stay in this state of consciousness, vector them in closer, bring them closer, bring them closer.

There is a group of beings right by this bush. Look with your inner sight if you cannot see them with your physical eyes. Close your eyes and see them standing here, all around us as far as the eye can see. There are several thousand extraterrestrial beings gathered in this field circumferentially around us. They are being sent and held here via sophisticated astral electronics. This is such a refined level of contact that the classified military operations cannot do anything but watch. Get on the right side of this change, my friends who are listening in the command centers... You have no other choices, and the time has come. Gaia's patience has been exhausted.

There are craft in the earth to our east emerging. There are several dozen ET craft coming up from within the earth as well. If you cannot see them with your open eyes, close your eyes and feel them with your heart and see them with your inner sight. They are absolutely here. There is a luminous senior ET being here beside me I have seen several times. Close your eyes and see him. Kindness is here; Shari is here; the ancient native peoples of this area are here. Note that the Pleiades are directly above us. There are civilizations from all these star systems and many we cannot see. The Great Spirit is speaking, the Winds of Change are blowing, the time of the Great Purification of Earth is at hand. The Earth is going to ascend to Her destiny, a globe holding a civilization of peace and enlightenment. We are just at the dawn – but this transformation is absolutely assured.

The energy continues to stream, and it will continue for as long as you all can take it. See in your inner spirit bodies the Light growing within you, and the Knowledge, and the Love. A beautiful, ruby red orb just appeared here before us, a Celestial ET object. Allow your mind to be pure, calm, and free of all distractions; be in this moment. And now place yourself at service to Peace. They are asking that each of you consecrate yourselves to that, the Most Great Peace. First, will be the lesser peace, which will be a geopolitical peace, and then the Most Great Peace of Enlightenment. And we are the dawn-breakers ushering that time... It may take a hundred and fifty years for that Emergence, out of 500,000 years. So, no matter how imperfect we may view ourselves on one level, on another level it is all perfect, with all the potential for the next half a million years streaming through us. Stand with God, find strength, and be with your ancestors and these ETs. They are our brothers and sisters in the stars, and the Great Spirit is gathering all these forces for the enormous transformation that is occurring on this planet, the pace of which is going to rapidly increase in the coming months and few years.

Trudy Guyker
About thirty seconds ago, I saw a really brilliant cobalt blue, elliptical shaped light about fifty feet away. I have never seen a color quite like that; it was absolutely gorgeous!

Dr. Steven Greer
They are Celestial ETs, Emissaries of the Dawn, Protectors of the Earth, Guardians of the Divine Plan of which we are all a part. You have to answer this Call; you all have to answer it. Enough of the lassitude and smallness because it is time to step into your spiritual power. We have all come from humble backgrounds. Open your heart to that and be wise within yourselves.

As soon as we sat at the Hidden Valley site, I closed my eyes and went instantly into Brahman Consciousness, the level beyond Unity Consciousness, and saw the entire creation as a Cosmic Egg. We have help available to all of us. If you ask for it, you will receive it. If you do not ask for it, you will not. They are calling us, but you have to say yes. Many are called, but few choose to *answer* the call. Remember, no one is a "Chosen One." It is about you choosing to *be one*. You have to choose that. See all of this as the Cosmic Mind; it is all awake. Your whole body is pure Awakeness. Awaken in your body. If you feel cold or hungry, tap into that inner source of infinite energy, because that infinite energy is within you, and you can stream it through you, creating infinite amounts of energy as heat and light.

This is what you are called upon to do, because in truth, your limitations are what you have created. Whatever limitations there are, you can let go of them as easily as you cling to them – if you connect your soul to the Great Spirit and ask for that help. And know that you are not alone. We are all doing this together; we are all doing this as we love each other. We stand in a circle filled with the love of one another. How beautiful it is, out here under the stars with these transmissions from Onion that are happening at this very instant!

Events are going to transpire soon in which everybody on the planet will know we are not alone, and those of you who know the truth will have to speak the truth to those with whom you live, because less than one in a million people on the planet knows the truth about who these beings are and why they are here. So you have to be the ones to speak, because if you do not speak the truth, there will be others who strive to deceive the masses. So you must be the ones to speak the truth, and a good truth it is. Let us make a circle here, put our arms around each other for a moment. There are twenty-one of us here. Everything you need to know has been downloaded non-linearly in these transmissions tonight, so you will meditate on that and have it unfold within your awareness, beyond language. Pure Knowledge, Healing, and Truth are all very simple. One life, one mind, brothers and sisters together on earth and in space and within the Celestial realm, all working together, toiling in the vineyard of this beautiful planet. How wonderful to be here now. God Bless you all.

[Dr. Greer sits to rest only a few moments, and then the experience continues.]

Another wave of contact is coming. A gathering of the Concourse on High and the Celestial Army of Light to transform humanity is coming. They are all here. Stay with the Divine thoughts. There are more extraterrestrial spacecraft arriving, thousands of them are approaching.

The Great Gathering is occurring. See it in your inner sight. They are nearly materialized here. All of you are assigned a task: to be of service. Jesus Christ, all the Avatars and all the Celestials are here, rank on rank approaching, coming to the earth.

The time for the Transformation of Earth is at hand. Do not ever forget this for as long as you live. They are manifesting and materializing, and we thank them for their presence. The transformation of this planet is very, very close at hand. You must leave your mundane lives behind and step into service. Free yourself from all of your attachments, whether it be money, prestige or anything else. Your lives are starting a new chapter... Forget all that you think you know about what you should be doing and contemplate this as if you were just born on this planet tonight. Shake off your stupor. Step into the light of what you can achieve. Time is actually very short. Conventional life must be transformed because all of you now must become extraordinary, not ordinary. Embrace that with passion, purity, and a willingness to sacrifice, to give, to be selfless – because now you have all been given everything you need. It is the time of the Great Awakening – the Great Awakening within us. It is, in fact, a new Creation, a new world from the innermost spirit. It is our sacred task to be completely at service, free from all attachment, turning only to the Great Spirit within us, free from all limitations, all fear, filled with joy, completely committed, at service to the Divine Plan, the Vision that must guide the world.

God Help us all. We need your help, and we need each other. All things are possible in this, the Divine Cycle of Fulfillment. All of our ancestors are here, going back to the beginning of humanity, and all of our future children are here as we are gathered at the morn of eternity together in this sacred place. And the infinite tree of life is renewed, and we are bearing new fruit, and a new Creation has appeared, and within the Empyrean Realm it exists in its completion. And so it is up to us to manifest it and to be a vehicle, a pure vehicle, for its establishment. Do what you can to work together to manifest that intent and the power of the Divine One.

These transmissions will be recorded and shared with the planet, for in spirit every single person on this planet is here to bear witness to this Great Transformation, and they will remember these days eternally, and all their children, and all that come after them are watching, waiting, and honoring those who serve. Be as unrestrained as the wind and put yourself completely at service to that Vision. Ask the Great Being how you may be of service;

and when you see that, embrace it with all your heart, freed from all doubt, all limitations, with all your being. Walk the path of service to Universal Peace and to humanity. No matter what may befall you in the path of service, it is honored eternally. It may not always be easy, and the right path often is not, but your eternal soul will be grateful. You are all greatly loved for your service.

Now we are remembering our purpose, and in that radiant and beautiful morn which is the dawn of eternity, we are all known by the Divine Being. We knew ourselves and our mission, and now we are awakening to that mission and to our true selves. We join together in the love of God and of one another as we establish on earth a new world, a Divine Civilization, an enlightened people, a just society. And if you take one step in that direction, the path will open into eternity. But you must put yourself in motion, awakened, and work, serve, and love together – then all of this will be possible. You have been given everything. Only when you let it pour through you, does it continue to pour into you, because this divine power you cannot hold onto and covet. This knowledge and truth must flow through you, heart to heart, mind to mind, and if you let it flow through you, it will always be replenished, for It is infinite. If you try to grasp it, it will vanish, and this is the mystery of sacrifice, and the joy of giving.

Serve the truth and speak the truth, no matter if you are vilified and no matter what may befall you, because in time we all shed this physical garment, but our souls are eternal. The earth is ready to be transformed, and every atom of the earth is made anew. God Bless all of you, and we are grateful for your service. Now listen within your inner soul, and open your heart to the message, and find your own vision and voice to the path that your own life must take. Be strong. Be faithful. Have courage. Be kind. Love one another and see the light of the Divine Being in all beings. Turn to the Great Spirit and ask what you must do. Fear not any challenge because you are always eternally supported and protected.

There are beings approaching, and we welcome them here. See that each of you has a guide, a source of protection and inspiration. How blessed we are to be at service at this time.

And so we must give gratitude and thanks eternal to the Great Being, that vast ocean from whence we have come – pure Cosmic Mind. We are always one with It, and if we put ourselves completely at service to this Great Being, the entire power of the vast ocean will be at our service, making us a pure channel for Divine Light.

Female voice
This is absolutely no coincidence that it is happening now. This is one of the most pivotal moments in our history. So, I hope people do not walk away from here and forget this. It is meant to be life changing.

Linda Willitts
It is really heralding the New Era. And the Universe is rejoicing.

Dr. Steven Greer
Yes, it is the herald of the New Era. This is the herald of the new era. It is absolutely upon us. See the excitement and joy in all realms. They are just jumping out of their electromagnetic skins! Each of us must be that herald. At first, there are only a few voices, and then thousands, and then millions, and then billions. The Universal Avatar is present and all of these extraterrestrial civilizations are acting as enlightened step-down transformers, just as we are the transformers for Earth. It is not to be held, but to be given; not to be remembered alone, but to be shared with all whom you know, from heart to heart.

The singularity of knowledge and its completion is within us. All of our souls bear witness to these transmissions that keep streaming forth. All who dwell on earth at this instant see that these words, this energy, this consciousness is awakening within us. All six and a half billion people, every soul, every mind, every body is being suffused in this cosmic light and knowledge as a continuous stream of pure consciousness and celestial knowledge.

The time for the healing of the earth, the reforming of earth into a new world, has arrived, and no temporal force, no military, no potentate can in any way thwart the inevitability of the Divine Plan unfolding on earth. So great is the power gathering within the earth, within her people, within the Angelic realm, and amongst the peoples from all the star systems of the Cosmos, that the outcome is assured and this transformation is imminent. In this certainty, and in this knowledge, go forth from this place assured of the outcome. The vision of a new world is within you, the wondrous sciences long withheld from the people of the earth will be unveiled; the foundations of a just and enlightened civilization will be established.

Know that this is an era of unbroken Universal Peace that shall endure for at least half a million years, until such time as every man, woman, and child on earth is in God Consciousness and living the life of enlightenment. And in that time, we will be extraterrestrial peoples to other worlds, and so this cycle shall continue forever – spreading knowledge and enlightenment in a creation that has had no beginning and has no end. It is pouring forth eternally from the Great Being standing within all things. Behold all the veils falling away. See the reality of what is within us and around us.

Female voice
This is like a major celebration. Really, I am sharing their joy with us, and they are really making a big point, too. And I get the sense that this can go on for hours or more.

Dr. Steven Greer
This will never end because now the connection has been made, and from this point forward it will be unbroken. Before it was given at intervals, but now the message will be continuous until the establishment of a peaceful civilization on earth is achieved; and there is no turning back. Remember this always and be faithful to what you have learned. That is how you honor it. God Bless all of you.

Male voice
Thank you for sharing it, Dr. Greer, and for translating for us.

Orion Transmissions continue
Joshua Tree National Park, Geology Tour Road
November 7, 2008
Background Information

The transmissions started as soon as we arrived at the Geology Tour Rd site and continued for approximately 45 minutes with

42 people witnessing the event and Dr. Greer's translation of the transmissions on site. The electromagnetic detectors were silent until Dr. Greer arrived...

Dr. Steven Greer
The transmissions are beginning. The Orion Constellation is up and has just cleared the trees. So now, we are all in cosmic awareness together with clear minds. I was told that they would be here as soon as we arrived on site. Wow, the tones just shifted to another band. They are going back and forth between two separate bands simultaneously! The ET beings are here astrally. There is an enormous spacecraft here, and it is actually a double pyramid. There are two of them together, with their bases connected. It is very, very significant, and I was told that earlier in meditation that "We will all be with you tonight." All interstellar civilizations are here with us tonight. They love this group! They are very excited tonight. I think you need to understand that all of you can connect to the Beings that are creating these electromagnetic tones...

Who is transmitting? These are our friends, brothers and sisters from other star systems, and they are here to connect with each of you. Ask and they will tell you. Open your minds and let go of your limitations. They want you to be clear tonight. Be free and as unrestrained as the wind. Let your mind open. This is awesome! I smell carnations now!

Multiple voices
Yes, I do too!

Dr. Steven Greer
The Celestials are coming. We have the extraterrestrial beings and the Celestial beings here – the Angelic realm. The earth is transforming. The time is nigh for the big changes on Earth. The time of the Great Purification has arrived. It is here. We are in an etheric ship and then within that, there are many other beings shifted on different frequencies. They are almost materialized (because the detectors are picking up electromagnetic energy). It is very directional and they are communicating telepathically now with everyone. There was just a blue-white orb that appeared.

Contact: Countdown to Transformation

Male voice
There's a huge being behind you, Dr. Greer.

Dr. Steven Greer
They are saying, "Welcome to the Universe. Welcome to the time of Universal Peace. The biggest transformation in the history of the earth's multibillion year existence is at hand."

We can see visibly now an exoatmospheric vehicle and they are confirming what I am saying. Please listen. This spacecraft we are seeing is the Master Control craft from the Deep Space Center. And we are being bathed in Celestial Knowledge and Light. Listen now! Various frequencies simultaneously can be heard! Now see the craft that is here around us in your astral, celestial vision, and the beings who are here. Open your hands like this and let their energy pour into you, the knowledge of this transmission.

Thank you! Did everybody receive that?! This is all about the energy, pure packets of Celestial Knowledge, pouring into all of you. They are here to deliver this massive download to us. How beautiful. Thank you!

Dr. Jan Bravo
The object in the northeast is gone.

Dr. Steven Greer
Did everybody see that golden globe? There was a huge golden ship for about five or ten minutes out there to the northeast.
[Multiple voices confirm this comment.]

Dr. Steven Greer
When I turned and made the antenna, there was a continuous download. All of you have received this energy, and it is in the bioelectric field of your body and soul. It will be unveiled within you in the coming months and years – and for the rest of your lives. It is very, very, very abstract. I do not know how to describe it except as I have this week, but it is the vision and the knowledge of everything that will occur in the next 500,000 years. Now, I would like for people to share their experience in meditation

tonight, and your experience in these transmissions as well. Open your heart and mind and share.

Dr. Raven Nabulsi
Right above this Joshua tree in the east, about twenty feet above us, a translucent orb appeared that was a rounded diamond shape and a fuchsia color.

Linda Willitts
I still see scintillating sparkles in that area.

Trudy Guyker
During meditation it was like I became very small and I was right up against a female eye. I was looking at the left side of a female's face, right at her eye from the side, and I must have been an ant's size because the eye was huge, and I felt that it was the eye of an Egyptian woman. It was not quite the elaborate makeup of an Egyptian, but there was eye shadow and I feel that it was an Egyptian woman. She was just gazing out, and so I am wondering if there is some connection between that and my meditation seeing Anwar Sadat.

Linda Willitts
In last night's meditation, Trudy and I saw another pyramid, too, like an Egyptian pyramid.

Dr. Steven Greer
I saw two superimposed pyramids here, which is of course the pyramidal shape from Egypt.

Female voice
I was shown in my meditation some Celestial beings. I asked if they would join us tonight and they said, "Dear One, we are always with you," and I said, "Sometimes you feel closer and sometimes you feel farther away," and they said, "That is a perception gap, not a reality gap." And they showed me an ancient mound and I thought, Greece, and they said, "No, it is the Mount of Olives, and this is where it all began."

Dr. Steven Greer
Right. I have been there.

Female voice
What began there? I have no idea. Do you know?

Dr. Steven Greer
That whole area of the world is where so many Avatars have come so there is an ancient connection to that area. I have been there many times, and an amazing energy exists there, which is what they were referring to. The cycle we are beginning now involves the creation of a new humanity. We are really blessed that you were given that image. It is really a very accurate image.

Second Female voice
In my meditation tonight the energy came in as I was repeating the mantra. During the course of that, I had the vision of Hathor and the look was one that I have seen many times before. And they said, "We are here. It is time."

Dr. Steven Greer
How many people saw the strange craft that was in the sky during the transmissions?
[Multiple assent]
We had that for hours and hours in Charlottesville, and felt that we had a continuous stream of celestial Consciousness pouring into us from the craft. And as we were driving into the Park to come here, there were vortices of energy ahead of the car, as if we were being escorted onto the site the whole time we were driving in. What else did people see in their meditation?

Female voice
I saw an eye also, but it was just an eye.

Dr. Steven Greer
That is an image many people get. It is the symbol of the Eye of God, the All-Seeing Eye, the eye that is within us, the Conscious Mind whereby you can see anyplace. The All-Seeing Eye is a great experience.

Look! There was a huge, golden orb right over the field here that actually lit up this little hilltop. Did you all see it? It was golden red; it was more gold than red, and a spray of light.

Linda Willitts and several voices
Yes!

Male voice
Yeah, I saw it go down too, like a laser almost.

Second male voice
So how many people saw the eye? The Eye in hieroglyphs is called the eye of Horus and it has to do with psychic and spiritual vision. And it could mean that everyone's getting blessed with that spiritual, psychic vision.

Dr. Steven Greer
That is correct. That is what this whole week is about: activating these capabilities within all of us, and being ambassadors to the universe and agents of transformation on this planet, because that is what we are here for[123].

Last year, when the Orion Transmissions started, I had this crystal out, and as I moved my body like an antenna, I finally locked onto Orion and then the transmissions became continuous. Remember?

Linda Willitts
Oh, yes. I will never forget!

Dr. Steven Greer
Well, Orion and Sirius figure very heavily in both the Egyptian traditions and in the Vedic traditions. Ted! Did you just see that big orb there?

Dr. Ted Loder
Yes, I saw it. I just caught it out of my peripheral vision, because

---

[123] See earlier section regarding the ET 'eye' that appeared at the home at which we were staying outside Joshua Tree National Park in November 2008. (SG)

it was to the side of me, not in front of me.

Dr. Steven Greer
It was brilliant and huge. The area it lit up was really amazing. It had a reddish golden quality – pure, beautiful light. They are all going to be here, and what we are seeing are different expressions of the ET presence. This is the Gathering, and when they told me tonight, "We will all be with you tonight," this is what that meant.

Debbie Foch
There is a high-pitched continuous tone now!

Dr. Steven Greer
Yes. A pure tone, from which all creation emanates: the primal thought, sound, and tone. Anyone, if you ever experience it in actuality, it is the most astonishing thing of your life.

Male voice
I was convinced that we would have another manifestation of the fragrance, and the rosy glow in the sky, which I have already seen. And there was something above us causing a burst of light.

Dr. Steven Greer
I saw that also. I was waiting for someone to say that, and as you are speaking, there is a being opposite you, in the center of the circle, that lit up as you started speaking, so I knew you had something to say.

Male voice
I think everyone will have an experience, a personal experience of loving – some way that is meaningful to you personally and sustain you as you go home.

Dr. Steven Greer
There was just a blue-white flash of light – right over the group about fifteen feet up in the north-northeast. I just saw an area in the sky that is circumferential around us and has an increasing matrix of energy – like an old fashioned black-and-white TV on the "fritz,"

but finer than that. It is suddenly increasing. When you meditate, your senses become very refined and you can see the essence of things. It is called Celestial Perception, when you eventually can see the finest Celestial energies, and it literally is a refinement of the neurophysiology that is wired into the consciousness and the mind. Have you experienced that in your lives?

[Multiple assent]

As I said, there are multiple ET craft present; many are superimposed in this exact space in various frequencies. Some are incredibly fine, at the near Celestial level of resonance, all the way to ones that are virtually materialized. My own feeling is that the golden orb that we saw earlier, and the one that we just saw, are the same ET craft moving in closer.

They want you to make a quiet connection to them – then a clearer and clearer connection, and build on that as you continue doing this work wherever you live. You are going to see more of their presence – manifesting as electronic, or materialized, or burst of light, or tone. They want you to develop your ability to see their presence with your inner sight even as your eyes are open. As I was saying that, I suddenly saw superimposed over the area where Procyon and Sirius are, a pink-red light that turned both those stars red. It was a very interesting phenomenon. So invite them to come, and invite them to manifest in any way they can, and then they will invite you into their dimension of light, and etheric energy.

Trudy Guyker

I was trying to understand some of the transmissions, and I feel the very last thing that was said in that continuous burst was "The greatest of all is Love."

Dr. Steven Greer

The greatest power, the greatest experience, is love...

There are numerous ET beings here. These are highly evolved God Consciousness interstellar beings. That was a different band on the detector, just as I said that! It's confirming the words...

We must put ourselves completely at service to the establishment of Universal Peace. And if you open that door, all will be possible. The time has arrived for Universal Peace on earth, the establishment of a Divine, enlightened civilization.

Do not be afraid, no matter what happens, because these Beloved Beings are always with us, and we are very much loved by them, even as we love them. Open your heart chakra and send a ray of love out to Orion and Sirius. And send the love and beauty of humanity to the Universe, and see it being returned from all these beings who are gathered here.

Todd Goldenbaum
Another object just dropped down out of Orion.

Dr. Steven Greer
There was an object that phased in near that Joshua tree. South-southeast at the level of the tree, there was an orb, which is a spacecraft filled with beings, shifted dimensionally into the etheric, and they are communicating with all of us. They want you to see them and feel them. The time is quickly approaching when the entire world will know we are not alone and all the warfare on the planet will cease. It is the biggest transformation in history, and we will bear witness to it.

The transmissions are coming from Orion, but these beings are here from many, many star systems throughout the Cosmos. They are the Interstellar Coalition, and they are indeed our brothers and sisters from the stars. They are calling you to join them, and this whole event for the last few days has been the heralding of the imminent establishment of an entirely new era on earth, the ninth great cycle, and we have entered it together. We are joined with them in prayer for the Earth and her people, and we turn to the Great Being, the Source of all life, giving thanks and asking for guidance. And we know, whensoever we call on that power, it will be with us and within us, and surround us all the days of our lives. This is a call for all those who bear witness to this, the Orion Transmissions, to completely turn their lives to this Transformation of life on earth and the establishment of Universal Peace and a Divine Civilization.

Now there is a beautiful being in the center of our circle, in front of me, and he wishes all of you to know that you are all greatly loved. And that we must love one another and see continuously this Grace flowing through us to Earth and Her people. And so long as we let it flow through us, it will continue, for this is a Divine Power that cannot be held, but only given. See it flow through you – your hands, your body, your minds, your souls, your hearts – to all those who dwell on Earth. And behold every heart and mind on earth filled with this new energy and light, blessed eternally in peace. As we live together in this sphere of life: One life, One mind, brothers and sisters, together eternally.

Stay focused on the transmissions. They are becoming more intense. Take them in. It is pouring forth from Orion. No force on earth can deter this outcome. We walk with the power of the Unseen and the Infinite Being within us and around us.

Receive it and let it flow through you now, to all those who dwell on earth – a Divine Healing, Celestial Power to every man, woman, and child, and to all of our leaders, and all of our friends. Open all your chakras, your mind, your heart, and let it flow! All the Earth is enveloped in this light, and the entire force of the Universe is focused here at this spot, spreading forth around the globe to every man, woman, and child, every nation, every people – a continuous stream of Celestial Knowledge and Love – Divine, Pure Love, Protection, and Guidance. The Great Awakening is Now! All six and a half billion souls are awakening in this, the Divine Moment.

And all those who are gathered here will bear witness to these events. And as time goes forward, you will behold the most wondrous transformation in your lives and in the life of the world. Now the entire earth being, Gaia, is awakening, and She is rejoicing with the Heavens, as the culmination of all Her cycles is now at hand.

And all the colors will blend into one and there will be one People of Earth who see they are brothers and sisters of the Peoples from the Stars. Every civilization capable of interstellar travel is represented here now. There is a great rejoicing within the Earth and Humanity and the Heavens. Feel that joy in your heart, and live it for the rest of your lives. Share the wisdom you have been given and work tirelessly for the establishment of the New Kingdom of Peace and Enlightenment on Earth.

We swim in an ocean of Light. Our minds are the fullness of Infinity, and our hearts are filled with the Golden Light of Eternal Love for the Great Being and for one another. And behold the Light shimmering around us in this circle. Rank on rank, the Star peoples and the Celestial Beings are gathered here in this, the Gathering which heralds the establishment of the New World. And continuously in your soul, call out to the Great Spirit for guidance and protection and strength. Feel that love and that joy and that eternal bliss as we go forward from this place into the world, and the cities and the towns and the continents, each of us fountainheads of knowledge, of guidance, of service to the cause of Universal Peace, enlightenment on Earth, and the Oneness of all people.

Here it is coming through us. Receive it! Transmit this energy to the entire planet: all your loved ones, all your ancestors, all your friends, and all that they know throughout the globe. This Divine Knowledge is coming: Pure love, Eternal life, Transformative Power. The transformative power of Enlightenment and Divine Love. Feel the joy of service as you find within yourselves the ability to manifest this Great Light. And if you turn to that guidance and light within you, you will be freed of every limitation, and every obstacle will melt, and the path will be clear. How blessed we all are to be here now. All of these civilizations who are gathered here wish to tell you how cherished you are in their minds and hearts. For you have picked up the mantle of service, and have found your way here...

Never look back, but be in the eternal perfection of Now, and be at service to the vision within us, the world we know that is manifesting, for it is already perfected within the Empyrean Realm of the crystalline consciousness within us. And now it is time for its manifestation through us into the world – have no doubt thereof. Each of you is being called to service, but only you can answer that call. So with purity of heart and faith that the Great Being is with you always, take up that work and know that you will never toil alone, and even if you do not perceive it at all times, this Divine Being, these Star People, and the Celestial Realm are with you and surround you forever.

They are calling each one of you. See that here, at this moment, are present all these Star People and all of your ancestors. And now see all those beings that will come to earth over the next five hundred thousand years as their souls reside within the matrix of the Great Being. They thank you because they, too, are with us now – all beings now present – from the future and the past, as we are gathered into One Great Being. We are all One in Spirit, eternally. Feel the love of those not yet born into this world as they honor our humble service at this crucial time in the evolution of the earth and the people of the earth. See that they are here as well, and see that we have opened the gate for them to come into a world of Peace to evolve here into a state of God Consciousness, and to become a Divine civilization together in eternal Love and Peace on Earth. How beautiful and Blessed is this time! See that the blessing is continuous, and the outpouring will never cease.

And what began last year at this time, on these dates, has now become an unbroken stream, as the Quickening is here. The transformation is at hand, and in fact, a year of life on earth now, will be more significant than a thousand years in the past. Such is the Quickening. Such is the power of this Transformation.

[The group takes a break here, and then reconvenes.]
Todd Goldenbaum
The faster and more intense the radar detector signal is, the nearer and stronger the source is.

Dr. Steven Greer
The radar beeps indicate pulses of knowledge... This started last year when I was holding the crystal toward Orion and it opened that channel of connection. This year it is amplified because we are closer to the transformation. In the past the radar detectors

went off if a being or craft were in the area, but not continuously.

Female voice
Another phenomenon that has been happening with all these transmissions is that time is distorted.

Dr. Steven Greer
An hour goes by but it only seems like 5 minutes. Tonight started as soon as we formed the circle and I got near the radar detectors. It is really profound.

Linda Willitts
The radar detectors change their volumes and "speak" in louder and softer voices during the transmissions. It is amazing.

Dr. Steven Greer
It is almost midnight. We have been here 3 hours, though it is hard to imagine. I would like people to share what they experienced while the transmissions were happening. All of you are being illumined from within, and also from outside as we are being bathed in a Celestial Light. This Celestial Light is real. It is physical as well as spiritual. It is an ancient function, and we just happen to live in a time where there are devices that help us see it. It is physical as well as spiritual energy, which is why some people are having physical, emotional and mental sensations, as the chakras are opening to the knowledge.

The transmissions that are continuing from Orion are very abstract, but they are, as I mentioned earlier, about pure energy, pure knowledge, pure spirit, and contain the seeds, the essence of everything for the next 500,000 years. It is also, most importantly, a call to service.

Much of the energy here is a tremendous rejoicing and happiness, a deep spiritual peace that comes with knowing the long years of human ignorance and war are closing so a period of unbroken peace and eventual global enlightenment can be established. That has never happened on the earth before – not in her five billion year history. So, it is a completely amazing cycle, and an amazing time to be alive on earth!

Female voice
This is exciting! When the transmissions started and the pace quickened, the more excited I became internally. My heart revved up and the energy started to soar, and then I went into this cosmic state, like I was connected to a light socket, and it went on for quite awhile. It is so joyful, it makes my heart flutter. I am so happy. And I do not know how to explain this.

Dr. Steven Greer
It is an electromagnetic flux, and an evidence of their presence, as they pour energy through these detectors and our bodies. My purpose when I do these trainings is to model what is happening so that people understand all the ways that you can make contact with these beings.

Male voice
If you had not given us the initiation in the cave yesterday, we would not be as receptive to this wonderful energy coming down from heaven as we are right now.

Dr. Steven Greer
I am very honored that I can share these transmissions with all of you. The words I spoke came from the Spirit that I was receiving. Within each of you exists your own knowledge and your own translation because it was pouring forth through everyone. All of you can do this on your own...

Remember, there are an infinite number of ways advanced civilizations, working through various intermediaries, can make contact with you. An actual craft or being seen is just an outward manifestation of something much more profound that is deep within pure consciousness and spirit and has to do with this extraordinary time and this quickening of the transformation.

Male voice
Every time a transmission comes, my body just takes in a huge breath – deeper than I ever knew a person could breathe in – as if it's storing up for use later on.

Trudy Guyker
Somewhere in the meditation I saw a flotilla of nine craft.

Dr. Steven Greer
Nine is the number of fulfillment, the highest digit. In the Zen Dome last year Trudy saw a gathering of the forces of the Godhead, and all of the Angelic beings. That is exactly what is now manifesting.

The outcome is assured. It does not and cannot happen by itself, but requires us as the children of Earth to be the means for that change and transformation. The extraterrestrial beings cannot land here and make it happen or force it...
We are the primary agents for the change and the transformation because we are in the physical plane; we are living and breathing the free air of Earth together, and we are the children of Earth. So it has to come through us, even though the source of the inspiration may be Celestial and extraterrestrial and Divine. It is very personal because each person must choose to make that transformation. It is a beautiful mystery and humbles us, and yet has enormous power.

Do not think that we need ninety-nine percent of the world working on this in order for it to happen. That is not how significant transformation happens. It is always done with a relatively small number. Do not underestimate the effect you, as an individual, are having. When you are in right action, great change is created, despite our imperfections, weaknesses and limitations.

Male voice
So what you are saying is that we are the bridge between heaven and earth?

Dr. Steven Greer
Absolutely. We are the means for that transformation, and the ETs are very happy when we put ourselves at service. Do not be concerned whether you can carry a thimbleful or a gallon or half the ocean. If everyone carries what they can, then it will happen. Everyone has gifts and abilities, so it is about stepping into the state of service and providing what you have to the work.

When people are all linked up together in a coherent state, seeing and feeling what we are feeling tonight, every atom of the earth is revivified – every heart on earth. That is really true. That is the mystery of the non-locality of Mind, and the interconnectedness of all. I could see that happening through this small group as the Orion Transmissions were streaming through us.

We have been trained in our society to be very acquisitive, but actually that pulls us down. If we let spirit and love come through us and give it back, then it is continually renewed and gets stronger and more beautiful. That is the power of love and forgiveness flowing through you. So view yourselves as pure channels and let it flow through you to the world and to others. Be as pure and innocent as a child, and it will flow forever through you...

As we leave now, view yourselves as true Ambassadors of Peace and Enlightenment to the entire Universe, and to the World. Ask for guidance in your service so you may find it and fulfill your destiny. It has been an honor to be with all of you. You are such a beautiful, sweet, spiritual group, and I consider you all my friends and family. I wish you safe journeys. God Bless all of you, and I hope to see you again soon wherever it may be.

Appendix

Basic Levels of the Cosmology

February 2007

Disclosure Project Witness Recalls Incidents

Dr. Steven Greer
Arnie Arneson is a Disclosure Project Witness whom we were delighted to have with us at The CSETI Experience.

Arnie Arneson
I came to the CSETI Experience because I had to find out about the CE-5 concept. I did not know anything about it. I knew the Disclosure aspect, and I will mention my impressions of the CE-5 later on. I was actually introduced to the Disclosure Project by listening to the Art Bell Show. I happened to hear Bob Salas one night on the Art Bell Show talking about his experience with the Missile Shutdown at Malmstrom Air Force Base., caused by a UFO. I was surprised that someone else knew about such things. It had happened to me back in 1967.

The person who followed Bob Salas on the show was also named Bob. Art Bell doesn't like to use last names so I kept hearing "Bob, Bob," and it finally clicked. The second Bob was my first supervisor at Boeing. He had retired and lived a mile or two from me. The next day, I made contact with Bob Salas up in Belleview, which is not too far from where I live in Auburn, Washington. He was very reluctant to come into Dr. Greer's Disclosure program, but I finally convinced him to do it.

As for myself, I was in the communication center at Malmstrom in March of 1967, and I saw the message come forward saying that the missiles had been shut down. Bob Salas was in the bunker and his airmen above were his security police. They told him there was a UFO outside the missile site, and that was a secondary effect of their presence.

I also contacted Bob Kamimski, my manager at Boeing, and we had breakfast together several times. He was the engineer chosen by Boeing to inspect the missile silos of the missiles that went down cold. During breakfast he said the missiles were perfectly clean; they did not go down by themselves but were shut down by something. He added that Boeing received a message from the Air Force half way through the investigation. The contents of the message were: "Stop the investigation and do not, repeat, do not, send us a report."

After I heard about Dr. Greer I sent a letter to him, not expecting much to develop. When Dr. Greer and his cameraman came out to interview me in Seattle he said he was going to interview 500 people and select twenty. I honestly did not expect anything more to develop. I do not know why he happened to key upon me, but I do appreciate it and will never forget the experience. I had an opportunity to spend a week in DC with all the other Disclosure Project witnesses doing the Press Club event and visiting Senators and Congressmen who did not have a clue.

Conversation with Adolph Raum

My last year in the air force, I was stationed at Wright-Patterson Air Force Base as Director of Logistics. Since it was my daughter's last year of high school, I left my family back in Oklahoma City, and I went by myself to Dayton, Ohio. A lady of English descent, Chris Whedon, lived near Dayton in a country mansion. She had a room for me, and I became something of an "adopted son," helping her cut the grass and wood since she was in her 70s.

Her deceased husband was Lieutenant-Colonel Spence Whedon, who was highly regarded in the Wright-Patterson Air Force Base community. He briefed the generals about all the UFO tapes and incidents during the Roswell time frame. I think he was the commander of the technical intelligence squadron the same time that the Roswell crash victims were transported to Wright-Patterson. I have a taped interview between Lieutenant-Colonel Spence Whedon and Major Donald Keyhoe[124] of NICAP[125] fame.

---

[124] Major Donald Keyhoe: http://en.wikipedia.org/wiki/Donald_Keyhoe
[125] NICAP (National Investigatory Committee on Aerial Phenomena): http://en.wikipedia.org/wiki/NICAP

Chris Whedon had parties at least every two weeks at her Dayton home. She had many retired friends over for dinner and a few drinks. One attendee was Dr. Adolph Raum, who was born in Switzerland and was 86. I do not know what his capacity was at Wright-Patterson, but he took a liking to me. He was involved with the first A-Bomb test in the US and knew Dr. Oppenheimer personally. He was highly respected amongst the houseguests at Whedon's. We became very good friends. One night after a couple of drinks, I thought I had his confidence and asked him about the little green men at Wright-Patterson. Immediately his face turned ashen white and he said, "All I will say is that they were not weather balloons." Then he became very stern and said, "Arnie, we will never talk about this again, do you understand?" I am firmly convinced I touched a nerve.

An Unforgettable Character

Another experience occurred at Davis-Monthan Air Force Base back in the mid-70s when I was on an inspection trip there. First I want to go back to when I was about four years old. I had a dream which I have with me to this very moment. I was in a circular craft of some kind above the Earth. All my dreams are in color, so I could look down and see the Earth; the clouds and everything were in color, and that is all I saw. Returning to the '75 inspection trip, on my first night there I was at the officer's club and all the tables were filled. I was sitting at a table with two chairs when a young captain walked over and asked to sit with me.

We sat and talked. After we finished the meal and had a drink or two, out of the clear blue sky, he told me that I had a dream that was bothering me. He described my dream exactly as it was and told me that one of these days I would see the color of the uniform I was wearing and would see more details about what was in that craft. I have no idea where he got that information. I looked for him while I was there doing inspections, but I never saw him again.

Dr. Steven Greer
What year was that?

Arnie Arneson
Around 1975. I did not broadcast that conversation. Had I put

out that kind of story, I would no longer have had a Top Secret Clearance, I can guarantee you.

Extraterrestrials and Energy: An Integrated Problem
Dr Steven Greer

Extraterrestrials, energy and propulsion are all one big issue, though many people fail to see the connection. In the past there was insurmountable inertia surrounding these topics. The new energy people judged the extraterrestrial issue as nonsense, while the extraterrestrial and UFO researchers wanted nothing to do with the new energy and propulsion information. What they did not and often still do not understand is that all of it is an integrated problem. The secrecy in one area is the same as the secrecy in the other.

I think people now know that we are running out of time and cannot ignore these issues any longer. The world is submerged in a huge number of interconnected crises. I liken it to when you are going down a runway and you hit the point where you have to take off or run out of runway. You either have to shut the jet down or take off. Our civilization is at that point and we have been there for a while. This is a do-or-die time, and we do not have another generation to hand it over to.

All the News is Not the Way Things Really Work

An issue not known publicly was that the Bentwaters RAF[126], at Rendlesham Forest in Suffolk, England was supposed to be non-nuclear, both by treaty and agreement. British protesters were raising hell about the fact that there were American nuclear weapons in England. Rendlesham Forest was always presented to the public as being nuclear free, when in reality they had many nuclear weapons based there. That is why the pyramid-shaped ET vehicle landed at Bentwaters. It was a hot nuclear area and a first-strike launch facility.

I met with a military and national security affairs writer from the Washington Post years ago. He told me he had a whole file on all

---

[126] RAF Bentwaters is a former Royal Air Force station about 80 miles NE of London, 10 miles ENE of Ipswich, near Woodbridge, Suffolk in the UK. [http://en.wikipedia.org/wiki/RAF_Bentwaters]

the material related to ultra secret black projects.

I asked him why he did not write an article about such projects, and he replied "Nothing important is ever published in the Washington Post or the New York Times." When I asked about the fourth estate he said it had been dead for decades. He was very glib and was actually working as an intelligence operative. They often use journalists as their cover. This same fellow told me about the human cloning experiments and creation of the PLFs (Programmed Life Forms)[127]. He knew about all this information and had files on much of this, but would not publish anything on it.

'Star Wars' Scenario: The Fear and Hatred Paradigm
Dr. Bill Clindenen
Why would the powers-that-be want an interplanetary war, when there is no way that we could win it?

Dr. Steven Greer
They want an interplanetary war for the same reason we stayed in the Cold War with mutually assured destruction when there was no way we could win. There are interests that benefit from a $1 trillion per year expenditure on military-industrial activities. The pawns that end up spending their lives in that game do not understand that behind the scenes, a permanent government, not an elected government, keeps the war machine moving. It is about control and a focus on fear to keep people doing their bidding.

Werner von Braun described it when he said that we would go from the 'Cold War' to 'Nations of Concern' to 'Global Terrorism' and eventually to a 'Threat from Outer Space.' Always focusing on a threat keeps people's attention and justifies not only the expenditures, but also the control that goes with fear[128]. Demagogues, whether they are political, religious or industrial, control the masses chiefly through fear. It is very effective because humans are hard-wired in their primal brain to respond to threats from the unknown.

---
[127] PLFs: Greer, *Hidden Truth* (2006), pp. 37; 235-236.
[128] Greer, *Disclosure* (2001), Carol Rosin testimony, pp. 255-261.

Examples that everyone knows about are things that were done to demonize Jews during the Third Reich. Nazis created posters saying Jews were planning to use the blood of non-Jews to make matzo meal for Passover. This same type of disinformation is now being shared among Islamic fanatics in the Middle East – the same Elders of Zion perspective[129]. It is horrible – but horribly effective.

By creating a 'boogie man' and fear, a population can be controlled through fear and hatred. It is very nasty, and very much a part of how large cartels have been able to consolidate power and control large numbers of people. The 'control drama' they plan to eventually unfurl represents the ultimate threat: Instead of the threat arising from one religion, race, or economic ideology, it will be from another planet. General Douglas MacArthur suggested the notion of an eventual interplanetary war on several occasions[130]. As in the movie *Independence Day*[131] the myth is that we will be attacked by the "aliens," and all nations must rally together to wage global war against the "aliens." This is the jingoism and demagoguery of those who wish to control the masses through fear and hatred. It is a defunct, moribund, and corrupt operating paradigm, but it is still very much alive.

The UFO subculture has been totally infiltrated by counter-intelligence interests to put forward frightening scenarios and gross disinformation so that people will learn to hate extraterrestrials – even if only one of the species. It is the same paradigm that says if there is even one nation of concern in the Middle East, we must go to war. This scenario has been planned since the 1950s. I have seen the support documents and have witnesses who state that this is the covert long-term plan of Majestic[132].

It is very easy to stampede people using fear. Look at the aftermath of 9/11 and the freedoms we lost in its wake. The media, the political establishment and the masses totally took leave of their senses while we preemptively invaded Iraq. The consequences of the Iraq war are horrible – much worse than Viet Nam[133].

[129] Elders of Zion: http://ddickerson.igc.org/protocols.html
[130] Douglas MacArthur notion on interplanetary war: http://www.snopes.com/quotes/macarthur.asp
[131] "Independence Day:" http://en.wikipedia.org/wiki/Independence_Day_(film)

The cabal knows that the ultimate trump card to play is the extraterrestrial card, and it will be used with predictable negative spin. Disclosure that we are not alone in the universe will be played in a way that shows other star cultures as a threat. So, instead of collecting money from just a few nations, they can drain it from six billion people to create space weapons and target extraterrestrial vehicles.

The issue is not even about whether such a war could be won. It is about whether or not conflict can be expanded in order to amass greater centralized power and control internationally. Over 90% of all the cases and information in the UFO civilian subculture is false information created to prepare the masses to accept the costs of a future conflict in space. I have been able to track where their funding is coming from and see the agenda behind it. Sadly, we are creating our own reality by believing such dangerous lies.

Here is the choice we face. We can create a star wars scenario as above – or we can choose to finally emerge from adolescence into a mature human civilization that values peace. We are on the verge of a turning point going from the end of adolescence into the maturing of the human race. Stepping back a little, and looking at our evolution from a *cosmic* point of view, humanity is in its late adolescence with all the fear, rebelliousness, dysfunction, and violence associated with that stage of development. Now, it is time to grow up; it is time for childhood's end…

I am optimistic that we will make it through this tumultuous period and evolve into a world civilization that is peaceful and worthy of being an interplanetary civilization. The CE-5 Initiative is a prototypical program to create the foundation for such a time. Major world governments are now supporting such a view and wish to adopt this as policy, which I see as a very positive step forward.

The permanent transnational group of 200 to 300 policy makers with enormous power within the industrial and super-secret

---

[132] Greer, *Disclosure* (2001), Carol Rosin testimony, p. 256; Carl Czysz testimony, pp. 517-518.
[133] Iraq war consequences: http://www.worldscibooks.com/general/5381.html

military intelligence world does not want this positive paradigm to emerge. They have the capability to interfere with anything that we try to do, including the use of space and airborne weapons systems to target any ET craft that approaches for a CE-5. That kind of suppressive activity began as early as 1993.

Are the ETs Hostile?
Dr. Steven Greer
In 1993 when I went to Wright-Patterson AFB to meet with Colonel Canola and some others, someone asked if these extraterrestrial visitors are hostile. I replied, "If they were, you and I would not be having this conversation. They have been targeted, tracked and shot down by humans since at least the 1940s. *If* they were hostile, they would have cleaned our clock by now! It would have been point, set, match, and over before I was born in 1955."

If a civilization that has the capacity to transfer huge spacecraft and people through interstellar distances at multiples of the speed of light wanted to destroy us, it would have been over a long time ago. That is obviously not their intention. The fact of the matter is that the Extraterrestrials are not hostile. However, they are gravely concerned about our behavior and our hostility, but they will not interfere in our affairs unless a worst case scenario develops...

Stand in the shoes of these extraterrestrial civilizations and imagine this: A civilization goes from horse and buggies to landing on the Moon and from muskets, rifles and machine guns to hydrogen bombs in one person's life span. My grandmother was born in the Reconstruction era in the late 1800s in the South. Her son, my uncle, helped put the first man on the Moon with the lunar module. We have combined enormous technological developments with incredibly horrifying destructive weapons and an unchecked, chaotic international situation. You would have to be insane NOT to have concern about where such a civilization as ours was going, because our technological capabilities have far outstripped our social and spiritual maturity.

People with spears or muskets are one thing, but it is truly dangerous when they can detonate hydrogen bombs, and are aggressively weaponizing space. Obviously that type of behavior generates concern. However, the fact that the Extraterrestrials are concerned about our technology outstripping our maturity does not mean that they are hostile toward us. They are rightfully concerned and disturbed at the path we have taken, as would be any thinking, rational, sane person.

When I asked Disclosure Project witnesses about the ET vehicles seen over Minot, North Dakota, and other places where there were more than a dozen intercontinental ballistic missiles rendered inoperable, they told me they thought ETs were warning us not to go to nuclear war. And this same type of event was happened in Russian nuclear silos.

Any yet in all of these warnings, they did not actually destroy anything. They are peaceful and act accordingly.

Arnie Arneson
In the case of the Russians, the ETs actually took launch control of the missiles themselves. In our case they just shut them down and confused the military.

Dr. Steven Greer
I remember that. The ETs took the reins from the Russian's hands to demonstrate they could control launch/no launch of the missiles.

The ETs' position is clear if one analyzes the nuclear situation. Colonel Ross Dedrickson and others have said that every nuclear facility, weapons storage area and processing plant has had ET craft flyovers. Each one has been visited and tracked, including Los Alamos . . [134] The nuclear issue has been of great concern to the extraterrestrials because it could get out of control very easily through a miscommunication or misperception. It is a hair-trigger sensitive situation.

They are concerned about our hostility, but they're not hostile towards life on Earth. The evidence suggests these extraterrestrial

---

[134] Greer, *Disclosure* (2001), Colonel Ross Dedrickson testimony, pp. 191-193.

civilizations have been observing development of life on Earth for millennia. While they do not have any interest in destroying Earth and engaging in war, they likely do have a very great interest in monitoring a dysfunctional world civilization so that these kinds of weapons are not unleashed in the rest of the universe.

I have been told there are civilizations at our level of technological development that do not even have a *concept* of war. They do not fight. They do not have that murderous monkey[135] paradigm. This is a very key point. The CE-5 Initiative represents a far better way than the 'us vs. them' paradigm existing on earth.

More Complex Levels

'Grays' and 'Reptilians:' are Not Terms That Should Be Used
Dan Krevitsky
Of the 50 or so civilizations that are visiting us, is it mostly the Pleiadians and the Grays that are interacting with CSETI or are the others interacting as well?

Dr. Steven Greer
We do not refer to the Extraterrestrials as 'Grays,' 'Pleiadians' or whatever. Those are terms used in the UFO subculture and mythology and are neither accurate nor respectful. We honor all types of beings we have met and respect the consciousness common to all of them.

Interplanetary Racism
We do not discriminate against any extraterrestrial civilization. We invite all civilizations capable of coming here to interact with us on the plane of this cosmic level of awareness. The aim of such interaction is communication, peaceful exchange and diplomacy.

Within the so-called New Age and UFO subcultures there are the "good aliens" and the "bad aliens." This is actually interplanetary racism. We must go beyond that mind set.

---

[135] Chimps murdering chimps: http://www.gather.com/viewArticle.jsp?articleId=281474976794596

On the other hand, humans have created artificial life forms made to look 'alien' that are entirely manmade. Some look like 'greys' or 'reptilians.' Such PLFs – programmed life forms – have been around for decades and are used in paramilitary abduction programs to deceive the public – and policy makers.

Recently, a few people have surfaced from Dulce and other facilities with accounts of such creatures working along-side humans in classified programs. These operations are highly compartmented and such witnesses do not realize that they saw the manmade 'aliens' and witnessed such stagecraft. Now the UFO subculture is all abuzz regarding the evil aliens working with the evil secret government in some grand conspiracy. It is nonsense and very clever disinformation – but highly effective.

Numerous top-secret witnesses have independently confirmed to me the manmade nature of these PLF 'aliens' – and described the 'stagecraft' of how they are used in abductions, mutilations and other frightening programs to create the specter of evil aliens. Some of these witnesses specifically worked on 'growing' the PLFs and saw how they were made – by man! And so, most of what people hear and see on this subject is manmade disinformation and not ET at all!

In July of 2008, we visited Stan Romanek and discovered that he was being targeted by such PLFs – but everyone around him was convinced they were real ETs! We heard the audiotape recording of an intelligence officer – using a computer generated British woman's voice Stan calls 'Audrey' – specifically warning him that the creature was "one of the fake ones!" and that a chemical had been sprayed at him to make him lose consciousness! This intelligence officer was trying to warn him and the UFO researchers of the PLFs and fake abductions – but they had no idea what Audrey was trying to say: They had no ideas PLFs existed and are utterly manmade stagecraft! (I personally believe Audrey is someone who may have known Stan's father – who was in the Air Force – and they are concerned that a cell is targeting Stan...)

In short: Please do not be deceived. The intelligence community and Majestic are fully capable of creating false flag operations designed to engender hate and fear. It is what they do! And how they maintain power...

But knowledge is true power. If you know that advanced ARVs and PLFs are used in such stagecraft, then you can discern the real ET presence from the dominant "false alien" scenario. It is time to wake up!

Dr. Bill Clendenin
I suppose political leaders do not see any political relevancy to this?

Dr. Steven Greer
Actually these leaders do see the relevancy, but they are terrified of how big an issue it is. That is my point. It is not that they think it unreal, trivial or irrelevant. It is as Laurance Rockefeller said to me; the issue is so global, the implications so vast and so profound that no aspect of life on Earth will be unchanged by its revelation and disclosure[136]. Politicians do not feel up to the task of taking it on. That is exactly what happened with Bill Clinton after I briefed his team and his CIA director. He was terrified of the implications and sent one of his closest friends to my home to tell me they were convinced that if he were to do what I recommended by issuing an Executive Order to examine, get control of, and disclose this information, he would end up like Jack Kennedy. I laughed, thinking he was joking, but he was serious. It has been kept secret not because it is silly, but because it is so enormously profound. The interests that would be affected are so influential – oil, energy, orthodox religious leadership, geopolitical power, world banking, etc. – and all of this would be substantially impacted.

Religion and Science
Terry Underwood
Is there a process that humanity has to go through to accept its past? Our past is not what we have been taught. Humanity's past is much different than the history books I read as I was growing up. In order to be able to handle receiving ET information, we have to

---
[136] Greer, *Hidden Truth* (2006), p. 102.

be in a different state of mind than most of us learned.

Dr. Steven Greer

Past or present does not matter. Development of higher states of consciousness is required no matter what you are dealing with. Certainly, most of what is taught in history, organized religion, science, archeology and theology is wrong. One does not endear oneself by saying this perhaps, but most of what is taught is just not correct. It is <u>useful</u> to someone, however, because it keeps the masses ignorant and controlled.

Dan Goldin[137], the head of NASA, made a comment to one of the five directors of NASA whom Dr. Ted Loder and I got to know. While flying in his NASA jet, Goldin looked down on the earth's population and said, "The masses are asses – they don't need to know this information…" That is the prevailing attitude, but my point is you do not have to be an ass, even if they regard you as one! He came out of SAIC (Science Applications International Corporation), one of the crown jewels in the classified contracting world. He was recruited from there to be Director of NASA and knew about black projects and the ET presence, of course.

Dr. Bill Clendenin

As a psychiatrist, I work in mental health with people who need to change but really do not want to. Most humans are not really evolved spiritually from what I see. I have observed the vast majority of people do not change unless they are dragged kicking and screaming into some other reality. People change when they have tremendous adversity or pain, and maybe that is what the universe is setting up now. Maybe we are being put in a situation where we have no choice but to open up to moving into an advanced reality, a better future.

I meditate, and one of the things that came to me one day seemed to be quite profound. It had to do with the biblical concept of ascension in which Jesus supposedly ascended into Heaven in physical form. What came was that ascension is not physical, it is

---

[137] Dan Goldin: http://www.space.com/news/goldin_final_011116.html

an ascension of consciousness of awareness. That seems to apply in the way you have talked about consciousness.

Dr. Steven Greer

I woke up one morning and checked my messages on my cell phone. There was a message from a wonderful, pure hearted and very interesting man. He and I had a meeting with a very deeply involved intelligence operative some years ago. The operative had resurfaced in Europe. He called because he had learned about a catastrophe soon to happen on Earth that would devastate the planet and the human race. He was begging me to ramp up Disclosure and contact. He felt it was the only thing that could give a glimmer of hope and understanding to what was about to befall our civilization. I share this because since my childhood I have been shown various disaster events.

The Native peoples call it, 'The Time of the Great Purification and Cleansing.' It will move humanity into another level of consciousness and spirituality. I say this not to disturb or frighten anyone. That is not at all what this is about. It is about positive change and spiritual growth. I took this man's request very seriously. The same request has also been coming to us periodically from members of the intelligence community. At CSETI we enter into Cosmic Mind and seek to see what, where and when such events might occur, and what courses of action we might take. We usually get pieces of information rather than clear scenes, but these can be combined to give an idea of what might be coming.

As they say in the Vedas[138], there are the three gunas, – forces in nature. One is 'satva,' the force of creation and positive motion. Second is 'rajas,' the maintenance or neutral force. Third is 'tamas,' the destructive force that tears down. All matter is affected by these three forces. An oak seed sprouts and grows by satva, maintains itself by rajas, and eventually dies by a tamasic process. But the seed sprouted originally in the dirt, made by the breakdown of material – tamas.

---

[138] Three Gunas: http://www.sanatansociety.org/ayurveda_home_remedies/ayurveda_three_gunas.htm

Great changes are coming, but only so humanity can become firmly established on the path of universal peace, enlightenment and a very advanced civilization...

Astronaut Neil Armstrong Saw ET Craft on Moon[139]

Norm Fletcher
Did Neil Armstrong say we were warned off the Moon?

Dr. Steven Greer
I've been told Neil Armstrong did say that. Quite a few ET spaceships were fully materialized on the crater near where the lunar module landed. At a CSETI training at Shasta we met a man whose wife worked as an alumna with Neil Armstrong, raising funds for Purdue University. He told us that Neil Armstrong told her that the crater was crowded with ET vehicles when they landed on the moon.

The Moon landing was actually a result of the Cold War, a result of our panic over Sputnik and the subsequent space race.
The requirement for acceptance into the group of interplanetary civilizations is the planet must be peaceful and unified in purpose. We must be able to go into space peacefully and unified, rather than as tribes trying to blow each other apart. On Earth we are not that advanced yet. We should have been 100 years ago, and we desperately need to get there. But until we choose peace, it simply is not an option to colonize Mars or any other planet in space.

The larger interplanetary society will not allow us to export our current violence and retrograde human behavior beyond Earth. Since that attitude was the consciousness behind the Apollo space race, the Extraterrestrials made it clear that we were not welcome to proceed until we got our act together on this planet. That is the real reason we did not go back to the Moon or finish the twenty scheduled Apollo missions. Cuts in funding were secondary, not primary.

It is not wise to allow a civilization whose technologies have

---

[139] Neil Armstrong speech at White House, 1994: http://ufowatcher.blogspot.com/2007/06/neil-armstrong-speech-at-white-house.html

surpassed their spiritual and social development to go rampaging through space. There is a universal order and a universal law that prohibits that. So far we have refused to accept the responsibilities of a mature civilization, the hallmark of which is a peaceful world.

The head of Army Intelligence disclosed to me they had detected extraterrestrial bases and activities under the surface of Mars that were not human. While there are old facilities and monuments there, there is also current activity that is very much extraterrestrial.

1970s Dream of a Possible Future

A lucid pre-cognitive dream that I had in the 1970s involved a future ET-landing event. I was at a place that looks a great deal like White Sands. There was a daytime CE-5 at which we were the lead contact team to vector in an extraterrestrial vehicle. In attendance were a major group of world leaders and wise elders with the *full support of the US military, including the air force*! The event was being recorded and broadcast "live." An egg-shaped craft descended and landed. Out came a very wise extraterrestrial elder whom represented a coalition of extraterrestrial peoples. I will never forget it. It was so lucid and clear that is was like looking at the room in which I am sitting. I am anticipating this event will happen.

Our work together over the past 18 years has created the possibility of this Contact event becoming reality.

The Struggle to Maintain the Vision

My biggest single struggle since 1990 has been not letting people hijack our efforts for their own agendas. Many people have childishly adopted racist archetypes, and as a result are just recapitulating the tribalism and racism of Earth. This is not what we need to do as we step from Earth into space. We need to leave that primitive thinking behind. That is a key principle of the CE-5 Initiative.

One of the hardest tasks I have had is seeing to it that the people who attend these expeditions as diplomats have the appropriate consciousness and purpose. We must be coming from a place of higher consciousness – of unprejudiced interplanetary diplomacy.

A place of higher consciousness means being peaceful rather than wanting to shoot a vehicle down to get the technology, or wanting to meet one type of extraterrestrial but not another, or wanting to make an alliance with one group only, etc. Such tribal nonsense has been the bane of human civilization for thousands of years. That divisive thinking needs to be transformed into a new vision of universal Oneness.

Briefings; Questions/Answers
Dr. Steven Greer
The world advances when people know they can act.
Margaret Meade reminds us not to underestimate what a few dedicated people can do to change the world and that every important change started with only a few such souls. From the genesis of CSETI in 1990 through these early days, the biggest challenge for me and for everyone trying to help was to be able to view themselves in the capacity of someone who could *do* things – be it CE-5s, Disclosure, or meeting with well-placed people in government and the military.

Once you say you *can do* something and put one foot in front of the other, the doors will open every step of the way. That does not mean it will all be easy! The effort has been equivalent to climbing Mt. Everest from 20,000 leagues under the sea as the starting point. We are working for change as enormous powers work to stop us, and they represent the most powerful vested interests on Earth. But it is time – and no force on Earth can deter the inevitable transformation of life to its next level of evolution. We are moving with the flow of the Universal Purpose…

Briefing Senator Claiborne Pell
Dr. Steven Greer
The Disclosure Project and the CSETI CE-5 Initiative are deeply integrated, though many people do not even know they are related. In the 1990s I was asked to do a briefing for the Board of Directors of the Institute of Noetic Sciences (IONS)[140], which was founded

by Astronaut Ed Mitchell. After the briefing, I met one of the people who had been involved with this group for years, Senator Claiborne Pell of Rhode Island, former Chairman of the Senate Foreign Relations Committee[141]. He flew out from Washington just for this dinner meeting held at a wonderful home on a hilltop next to George Lucas' Skywalker Ranch in California[142].

Senator Pell had been following our work. He was good friends with Laurance Rockefeller, whose people had been at our gatherings at Crestone, had seen the encounters and had reported these back to Laurance. He said he had wanted to know about the ET subject since he entered Congress in the 1950s, but was never able to get an answer to any of his inquiries through normal channels. I told him he was in good company because even the President and the CIA Director were not privy to that information. I also informed Senator Pell that I had briefed the Head of Intelligence for the Joint Chiefs and given him the project code numbers and names for these illicit projects.

Senator Pell was very frustrated by this situation and asked me to come to Washington to brief his staff on the subject. We began talking about the philosophical and existential aspects of this, and I told him about the CE-5 Initiative – about making contact with these extraterrestrial civilizations. His eyes got very wide. Pointing to the stars above our heads, I told him it was a shame that he was the Chairman of the Senate Foreign Relations Committee of the most powerful government in the world and yet was being denied the most significant foreign relations issue in history! He looked at me through his horn-rimmed glasses, blinked, and exclaimed, "Well, Dr. Greer, I'm afraid that you might be right!" It was a very emotional moment. Here was a man who epitomized noblesse oblige, who had been in the government for many decades and who would have been the perfect diplomat to interact with the ETs – but he was denied any information about it until our meeting...

Experience with Dorothy Ives

Burl Ives, the famous actor and singer, got his Oscar for "The

---

[140] IONS: http://en.wikipedia.org/wiki/Institute_of_Noetic_Sciences
[141] Claiborne Pell: http://en.wikipedia.org/wiki/Claiborne_Pell
[142] Home of Paul and Diane Temple.

Big Country," with Gregory Peck, Charlton Heston and Jean Simmons[143]. His wife, Dorothy Ives, attended a talk I gave at a conference in Colorado. After the conference, we went to the McGuire Ranch in Wyoming to engage the CE-5 protocols for contact. Within moments, a craft approached and hovered at the top of a cloud formation, and began signaling to us. It was twilight, not yet dark, and you could see the ship very clearly. She realized the contact protocols worked, and decided she would become an Ambassador to the Universe.

She and Burl lived in Anacortes, Washington, in a beautiful home on the water. Some time after she got home, Dorothy and her teenage grandchild sat and practiced the protocols. She went into deep consciousness and invited the ETs to visit. Suddenly, a beautiful, circular object came in, and played peek-a-boo in and out of a nearby cloud. The child said, "Grandmamma, there are space people here."

Subsequent to that, in January of 1994, she said that the morning of the Northridge earthquake in southern California she got up about 4:30 in the morning and went downstairs. She saw a disc-shaped, circular, golden ET craft literally hovering right over their courtyard, about 30 feet above the house. A bluish light was shining on her from the craft as she stood in the foyer, and ET communications were streaming from this craft communicating directly to her mentally, saying: "Do not be worried. Do not be afraid. We are always with you. You will be protected."

It was a very close encounter. She felt an urge to call her best friend in LA who, at that moment, was in the Northridge Earthquake[144]. The *identical spacecraft* was outside her friend's house with the light streaming through the window and telling her friend not to be afraid and that she would be protected. Dorothy wondered if it was one craft or two, and I explained it was one craft bi-locating. ET craft can bi-locate, just as human masters in the Himalayas have been known to bi-locate their bodies and appear physically to multiple people at the same time[145].

[143] Burl Ives: http://en.wikipedia.org/wiki/Burl_Ives
[144] Northridge Earthquake: http://en.wikipedia.org/wiki/Northridge_earthquake
[145] http://www.angelfire.com/realm/bodhisattva/seshadri.html

The extraterrestrials were demonstrating bi-location and were also saying that in the event of a world emergency, they would be with Dorothy and her friend to protect them. She told me it was the most comforting and peaceful experience of her life. Nothing like that had ever happened to her until she began practicing the CSETI protocols, and suddenly it was like a veil lifted for her. I think it's important to realize that anyone can do this work because within each of us the totality of the universe is folded. All of us are universal resonators, and all of us are universal beings. As soon as you realize this and *accept* the role of an ambassador for universal peace, doors open in astonishing ways.

ET Crafts Targeted by Neutrino Light Detector Invention
Dr. Steven Greer

A former military officer I know was on the board of directors of a company whose founder and inventor had developed a 'neutrino light detector', detector,' a device that detected subtle, sub-electromagnetic emissions associated with extraterrestrial vehicles when they were in a dematerialized form. This detector was stolen by the NRO, National Reconnaissance Office, for use in their detection satellites so they could target ET vehicles prior to their full materialization. I know this for a fact, as I have met the inventor, who is a very accomplished scientist.

Of course, CSETI is doing its work on a relatively low tech level. One thing I need to emphasize is that this entire project from its inception to the present has been an unfunded, volunteer, un-staffed, citizens' diplomacy effort. We have gone all over the world doing this work without an office, without a staff, without equipment, and without a budget. And yet, we have not been limited at all in what we can achieve in actual contact. This is a very important point. We do not have access to the secret arsenal of the vast military industrial consortium dealing with the ET presence and free energy subject. They have been developing electromagnetic systems, anti-gravity and free energy systems since the 1940s. Nor do we have the hundreds of billions of dollar of funding they have illegally obtained over the last few decades. But what we do have is what the extraterrestrial civilizations are looking for – an unprejudiced mind and heart, clear intent and a peaceful purpose. That is all you need, and if you have it, you can do the CE-5 work and make contact wherever you are.

Terry Underwood
Do ETs have the ability to recognize 'poor intentions' as humans speak or do extraterrestrial capabilities go beyond speech?

Dr. Steven Greer
When there is an extraterrestrial event happening or about to happen, and if there are people on site with conflict-oriented or fear-based intentions, the event will not take place until those people leave. ET technologies that interface with consciousness are quite good at detecting such intentions.

The success of attempted Contact is primarily related to those present having the right intent. For example, mere curiosity is not enough because the ETs are not here to provide entertainment! We must understand there is a higher purpose to contact. That purpose is to create the foundation for future, peaceful relations between humans and other civilizations. If that understanding is present and sincere, amazing interactions will often occur.

The extraterrestrial people we have had contact with have been uniformly peaceful, respectful and gentle. Go without and beyond fear and prejudice and you will be amazed at what can happen!

Q&A About ET Knowledge of Earth Civilizations
David Alfassi
Do the Extraterrestrials know about the history of past civilizations on Earth? Would they be a good source to get that information?

Dr. Steven Greer
They have the entire record of Earth all the way back to when life first emerged here. The project dealing with Earth is an ancient one. Remember some of these civilizations have been extant and involved with the Earth in an active role for thousands, perhaps even millions of years. There is no doubt about that, so they have massive amounts of information.

David Alfassi

Did the ETs introduce mutations in the development of the human organism or is development sporadic or by chance like Darwin says?

Dr. Steven Greer

Both have occurred. There is no question that evolution occurs, and there is also no question that Homo sapiens has a significant gap in evolutionary history. My understanding is that at certain key times there have been genetic augmentations made to our capabilities. So it is not an 'either-or' question. By the way, this does not preclude the existence of a Creator in the sense of the Divine Being.

However, the ultimate augmentation happens on a different level than mere genetic. Let us consider a scientific method that is non-reductionist, while still scientific[146]. Based on evidence from ET craft that have been tragically shot down and retrieved and on the testimony of men who have actually seen them up close, ET craft are seamless. The ETs on board even had seamless clothing that was molded, formed and materialized around them.

Within the sub-electromagnetic resonance field of the etheric realm, you can create a blueprint or a template around which atoms will form. Once you have a template you can create or materialize what comes into linear space/time as a perfectly formed object. That is why the alloys and the other components in ET craft are so pure – beyond what can be made by current Earth technology. The ET objects are assembled at the sub-atomic level, at the finest level of form and energy. That is also why the light from these craft is so amazingly pure and unusual.

The same principle applies if we consider biological structures. The ultimate augmentation of higher biological life forms comes from the realm of *consciousness,* as the astral body manifests the physical body. In reality the flesh and bones body is a physical expression of a conscious template – the astral body of conscious

---

[146] The science of Causal Sound Frequencies used by Extraterrestrials has not been referenced in academic circles on Earth. It has been studied in black projects.

light. Within this astral, conscious body of light form exists the causal body of thought-sound frequencies.

This template in consciousness implies that at a fine resonance level, you can further refine and heal the physical body. That is why prayer, and inter-cessionary prayer and meditation/visualization have been shown to be efficacious in healing[147]. That is also why 'energy work' is effective. Our current society has very strong conceptual ties to the fixed, linear, time/space material realm. As a result, we do not understand that the material represents only the outer expression of the causative level of a body – or even ET spacecraft. The Causal Sound Frequency paradigm works very differently in the technology, manufacturing and manifestation of objects. While it is still a material science, it is a very advanced material science. The causative action occurs first within consciousness. Conscious mind and individuation flows from the Unbounded as a tone, a perfect tone, the song of each soul, and then manifests as the body of astral light, which further materializes as the physical body. The process is a seamlessly connected resonance frequency from the Unbounded to the physical body.

Thus, the state of awareness, thought and consciousness of a person- or a species- affects the outer bodily form – and the species can and does evolve through the effect of mind. Primacy of effect exists within consciousness...

I interviewed a man who was the captain of a Navy contract vessel in the early 1960s. They were retrieving intercontinental ballistic missiles (ICBMs) being test fired downrange in the south Atlantic. I have spoken extensively with this captain, but he will not come forward publicly because of the threats made against him. At the time of this event, the military was trying to improve the guidance systems and precision of ICBMs, but for some reason that they could not understand, the missiles kept missing their targets. They concluded this was caused by some form of external interference. Somebody while ET craft were observed in the area – *somebody* was trying to slow down the development of these fearsome weapons.

---

[147] Healing prayer: http://www.dosseydossey.com/larry/default.html

The 'somebody' turned out, of course, to be our ET friends who did not want us to go to DEFCON 1 and destroy this planet.

The captain was on duty one night when an ET craft appeared suddenly on radar. He contacted his command center, who also had it on their radar. Suddenly they saw a brilliant explosion in the sky, and then the object vanished from radar. The next morning they were vectored to the coordinates where the ET craft was last seen, and all that was left was a six-foot by six-foot pod floating on the ocean. The ET craft itself had sunk into the Atlantic. When the captain's crew retrieved this pod and opened it, they found four, thirty-nine inch tall Extraterrestrial Biological Entities.

The Extraterrestrial Biological Entities (EBEs) were rather handsome-looking men, according to the captain. He said they had the bronze skin color "of a Sicilian," no hair, no outer ears, fine lips and an almost vestigial nose. The eyes were almond-shaped and quite attractive similar to humans. They all had on one piece tightly fitted suits of some metallic like material. Unfortunately, they were all dead – none of the beings had survived the electromagnetic weapon that hit their vehicle.

The captain told me he could not see how these beings got into those one-piece suits that had no buttons, zippers etc. I explained that the uniforms materialized around the beings by using advanced technologies that assemble material objects from the resonant fields of energy around us. And that these technologies are linked to consciousness or thought-interfacing technologies.

He was ordered to put the bodies in the ship's freezer, and later a nuclear-powered submarine surfaced near them. Stern and frankly abusive men boarded his ship, and threatened that if anyone ever spoke of the event they would "disappear." They took the four bodies and the pod onto the submarine and left. The captain never heard anything else about it.

It was clear to the captain the ETs were interfering with these missiles and were trying to slow down the escalating international arms race. A similar story came from a Disclosure Project witness who was the missile launch officer at the ICBM launch control at Malmstrom AFB in Montana[148]. In that incident in 1967, multiple missiles in silos shut down in rapid succession and a glowing red object was seen hovering outside the front gate. An extensive investigation by the Air Force could not produce any viable explanation for the shutdowns. The witness got the sense that whoever those visitors are, they do not want us to be able to launch all of the intercontinental ballistic missiles. We had thousands of them, and if we had gone to DEFCON 1, the planet would have been a cinder floating through space.

Q&A On ET "Lack of Emotion"

Alice Sleight
What about ET capabilities for emoting? There seems to be a lot of disinformation that they do not have emotions.

Dr. Steven Greer
I want to make it clear that the ETs are emotional, very loving and very intelligent. However, different species have different ways of expressing emotion, as do various humans and human cultures. A huge variety exists amongst humans, and we are all Homo sapiens with the same genetic code. When we consider beings that have evolved in different planetary systems, there is going to be enormous variety. To cast Extraterrestrials as cold and unfeeling is untrue and is a "racist" characterization. Certainly there are different textures and expressions of emotion, in ET cultures. All of these beings have heart, mind, emotions, feelings and intelligence. They are more like us than not...

We need to experience the state of consciousness called the 'unity' or 'pure mind' state in order to *really* understand other species. Experiencing this universal aspect of consciousness is essential. The state of pure consciousness provides us the required compassion, stability, and anchoring in self needed for Contact. This state of spiritual oneness enables us to deal properly with the level of diversity in life throughout the cosmos since it gives us an understanding of the oneness of all beings.

---

[148] Greer, *Disclosure* (2001), pp. 167-171.

If you connect to this universal aspect of consciousness, every being you encounter, no matter how strange it may be emotionally or intellectually, will be seen as a friend rather than "alien." You will not be unnerved or frightened if you are established in this universal aspect of the unbounded Self – the eternal Self.

So the first stage of being an ambassador to all extraterrestrial people is having the understanding and experience of the cosmic mind within us. This universal, non-local, unbounded mind within represents the true anchor for our individual souls. It is the calm center in this whirling universe of change.

It also gives us the foundation for what we have in common with these ET beings. If you are functioning from this deep level of realization of the oneness of Mind, you experience that we are more alike than different. You are more aware of the likeness, and it is that awareness which is the foundation of unity. Hence the CSETI motto is: "One Universe, One People."

Understanding ET Technology

Dr. Steven Greer

It is a very big leap to go from a linear understanding of the extraterrestrial presence to a *complete* understanding of it. An aerospace engineer from McDonald-Douglas told me his research team knew there was a nexus between ET technologies, thought and consciousness. They knew the connection existed because they had seen it in so many reports. They had not figured out how it worked, but he told me that the CSETI protocols, based in consciousness, worked because ET communications use technologies interfacing with thought.

We are having real-time experiences with highly intelligent life forms whose technologies are already at the critical mass of artificial intelligence such that the entire spacecraft is conscious.

Many people think they do not have any remote viewing talent, but they actually do. Dreams are sometimes a remote view. The astral body in the dream state is pure and detached, so it can see and know things that are real and not limited to linear events. One can move off the space axis and the time axis as well. In other words, you can be sleeping, and also go to some place far away in both space and time. Many people have had such experiences because both space and time are transcended by the nature of consciousness.

A scientist once asked me how most people experience contact with extraterrestrial civilizations. I explained that the number one way that actual and real contact has happened between humans and extraterrestrial civilizations is the lucid dream state. Extraterrestrials use technologies that interface with consciousness seamlessly. In their faster-than-light travel through interstellar space, they pass through the astral domain – the etheric realm of the lucid dream state. The consciousness aspect of the ET phenomenon has completely baffled the scientists, and yet it is at the core of their science. The technology/consciousness synthesis is so advanced it is believed to be impossible by mainstream science. It is beyond magic to most people. And yet it will also be the future of science on Earth...

A Key Requirement for Contact
Dr. Steven Greer

When we do CE-5 work, the extraterrestrials actively look for people who are developed enough in consciousness to be able to function in a unified, coherent fashion. They avoid contentious attitudes and behaviors, and will even end an emerging contact when group coherence is lost. They have watched us fight for thousands of years and have no interest in such behavior. They are quite interested in human beings who work together in Universal consciousness. That is a key requirement for contact.

Norm Fletcher

You talked about electronic devices that our ET friends use as a means of communication non-locally. How much of ET thought is technological and how much is due to their refined state as conscious beings? How long have you known there was some technology for thought amplification? Are some of these beings more evolved or better equipped without using technology to communicate?

Dr. Steven Greer

I have known there is a technological interface with consciousness and thought since I was 18 when I had my first CE-5 on the mountain in North Carolina, in 1973. Extraterrestrial civilizations have certainly developed consciousness to the point of easily using technology/mind interfaces. The very advanced God-conscious ET civilization have also mastered the Siddhis and can accomplish many things with mind alone, as have some humans throughout history.

Coherent Thought vs. Random Thought

Just because one has a highly developed consciousness does not mean that it is always accurate. The only being that would be accurate all the time would be the Great Being, or the Universal Mind. Anything short of that is prone to variation of accuracy. For that reason, many of these star cultures have developed technological devices that detect coherently-directed thought associated with a purpose. They are not scanning for endless numbers of random thoughts from all beings in the universe. However, if you are looking directly at a craft or being and thinking towards it, they can detect it. The same holds true for transmitting. The crucial feature involved is that the thought has to be 'coherent' and emanating from a deep level of quiet awareness with strong intent.

That realization led me to develop 'coherent thought sequencing,' a deep state of consciousness centered in non-locality, having very strong, clear and directed thought with a clear intent and will. The directed aspect is very important. Those are the key elements to successful use of consciousness and thought.

Richard Haines of NASA and I studied[149] chance encounters in which a person happened to see an ET craft[150]. ET sensing devices would pick up that an intelligent human being was looking at them, and they would respond to that person. When the human thought, "move to the left," or "move to the right," or "come closer," or, "Ooh, I'm scared, move away," the object would interact with

---

[149] Haines, Dr. Richard. *CE-5: Close Encounters of the Fifth Kind.* (1999). http://www.ufoevidence.org/books/book95.htm

[150] Richard F. Haines. *CE-5: Close Encounters of the Fifth Kind* (Naperville, IL: Sourcebooks, 1999).

them accordingly. That has been documented hundreds of times.

Extraterrestrial vehicles can be materialized, dematerialized – or in-between these states – like hearing two stations at once on a radio as you change frequencies. The spin and resonance frequency of the craft are a little bit out of phase with our linear space/time. The vehicle looks very physical and materialized, yet it can go straight through solid matter, because solid matter is mostly empty space.

If you collapsed all the solid matter of your body, it would fit on the head of a pin. So there is nothing to keep one bit of empty space from going through another bit of empty space if it can shift a little bit out of resonance frequency. That is how objects that appear to be solid materialized objects can go straight through other solid materialized objects. They can shift their resonance frequency and spin.

In a paper I wrote in 1991, "A Comprehensive Assessment of the UFO/ET Subject," I described the consciousness-assisted technologies and the technology-assisted consciousness that is the central operating paradigm for interstellar civilizations[151]. The central science of these technologies is consciousness and mind in its interface with the cosmos with space, time, matter and electromagnetism. After I had written this paper, it made its way through the CIA and aerospace firms, like Lockheed Skunk Works, McDonald-Douglas etc. I got a call from an engineer, Dr. Robert Woods, who became one of our Disclosure witnesses. He had been asked personally by McDonald to look into ET technology, specifically into the anti-gravity and electromagnetic aspects.[152]

One of the cases he was particularly interested in happened in Baja California in the 1960s. Someone had an encounter with an ET craft that had landed, and an ET was wearing a dark box in front of its abdomen. Thoughts were coming directly from that box into the mind of this witness and he could think directly in to it, so the extraterrestrial knew everything that was being projected. Dr. Woods asked me how I knew about a nexus where

---

[151] Greer, *Extraterrestrial Contact* (1999), pp. 11-16.
[152] Greer, *Disclosure* (2001), Robert Woods testimony, pp. 433-440.

electromagnetism, magnetic field flux, consciousness, thought and anti-gravity all come together. I explained that I had direct experience with the ETs on that issue in 1973. The ETs have strong sensing capacities, but these capacities are mediated through extremely advanced technologies. We are dealing with civilizations thousands to millions of years more technologically and socially developed than we are. Accordingly, every manifestation of their technology would look like magic to the most advanced physicist at Cal Tech or MIT.

While much of this sounds fantastic to the average person, it is actually information that has been known in certain aerospace and classified circles since the 1940s. It is a shame that our children are not being educated with the science of consciousness, electromagnetism, magnetic field flux and the real cosmology. Without that knowledge we have two hands and one foot tied behind our back trying to hop into the future.

Question on Types and Purposes of ET Craft
David Alfassi
There seem to be so many different kinds of ET craft. Do they come and go from their origin or do they stay near earth? What do they do? Are they waiting for us to call them? How does it work?

Dr. Steven Greer
There is no one answer to that. Obviously, they have a very important mission with planet Earth. If people are conscious and aware of them they may interact, but often they are carrying out specific tasks. They may be monitoring Earth's tectonic plates or observing a weapons storage area outside Los Alamos, or trying to mitigate some other Earth problem. My understanding is that a very large number of extraterrestrial civilizations are represented, and they are all working together. There exists in deep space an interplanetary center from which they come and go by resonantly shifting beyond the speed of light and appearing in another point in space. One of the goals of this book is to describe and explain manifestations of these extraterrestrial technologies experienced in our CSETI trainings and expeditions.

As to why they would be here, there are a thousand answers. One reason is because we are deliberately inviting them to cultivate with us the higher purpose of interplanetary, universal peace. The primary reason we have had so many expressions of extraterrestrial intelligence is the state into which we deliberately enter and from which we function. We recognize that the source of conscious intelligent life in the universe is One Awake Being, an awake mind within us. That unity state of consciousness is at the heart of all spiritual traditions, Christian, Jewish, Buddhist, Hindu, Muslim, Shamanic, Native American, etc.

I think the ETs have a compelling interest in interacting with humans who understand the interconnectedness of all things, and they have shown us that. I think it is also why we have been protected, why we have had such amazing experiences with them, and why we will continue to have contact. From the inception of CSETI, they made it clear that they would give full support for what we are doing. We have not been disappointed. It is important to realize that they are not dolphins at Sea World trained to do tricks to entertain curiosity seekers and dilettantes. If there is a sincere desire to have this sort of contact for a higher purpose beyond one's own selfish curiosity, you will find there will be astonishing ways that they will appear.

They are here to understand us, to assist us, and to eventually build a bridge between humanity and other peaceful civilizations. The people of Earth are certainly not peaceful yet, but some day we will go into space in peace. That is Earth's long-term mission. What could be more exciting and beautiful than Earth reaching its fulfillment? While there are certainly other specific reasons craft may appear, this is the heart of what the extraterrestrials are interested in – the establishment of universal peace.

The Mosaic of Information from ETs
Dr. Steven Greer

One reason why everyone in a contact group needs to share his or her remote viewing experience is because we have found that the ETs often will give one packet of information or fact to one person, another packet or fact to another, another to a third, and so on.

They want to see if there is coherence and unity of purpose in the group, and to see if all group members will share with each other in an openhearted way. When that happens, the whole mosaic is made clear and ET contact is increased – or an important message is conveyed which otherwise is lost.

David Alfassi
You mentioned that in the Rendlesham Forest incident in England, the so-called ETs could have been visitors from the future. Can they actually go into the past and change the evolution of events?

Dr. Steven Greer
They do not do it directly because of the nature and complexity of the Akashic Record. The most they can do is show up when events reach a critical point and hope to cause a change indirectly. The process does not work the way you would expect from watching or reading science fiction on time travel.

My impression from talking with the military officers present at the Bentwaters landing was that the 'visitors' there were concerned about the fate of humanity and what might happen if we did not get control of the nuclear arms race. The incident was an expression of concern. They did not go in there to take the nuclear weapons out. Obviously, if you have that ability, you could just rewind events back to when the first error was made and just make sure it did not happen. Apparently that is not possible – or advisable.

David Alfassi
But if they came from the future, then they were obviously at the point of the future that was there now. So is the 'now' only relative to the particular perspective of who participates in it? In other words, does everybody have their own 'now,' and the 'nows' are unrelated to each other?

Dr. Steven Greer
No. The 'nows' are related. It is a complex fractal. It is a quantum hologram, and every part of it is within every other part and affects every other part. That is why it is very important to understand the old saying, "As above, so below. As below, so above."

There is a connection between what happens on Earth and what happens in other star systems far away. Most people listening to Carl Sagan speak about 'billions and billions' of light years got the impression distances are so great that interaction with other life forms just could not happen. That line of thinking is wrong. If you understand non-locality and the quantum hologram aspect of life, what happens on earth very much affects and impacts the entirety of the cosmos.

We are not some island floating in space, unconnected and unrelated. Non-local levels beyond the speed of light produce subtle effects that are very real and have an effect in vastly distant locations. So in reality, the whole cosmos weeps when terrible things befall the Earth and humanity. The more highly evolved a civilization is, the more aware it is of the deeper celestial and astral levels where Earth events are known and actually felt. Conscious mind and the more subtle emanations of consciousness represent a blossom unfolding. The totality and completeness of the universe is within that individual flower.

The process of individuation – where from the Unbounded, our individualities emerge, first from the level of the causal, tonal thought, and then our astral bodies of light manifest and then our physical bodies materialize – is like a blossom unfolding from within. So something happening to an individual can be felt by all. Events happening to a whole planet with billions of people are felt. This is the heart of universal compassion. This is the compassion of the Buddha manifested at the cosmic level. Truly wise people see the interconnectedness that exists rather than falling for the illusion of separation. Modern sciences are excellent at breaking structures and processes down in a linear fashion (reductionism) but the headlong pursuit of reductionism has caused us to lose the whole. We have overlooked the integrative function of consciousness or spirit. We have failed to understand the non-duality of reality.

An integrated, conscious reality affects all of relative existence at all strata from the finest celestial manifestation to other planets. If you look at a cosmic extrapolation of Rupert Sheldrake's morphogenic fields[153], you realize that his concept works at all levels. That might help one understand why there is such ET interest and concern about what is happening on Earth.

A British intelligence agent I met had been providing information on the ET presence to Prince Phillip and Prince Charles, as well as Lord Mountbatten before he was murdered. He said "When we started detonating thermonuclear weapons in the atmosphere of Earth, we kicked a cosmic hornet's nest!"

Colonel Ross Dedrickson[154] started in the air force and became a senior official of the Atomic Energy Commission, which preceded the Department of Energy. He was in charge of inspecting all our nuclear weapon storage facilities. He told me every single one of them was being monitored by extraterrestrial vehicles due to their deep concern over nuclear weapons. Such concern has been reported independently as well[155].

Arnie Arneson was involved in the Malmstrom Air Force Base nuclear silos incident in 1967 in which an ET craft took multiple ICBMs off line, rendering them un-launchable[156]. The same morning another ten were neutralized at a squadron 30 miles away[157]. Around that time the Soviets also lost launch control of their missiles at the control center. The extraterrestrial civilizations were warning us not to blow up this beautiful planet, and demonstrating that they could intervene. Destroying Earth would have effects on deep levels of consciousness and reality elsewhere because all life is connected. Earth is not as separated in space as many of us would like to think. It is a very deep issue to contemplate.

Question on Creating Events from Mind
Alice Sleight
You have made comments about how we can create reality. Please elaborate.

Dr. Steven Greer
A few people have suggested that CSETI events are created in our minds[158]. That is true, but not in the way they suggest. What they

---

[153] Morphogenetic fields are defined by Sheldrake as the subset of morphic fields which influence, and are influenced by living things.[http://en.wikipedia.org/wiki/Morphic_field - Morphogenetic_field]
[154] Greer, *Disclosure* (2001), Ross Dedrickson testimony, pp. 191-193.

do not understand is that the conscious mind is a singularity. There is only one conscious mind in all of the cosmos. Everything is consciousness phasing and resonating as any particular thing. As the Vedic tradition says: "All This is That."

In reality, all matter is consciousness resonating as a specific object. On one level you can see it as a 'discrete' object, and it is. On another level of consciousness – unity consciousness – it is actually consciousness manifesting as a 'discrete' body, or stars, plants, wood, minerals, etc. So from the point of view of a cosmically awake person who is aware of Cosmic Being, everything is emanating continuously from mind, and thus we create form and events from Mind.

Each person, then, is the Universal Being – and can manifest from within this state of Oneness. But this emerges from beyond the ego – now we are speaking of the Great Being standing within all of us as One...From that station in awareness we can manifest all.

Question on Bright Flashes
Alice Sleight
We have seen bright flashes in the sky at trainings. Would you please repeat your interpretation of what these might be?

Dr. Steven Greer
Often we see bright emissions of light – electromagnetic radiation – as a sphere or a point of light. These can be the actual craft appearing as they phase shift into our space. But another possibility occurs when a craft in the area begins to interface with the space/time continuum. The energy of our astral bodies is finer than the energy of an extraterrestrial craft when it is shifted beyond the speed of light. There are gradations of etheric and astral energy, an almost infinite number of gradations. It is similar to the endless number of frequencies in the electromagnetic spectrum of light. It would be like having a rheostat for those energies. If you turn it one way, the craft or being is fully materialized. Turn it the other way, and the craft or beings are beyond the speed of light, and

[155] http://www.cufon.org/contributors/DJ/Do%20Nuclear%20Facilities%20Attract%20UFOs.pdf
[156] Greer, *Disclosure* (2001), pp. 176-179.
[157] Greer, *Disclosure* (2001), p. 169.

you see nothing. You might also be at a point between frequencies where you sense both.

So the craft or being can be both 'here' and 'there.' We see the light emissions as flashes. Once it shifts in one direction, you might see the actual outline of the craft as a foggy astral shape, and you might even see its lights. If it shifts further, it will be a completely materialized craft. It can do that instantly or in fine gradations.

Often when not fully materialized, we see the complete outline of the craft because they are close enough to the frequency of our material space/time to emit lights. Sometimes their craft buildup energy that will emit a flash of light, and that is a very important thing to watch for. At Shasta we saw a red orb hanging in a tree, and there was actually a craft there. We have had visible lights float right in through windows and come into rooms and lecture halls when we were speaking.

Describing the Indescribable

Alice Sleight

In your book, *Hidden Truth – Forbidden Knowledge*, you did a great job of articulating some of the esoteric features of contact with extraterrestrial technologies and civilizations. I found I needed to read it many times over, but each time, I understood more of the ideas.

Charlie Balogh

I think that when you try to describe something that is so experiential in consciousness there are no words adequate to describe it fully. So you do your best to put words around a description to create the concept and recreate the energy. That is probably the most difficult aspect of all this.

Dr. Steven Greer

It is enormously difficult when the territory is not well known. One of the big problems with much of learning is that people confuse the roadmap with the place. A map of Palm Springs is not Palm

---

[158] As an example: http://www.csicop.org/si/9709/sheaffer.html

Springs. People forget that about language. They get lost in the intellect and in the symbols and forget to focus on the reality of what the symbols are trying to convey.

Language can be very powerful, but you have to go beyond the language into the experience. Even the best teacher is only able to provide an opening to the doorway that you must go through so you can experience the reality yourself. Otherwise, it remains only an intellectualization.

The CSETI philosophy is to give people the tools, articulate the techniques, enhance understanding and encourage individual exploration. That is why CSETI is so decentralized and lacking a bureaucracy. You just go out, form your own Contact group, and explore. If you have some great experiences, let me know. I would love to hear about them. But you must do it yourself – and explore!

The next 500,000-year cycle is the cycle of the fulfillment of the potential of humanity. One of the cornerstones of that fulfillment is for individuals to take full responsibility for their spiritual development, experience and knowledge. They must not allow themselves to be passive and infantilized by a priesthood, leaders or authority figures. A certain amount of true (and not feigned) humility needs to accompany a spiritual teacher. Let us share knowledge and wisdom, open the door and point the way with some techniques, then let people find their *own* path.

Contact Event with a World Government

CE-5 with a G7 Country

Dr. Steven Greer
We have been in communication with a major government at the highest levels, including the President, the Minister of Defense, and the President's scientific adviser. They are very committed to supporting an ET contact event and have written us a commitment letter. Such an event could not have happened ten years ago. The fact that this would even be discussed in the corridors of official power in a G7 country is quite a breakthrough. The letter from

their Ministry of Defense asks CSETI to set up the conditions to precipitate a Close Encounter of the Fifth Kind.

The fact that they have invited CSETI to be the primary contact team is because they know we have had actual contact. This project would be done in cooperation with their air force, space agency, intelligence community, political leaders, and scientific leadership, including Nobel Prize-winning scientists. The purpose of this encounter would be for the leadership of that country to make peaceful, diplomatic contact with these extraterrestrial visitors. The contact would be followed swiftly by a global announcement and broadcast where possible.

This book is an important vehicle to communicate the true nature of ET contact experiences to the public – and other governments of the world. Sharing the rich tapestry of these experiences provides insight into how real ET contact happens.

Peaceful Context Vital

This contact is fraught with risk, potential setbacks, and danger, so I have made it clear to this government and its leaders that unless this event is conducted in a way that redounds to the benefit of the entire human race and within a framework of peaceful contact and peaceful interaction, it will probably not happen. This meeting must be carried out appropriately so we do not repeat the errors of the last 60 years...

One of the most important things I have discussed with this foreign government is the nature of the rogue element that has access to incredibly sophisticated weapons, is transnational, extremely powerful and well funded. The chief counsel for the head of the Senate Appropriations Committee, who held a top secret clearance told me personally in 1994, that there was upwards of $100 billion a year going into projects they had no way of tracing. He also told me that he gotten close to uncovering the clandestine operations dealing with UFOs, but that there was a lead wall of secrecy around it. He said, "Dr. Greer, you are dealing with the varsity team of all black projects. Good luck."

A man I know designed and built the early 'star wars' platforms we put into space in 1965. These platforms had high-powered longitudinal weapon systems. He worked for Hughes and virtually every aerospace contractor at the time. Those weapons were fully functional when many of us were children. He excitedly told me about how great it was when they could actually get a "kill" – which meant hitting an ET craft and bringing it down. This is a horrifying thought, but he was programmed to think it was a success because his weapon system worked. Imagine the kind of covert weapons this group has today, over 40 years later.

For this reason, ET contact proceeds cautiously – and we always emphasize to these visitors that they should appear in whatever manner is safe for any given time and place...

Transnational Group Increasingly Progressive

Over the years we have had people from the leadership of this covert transnational group quietly reach out to CSETI . When I briefed President Clinton's people in 1993, they indicated about a third of this leadership policy group supported what we were recommending. Now the fraction is more than half. There is still a ruthless, vicious minority in this group who would like to wreak havoc, but it is not a majority anymore. We have been encouraging those who have a more progressive view of the future to join us in Contact and Disclosure. Now it looks like they have reached a critical mass within the cabal, which is both exciting and yet also fraught with peril.

But the potential benefits to humanity resulting from an open, formal contact event of this nature involving a major G7 country far outweigh the risks involved. Such Contact will lead to official Disclosure, which in turn will open the doors to the new energy technologies.

A Paradox

Sarah McClendon's Conversation with Bill Clinton

Arnie Arneson

When we were at the Disclosure Project event in Washington, D.C., several of us were having dinner. Reporter Sarah McClendon had a conversation that is related to Dr. Greer. She has since passed on, but she had a conversation with President Clinton one day and asked him, "When are you, as President of the US, going to release some of this information to the public?" He bent over to her and said, "Sarah, there is an element of the government that I have no control over, and I can do nothing." She claims Clinton said those words to her.

Dr. Steven Greer

When she told me this story Sarah McClendon was incredulous. I assured her this was normal for people at the highest level of governments, many of whom have had the exact same thing happen to them. Many have received proof-positive evidence of these matters and even of current operations. I have found that the people who are not in the loop – mid-level apparatchiks who think they know everything – are the only real skeptics. The senior people are not so hard to talk to because they often know it is true. I have never had a problem getting an admiral or a four-star general to acknowledge this subject is real – even though they are being denied access to current operations. It's an interesting paradox, and not one you would expect.

Index

A

ABC News, 260-264
abduction squads, 46
abilities to sense, 255
abundance, 22
advanced technologies, 43, 206
AERO (Advanced Energy Research Organization), 21, 219
Akashic Record, 45, 187, 206, 434
Alien Reproduction Vehicles (ARVs), 26, 46, 118, 145, 149, 154, 230, 293, 326, 414
aliens
    as ultimate enemy, 408
alleged object
    aurora borealis, 212
    bird, 289
    cloud, 188, 207
    headlights, 258
    satellite, 199, 259
    star, 231, 287
Alton Barnes, England, 33, 46, 93, 293, 326
Altshuler, Dr. John, 53
Ambassadors to the Universe, 121
Ames Research Center, 41
Andrews, Colin, 25, 33, 37, 46, 98, 106, 143
anechoic chamber, 297
angels, 205
    escorts, 84
    guardian beings, 88
animal experiences, 125
    karmic repercussions, 178
animal interactions
    coyotes, 362
anomalous sounds, 18, 317
    deer-like, 318
    electronic tone, 336, 338, 349, 351
    metallic tone, 331
anti-gravity effect, 229

aquifer, 359, 366
arch of sparkles, 362
Arkansas, 120
armada (of ET ships), 370
Armstrong, Neil, 417
Army intelligence
    head of, 32, 328, 418
ascension, 416
Asheville, North Carolina, 128

astral energy, 43
    gradations of, 437
astral vision, 238
Atlimeyaya, Mexico, 74
Australia, 23, 277
avatar being, 79, 89, 135, 171, 175, 248, 254, 282, 305
    the Ancient One, 285
Avatars, 267, 275, 383
awareness
    multiple channels of, 330

B

Baca
    aquifer underneath, 359
    encounter in winter, 38
    vision quest, 61
ball lightning, 18
Barge Inn, Alton Barnes, 143, 201
BBC (British Broadcasting Corporation), 25, 37, 80
Bearden, Tom, 64, 111, 165
Belgium, 29
Bell, Art, 34, 58, 154, 260, 262, 311, 403
Bentwaters RAF, 434
best available evidence, 80
Biefeld-Brown Effect, 26
Big Dipper anomaly
    stars disappear, 360
bio-electromagnetic field, 378
biosphere degradation, 21

black projects
    code names and numbers, 83
    interdimensional electronics, 157
black shelving, 22
Blanca Peak, CO, 53, 87, 359
Blink-182 (musical group), 66
blueprint of the future, 254
Boeing, 403
Bonny Bridge, Scotland, 60
Boutros-Ghali, Boutros (Secretary General of UN), 55, 63
Boynton Canyon, AZ, 157
Bradshaw Ranch, AZ, 145, 154, 157
briefing
    for Members of Congress, 80
Brown, T. Townsend, 26
Brown's gas, 319
Burkes, Dr. Joe, 41
Bush, Pres. George W., 223

C
cabal, 63, 111, 139, 287, 374, 441
California, University of, 145
Callahan, John, 262
Cambridge University, 46
Canada, 23, 52, 172, 221, 259, 324
cancer, 56, 63, 81, 98, 99, 113, 178
Canola, Colonel, 410
Card, Andy, 222
Carson, Polly, 106
cartels, 408
cathedral site at Mt. Shasta, 284, 367
Causal Sound Frequency paradigm, 425
Caux, Switzerland, 195
CBS News
    "48 Hours", 263
CE-5, 18
    animal interactions, 308
    anomalous odor, 300
    astral fog effect, 307
    bioluminescence (from probe), 315
    bubble in compasses, 299
    confirmation of, 199
    consciousness training, 25
    contact protocols, 37

crop circle, 34
deliberate contact, 19
exhilaration, 344
historical collection of encounters, 41
interactive aspects, 24, 199, 376
major, 76, 81
mediated event, 114
military helicopter episode, 348
new paradigm of deliberate en counter, 24
temperature anomaly, 299, 345, 352, 354
working groups, 46
CE-5 Initiative, 222, 409, 412
    ambassadors, 349
    defined, 22
    expeditionary effort, 25
    expressions of contact, 19
    futuristic, 21
    no limits, 34
    three components, 25
CE-5: Close Encounters of the Fifth Kind, by Haines, Dr. Richard, 41
Celestial beings, 388
Celestial Fragrance, 371
celestial mesh of energy, 62
Center for the Study of Extraterrestrial Intelligence (CSETI)
    purpose, 19
Chandler, Arizona, 81
Charlottesville, VA, 76, 128, 219, 313
Cheyenne Mountain, CO, 86, 104
CIA (Central Intelligence Agency), 320, 431
CIA Director, 32, 56, 328, 414
civilizations
    cosmic consciousness, 183
classified projects, 19, 26
Clinton, Pres. Bill, 80, 82, 120, 222, 414, 442
close encounter of the fifth kind. See CE-5
Close Encounter types, 23
Close Encounters of the Third Kind (movie), 333

clouds
    open above us during meditation, 111
Coast to Coast AM, 34
cocoon of silence, 88
code numbers (project), 420
coherent group, importance of, 255
coherent light, 48, 106
coherent thought sequencing. See CTS
Colby, Bill, 56, 81, 111
Cold War, 407, 417
communication device
    box-like object, 131, 139, 243
    crystal pyramid, 181
compass
    bubbles in, 359, 366
    magnetic field shifted, 93
Concourse on High, 88, 134, 136
confirmation, example of, 102, 147, 167, 214, 227, 251, 252
    shift of compass, 93
Congressional Briefing, 82
Connect Live, National Press Club, 224
consciousness
    and technology, 428
    Brahman, 382
    development of, 415
    focus on, 288
    higher, 335
    one's level of, 43
    unity, 382, 427, 433
consciousness assisted technology, 372
contact
    certain state of consciousness needed, 125, 138
    on mountain in North Carolina, 65, 71
Corso, Col. Phillip, 21-22, 173
Cosmic Consciousness, 58, 81, 124
Cosmic Egg, 136, 380
Cosmic Mind, 416
cosmology
    sharing the, 64, 87
Costa Rica, 235
counter rotating fields, 300
counterintelligence agents, 60
Craddock, Pat, 117
Craddock, Tony, 96, 117, 145, 147
craft
    accordion-like movement, 116
    acorn-shaped, 164
    bilocating, 421
    blue-green teal, 61
    boomerang-shaped, 104
    bottom of bowl shape, 336
    brilliant white, 365
    campfire-like plasma, 184
    chevron-shaped, 87, 91, 251
    cigar-shaped, 51, 188, 265
    circular, 59, 290, 421
    dematerialized form, 422
    diamond white, 103
    diamond-like flashes, 369
    diamond-shaped, 185
    disc with a dome, 138, 189, 220
    disc-shaped, 35, 54, 86, 87, 116, 164, 421
    disguised as car taillights, 41
    disguised as cloud, 97
    disguised as firefly, 163
    dome-shaped, 115
    egg-carton like bottom, 186
    egg-shaped, 55, 418
    enveloped by cloud, 97
    enveloping Greer house, 220
    glass-bottomed, 139
    God-conscious, 345, 367
    golden, 288, 389
    golden golf-key-like, 246
    golden red, 361
    gray amorphous, 318
    Hershey Kiss-shaped, 68
    inverted convex mirror, 292
    jewel-like, 48, 131, 190, 354
    lenticular-shaped, 375
    Mars-like, 353
    orange plasma light, 42
    orange-colored, spinning, 66
    pseudo-fog, 225
    pure, white, round, 336
    pyramid-shaped, 285, 406

red, 365
shape shifts, 49
sombrero-shaped, 61, 62, 248
spherical, 370
tetrahedral, 172, 308
three formed CSETI triangle, 31
triangular, 29, 39, 51, 60, 76, 81, 86, 87, 105, 117, 155, 171, 181, 192, 264, 308, 360
Crestone, Colorado, 48, 76, 359
first experience, 38
VIP expedition, 52
vision quest, 61, 64
Cromwell, Jamie (actor), 66
crop circle, 25, 33, 34, 37, 98, 197, 199, 201, 206
the Kite, 143
White Hill, 201
crossing point of light, 43, 44, 205, 314
key point, 44
through the veil of, 64
crystalline matrix, 65
CSETI
approach to classified operations, 158
contact protocols, 19, 39, 55, 68
first training(1993), 40
mission, 286
need for training expeditions, 37
purpose, 25, 196
success of, 26, 45
tones, 18
training materials, 277
unfunded volunteer effort, 422
use of "alleged" with events, 97
CSETI tones, 116, 193, 217
CSETI triangle, 301
crop circle, 34
crop circle in VA, 128
orbs in sky, 99
with 3 teams, 42, 167
CTS (Coherent Thought Sequencing), 29, 67, 81, 92, 146, 183, 239, 430
Cunningham, Neil, 80

D

Dalai Lama, 250
Davenport, Peter, 182
Davis-Monthan Air Force Base, 188, 405
Dedrickson, Ross, 411, 436
Deep Space Coordinating Center, 379
Defense Intelligence Agency (DIA), 85
DeLonge, Tom, 66
dematerialization
example of, 142
manifestations of, 43
Denver, Colorado, 119
Department of Defense (DOD), 82
Department of Energy, 436
Desert Hot Springs, CA, 66
Devas, earth, 132, 181
diplomatic contact, 25
Disclosure Project, 21, 78, 85, 120, 121, 209, 213, 218, 221
Press Conference, 224
Witness Testimony DVD, 83
witnesses, 157, 260
<u>Disclosure: Military and Government Witnesses reveal the Greatest Secrets in Modern History</u>, 17, 259
disclosureproject.org, 17
disinformation, 295
designed to sow fear, 35, 38
in the Middle East, 408
distinguish
ETV and ARV, 27
Divine Being, 380, 385, 424
divine consciousness, 79, 112
dolphins, 141
Atlantic bottlenose, 124
spinner, 124
dome of protection, 226
Dongo, Tom, 157
Dr. Death, 80, 83
dream
lucid, 80, 111, 120
elaboration, 234
precognitive, 39, 249
precognitive (possible future),

418
dysfunctional (society), 328

E

Earth as God-consciousness place in future, 244
Earth network reconnaissance system, 44
economic development
    hijacked, 21
Edwards AFB (Muroc), 20, 118
Eisenhower, Pres. Dwight, 20, 21
electrical storms, 228
electromagnetic (EM) field weapon, 269
electromagnetic effect
    Hawaii expedition, 126
    on compass, 36, 300
    with ET craft, 259
    with lights in manor house, 108
electromagnetic flux, 400
electromagnetic weapons systems, 422
    attempts against us, 82
    targeted on ETVs, 44, 326
electronic warfare systems, 22, 165, 171, 177
electrostatic charges, 36, 293
ELF (extremely low frequency) effect, 348
Ellison, Larry, 224
Empyrean Realm, 384, 397
engine
    internal combustion, 21
Enigma (vocal group), 62
environmental collapse, 21
ET
    angelic/celestial presence, 85, 302, 307, 309, 344, 351
    emotions, 427
    hearings on the subject, 80
    like to be called ETs, 216
    subject hijacked, 20
    topic—missing piece of the puzzle, 84
    underground base, 69
ET consciousness and technology, 378
ET technology
    anti-gravity, 431
    communication box, 139
    contained light, 259
    crystal pyramid, 181
    device interfacing with thought, 22
    energy emissions, 156
    monitoring nuclear activity, 411
    repairing plate tectonics, 147
    sensing coherent thought, 253
    thought box, 431
    took launch control of missiles, 411
etheric energy, 43
    gradations of, 437
ETs identified
    The Friend, 301
    The Loved One of Mt. Shasta, 303, 310
Eupan, Belgium, 29
Everglades, Florida, 57
evolution
    arrested, 21
experiencing events, 75
expose of ABC incident, 262
expressions of ET intelligence, 18, 103, 183, 302, 311, 433
    echo manifestations, 152
extermination, slated for, 63
extraterrestrial
    appearing in the flesh, 108
    appears to Greer & Adamiak, 100, 240
    assist humans, 433
    awareness of reactions, 36, 46
    base and spaceport, 54
    beings
        assigned to each person, 135, 257
        at the site, 31, 237
        radiating love & compassion, 93
    bilocation, 422
    communication through dreams, 50

contact, 23, 294
dematerialize at Pentagon, 84
desire for peaceful contact, 32
elders, 88
expressing emotion to us, 49
facility inside Blanca Peak, 89
guards, 88
hand merges with Greer's hand, 162
interaction with Mexican children, 74
interference with weapons systems, 425, 427, 436
met with Corso, 22
monitoring Earth, 432
playing peek-a-boo, 421
reconnaissance, 33
seamless clothing, 424
technological capabilities, 53
touch, 71, 91, 123, 128, 151, 153, 180, 301, 308
vehicle, 88, 104
Extraterrestrial Biological Entities (EBEs), 426
recovered by Navy, 426
Extraterrestrial Contact: the Evidence and Implications, 17, 23, 82
extraterrestrial intelligence
beings & ship in God-consciousness, 190
golden doorways, 132
interactive chirping with walkie-talkies, 193
manifest on CSETI expeditions, 17
touch an example, 71
extraterrestrial vehicle (ETV)
fully materialized, 21
extraterrestrial vehicles (ETVs), 18, 23, 230
assembled at sub-atomic level, 424
different states, 54, 437
four hovering, 31
hidden in plain sight, 189
materials, 48
seamless, 424
sense coherent thought, 253
targeted, 44, 426
thousands of sightings, 27
twin craft at Shasta (2005), 281
vs. ARVs, 26
Extraterrestrials and the New Cosmology (paper), 62
Eye of God, 391
Eye of Horus, 372, 392
Eye of Orion, 372

F

FAA (Federal Aviation Agency), 54, 262
fast walkers, 104
FBI (Federal Bureau of Investigation), 22
fear
stops an event, 46
Fibonacci sequence, 313, 314
field distortion, 173, 179, 314
Fire in the Sky movie, 38
Flagstaff, AZ, 157
flares dropped by military, 107
flashes (of light), 334, 337, 352, 437
floating onboard a craft, 71
flotilla (of ET ships), 368, 369, 401
fog-like anomaly, 187, 370
Fort Huachuca, AZ, 188
fossil fuels, 21
fractal (complex), 434
frequency
spin and resonance, 54
fugue state, 80, 203

G

G7 country CE-5 event, 324, 375, 439
letter from M.O.D., 439
Galbraith, Bootsie, 53
Gandhi confidants, 58
Garza, Santiago Yturria, 54
Gates, Bill, 224
gateway
for ET activity, 44
genetic augmentations, 424
Geology Tour Road, 373

geo-political instability, 21
George, Ambassador Jim, 250, 324
giant searchlight attracted ETVs, 24
Glastonbury Crop Circle Symposium, 206
global warming, 21
God-conscious, 379
God-consciousness, 89, 136, 172, 190, 244, 247, 302, 338, 377
   craft, 302
   seeing the celestial, 61
Godhead, meeting with the, 244
Goldin, Dan, 415
Gore, VP Al, 82
Grays
   not term used by CSETI, 412
Great Awakening, 384
Great Being, 23, 168, 200, 430
Great Sand Dunes, Colorado, 38, 52, 53, 229, 361
Green, Michael, 206
group coherence, 33, 429
Gulf Breeze, Florida, 31, 49
gunas, 416

H

Haines, Dr. Richard, 41, 430
hair standing up, 36, 71
Hairgrove, Bob, 57, 73, 147
Halliburton, 320
Hare, Donna, 130
Heathrow Airport, 99
helicopter, black, 170, 176
Hellyer, Paul, 221, 324
Henri-Chapelle, Belgium, 30
<u>Hidden Truth – Forbidden Knowledge</u>, 17, 23, 32, 82, 121, 235, 438
Hidden Valley, CA, 113, 186, 245, 332, 354, 382
hide and seek with the ETs, 197
History Channel, 262
hoax on American public, 265
Holloman Range, NM, 22
hologram (quantum), 434
Hoover, J. Edgar, 22
horse communication, 123

Hughes (corporation), 327
Hughes, General Patrick, 85
human potential
   advanced technologies thwarted, 21
Humpback Mountain, 370
hundredth monkey phenomenon, 45

I

Independence Day (movie), 296, 408
infrared camera, 76
infrared scope, 30
Institute of Noetic Sciences (IONS), 419
inter-dimensional technology, 19
Internet, 60
Interplanetary Center, 352
interplanetary racism, 412
interplanetary war, 36
interstellar capable
   meaning of, 43
Interstellar Coalition, 395
interstellar vehicles
   operation of, 43
Iraq, 408
Italy, 101
Ives, Burl, 420
Ives, Dorothy, 74, 421
Ivy Inn, England, 36

J

Japan, 36
Japanese television crew, 36
Jennings, Peter, 260
Joint Chiefs of Staff, 84
Joint Staff
   head of Intelligence, 83
Joshua Tree, CA, 61, 66, 113

K

Kamimski, Bob, 404
Kennedy, Pres. Jack, 222, 414
Keyhoe, Donald, 404
Kindness, ET elder & diplomat, 164, 220, 354, 355, 381
   cobalt blue ship, 121, 127, 138, 165

craft as orb inside house, 242
described, 119
fly-in, 170, 192, 198, 203, 208, 236, 275, 313, 364, 365, 369
golden light in NH, 160
small blue light, 347
spotlight in Crestone, 298
Kindness, ETs identified. *See* Kindness, ET elder & diplomat
Kingston, David, 206
Kitei, Dr. Lynne, 81
Kokopelli, 282, 285, 305
Kona, Hawaii, 122
Kucinich, Congressman Dennis, 221
Kundalini effect, 380

L

La Brea tar pits, 24
Lamb, George, 53
Laramie, Wyoming, 137
lasers, 25, 99
bounce off dematerialized craft, 143
light stops as if hitting dome, 111
stopped by something, 354
Lear Jet, 320
learning to see
subtle form, 198
levels of consciousness, listed, 244, 283
levitation, 230
learned skill, 94
light
celestial, 302, 389
green neon (cylinder of), 317
liquid, 55, 133
Livingston Manor, New York, 65
Lockheed, 431
longitudinal weapons systems, 327, 441
Lord Mountbatten, 436
Los Alamos, New Mexico, 50, 411, 432
Los Angeles, CA, 24
Lucas, George, 420
Luke AFB, 81

M

MacArthur, General Douglas, 408
Magic Creek, Crestone, CO, 250
magnetometers, 186, 197, 208, 216
Majestic Group, 80
Malmstrom Air Force Base, 403, 427, 436
mandala, 126
orb, 310
Mansell, Chris, 35
Marconi, Guglielmo, 18
Marlborough, England, 36
material structure of the cosmos, 19
materialized
craft, 311, 354, 431, 438
definition, 19
full, partial or subtle, 76
not seen by all, 43
not usual form, 43
disc-shaped craft at eye level, 35
three-foot high ET beings, 41
materialized spacecraft, 185
McClasky, Michael, 75
McClendon, Sarah, 442
McDonald-Douglas, 431
McGuire Ranch, WY, 137, 421
Meade, Margaret, 419
media, 408
big media corrupt, 262
coverage in Wickenberg, AZ, 44
mainstream, 82
pursuit in England, 34
topic treated seriously in Mexico, 74
Medicine Wheel Site, Mt. Blanca, 130
Meditation
shift in coverage, 171, 245
meeting
Col. Canola, 410
Eisenhower and ET at Edwards AFB, 20, 21
Paul Hellyer, 324
planned with Bill Colby, 56
Senator Claiborne Pell, 420
shadowy group near Pentagon, 219

UFO researchers in Crestone, 38
    with intelligence operative, 416
Mensa, 47
mentalis, 335
Mexico, 39, 76, 112
Mexico City, Mexico, 73
Meyer, Stan, 319
    device, 319
military
    helicopters, 143, 193
    installation
        underground, 157
    jets arrive after sighting at Mt.
        Blanca, 95
    reconnaissance, 46, 95
    suppression, 191, 290
        from NORAD at Cheyenne
        Mt., 86
    helicopters, 140
mind control, 82
mind-conditioning, 26
Minister for Environment
    Holland, 108
Minister of Defense
    Canada, 52, 221, 324
    G7 country, 439
Ministry of Defense
    England, 46, 108, 285
    European, 20
Minot, North Dakota, 411
Missile Shutdown (Malmstrom
    AFB), 403
Mitchell, Edgar, 420
MJ-12 group, 63, 112, 210, 329
modalities
    of ET-human interaction, 24
Montauk Project, 157
Monterrey, Mexico, 54
morphogenic
    field propagation, 72, 183
    fields, 435
motto: One Universe – One People,
    25, 428
MRA (Moral Rearmament Associa
    tion), 195
Mt. Blanca, CO, 59, 301
Mt. Graham, AZ, 188

Mt. Pinatubo, Philippines, 40
Mt. Popo, Mexico, 40, 73, 76
Mt. Shasta, CA, 25, 76, 140, 260, 438
    cathedral contact site, 302
    first training, 170
Murder, Inc., 80

N

Nakamora, Michi, 36
NASA, 41, 415, 430
National Press Club, 225
National Press Club event, 211
National Seashore, OBX, NC, 375
national security, 46
National Security Agency (NSA), 26,
    224, 328
Native American cave, Joshua Tree,
    121
Native American elders, 89, 132, 181
Navaswan, 345
Nazis, 408
near-death experience, 23, 65, 79, 89,
    125, 243, 245
need to know
    Cambridge professor example, 47
    Joint Staff admiral example, 83
negative ET perspective, 295
Nellis Air Force Base, 83
neutrino light, 19, 32, 44, 86, 197,
    422
New Hampshire, University of, 159
New York Times, 263
NICAP (National Investigations
    Committee on Aerial Phenom
    ena), 404
night scope binoculars, 29, 302
non-local
    fields and effects, 45
    levels beyond light-speed, 435
    unbounded mind, 428
non-local consciousness, 18, 68, 378
NORAD (North American Aerospace
    Defense Command), 86, 104,
    164, 228
Northridge Earthquake, 421
NRO (National Reconnaissance
    Office), 83, 422

numerological phenomena, 364

O
Obama, Pres. Barack, 371
Ocean, Joan, 122
oil wars, 21
Old Sarum, 201
Oliver's Castle, England, 34
Ong, Karen, 277
open contact
    failed attempt, 20
orbs, 318, 333, 364, 367, 438
    discussion of, 240
    visible amber, 87
Orion transmission, 351, 373, 378, 402
    Dr. Greer as step-down transformer, 353, 374
    quartz ball, 353

P
Palm Beach County, California, 58
paradigm
    combining ET & celestial, 287
Pell, Senator Claiborne, 324, 420
Pensacola, Florida, 31, 49
Pentagon, 219
    E Ring, 83
perception
    celestial, 44
perceptual abilities, 43
Perla, Diana, 55
phase shift, 27, 115
phenomena defined, 18
Philippines, 40
Phoenix Lights, 76, 81
Phoenix, AZ, 67, 80
photo
    Kindness' ship & Shari's essence, 121, 214
    vortex in crop circle, 201
Pine Bush, NY, 191, 360
pink
    associated with Shari Adamiak, 167, 211, 250
Pleiadians
    not term used by CSETI, 412

polar ice caps melting, 21
Pope, Nick, 46, 108
Popocatepetl. See Mt. Popo, Mexico
Port Townsend, Washington, 169
post-traumatic stress, 122
poverty
    80% of world's population, 21
power grab, 21
prayer, 168
prayer (inter-cessionary), 425
Prince Charles, 436
Prince Phillip, 436
probe, 33, 76, 139, 249
probe (communications), 313
Programmed Life Forms (PLFs), 157, 407, 413, 414
protection example, Mexico, 78
protection example, Outer Banks, 376
protocols
    CE-5, 25, 108, 121
protocols for ET Contact, 23
pseudo contact, 294
pseudo-abductions, 293
pseudo-mutilations, 293
Psychic Warrior, 117
psychological warfare, 82
    "evil ET", 295
    inuendo Greer a CIA agent, 60
psychotronic attack, 151, 177
psychotronic/radionics, 364
Puja, 288, 350, 360
Puja ritual
    at Shaman Cave, 354
    Charlottesville, VA, 318
pulsing
    of Joshua tree, 332
purification (with raindrops), 360, 362
purpose
    appreciate & understand cosmology, 169
    of this book & trainings, 168

Q
quantum vacuum, 93

R

radar arrays, 22
radar detector
    sounding on X and K bands, 95
    triggered in Joshua Tree, 116, 186, 378, 398
radio transmitted tones, 18
radionic transmission of cancer cells, 64, 178
rajas, 416
Rather, Dan, 263
Raum, Dr. Adolph, 405
realities
    beyond what most can imagine, 93
    can be flawed, 196
    perceiving simultaneous multiple, 141
    unique & shared, 42, 144
remote viewing, 23, 428
    of plane crash, 57
Rendlesham Forest, England, 285, 406, 434
reverse engineering
    ET craft and technology, 83
RMIT (Rapid Mobilization Investigative Team), 54, 65
Rock Point, Maryland, 56
Rockefeller, Laurance, 222, 414, 420
Rocky Mountain UFO Conference, 137
Rosetta stone
    of ET communication, 67
Roswell, 21, 22, 63
Royal Trust Lands, England, 34
Rumsfeld, Donald, 221
Russell, Ron, 98, 106, 108, 110, 164
Russian nuclear silos, 411

S

Sadat, Anwar, 390
Sagan, Carl, 315, 435
    SAIC (Science Applications Intl. Corp.), 415
Salas, Bob, 221, 403
Samadhi, 288
    seeing, 58
Sand Flats, Mt. Shasta, 269
Sangre de Cristo Mountains, 53, 165, 208, 299
Santa Claus, 35
Santa Fe, New Mexico, 50
Santa Rosa Island, FL, 31
satellite
    alleged, 51
satva, 416
saying
    "As above, so below. As below, so above.", 434
    "As ye have faith...", 51
    "The wise are those who speak not...", 61
scanning of intent, 33, 182
scanning procedure, 39, 248
Schiff, Congressman Steve (NM), 63
Schrödinger, Erwin, 23, 45
Schwartz, Bob, 262
scintillating light, 314, 337, 379
Scotland, UK, 60
Sedona, Arizona, 145
Selover, Bob, 131
SETI project (misguided), 315
Shaman Cave, 354
Shaman's Cave, Joshua Tree, 213, 288
shapes of ET beings
    all humanoid, 71
    ant-like, 141, 251
    bee-like, 141
    bird-like, 72
    Casper-like, 91, 135
    grasshopper-like, 129, 141
    insect-like, 71
    manatee head & face, 129, 171
    owl-like, 277
    praying mantis, 71, 141
    whale-like, 72
Sheffield, England, 195
Sheldrake, Rupert, 45, 435
Shenandoah National Park, 163, 317
Shostack, Seth, 315
Siddhis, 65, 204, 230, 252
signaling, 18, 24, 40, 55, 172, 184, 202, 216, 239, 260, 269, 294

electronic tones to our recorded ones, 116
in intelligent sequences, 31
sine wave of crop circle tones, 37
single mind of consciousness, 23
singularity of knowledge, 386
Sky Harbor Airport, 81
smell
    flower scents, 156, 250
    of crushed ants (formic acid), 70
social disruption, 21
sound
    high-pitched, continuous, 393
sounds, 163
    altered, 161
    arrows of sound, 166
    clicking, 161
    crop circle-like tones, 278, 289
    omnidirectional, 292
    sound event, 155
    underground craft, 217
South America
    ETV debris samples, 48
speed of light, 43, 44, 144
spirit world, 59
Sputnik, 417
stagecraft to deceive public, 293
Star People, 87, 89
Star Trek movie, First Contact, 66
Star Wars movie, 106
star wars scenario, 329, 409
State Department of the United States, 19
step-down transformer (electromagnetic antenna), 379
Stonehenge, 205
subtle vision, 44, 168
Sufi mystics, 26
Sufi parable, 51
suppression effort, 325
suppressive countermeasures, 32, 108, 287
synthesizer
    recreates crop circle tones, 37

T
tamas, 416

tamasic process, 416
Taylor, Busty, 99
technological development hijacked, 21
technology/consciousness synthesis, 429, 430, 431
teleportation technology, 259
Tempe, AZ, 82
temperature change, 140, 161, 180, 378
    enveloped in etheric ET craft, 110, 227
The Crossing Point (paper), 62
The Day After Roswell, 21
The Day the Earth Stood Still movie, 20
The Orion Project (TOP), 21, 219
The Phoenix Lights, 81
Third Reich, 408
Threfeld, Fred, 259
Tibetan bowl, 111, 362
    tones, 306
Tibetan Stupa, 250, 256
Titanic, movie, 146
totality of universe folded within us, 422
Tower of Babel, 284
trans-dimensional technology, 149
transformative energy, 338, 346
tree shaking from ETV phase shift, 115

U
UFO
    ARVs man-made, 26
    Congressional hearings (1968), 221
    hobbyist groups, 19
    literature, 294
    no such thing, 26
    propulsion system, 21
    research community, 100
    subculture, 35, 408, 412
ultra-sonic technique, 48
UN (United Nations), 19, 55, 63
Unbounded, 425, 435
Universal Consciousness, 23, 430

Universal Peace, 366, 395
USOs (unidentified submerged objects), 145

V
Vatican Observatory, AZ, 188
vectoring, 18
Vedic
    information, 65, 142
    saying
        "All This is That", 200, 437
    tradition, 244
video
    flashing lights, 209
    massive triangular craft, 172
video equipment
    fried, 37
visible spectrum, 43
volcano
    Mt. Shasta, CA, 302
    Popo, Mexico, 39
von Braun, Werner, 407

W
W.B., well-known billionaire, 80
walkie-talkies, 42, 194
Walton, Travis, 38
Washington Times, 222
Washington, D.C., 219, 221
weapons of mass destruction, 20
weather phenomena, 18
Whedon, Chris, 404
Whedon, Spence, 404
White Eagle Lodge, Crestone, 85, 226
White House, 222
white noise of space/time, 45, 132, 206
White Oaks Naval Facility, MD, 206
Wickenberg, Arizona, 40
Wilcox, AZ, 188, 248
Wiltshire, England, 47
Woodborough Hill, England, 34, 142
Woods, Dr. Robert, 431
Woolsey, R. James, CIA Director, 32
worlds of light, 94
Wright, Sandy, 53, 60

Wright-Patterson Air Force Base, 404
Wyoming, University of, 137

X
xenophobic intent, 39
X-files, 225

Z
Zapata Falls, Mt. Blanca, 85, 90, 130, 133, 257, 361
Zen Dome, 232, 401